CHAPTER 1

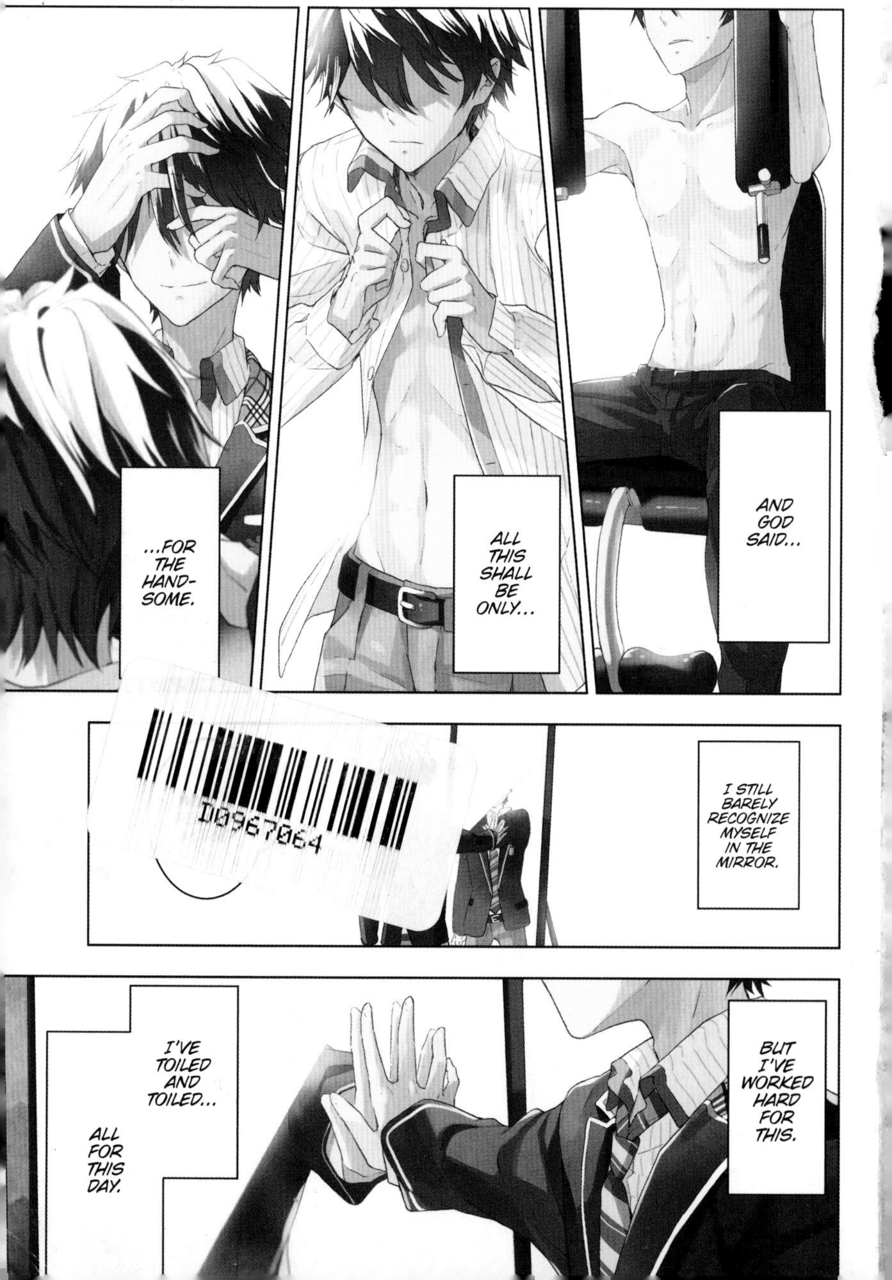
AND GOD SAID...
ALL THIS SHALL BE ONLY...
...FOR THE HANDSOME.
I STILL BARELY RECOGNIZE MYSELF IN THE MIRROR.
BUT I'VE WORKED HARD FOR THIS.
I'VE TOILED AND TOILED...
ALL FOR THIS DAY.

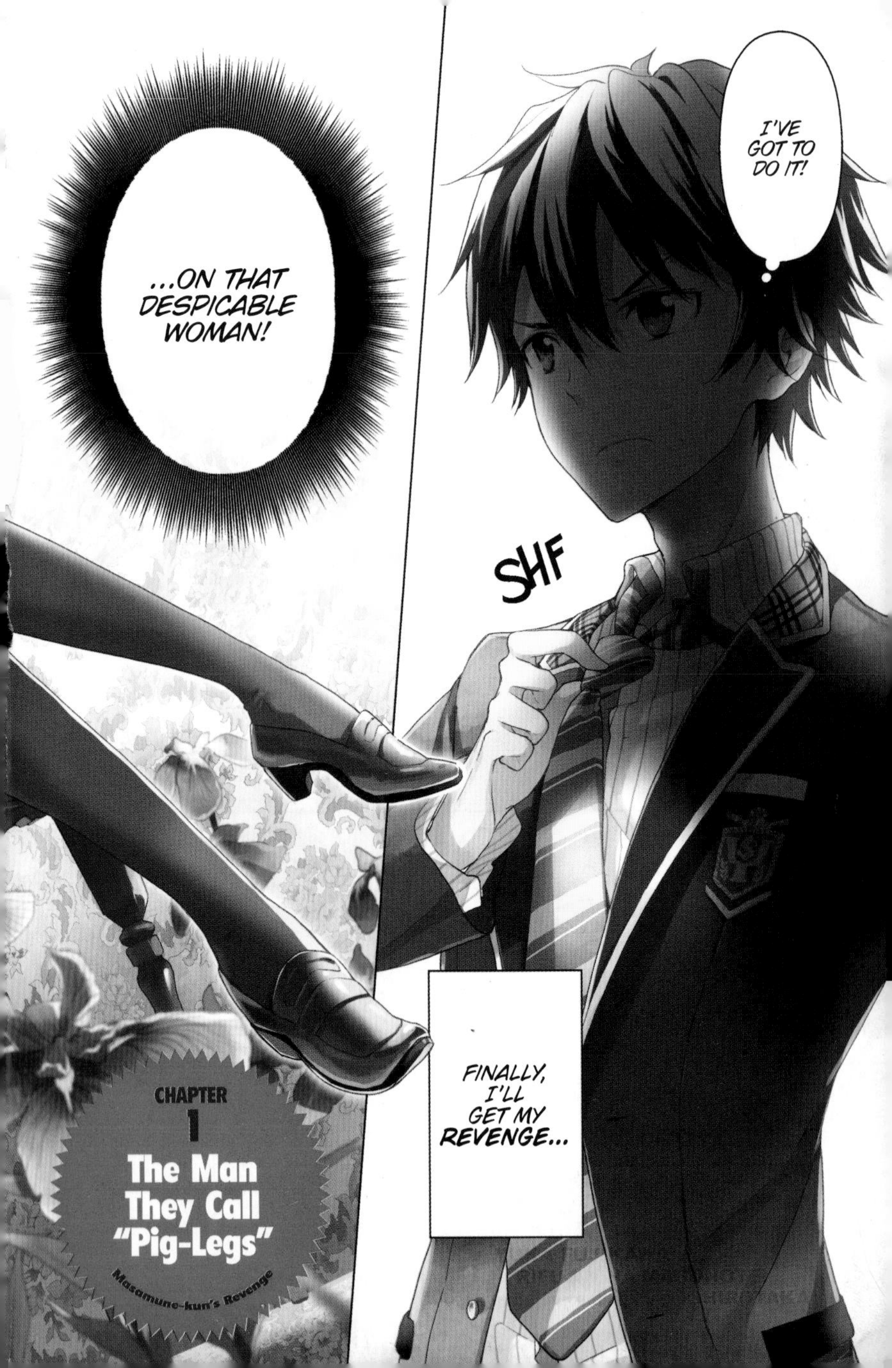
I'VE GOT TO DO IT!
SHF
FINALLY, I'LL GET MY REVENGE...
...ON THAT DESPICABLE WOMAN!
CHAPTER 1
The Man They Call "Pig-Legs"
Masamune-kun's Revenge

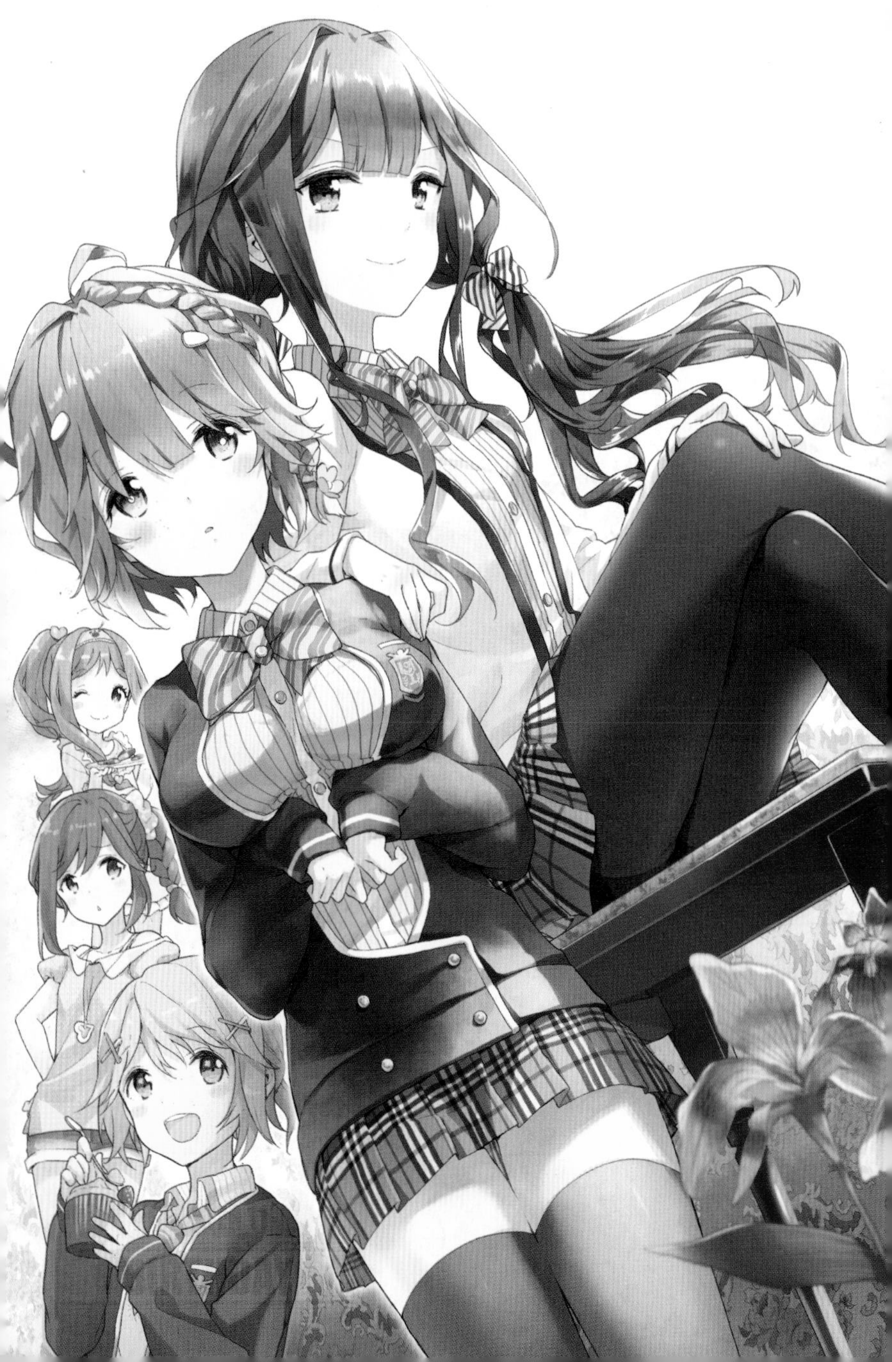

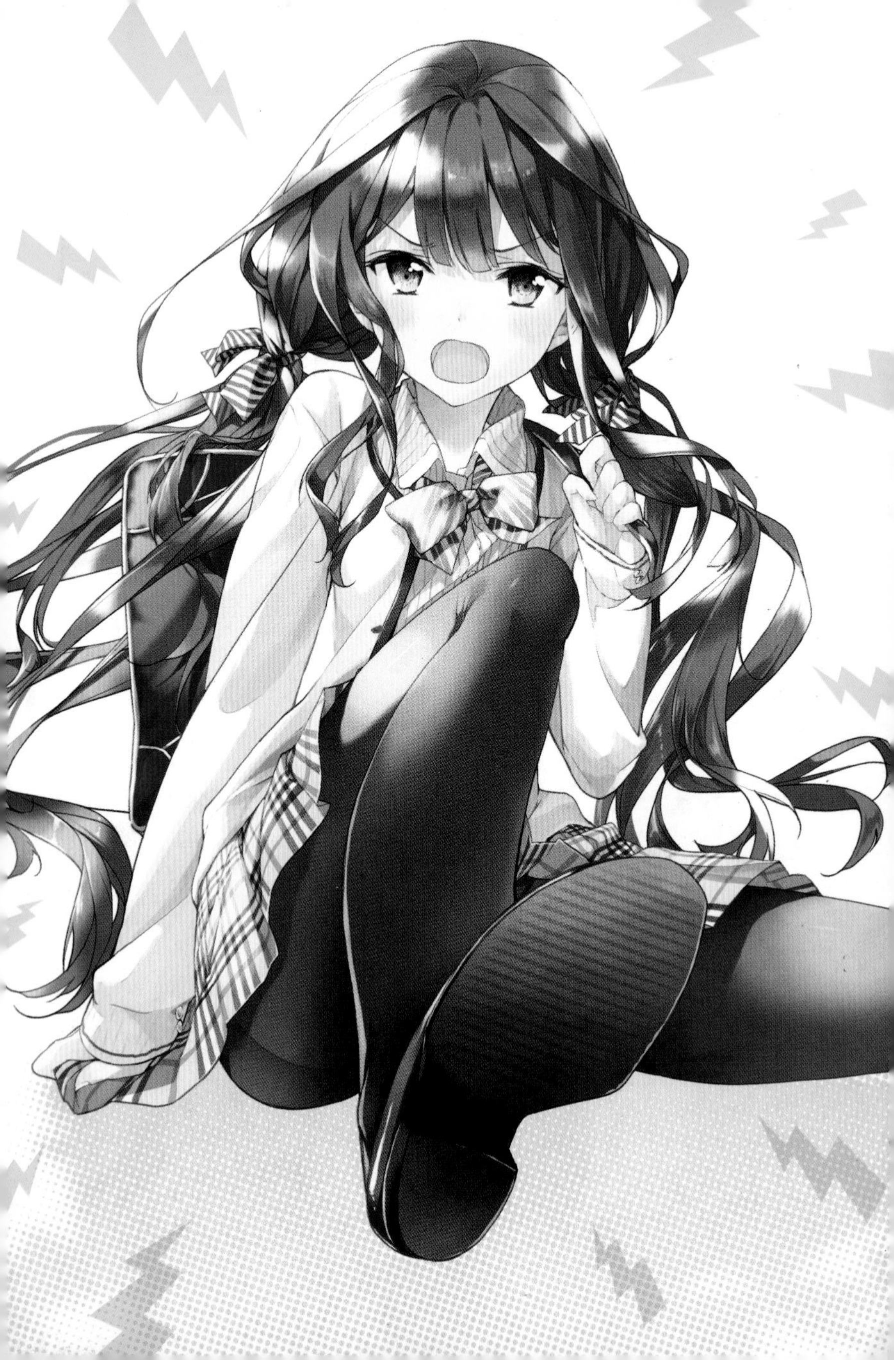

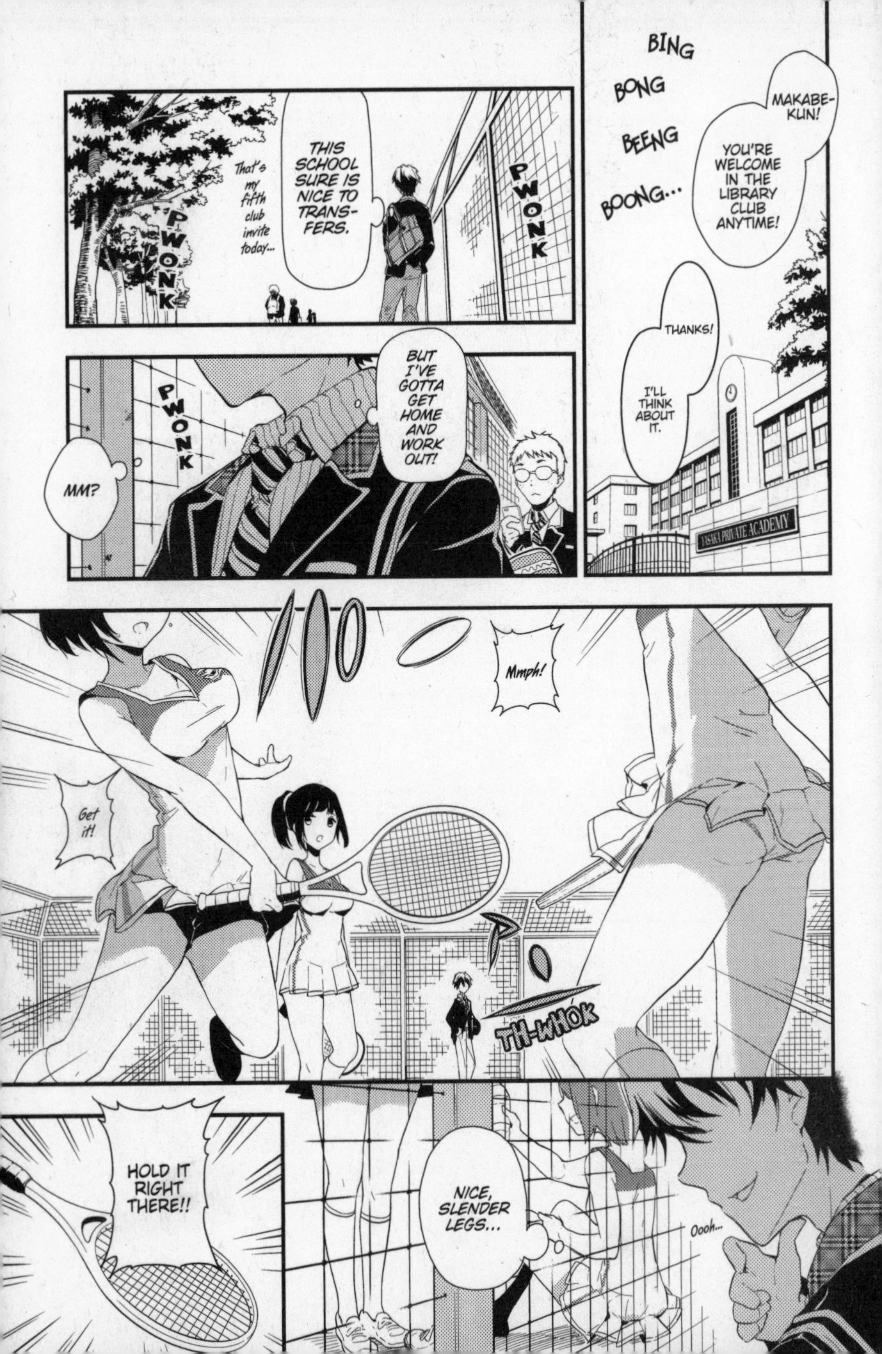
BING BONG BEENG BOONG...
MAKABE-KUN! YOU'RE WELCOME IN THE LIBRARY CLUB ANYTIME!
THANKS!
I'LL THINK ABOUT IT.
YASAKA PRIVATE ACADEMY
PWONK
THIS SCHOOL SURE IS NICE TO TRANSFERS.
That's my fifth club invite today...
PWONK
BUT I'VE GOTTA GET HOME AND WORK OUT!
PWONK
MM?
Mmph!
Get it!
TH-WHOK
Oooh...
NICE, SLENDER LEGS...
HOLD IT RIGHT THERE!!

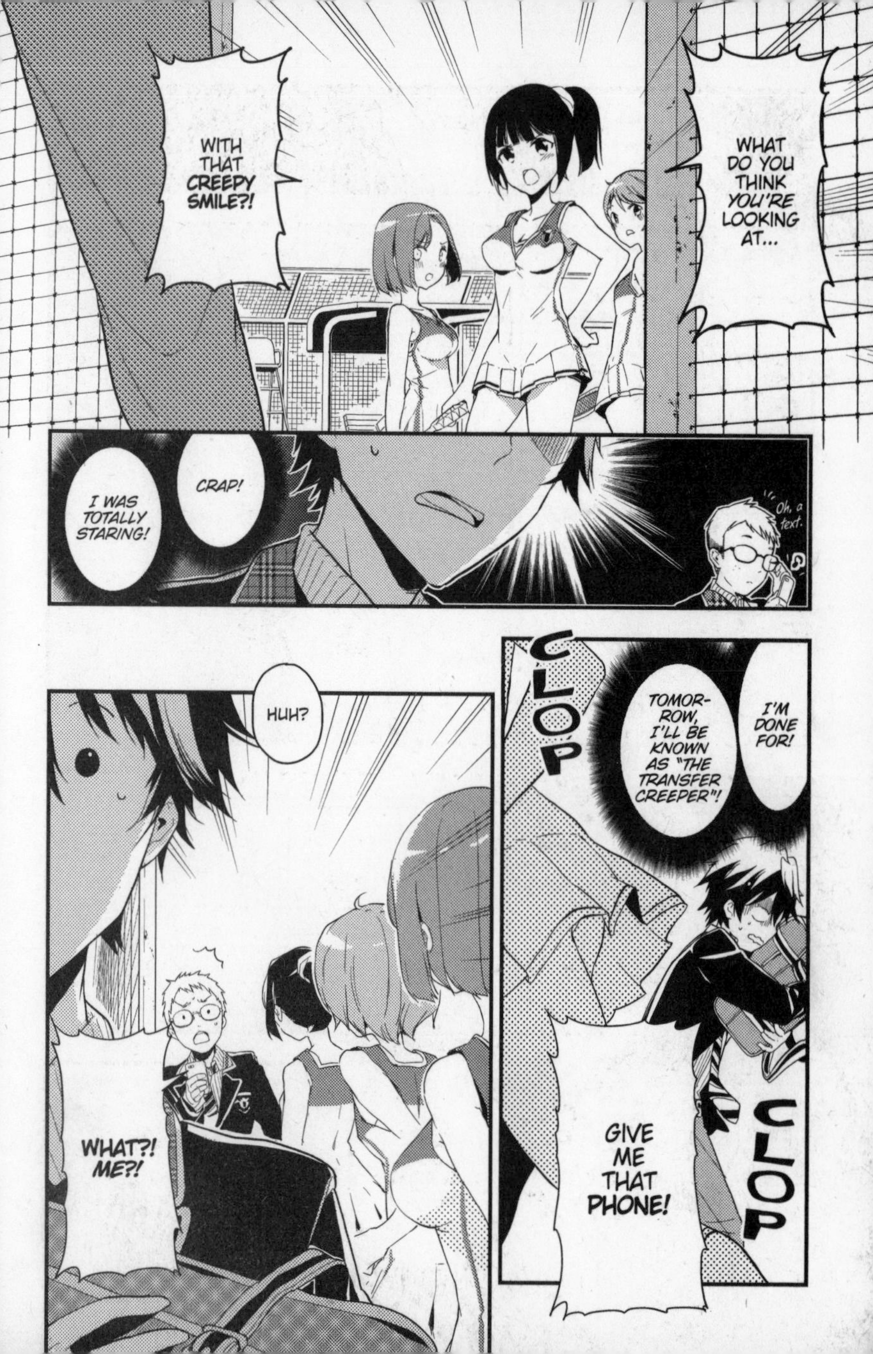
WHAT DO YOU THINK YOU'RE LOOKING AT...
WITH THAT CREEPY SMILE?!
CRAP!
I WAS TOTALLY STARING!
Oh, a text.
CLOP
I'M DONE FOR!
TOMOR-ROW, I'LL BE KNOWN AS "THE TRANSFER CREEPER"!
GIVE ME THAT PHONE!
CLOP
HUH?
WHAT?! ME?!

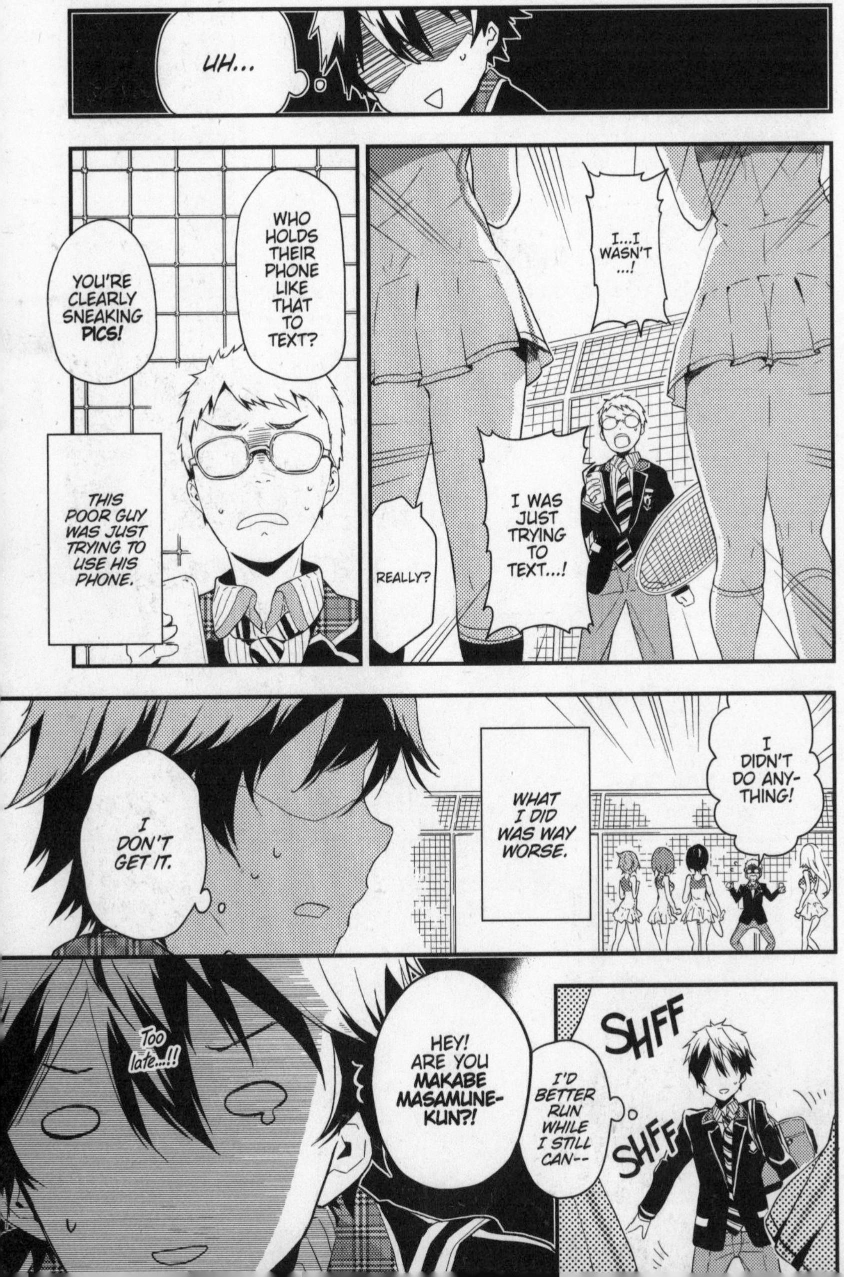
UH...
I...I WASN'T ...!
I WAS JUST TRYING TO TEXT...!
REALLY?
WHO HOLDS THEIR PHONE LIKE THAT TO TEXT?
YOU'RE CLEARLY SNEAKING PICS!
THIS POOR GUY WAS JUST TRYING TO USE HIS PHONE.
I DIDN'T DO ANY-THING!
WHAT I DID WAS WAY WORSE.
I DON'T GET IT.
SHFF
I'D BETTER RUN WHILE I STILL CAN--
SHFF
HEY! ARE YOU MAKABE MASAMUNE-KUN?!
Too late...!!

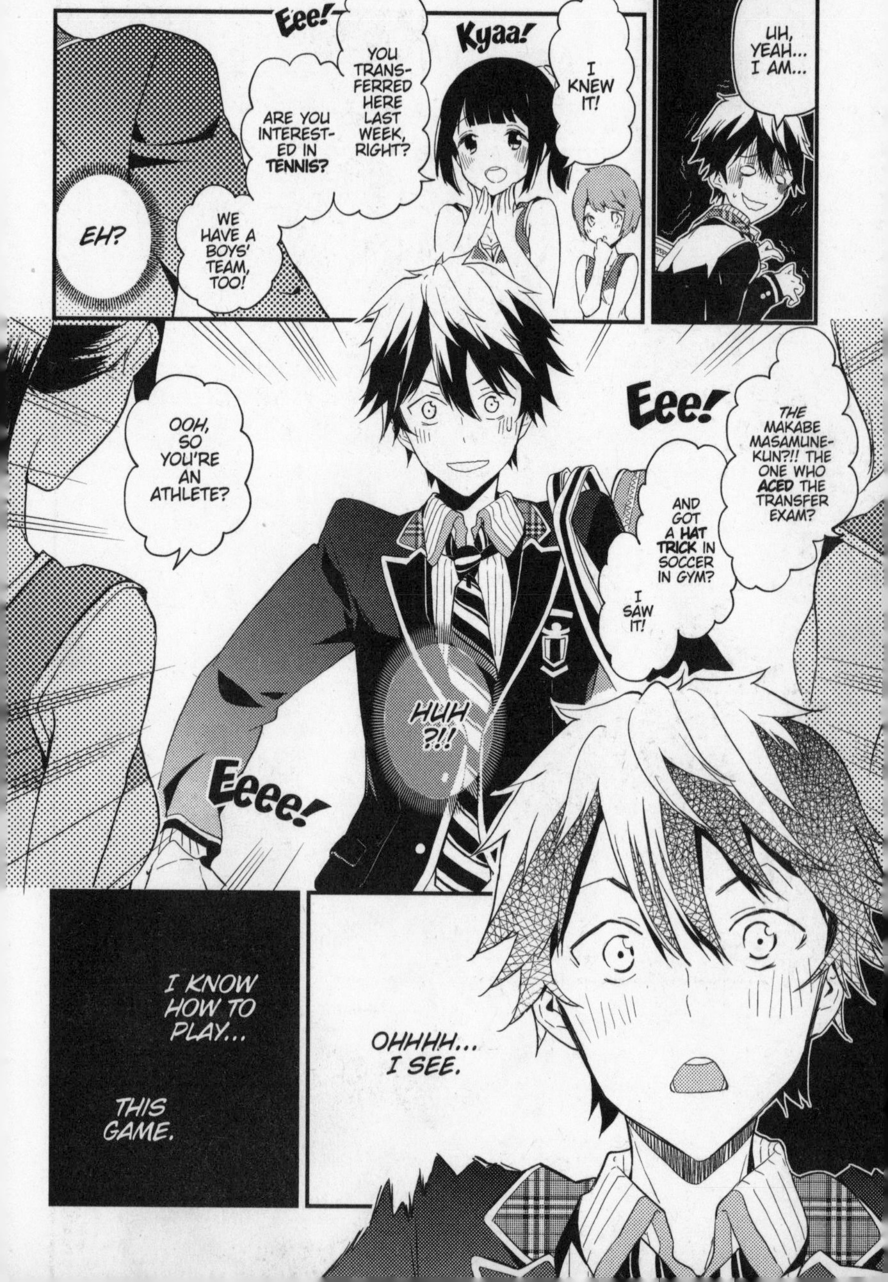
UH, YEAH... I AM...
I KNEW IT!
Kyaa!
YOU TRANSFERRED HERE LAST WEEK, RIGHT?
Eee!
ARE YOU INTERESTED IN TENNIS?
WE HAVE A BOYS' TEAM, TOO!
EH?
THE MAKABE MASAMUNE-KUN?!! THE ONE WHO ACED THE TRANSFER EXAM?
Eee!
AND GOT A HAT TRICK IN SOCCER IN GYM?
I SAW IT!
OOH, SO YOU'RE AN ATHLETE?
HUH?!!
Eeee!
OHHHH... I SEE.
I KNOW HOW TO PLAY...
THIS GAME.

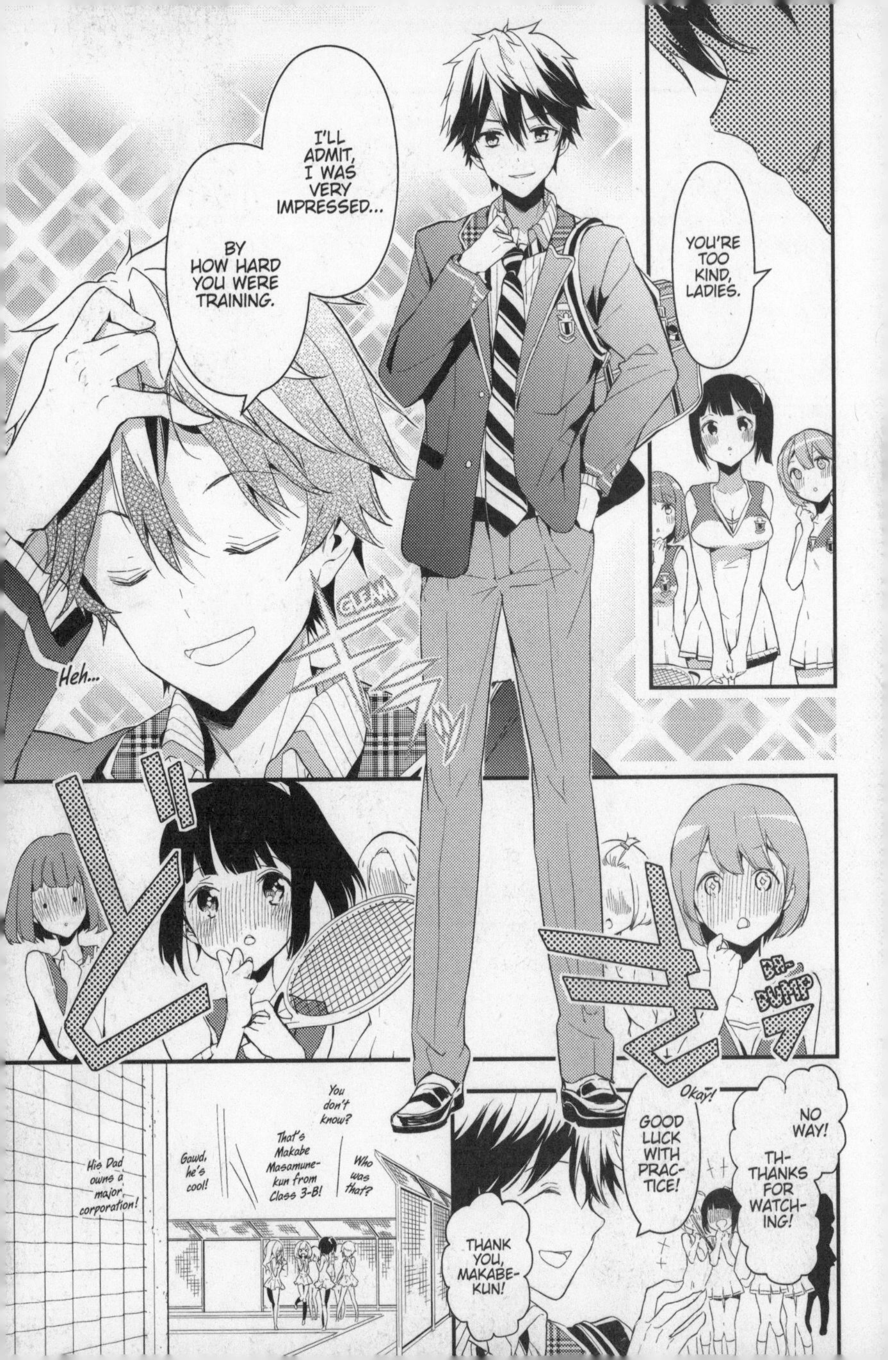
YOU'RE TOO KIND, LADIES.
I'LL ADMIT, I WAS VERY IMPRESSED...
BY HOW HARD YOU WERE TRAINING.
GLEAM
Heh...
BA-DUMP
NO WAY!
TH-THANKS FOR WATCHING!
Okay!
GOOD LUCK WITH PRACTICE!
THANK YOU, MAKABE-KUN!
Who was that?
That's Makabe Masamune-kun from Class 3-B!
You don't know?
Gawd, he's cool!
His Dad owns a major corporation!

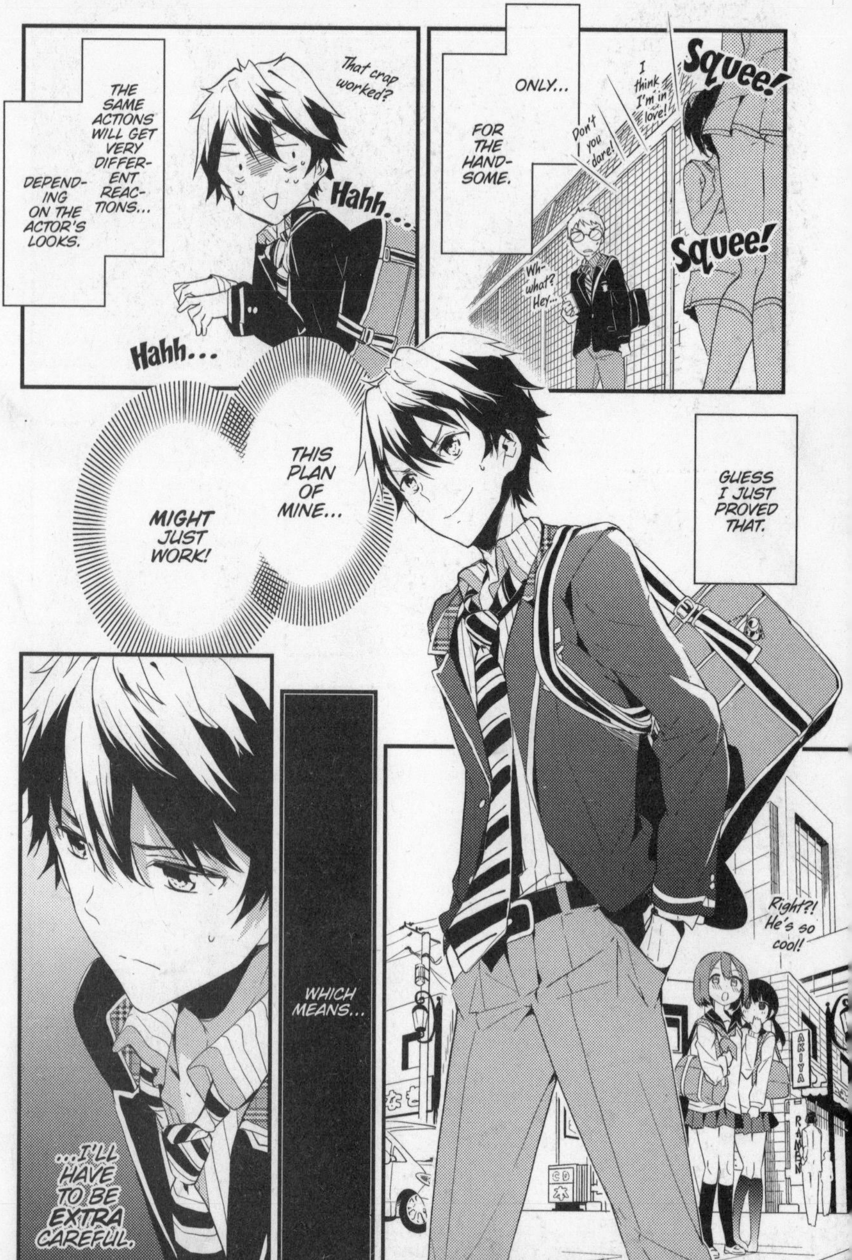
ONLY...
FOR THE HANDSOME.
Squee!
I think I'm in love!
Don't you dare!
Squee!
Wh-what? Hey...
THE SAME ACTIONS WILL GET VERY DIFFERENT REACTIONS...
DEPENDING ON THE ACTOR'S LOOKS.
That crap worked?
Hahh...
Hahh...
GUESS I JUST PROVED THAT.
THIS PLAN OF MINE...
MIGHT JUST WORK!
Right?! He's so cool!
AKIYA
RAMEN
CD
WHICH MEANS...
...I'LL HAVE TO BE EXTRA CAREFUL.

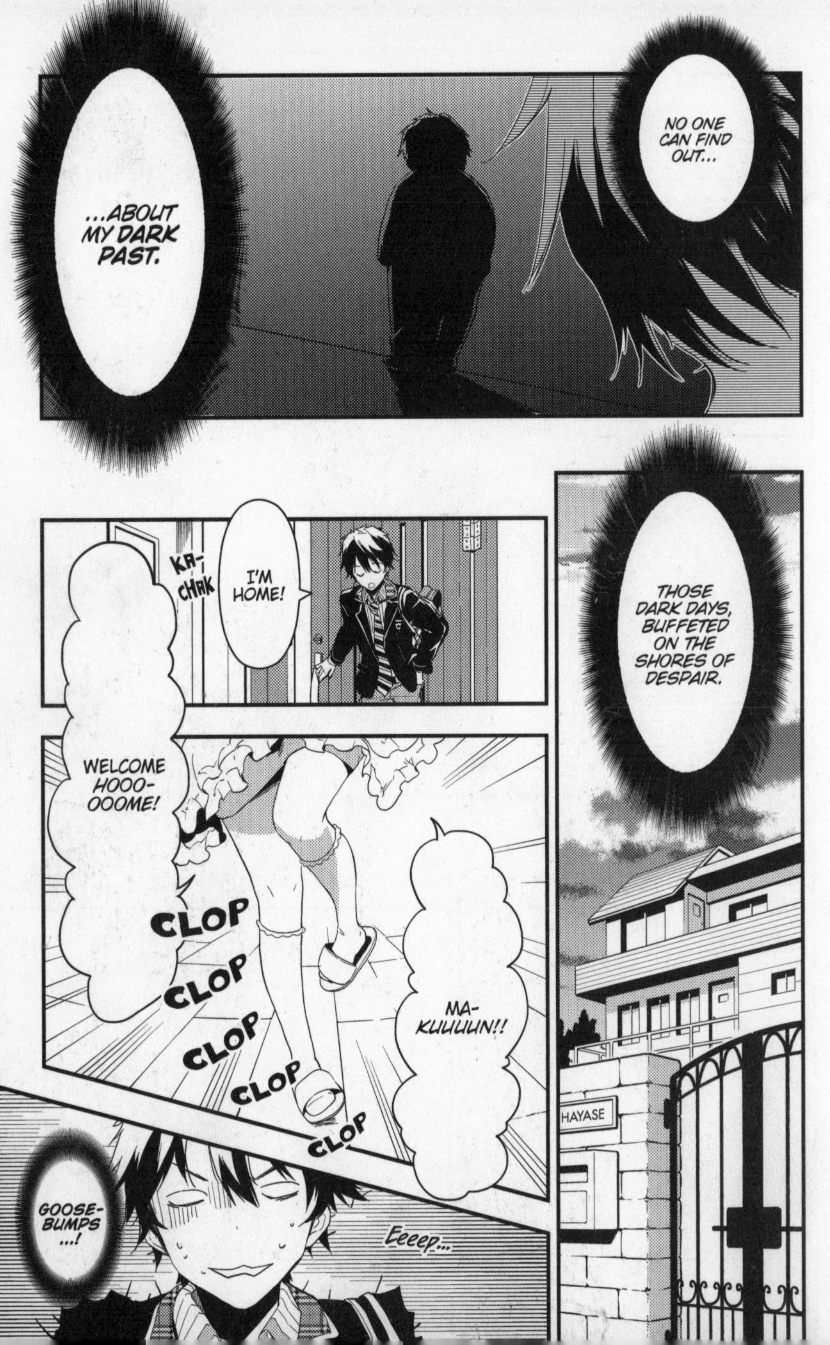
NO ONE CAN FIND OUT...
...ABOUT MY DARK PAST.
THOSE DARK DAYS, BUFFETED ON THE SHORES OF DESPAIR.
HAYASE
I'M HOME!
KA-CHAK
MA-KUUUUN!!
WELCOME HOOO-OOOME!
CLOP CLOP CLOP CLOP CLOP
Eeeep...
GOOSE-BUMPS...!

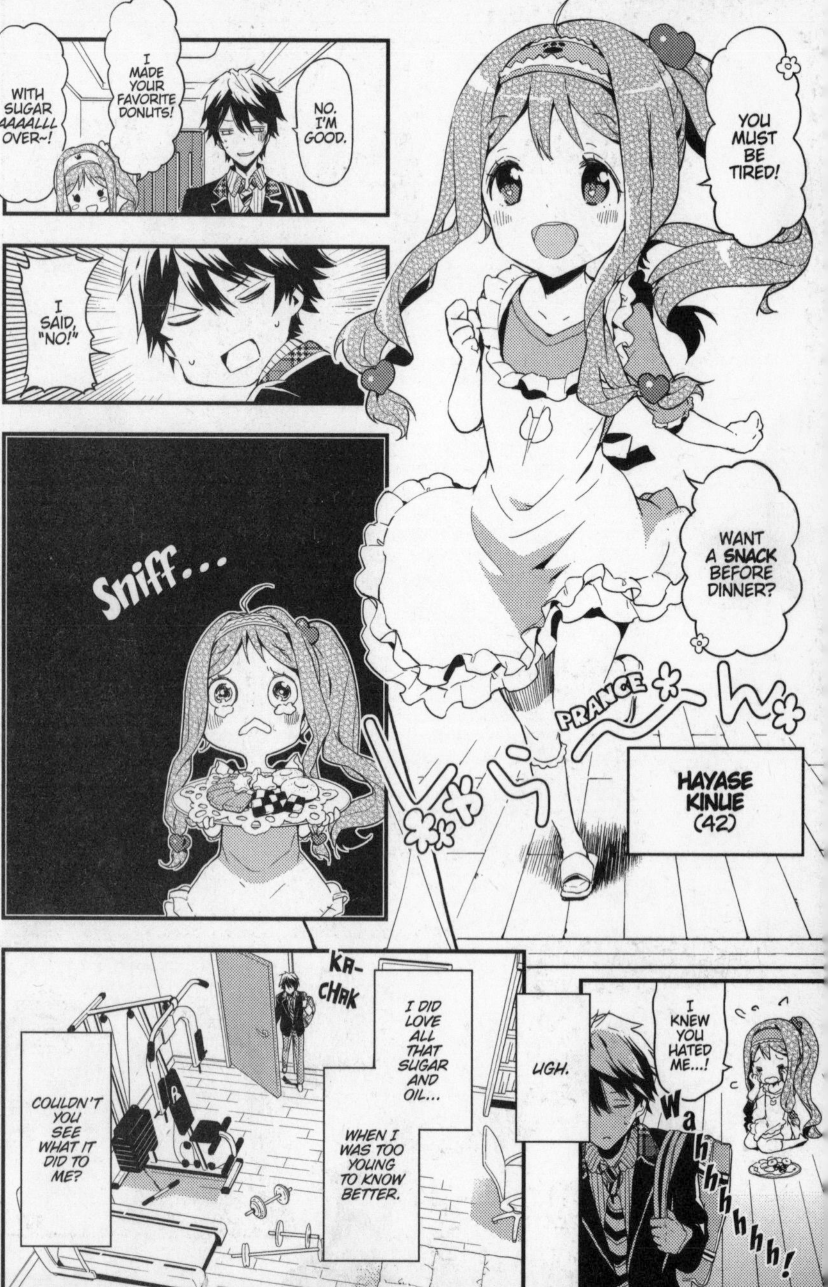
YOU MUST BE TIRED!
WANT A SNACK BEFORE DINNER?
PRANCE
HAYASE KINUE (42)
NO. I'M GOOD.
I MADE YOUR FAVORITE DONUTS!
WITH SUGAR AAAALLL OVER~!
I SAID, "NO!"
Sniff...
I KNEW YOU HATED ME...!
Wahhhhhhhhhh!
UGH.
KA-CHAK
I DID LOVE ALL THAT SUGAR AND OIL...
WHEN I WAS TOO YOUNG TO KNOW BETTER.
COULDN'T YOU SEE WHAT IT DID TO ME?

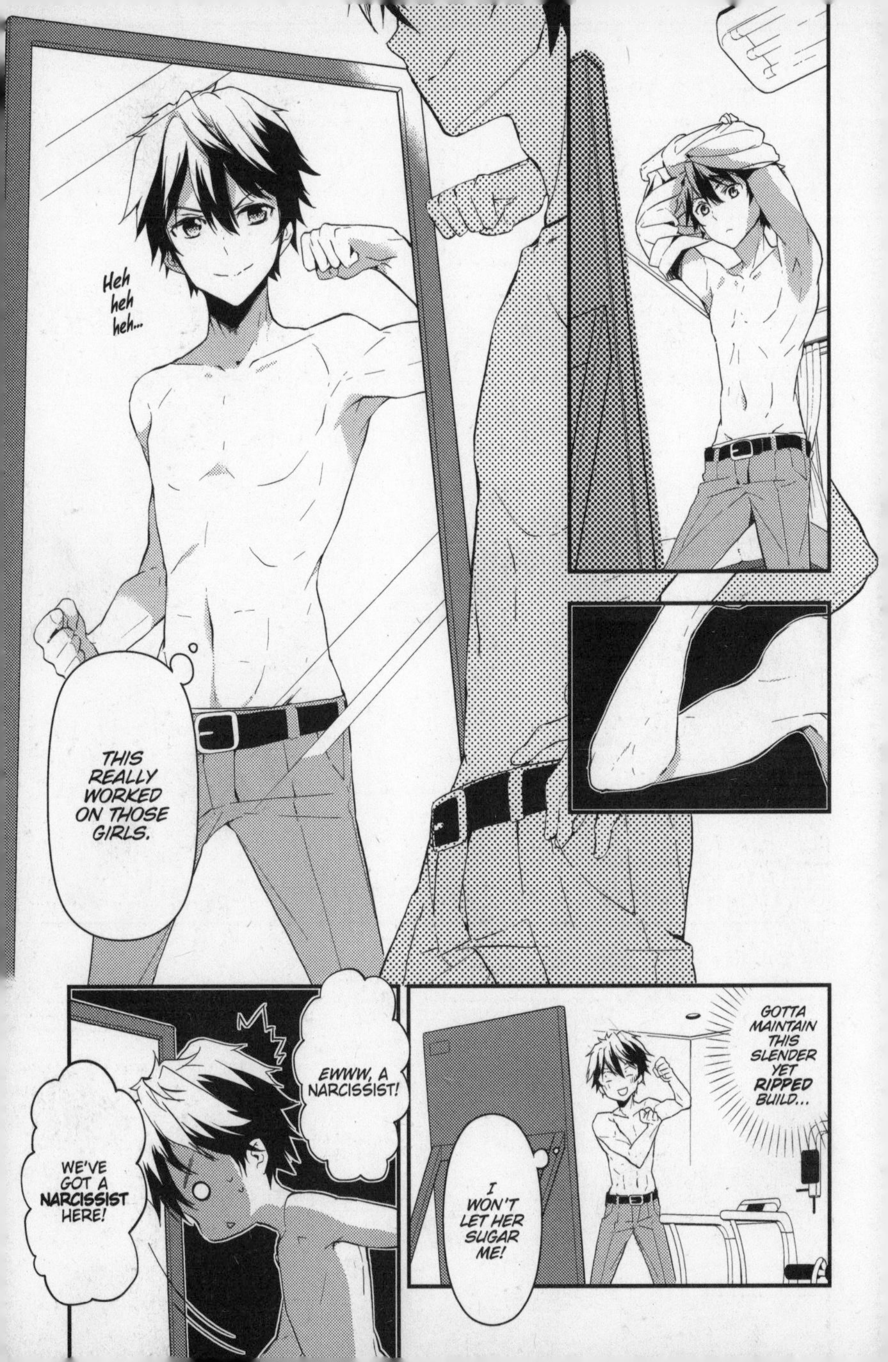
Heh heh heh...
THIS REALLY WORKED ON THOSE GIRLS.
GOTTA MAINTAIN THIS SLENDER YET RIPPED BUILD...
I WON'T LET HER SUGAR ME!
EWWW, A NARCISSIST!
WE'VE GOT A NARCISSIST HERE!

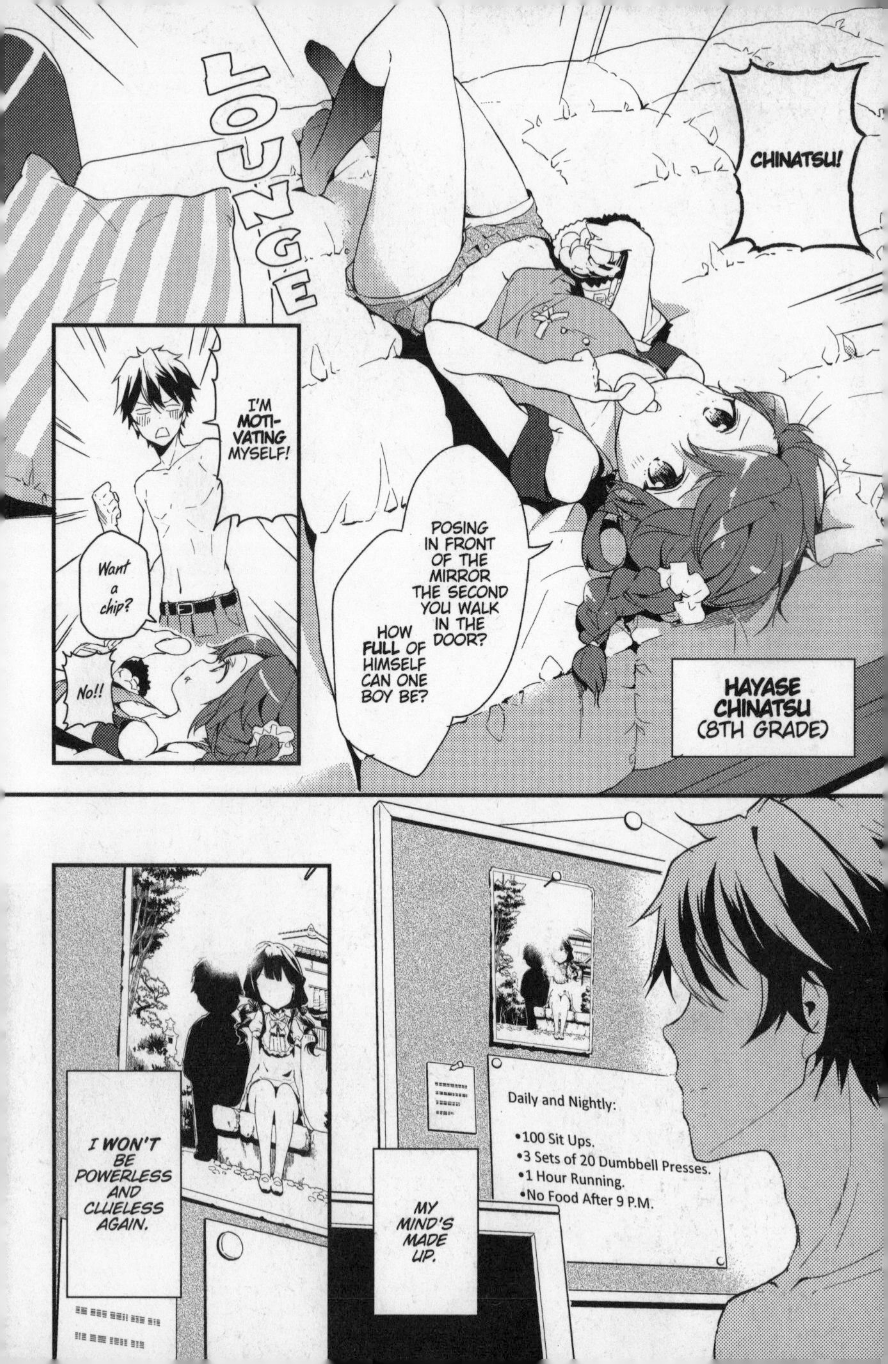
LOUNGE
CHINATSU!
POSING IN FRONT OF THE MIRROR THE SECOND YOU WALK IN THE DOOR?
HOW FULL OF HIMSELF CAN ONE BOY BE?
HAYASE CHINATSU (8TH GRADE)
I'M MOTI-VATING MYSELF!
Want a chip?
No!!
Daily and Nightly:
•100 Sit Ups.
•3 Sets of 20 Dumbbell Presses.
•1 Hour Running.
•No Food After 9 P.M.
MY MIND'S MADE UP.
I WON'T BE POWERLESS AND CLUELESS AGAIN.

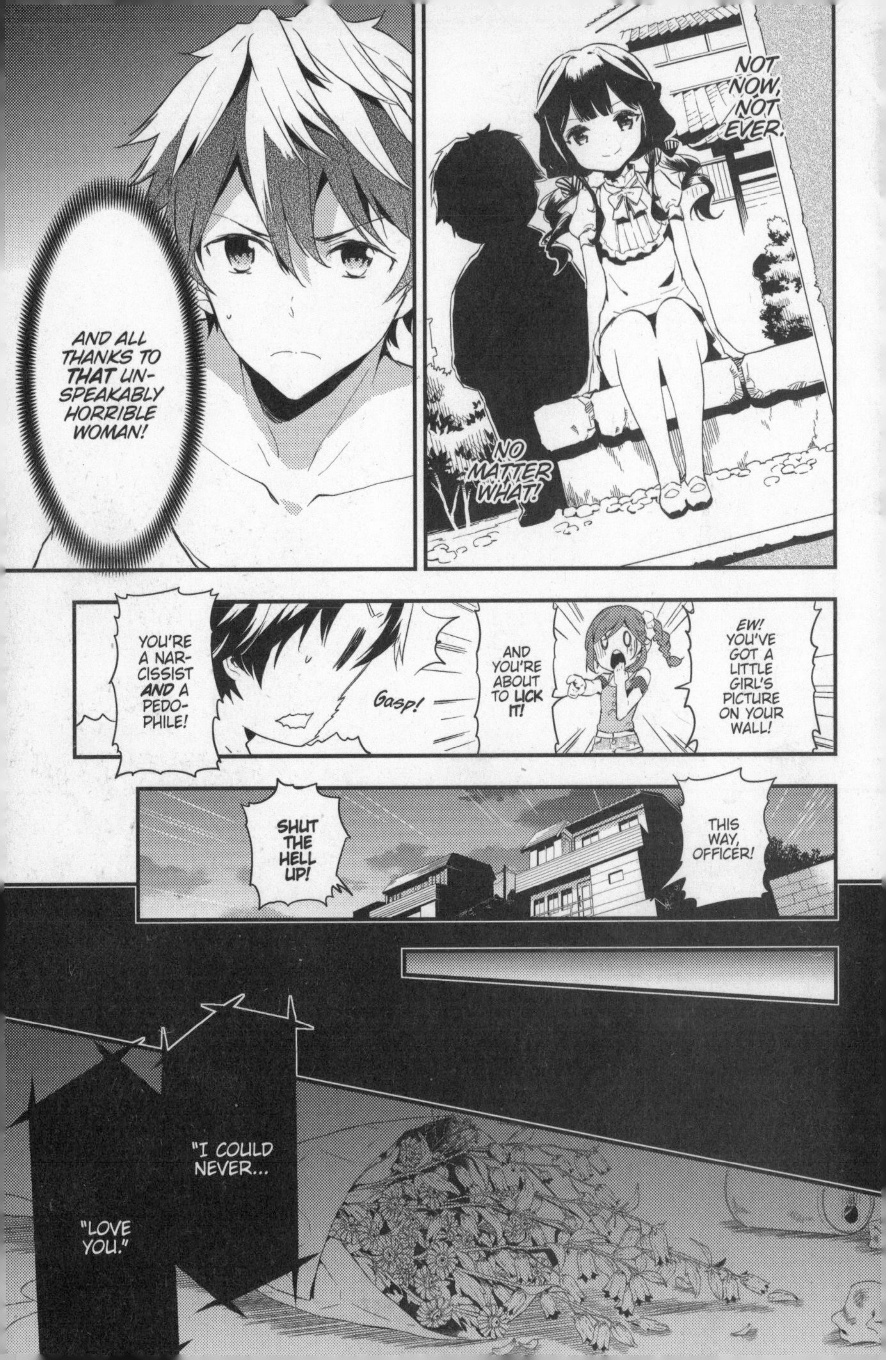
NOT NOW, NOT EVER.
NO MATTER WHAT!
AND ALL THANKS TO THAT UN-SPEAKABLY HORRIBLE WOMAN!
EW! YOU'VE GOT A LITTLE GIRL'S PICTURE ON YOUR WALL!
AND YOU'RE ABOUT TO LICK IT!
Gasp!
YOU'RE A NAR-CISSIST AND A PEDO-PHILE!
THIS WAY, OFFICER!
SHUT THE HELL UP!
"I COULD NEVER...
"LOVE YOU."

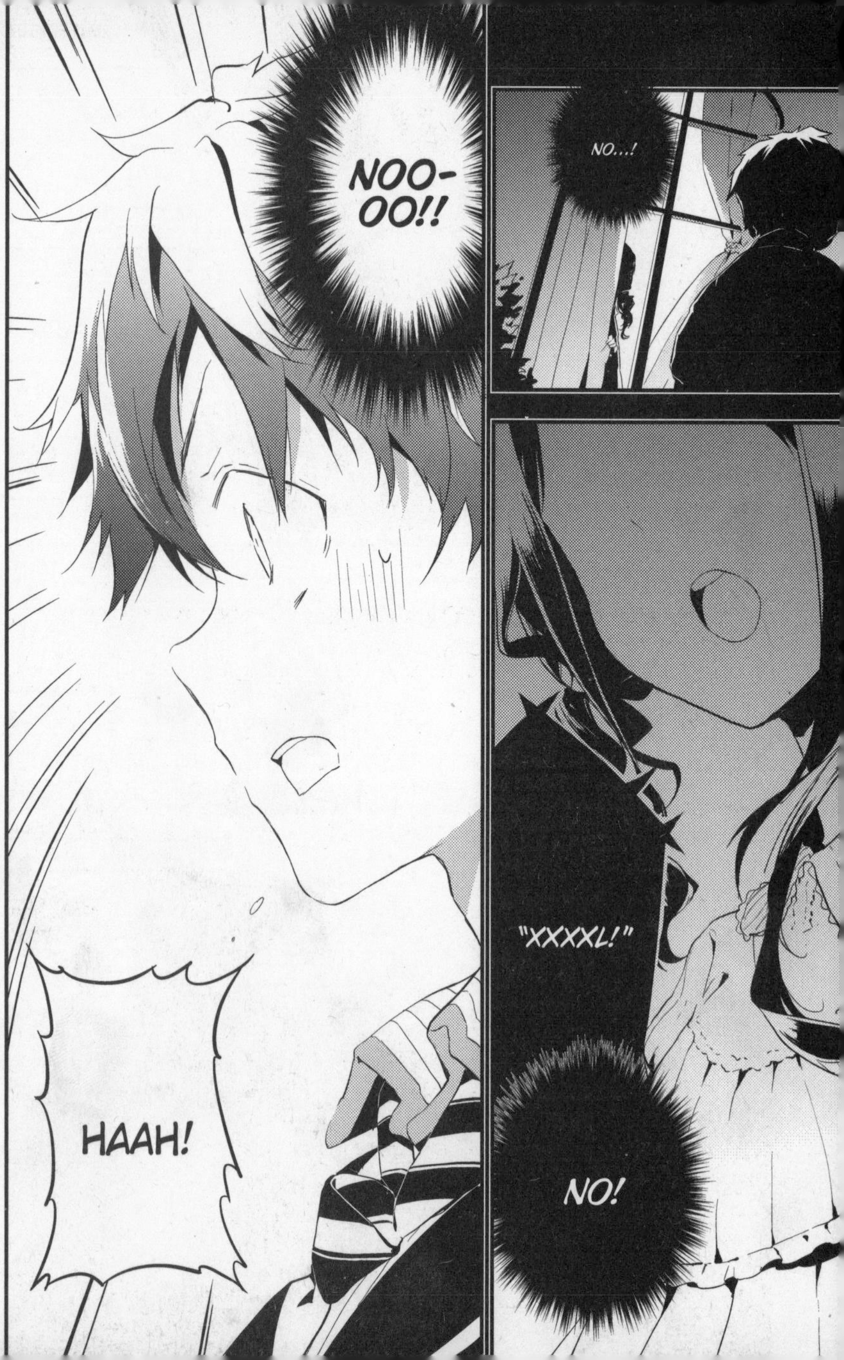
NO...!
"XXXXL!"
NO!
NOO-OO!!
HAAH!

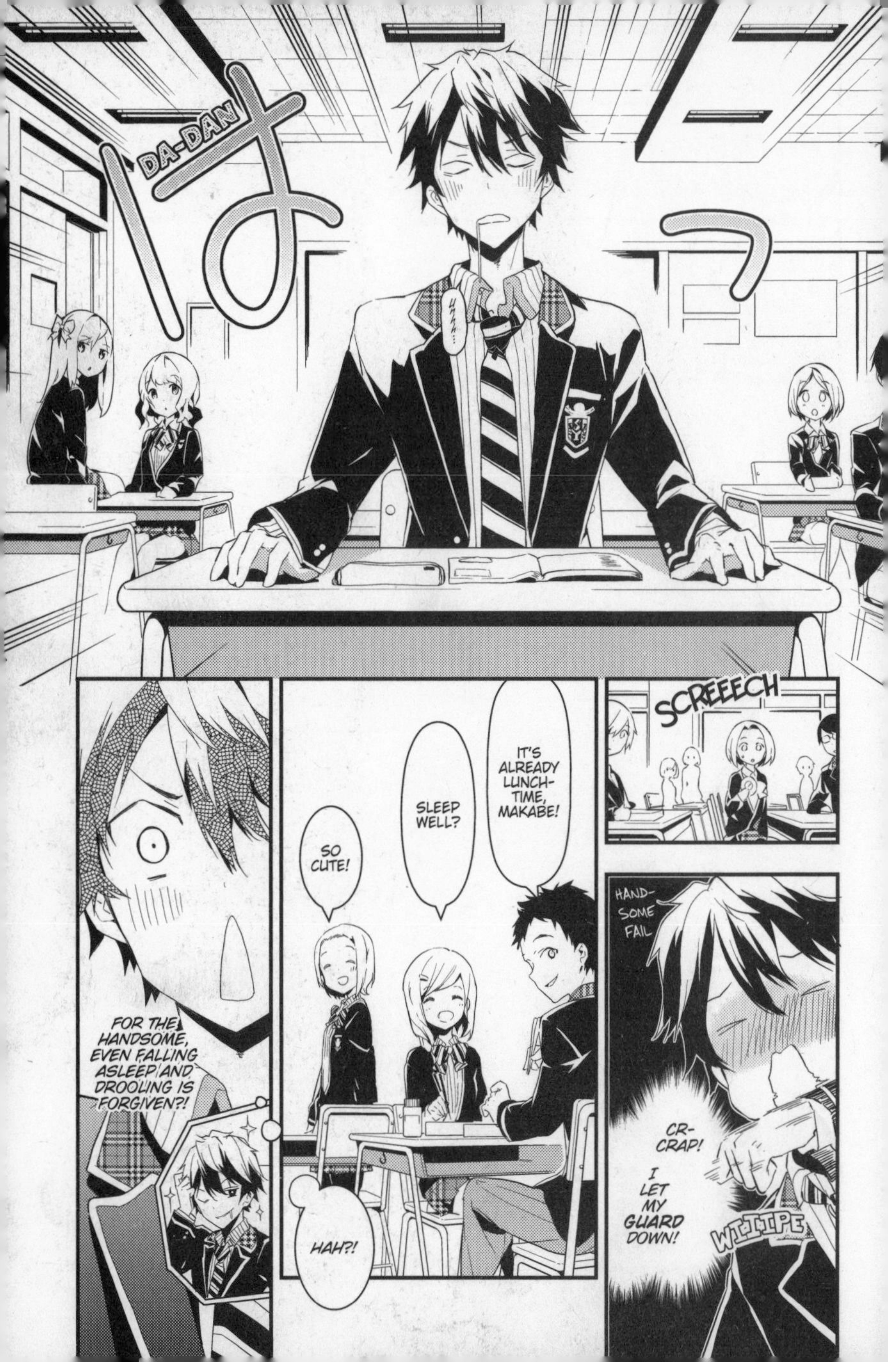
DA-DAN
はっ
SCREEECH
HAND-SOME FAIL
CR-CRAP!
I LET MY GUARD DOWN!
WIIIPE
IT'S ALREADY LUNCH-TIME, MAKABE!
SLEEP WELL?
SO CUTE!
HAH?!
FOR THE HANDSOME, EVEN FALLING ASLEEP AND DROOLING IS FORGIVEN?!

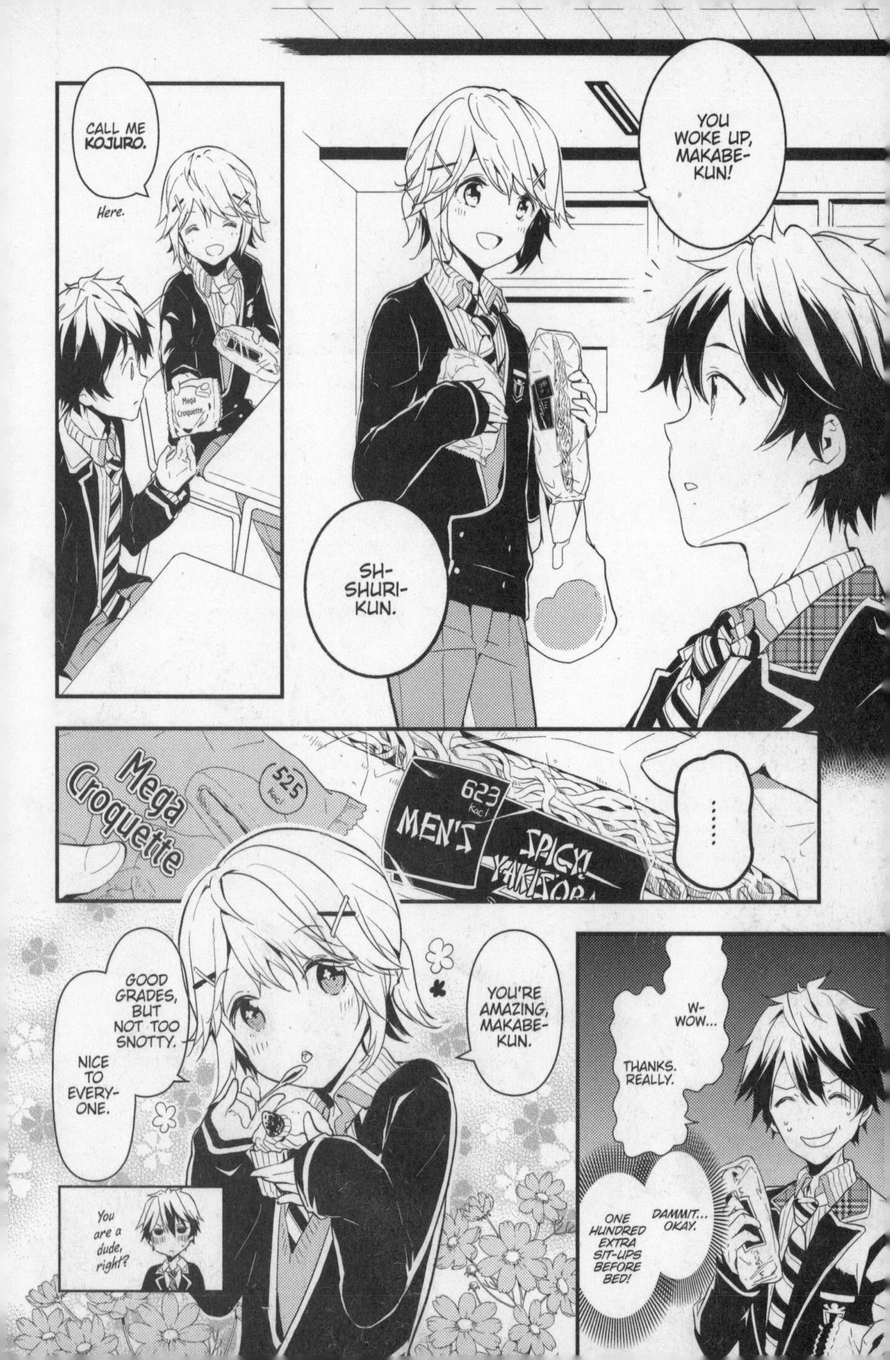
YOU WOKE UP, MAKABE-KUN!
SH-SHURI-KUN.
CALL ME KOJURO.
Here.
Mega Croquette
......
623
MEN'S
SPICY!
Mega Croquette
525
W-WOW...
THANKS. REALLY.
DAMMIT... OKAY.
ONE HUNDRED EXTRA SIT-UPS BEFORE BED!
YOU'RE AMAZING, MAKABE-KUN.
GOOD GRADES, BUT NOT TOO SNOTTY.
NICE TO EVERYONE.
You are a dude, right?

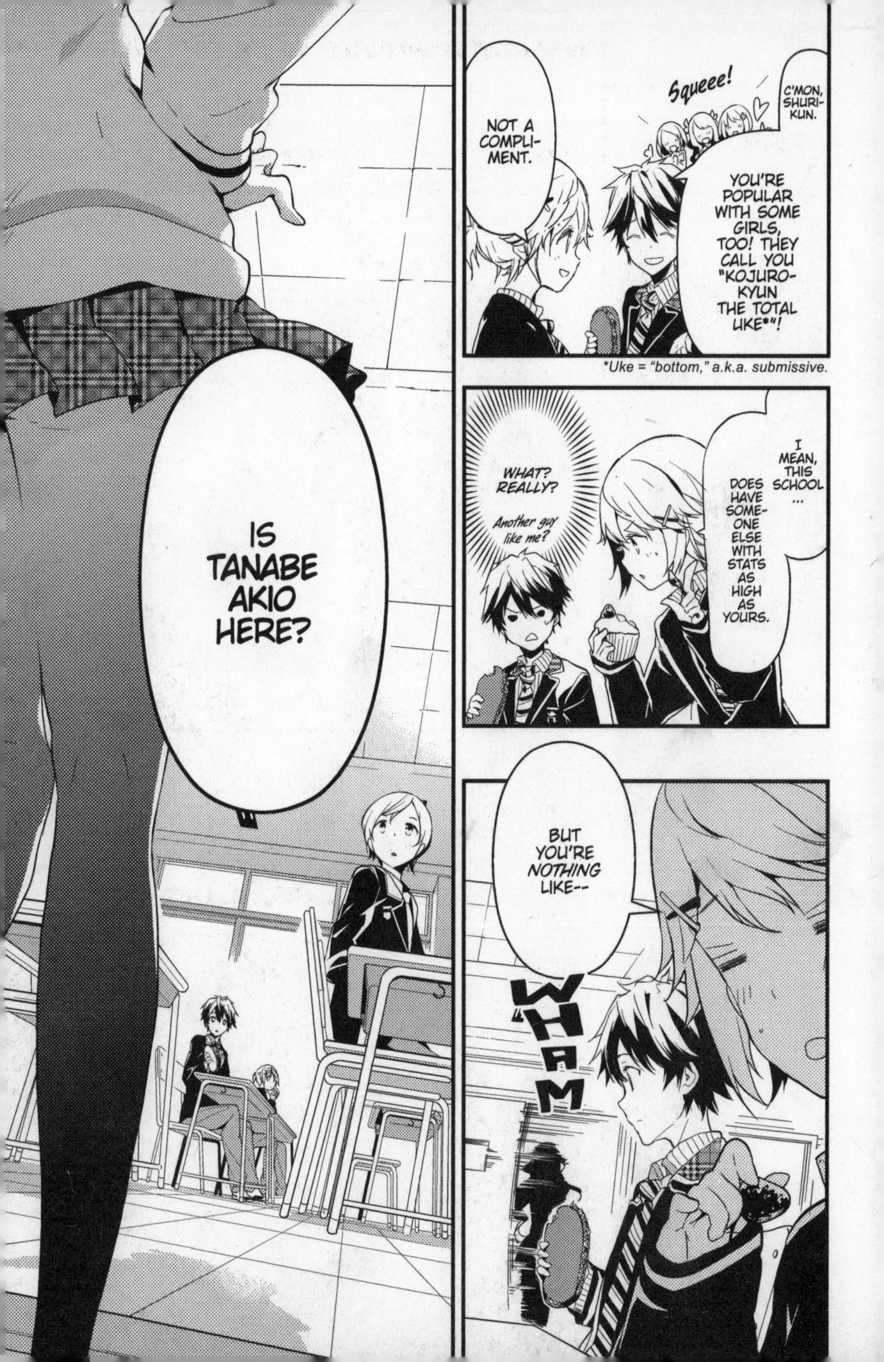
C'MON, SHURI-KUN.
Squeee!
YOU'RE POPULAR WITH SOME GIRLS, TOO! THEY CALL YOU "KOJURO-KYUN THE TOTAL UKE*"!
NOT A COMPLIMENT.
I MEAN, THIS SCHOOL ... DOES HAVE SOMEONE ELSE WITH STATS AS HIGH AS YOURS.
WHAT? REALLY?
Another guy like me?
BUT YOU'RE NOTHING LIKE--
WHAM
IS TANABE AKIO HERE?

*Uke = "bottom," a.k.a. submissive.

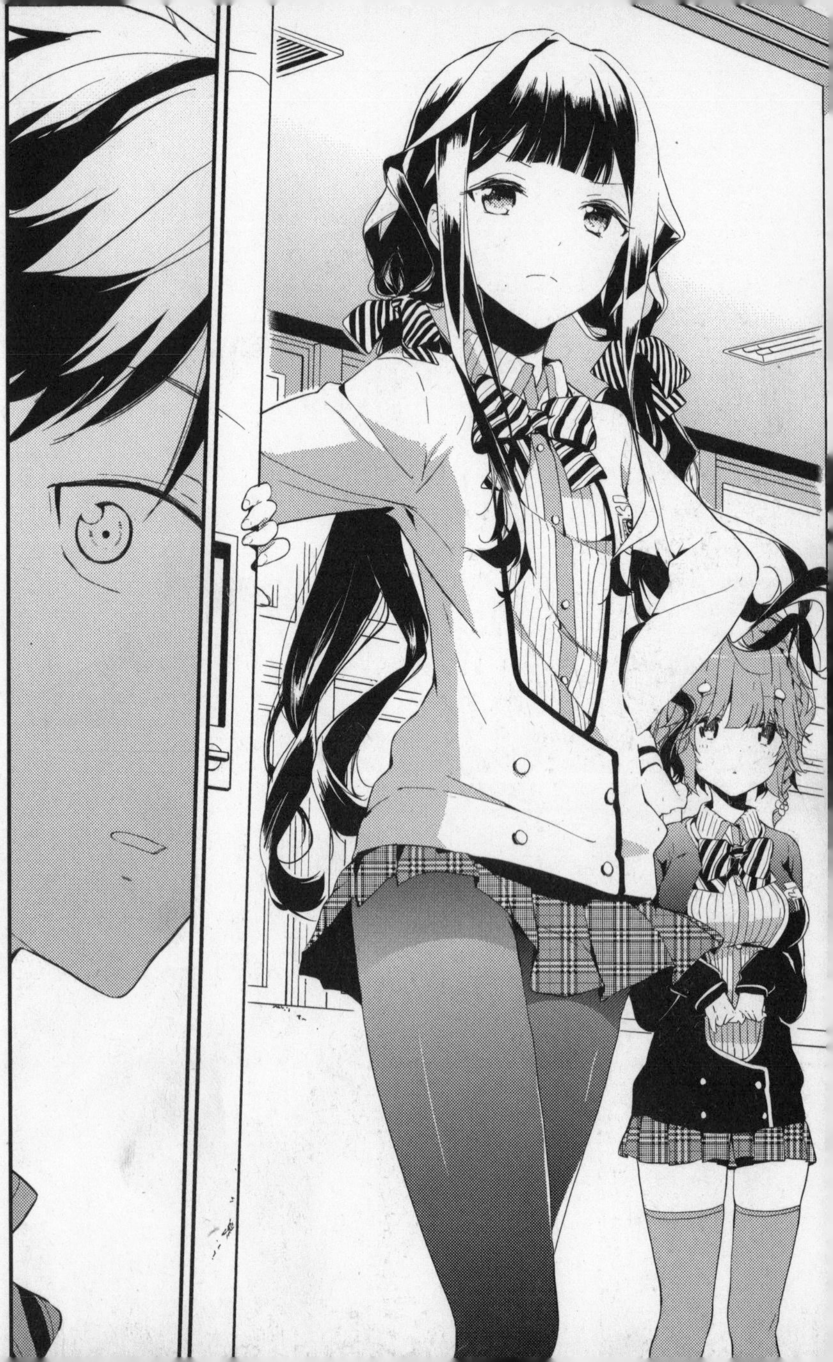

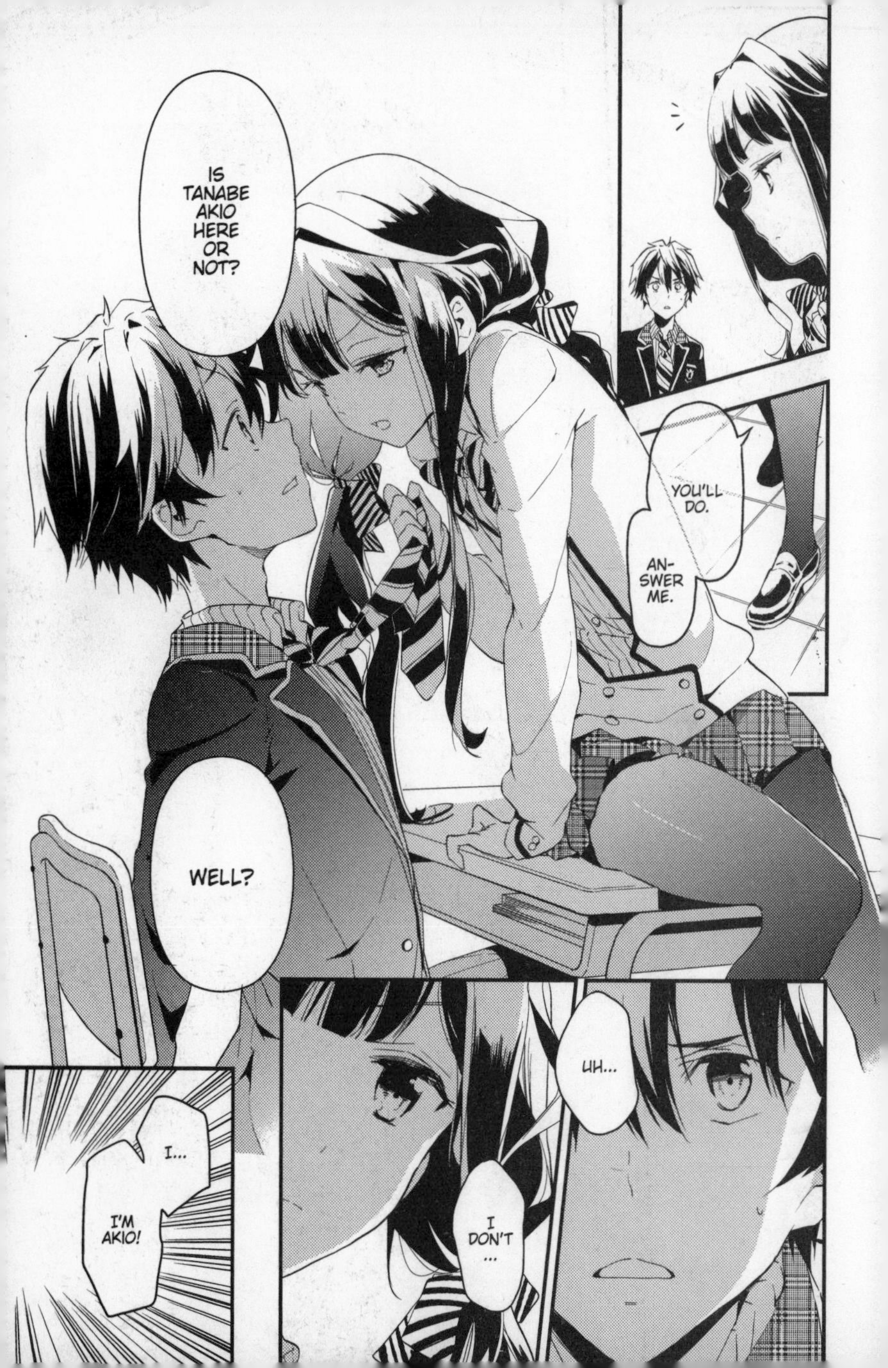
YOU'LL DO.
AN-SWER ME.
IS TANABE AKIO HERE OR NOT?
WELL?
UH...
I DON'T ...
I...
I'M AKIO!

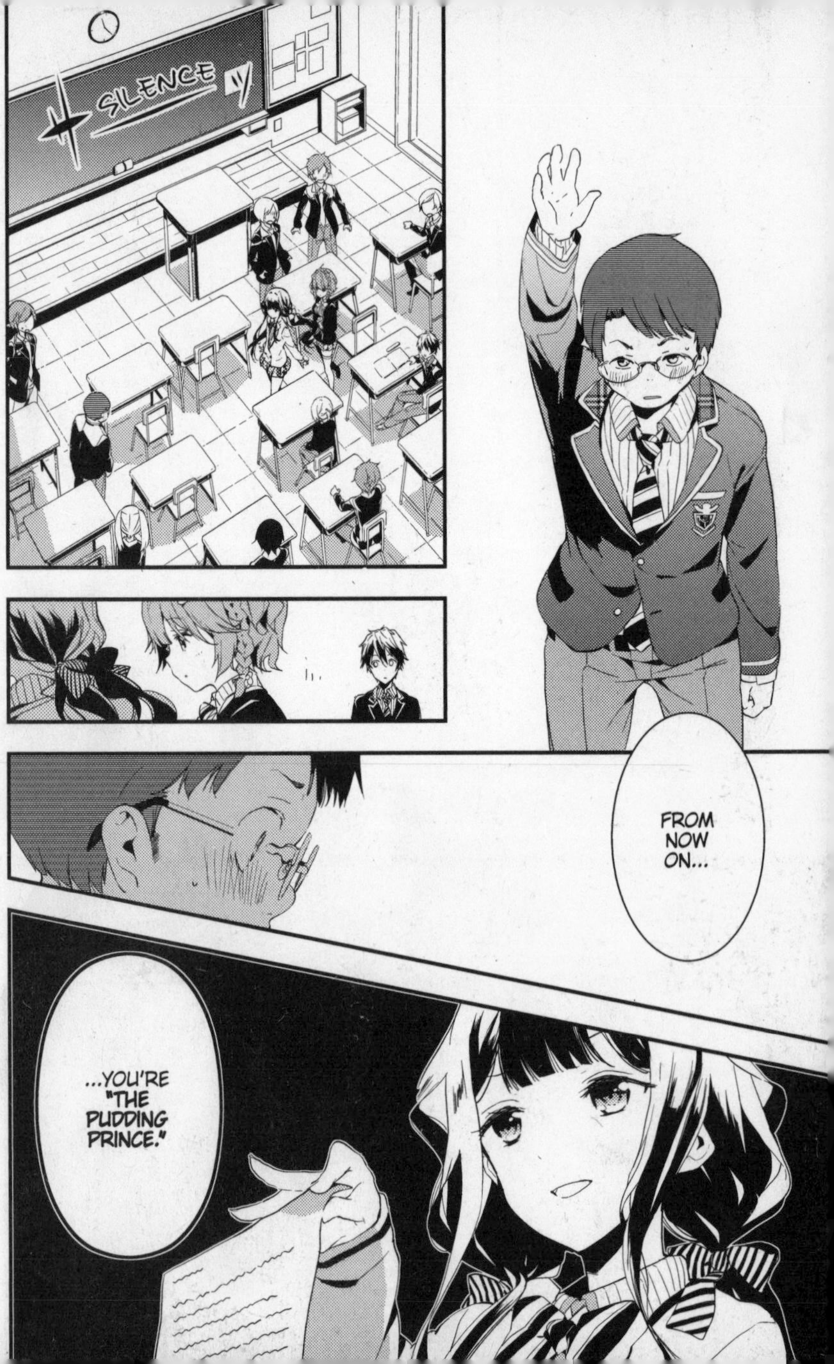
SILENCE
FROM NOW ON...
...YOU'RE "THE PUDDING PRINCE."

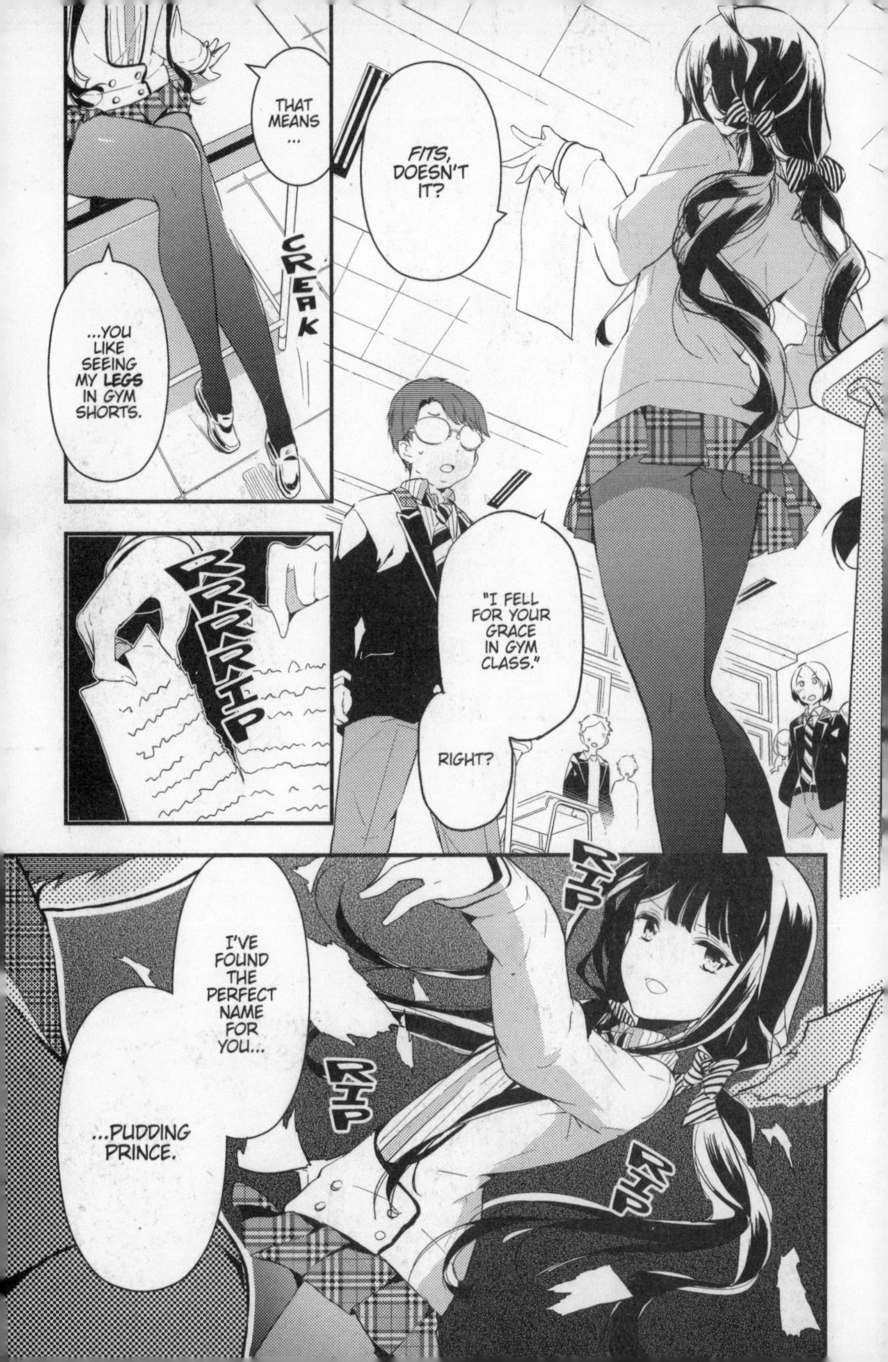
FITS, DOESN'T IT?
CREAK
"I FELL FOR YOUR GRACE IN GYM CLASS."
RIGHT?
THAT MEANS...
...YOU LIKE SEEING MY LEGS IN GYM SHORTS.
RRRRRIP
RIP
I'VE FOUND THE PERFECT NAME FOR YOU...
...PUDDING PRINCE.
RIP
RIP

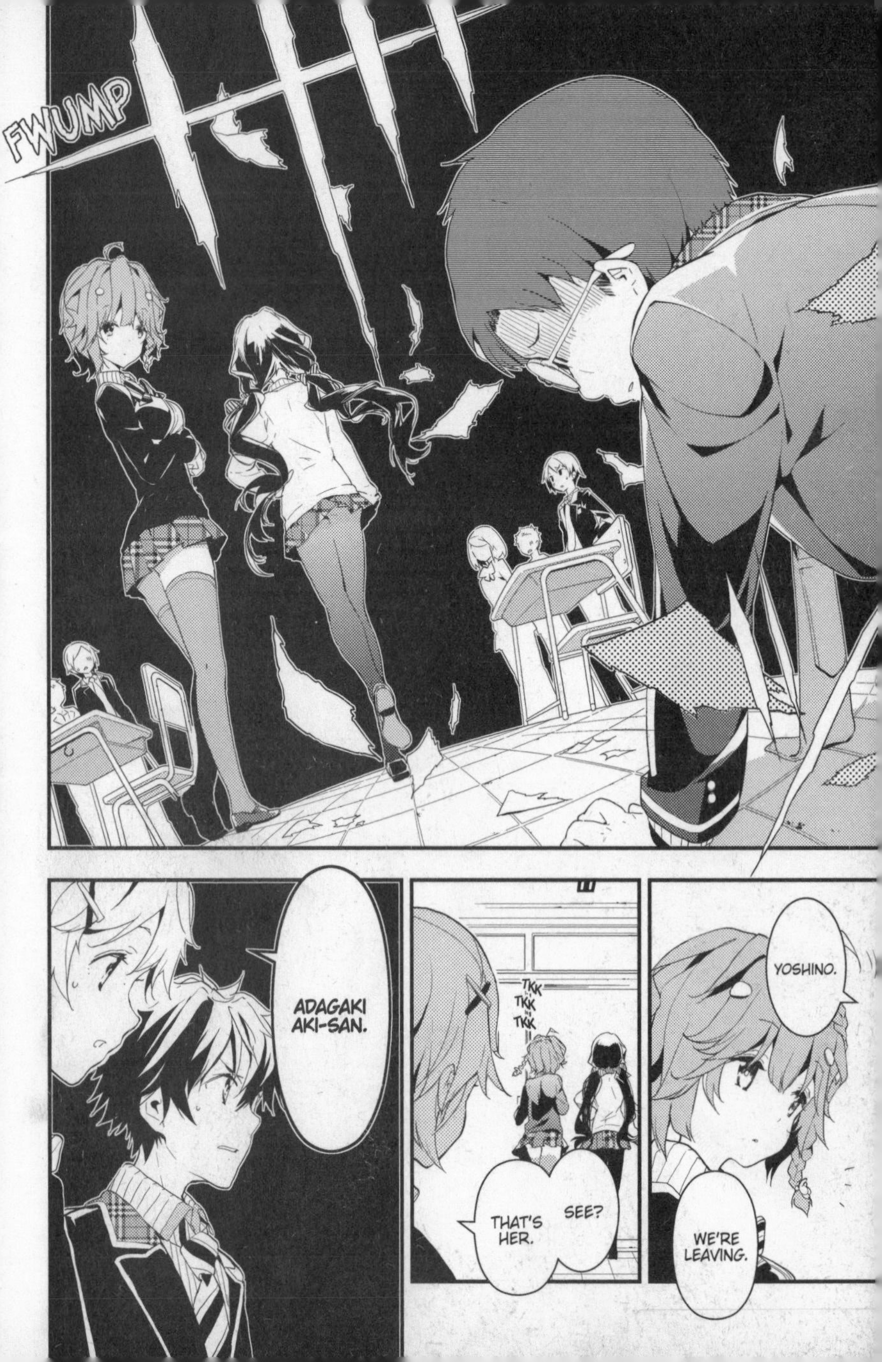
FWUMP
YOSHINO.
WE'RE LEAVING.
TKK TKK TKK
SEE?
THAT'S HER.
ADAGAKI AKI-SAN.

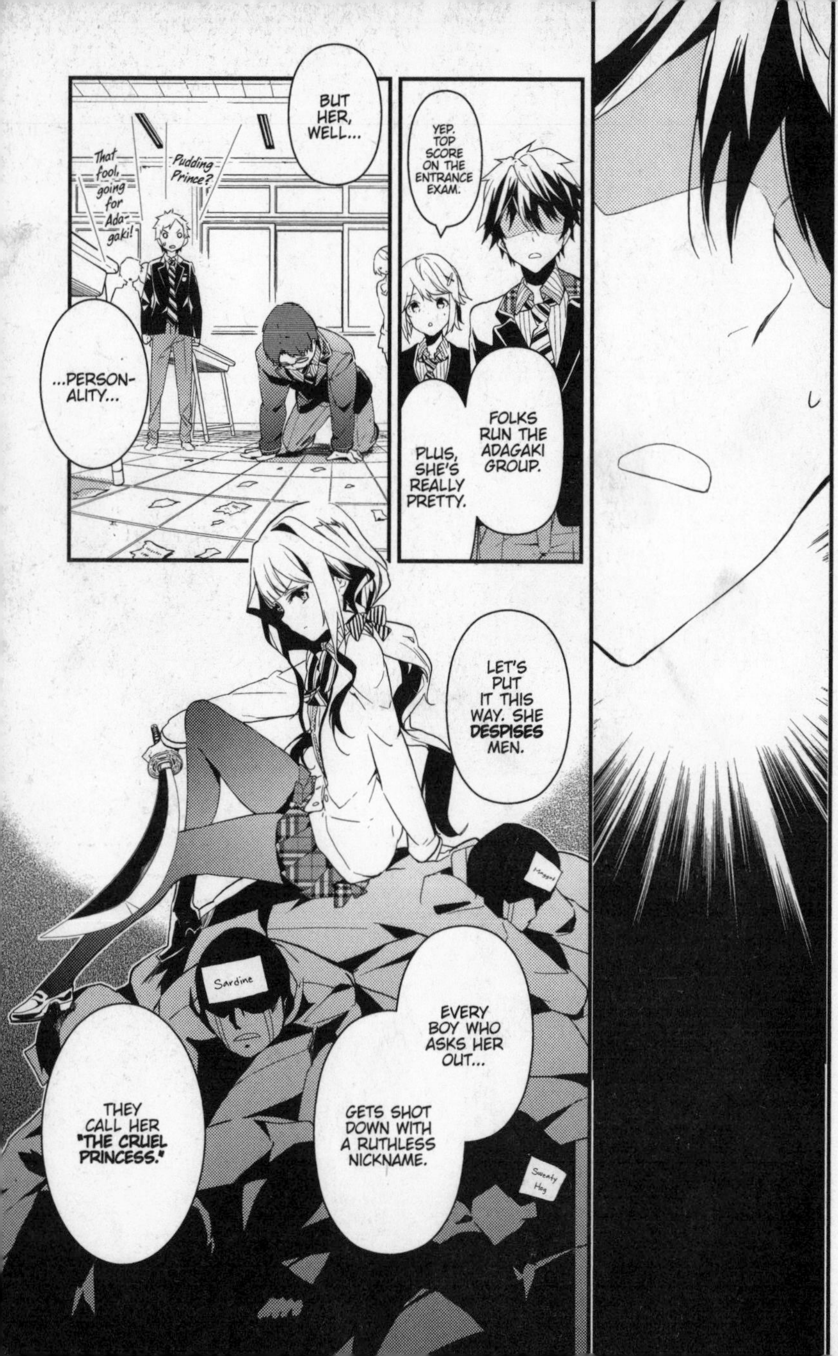
YEP. TOP SCORE ON THE ENTRANCE EXAM.
FOLKS RUN THE ADAGAKI GROUP.
PLUS, SHE'S REALLY PRETTY.
BUT HER, WELL...
Pudding Prince?
That fool, going for Adagaki!
...PERSONALITY...
LET'S PUT IT THIS WAY. SHE DESPISES MEN.
EVERY BOY WHO ASKS HER OUT...
GETS SHOT DOWN WITH A RUTHLESS NICKNAME.
THEY CALL HER "THE CRUEL PRINCESS."
Sardine
Sweaty Hog

I DIDN'T...

...EXPECT TO SEE HER SO SOON!

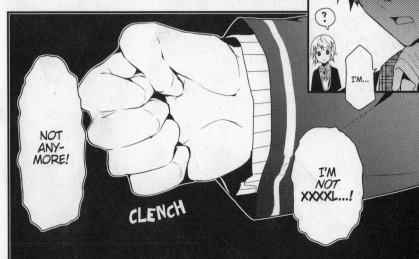

?

I'M...

NOT ANY-MORE!

CLENCH

I'M NOT XXXXL...!

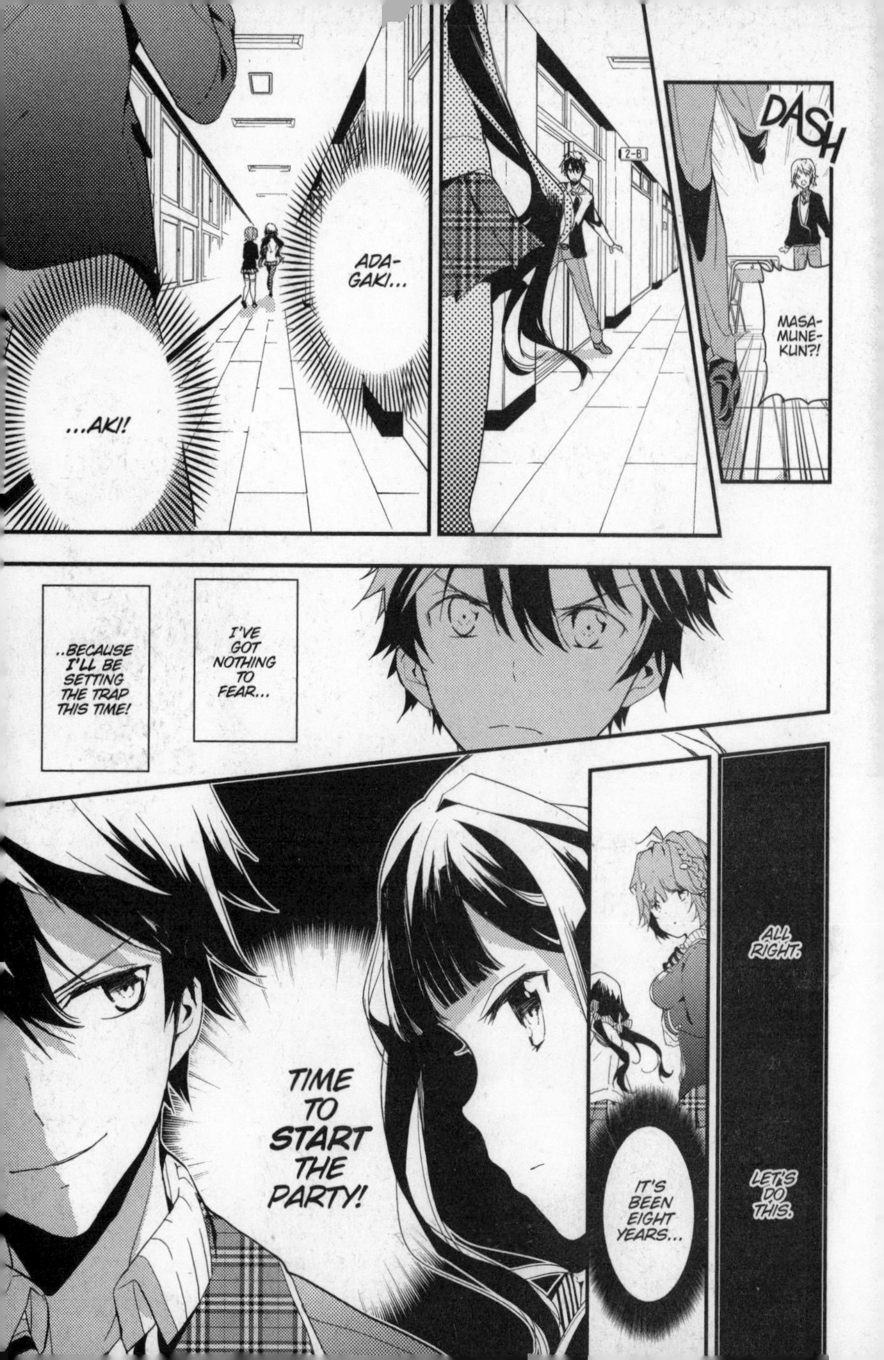
DASH
MASAMUNE-KUN?!
ADA-GAKI...
...AKI!
I'VE GOT NOTHING TO FEAR...
..BECAUSE I'LL BE SETTING THE TRAP THIS TIME!
ALL RIGHT.
LET'S DO THIS.
IT'S BEEN EIGHT YEARS...
TIME TO START THE PARTY!

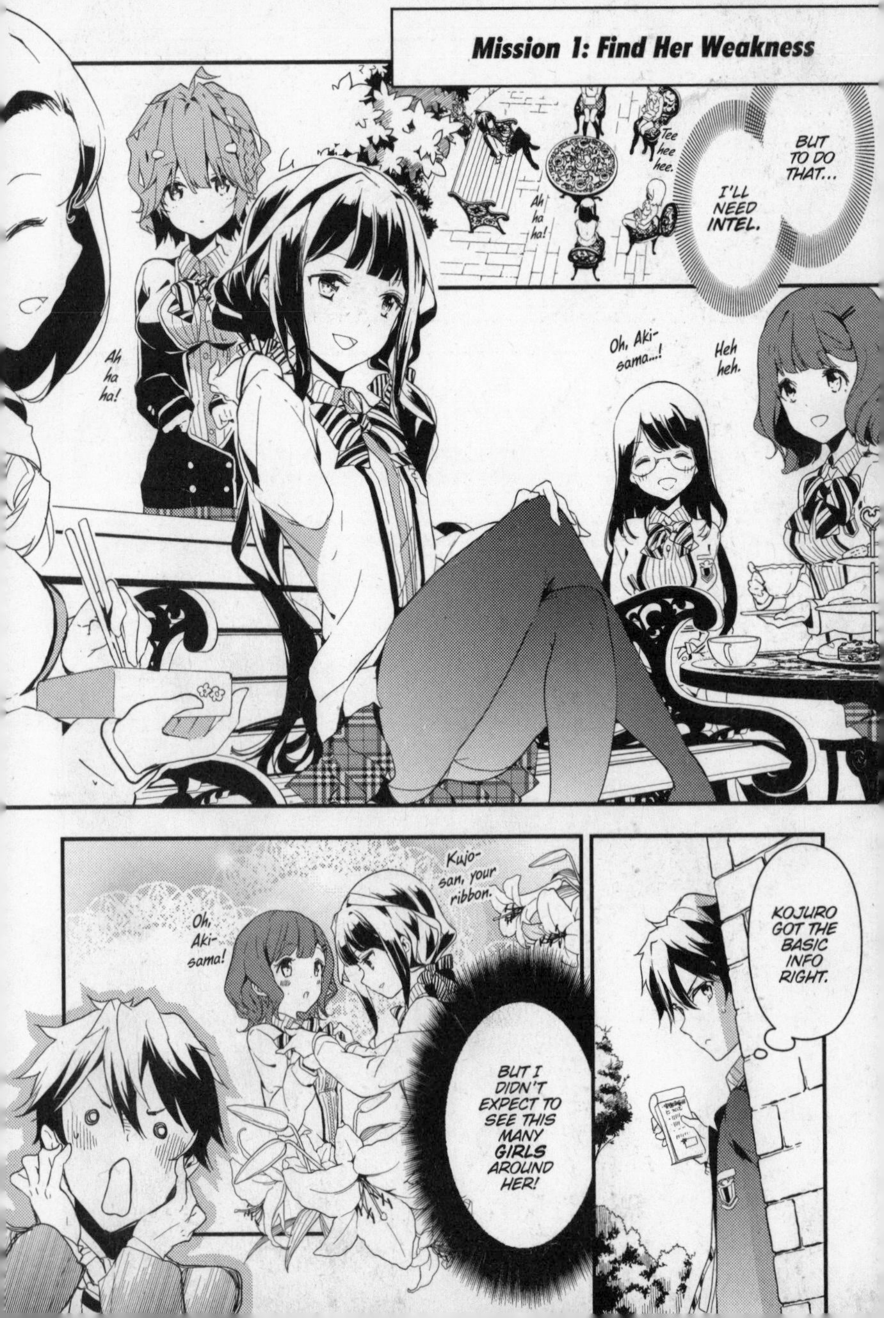
Mission 1: Find Her Weakness
BUT TO DO THAT...
I'LL NEED INTEL.
Tee hee hee.
Ah ha ha!
Heh heh.
Oh, Aki-sama...!
Ah ha ha!
KOJURO GOT THE BASIC INFO RIGHT.
Kujo-san, your ribbon.
Oh, Aki-sama!
BUT I DIDN'T EXPECT TO SEE THIS MANY GIRLS AROUND HER!

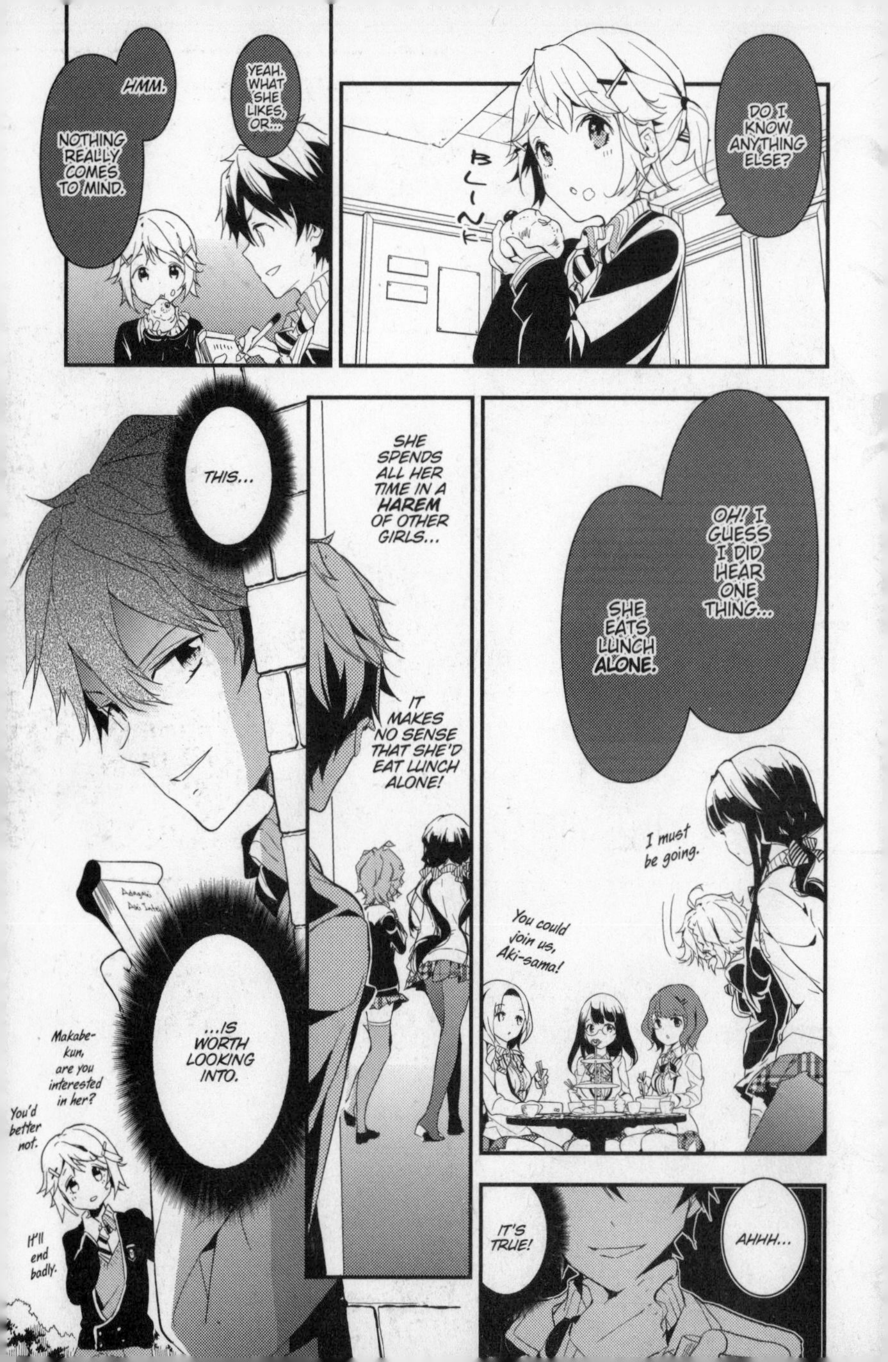
DO I KNOW ANYTHING ELSE?
BLINK
YEAH. WHAT SHE LIKES, OR...
HMM.
NOTHING REALLY COMES TO MIND.
OH! I GUESS I DID HEAR ONE THING...
SHE EATS LUNCH ALONE.
I must be going.
You could join us, Aki-sama!
AHHH...
IT'S TRUE!
SHE SPENDS ALL HER TIME IN A HAREM OF OTHER GIRLS...
IT MAKES NO SENSE THAT SHE'D EAT LUNCH ALONE!
THIS...
...IS WORTH LOOKING INTO.
Makabe-kun, are you interested in her?
You'd better not.
It'll end badly.

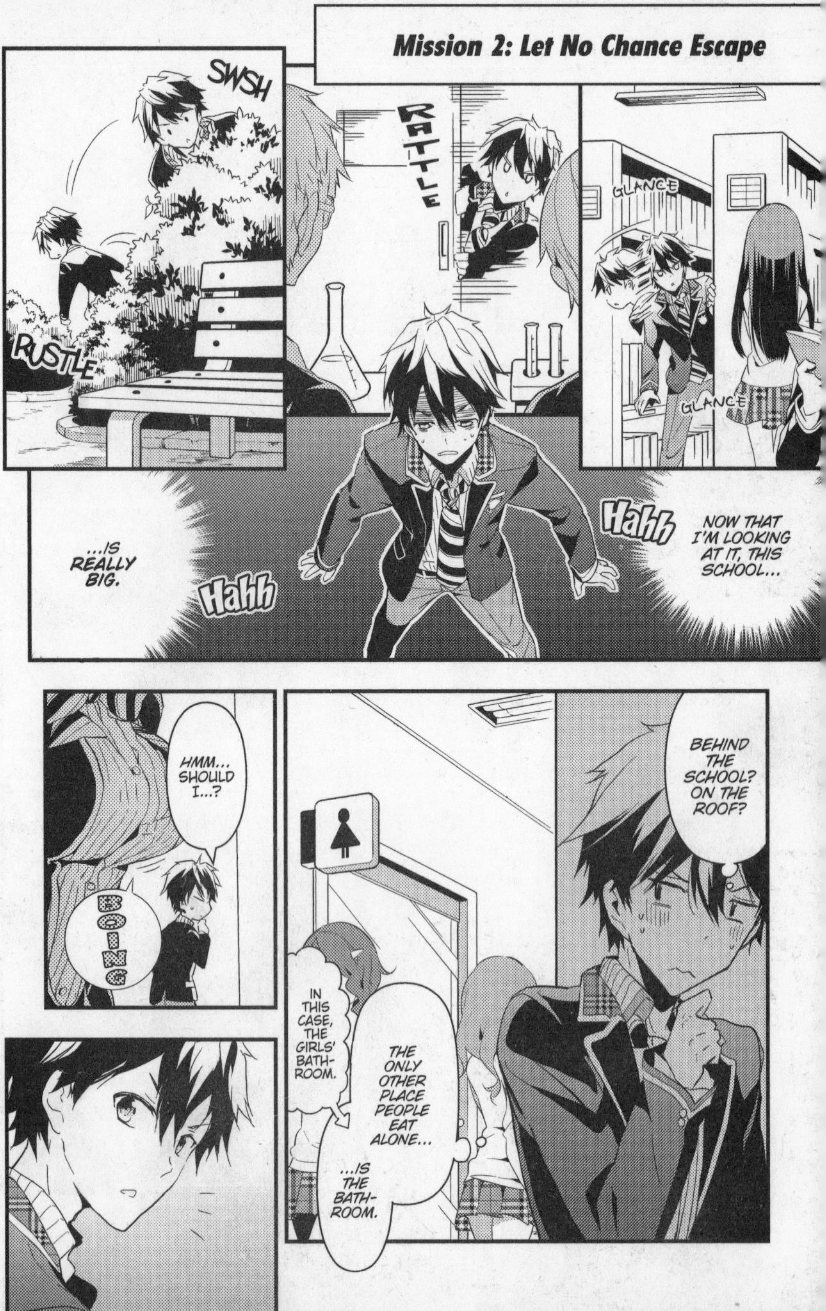
Mission 2: Let No Chance Escape
GLANCE
GLANCE
RATTLE
SWSH
RUSTLE
NOW THAT I'M LOOKING AT IT, THIS SCHOOL...
Hahh
Hahh
...IS REALLY BIG.
BEHIND THE SCHOOL? ON THE ROOF?
THE ONLY OTHER PLACE PEOPLE EAT ALONE...
...IS THE BATH-ROOM.
IN THIS CASE, THE GIRLS' BATH-ROOM.
HMM... SHOULD I...?
BOING

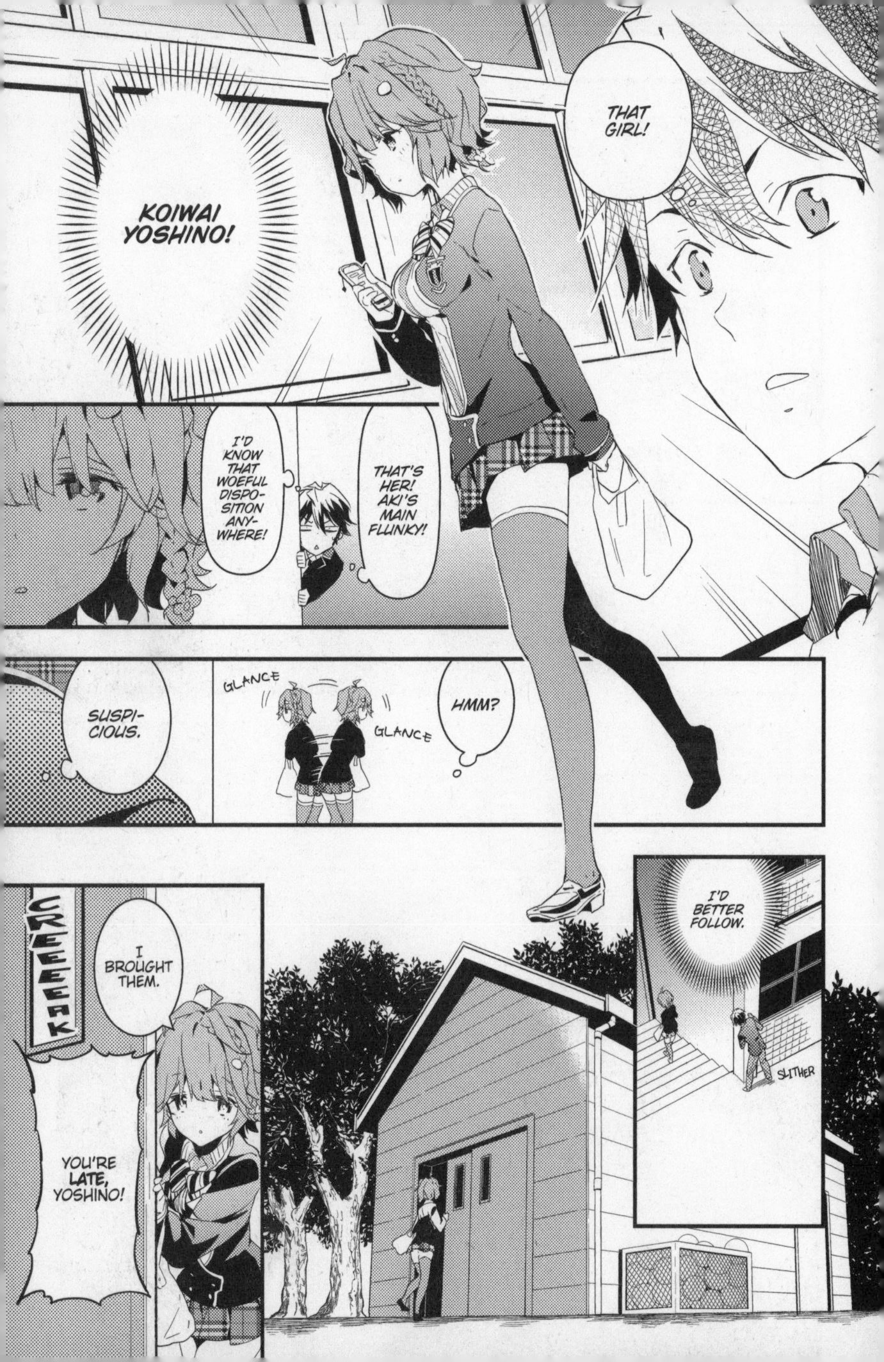
THAT GIRL!
KOIWAI YOSHINO!
THAT'S HER! AKI'S MAIN FLUNKY!
I'D KNOW THAT WOEFUL DISPO-SITION ANY-WHERE!
HMM?
GLANCE
GLANCE
SUSPI-CIOUS.
I'D BETTER FOLLOW.
SLITHER
CREEEAK
I BROUGHT THEM.
YOU'RE LATE, YOSHINO!

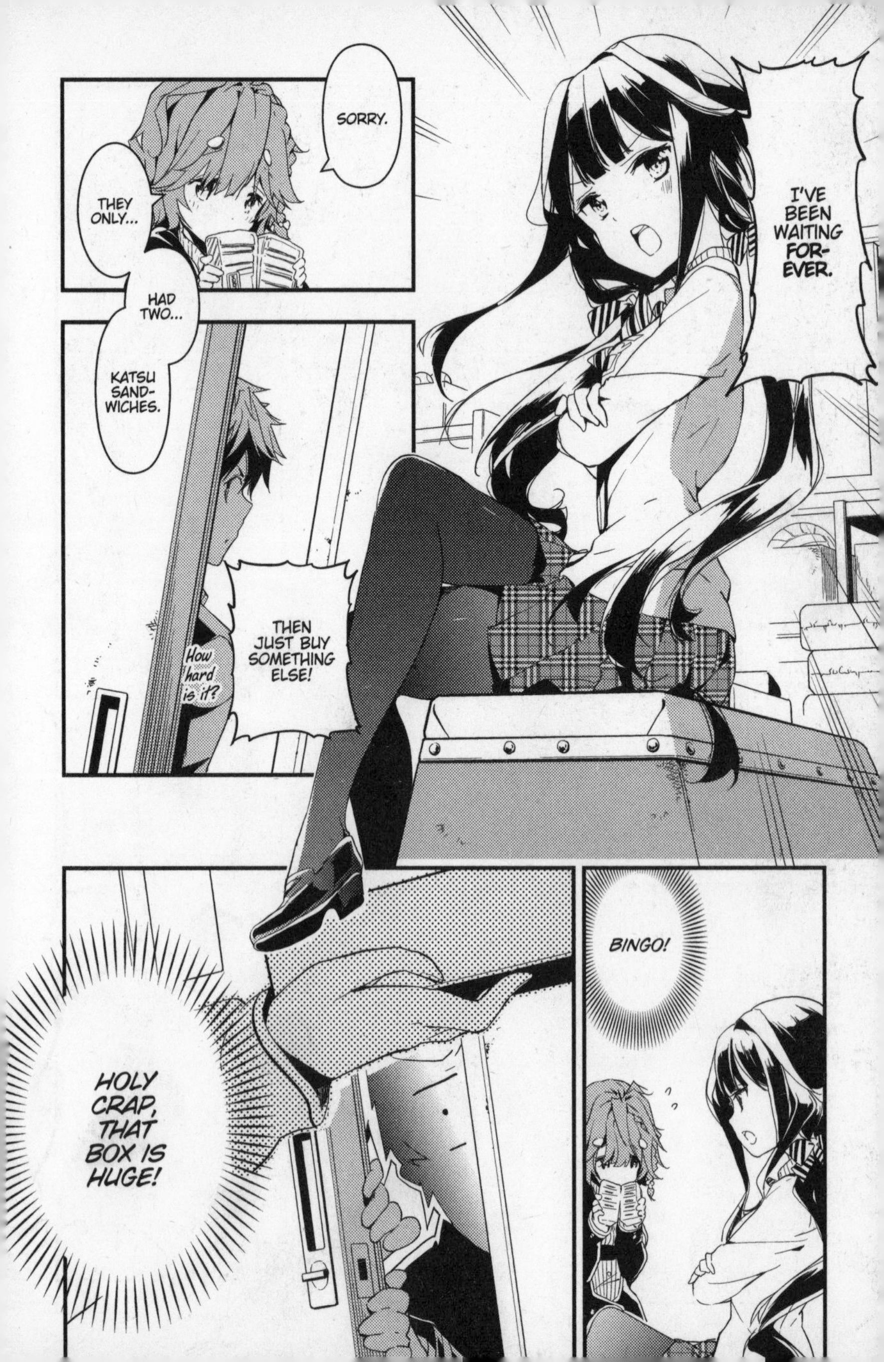
I'VE BEEN WAITING FOR-EVER.
SORRY.
THEY ONLY...
HAD TWO...
KATSU SAND-WICHES.
THEN JUST BUY SOMETHING ELSE!
How hard is it?
BINGO!
HOLY CRAP, THAT BOX IS HUGE!

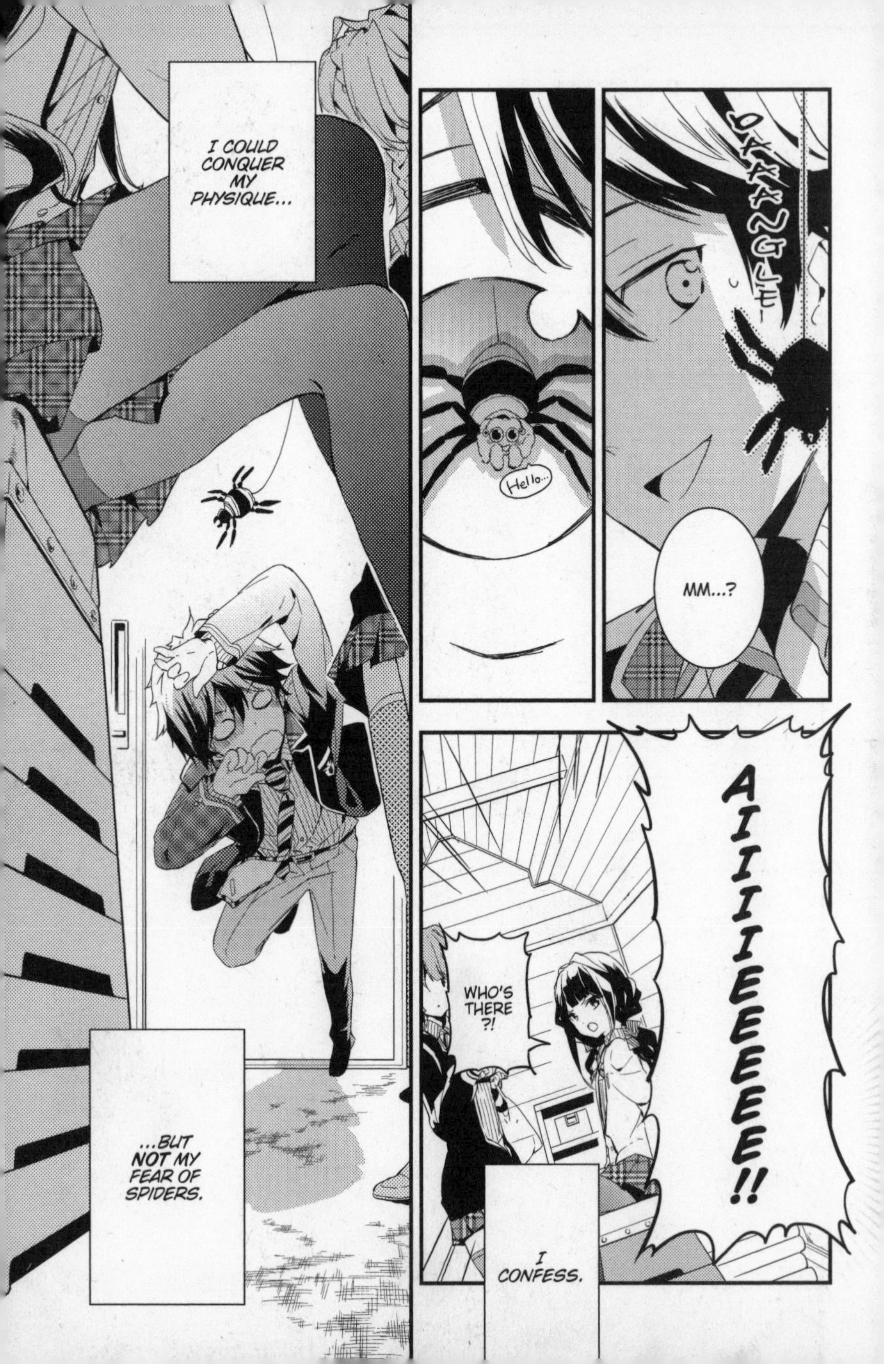
MM...?
Hello...
AIIIEEEEEE!!
WHO'S THERE?!
I CONFESS.
I COULD CONQUER MY PHYSIQUE...
...BUT NOT MY FEAR OF SPIDERS.

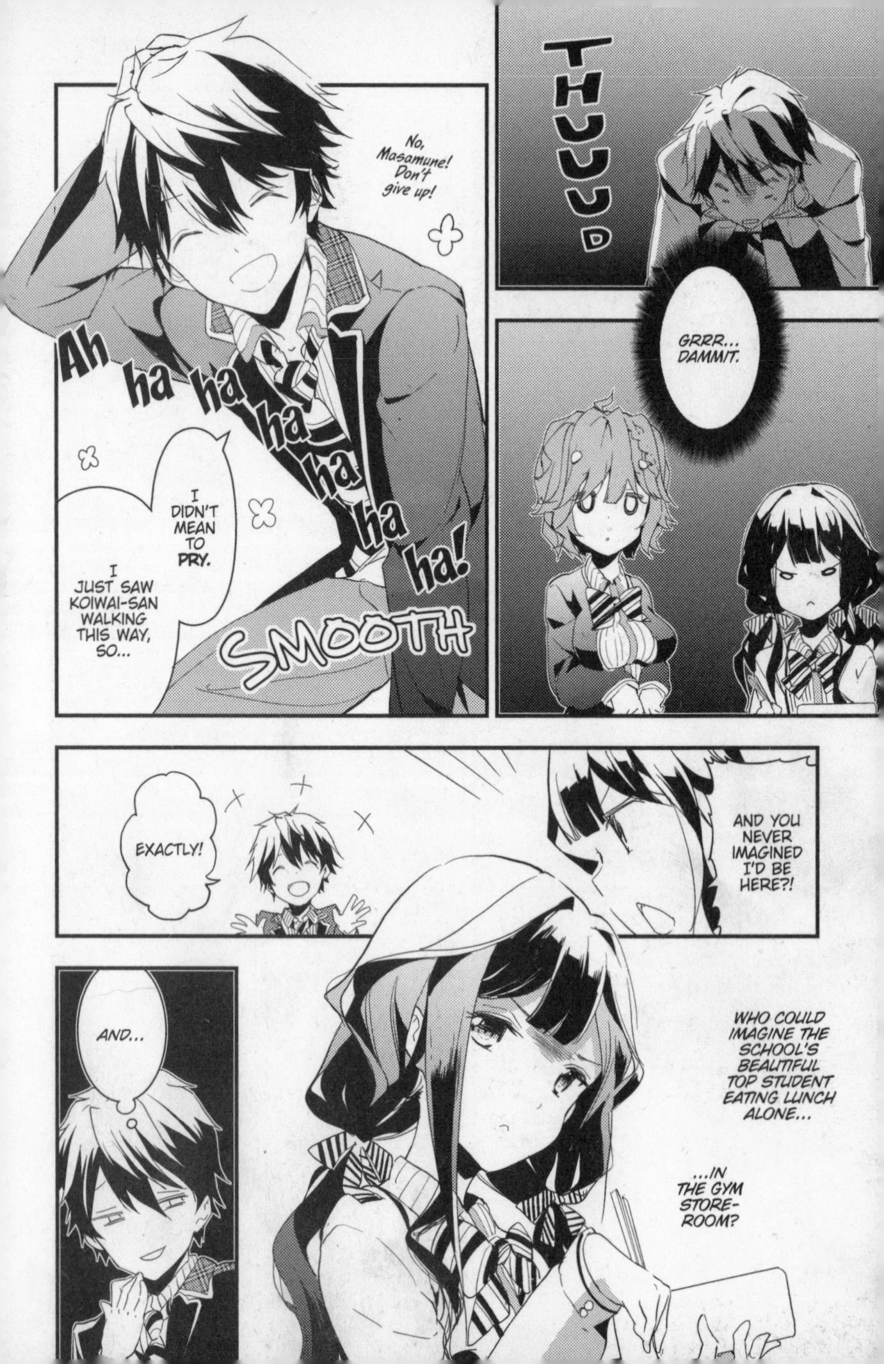
THUUUUD
GRRR... DAMMIT.
No, Masamune! Don't give up!
Ah ha ha ha ha ha ha!
I DIDN'T MEAN TO PRY.
I JUST SAW KOIWAI-SAN WALKING THIS WAY, SO...
SMOOTH
AND YOU NEVER IMAGINED I'D BE HERE?!
EXACTLY!
WHO COULD IMAGINE THE SCHOOL'S BEAUTIFUL TOP STUDENT EATING LUNCH ALONE...
...IN THE GYM STORE-ROOM?
AND...

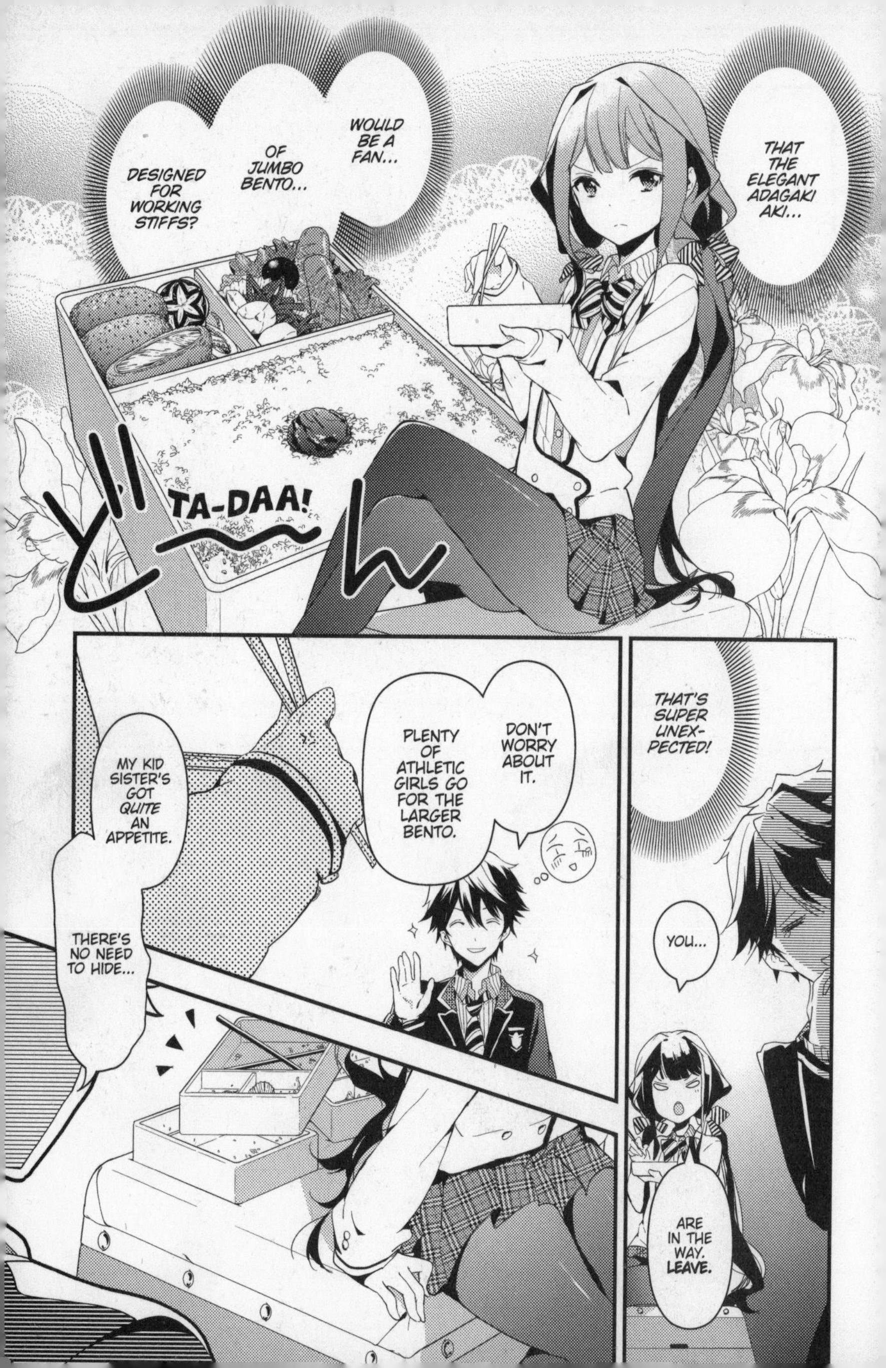
THAT THE ELEGANT ADAGAKI AKI...
WOULD BE A FAN...
OF JUMBO BENTO...
DESIGNED FOR WORKING STIFFS?
どーん
TA-DAA!
THAT'S SUPER UNEXPECTED!
YOU...
ARE IN THE WAY. LEAVE.
DON'T WORRY ABOUT IT.
PLENTY OF ATHLETIC GIRLS GO FOR THE LARGER BENTO.
MY KID SISTER'S GOT QUITE AN APPETITE.
THERE'S NO NEED TO HIDE...

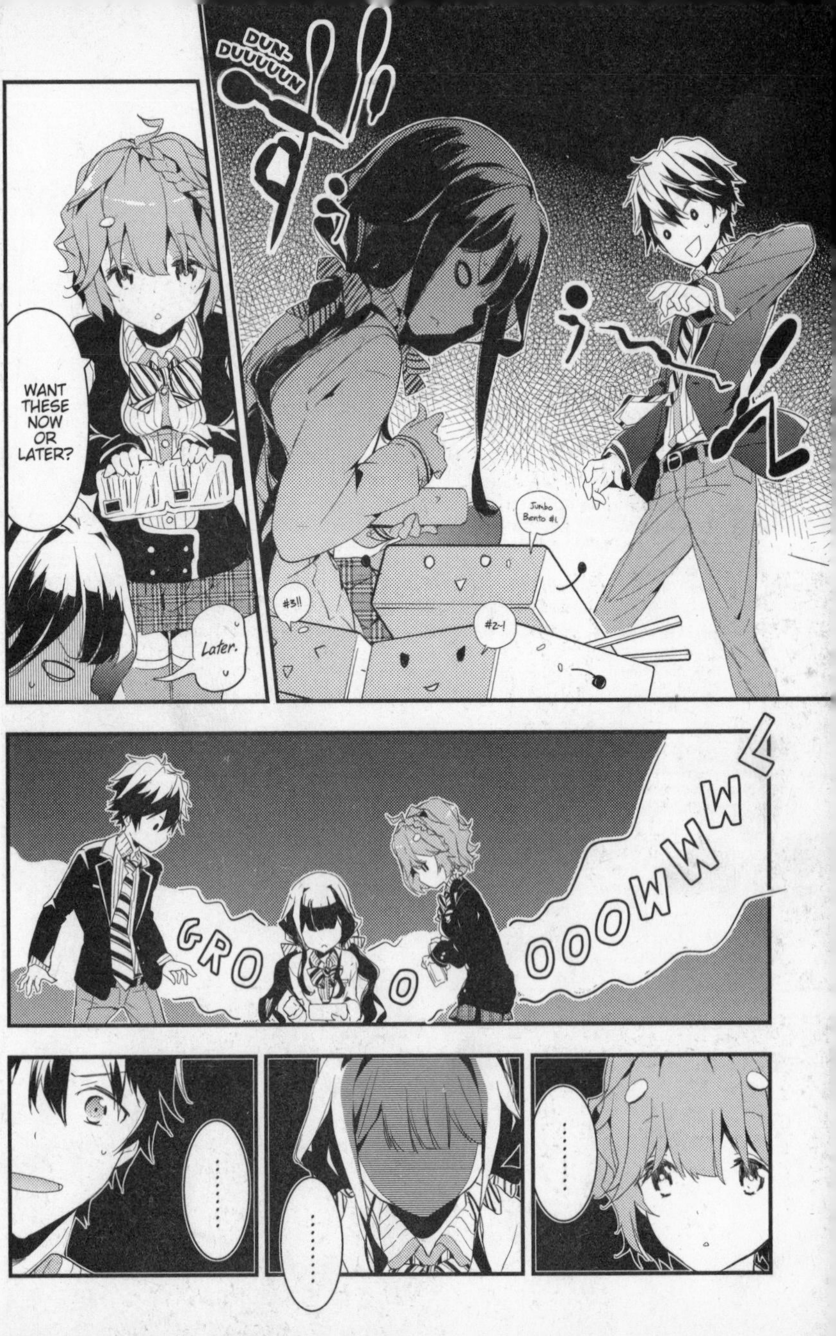
DUN-DUUUUUN
Jumbo Bento #1.
#2~!
#3!!
WANT THESE NOW OR LATER?
Later.
GROOOOOWWL
......
......
......
......

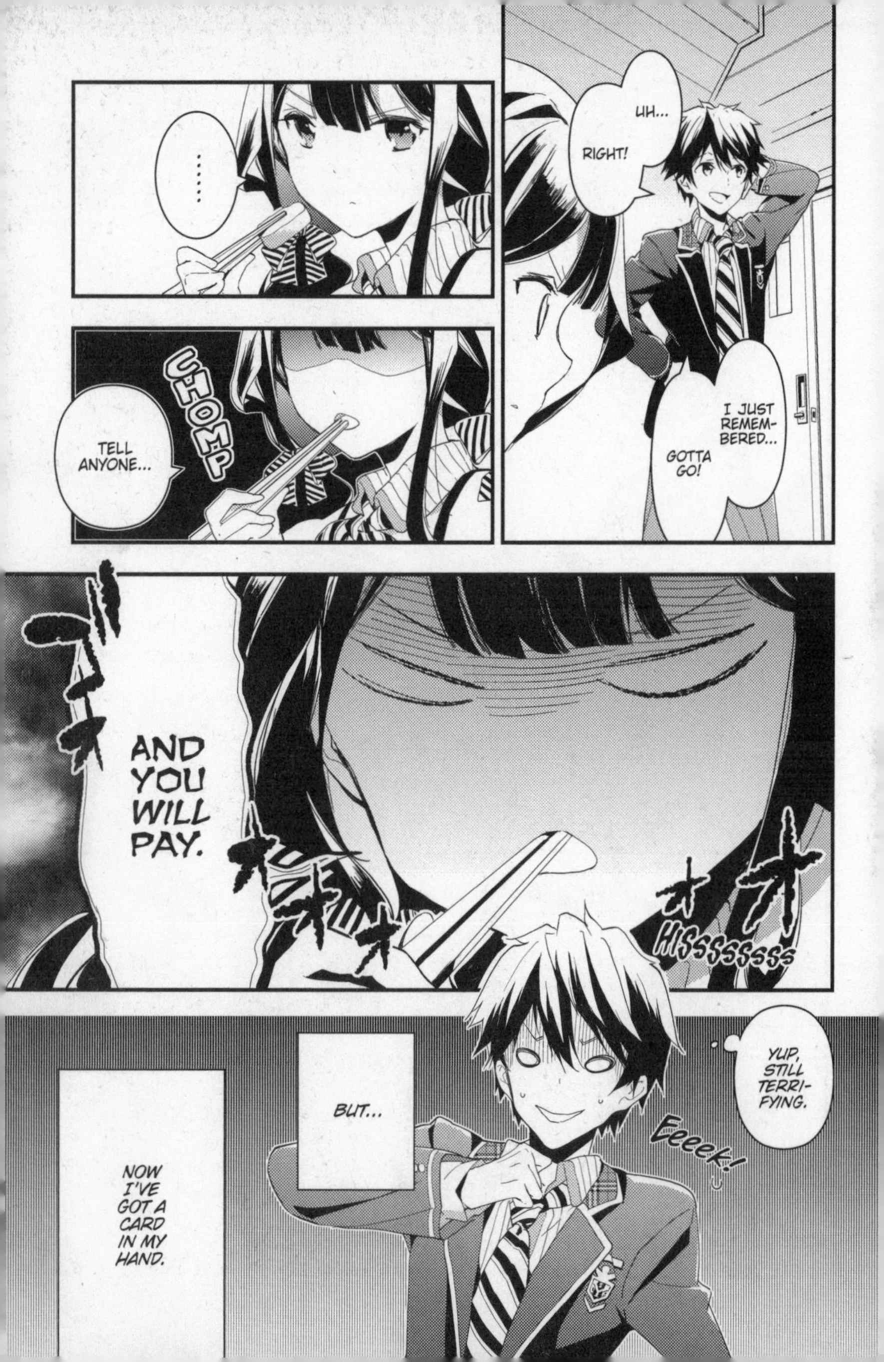
UH... RIGHT!
I JUST REMEM-BERED... GOTTA GO!
......
CHOMP
TELL ANYONE...
AND YOU WILL PAY.
HISSSSSSSS
YUP, STILL TERRI-FYING.
Eeeek!
BUT...
NOW I'VE GOT A CARD IN MY HAND.

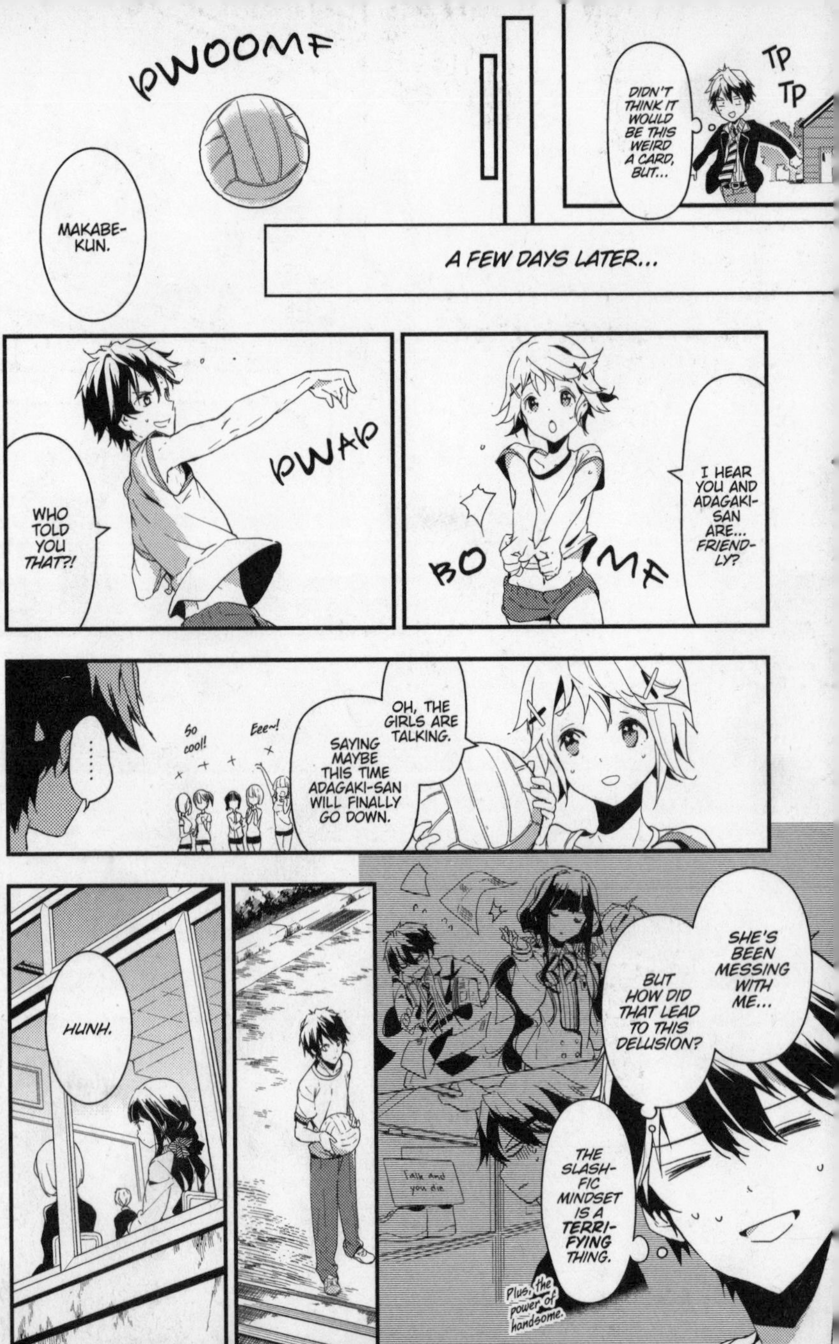
DIDN'T THINK IT WOULD BE THIS WEIRD A CARD, BUT...
TP TP
A FEW DAYS LATER...
PWOOMF
MAKABE-KUN.
I HEAR YOU AND ADAGAKI-SAN ARE... FRIENDLY?
BOOMF
PWAP
WHO TOLD YOU THAT?!
OH, THE GIRLS ARE TALKING.
SAYING MAYBE THIS TIME ADAGAKI-SAN WILL FINALLY GO DOWN.
Eee~!
So cool!
......
SHE'S BEEN MESSING WITH ME...
BUT HOW DID THAT LEAD TO THIS DELUSION?
THE SLASH-FIC MINDSET IS A TERRI-FYING THING.
Plus, the power of handsome.
Talk and you die
HUNH.

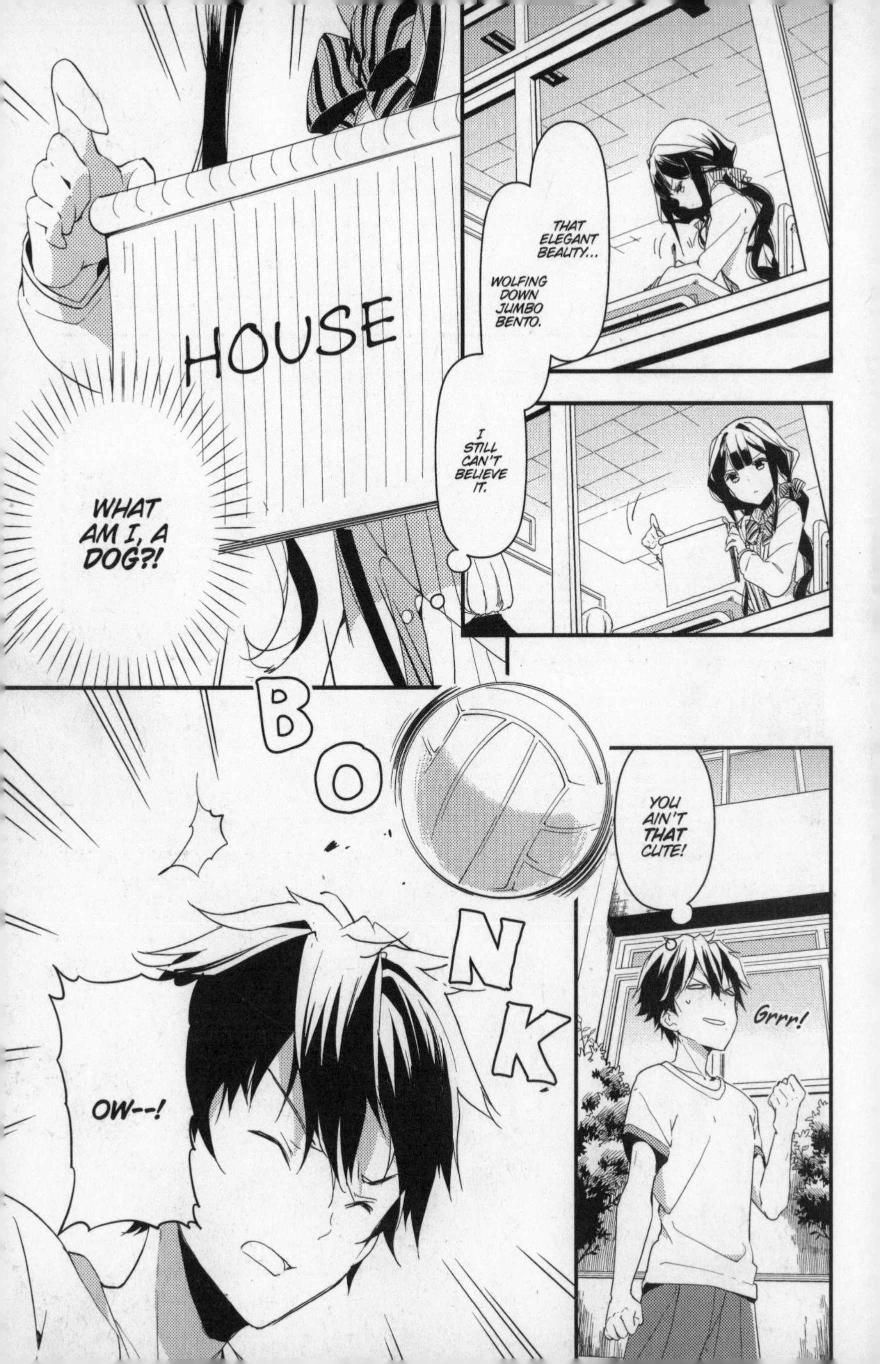
THAT ELEGANT BEAUTY...
WOLFING DOWN JUMBO BENTO.
I STILL CAN'T BELIEVE IT.
HOUSE
WHAT AM I, A DOG?!
YOU AIN'T THAT CUTE!
Grrr!
BONK
OW--!

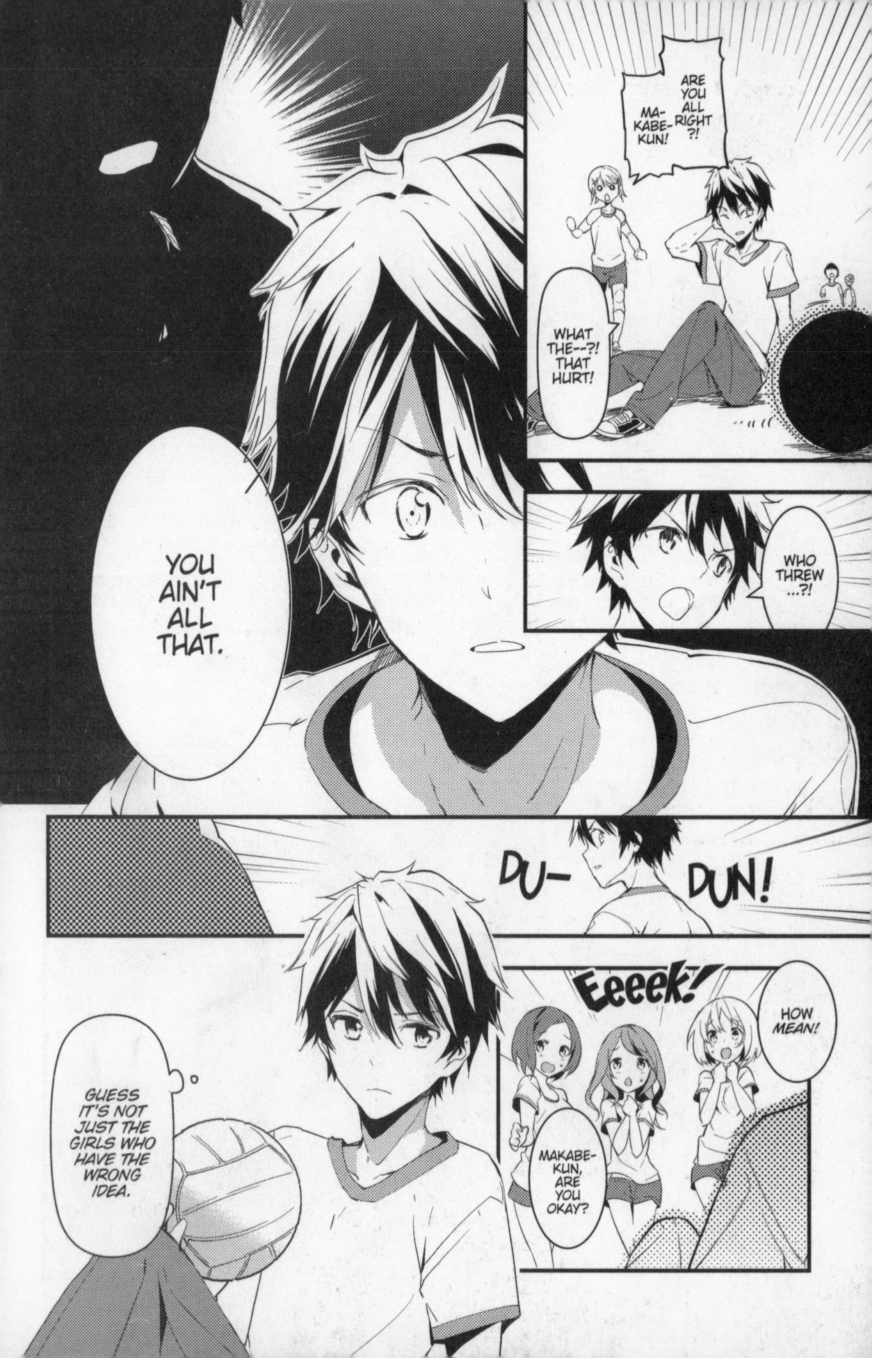

MAKABE-KUN! ARE YOU ALL RIGHT?!
WHAT THE--?! THAT HURT!
WHO THREW ...?!
YOU AIN'T ALL THAT.
DU- DUN!
Eeeek!
HOW MEAN!
MAKABE-KUN, ARE YOU OKAY?
GUESS IT'S NOT JUST THE GIRLS WHO HAVE THE WRONG IDEA.

Mission 3: Play Your Card Strategically

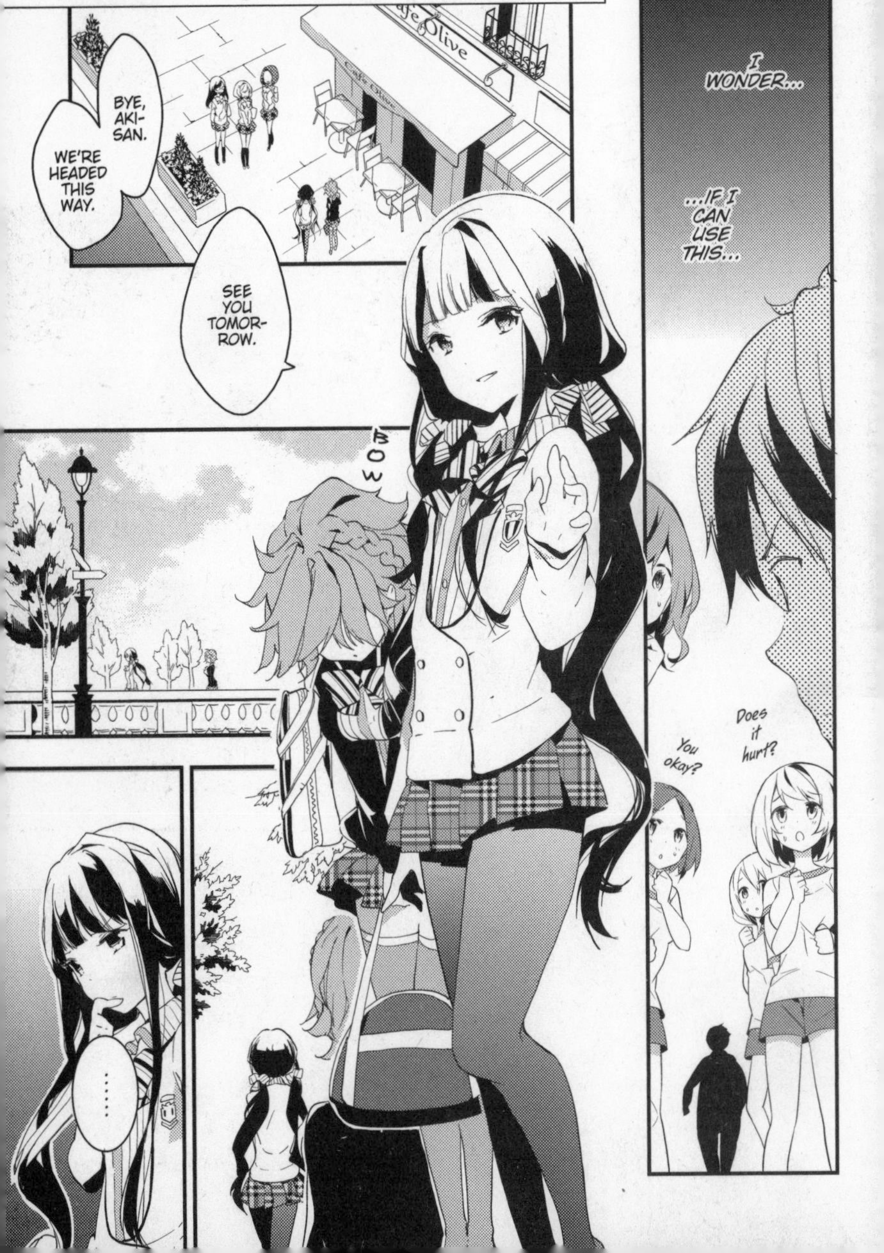

I WONDER...
...IF I CAN USE THIS...
Does it hurt?
You okay?
BYE, AKI-SAN.
WE'RE HEADED THIS WAY.
SEE YOU TOMORROW.
BOW
......

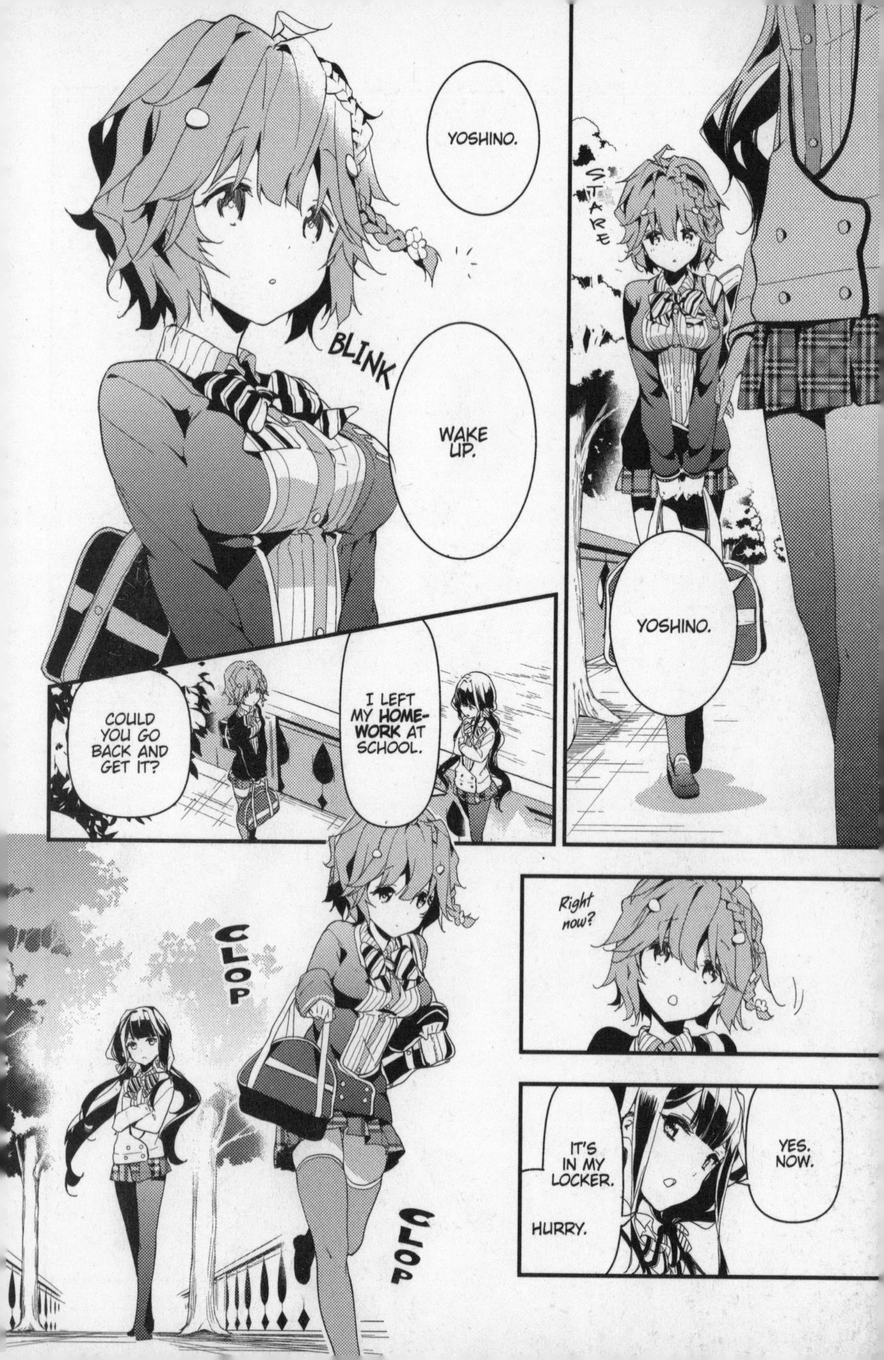
STARE
YOSHINO.
YOSHINO.
BLINK
WAKE UP.
I LEFT MY HOMEWORK AT SCHOOL.
COULD YOU GO BACK AND GET IT?
Right now?
YES. NOW.
IT'S IN MY LOCKER.
HURRY.
CLOP
CLOP

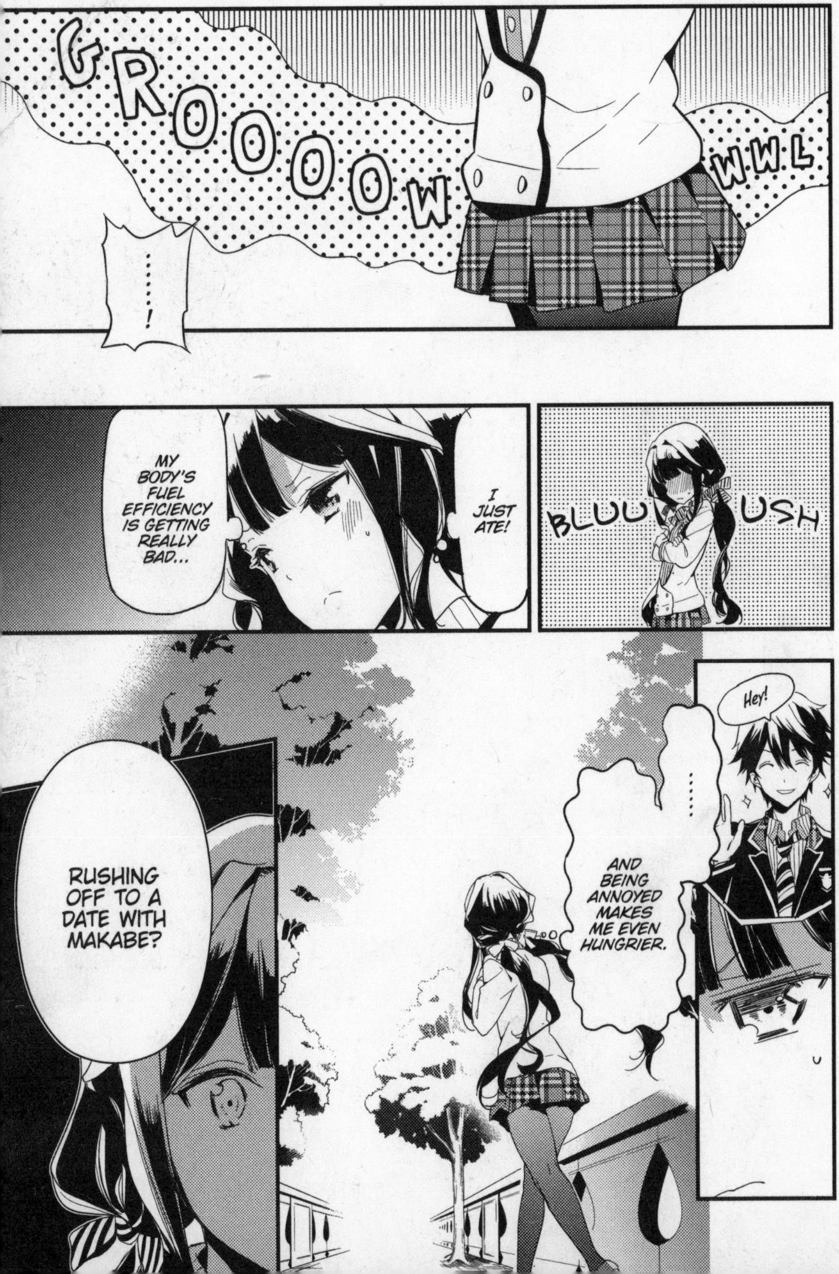
GROOOOWWWL
.....!
BLUUUSH
I JUST ATE!
MY BODY'S FUEL EFFICIENCY IS GETTING REALLY BAD...
Hey!
......
AND BEING ANNOYED MAKES ME EVEN HUNGRIER.
RUSHING OFF TO A DATE WITH MAKABE?

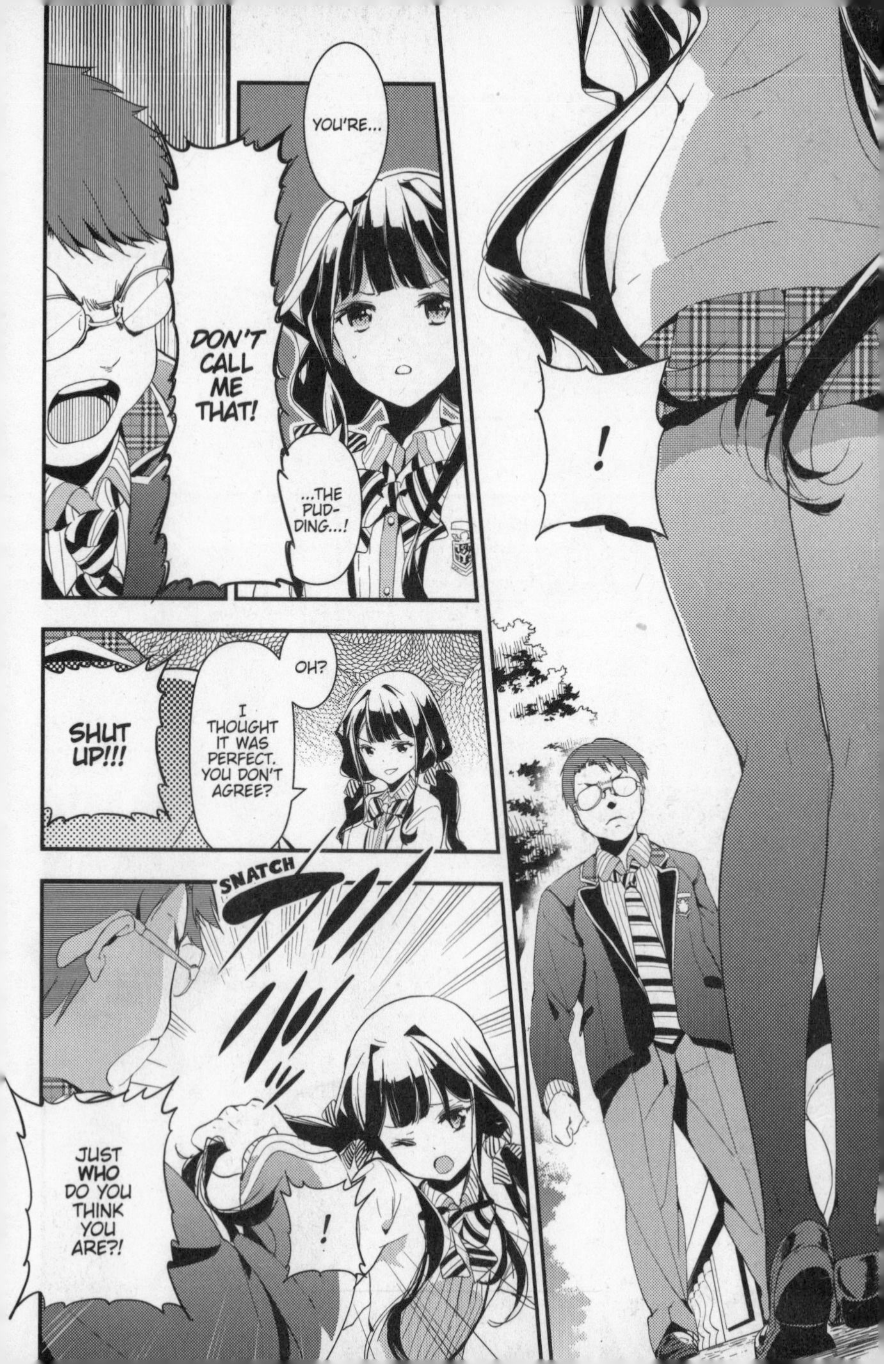
!
YOU'RE...
...THE PUD-DING...!
DON'T CALL ME THAT!
OH?
I THOUGHT IT WAS PERFECT. YOU DON'T AGREE?
SHUT UP!!!
SNATCH
!
JUST WHO DO YOU THINK YOU ARE?!

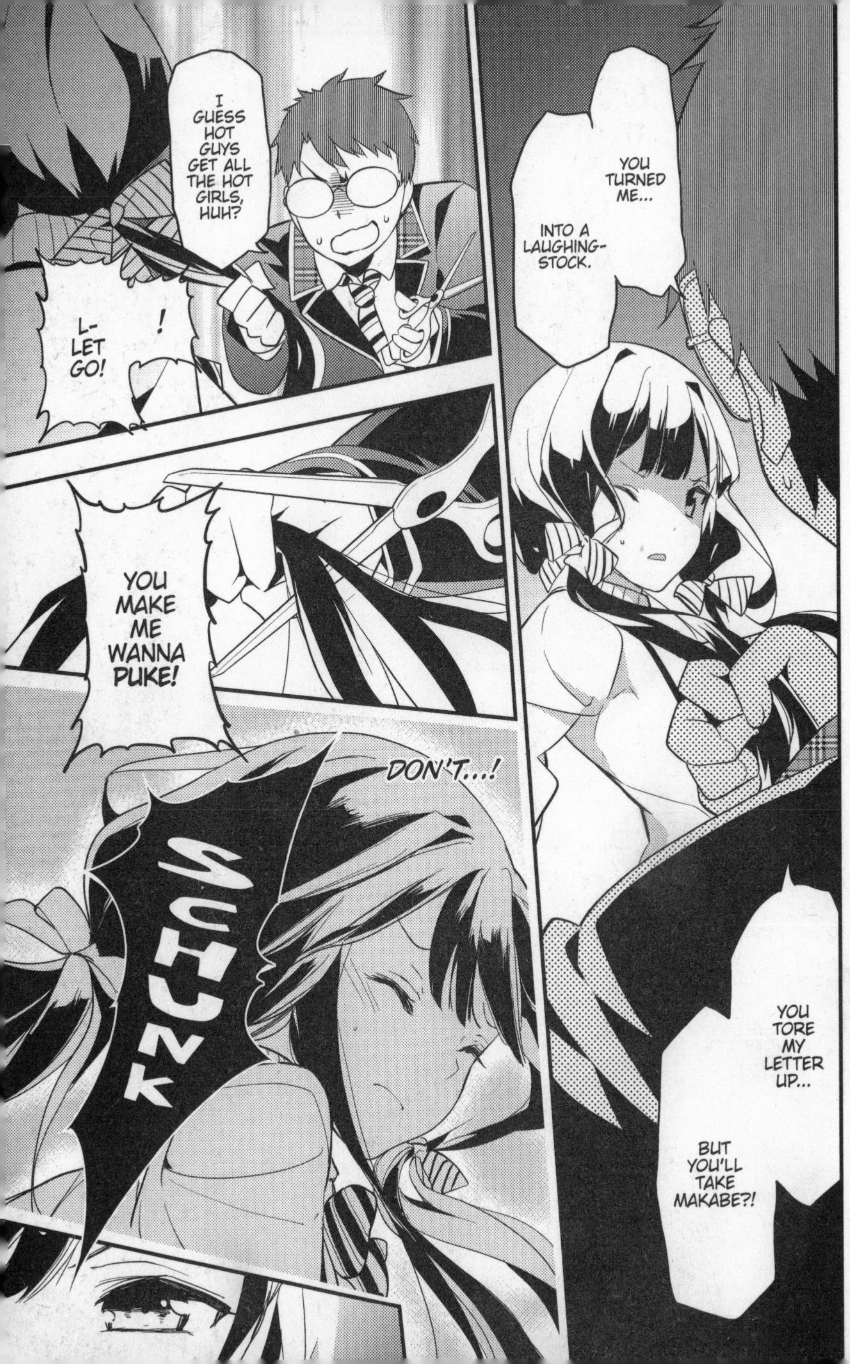

YOU TURNED ME...
INTO A LAUGHING-STOCK.
YOU TORE MY LETTER UP...
BUT YOU'LL TAKE MAKABE?!
I GUESS HOT GUYS GET ALL THE HOT GIRLS, HUH?
!
L- LET GO!
YOU MAKE ME WANNA PUKE!
DON'T...!
SCHUNK

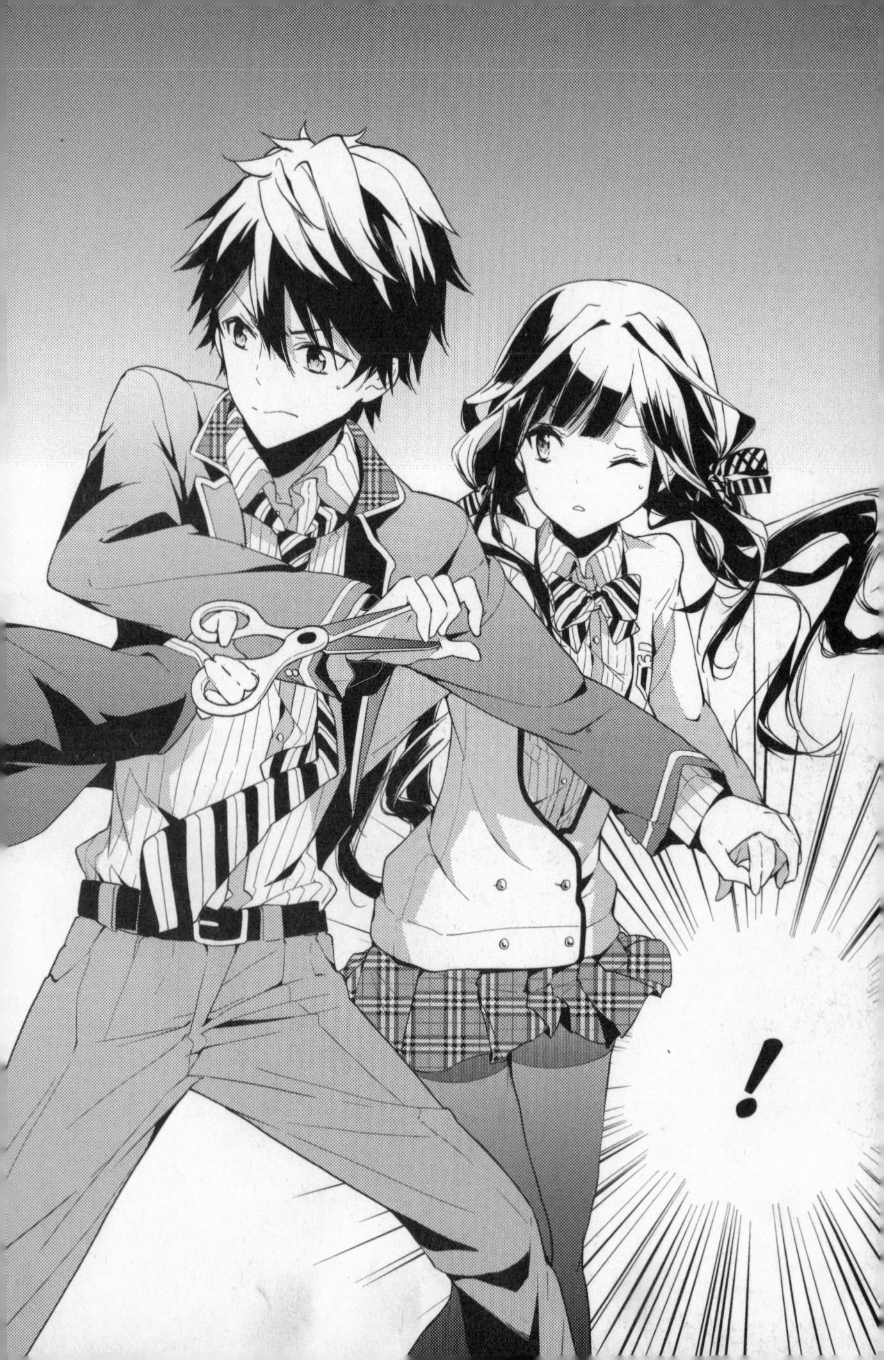
!

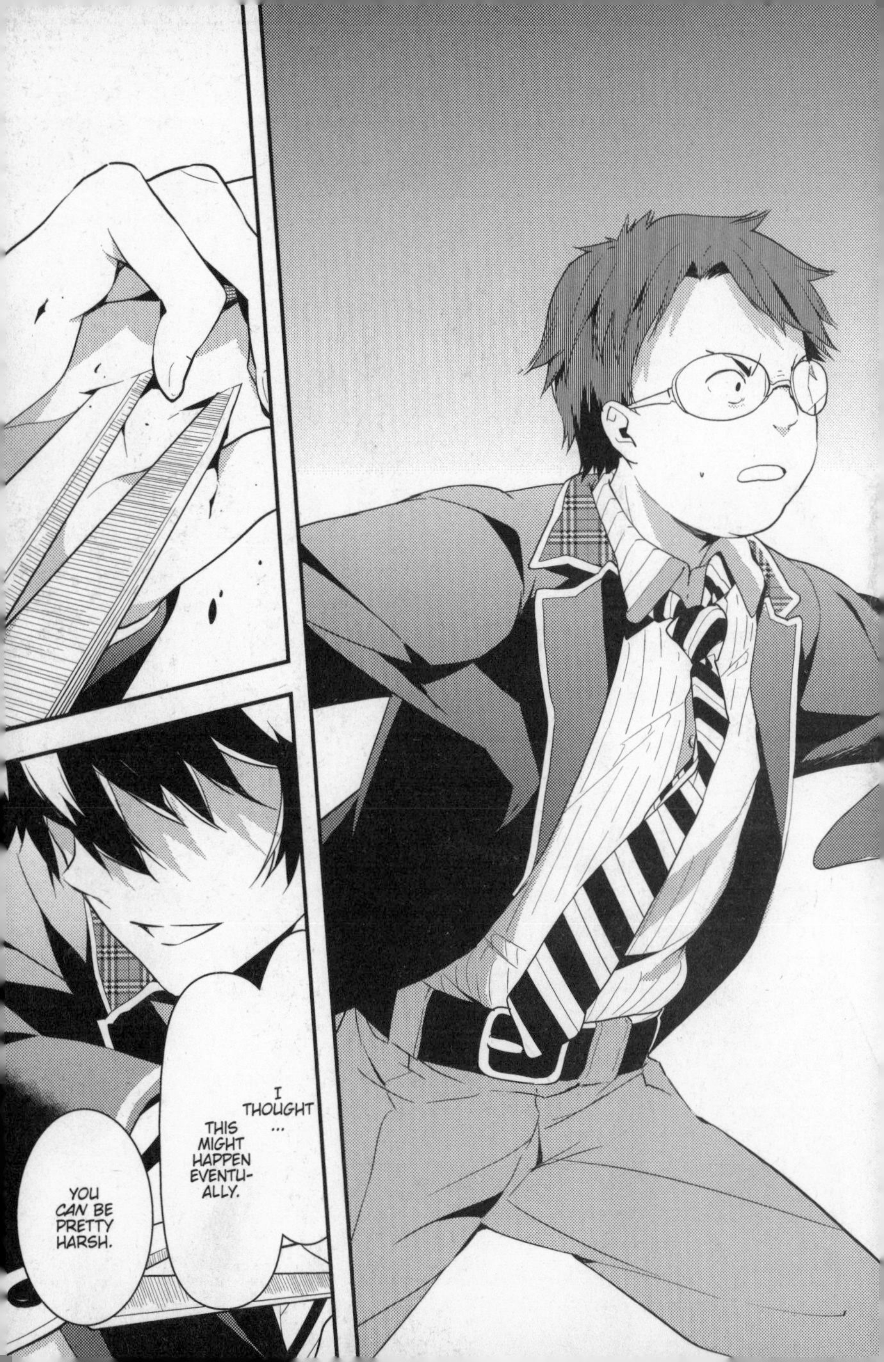
I THOUGHT ... THIS MIGHT HAPPEN EVENTU-ALLY.
YOU CAN BE PRETTY HARSH.

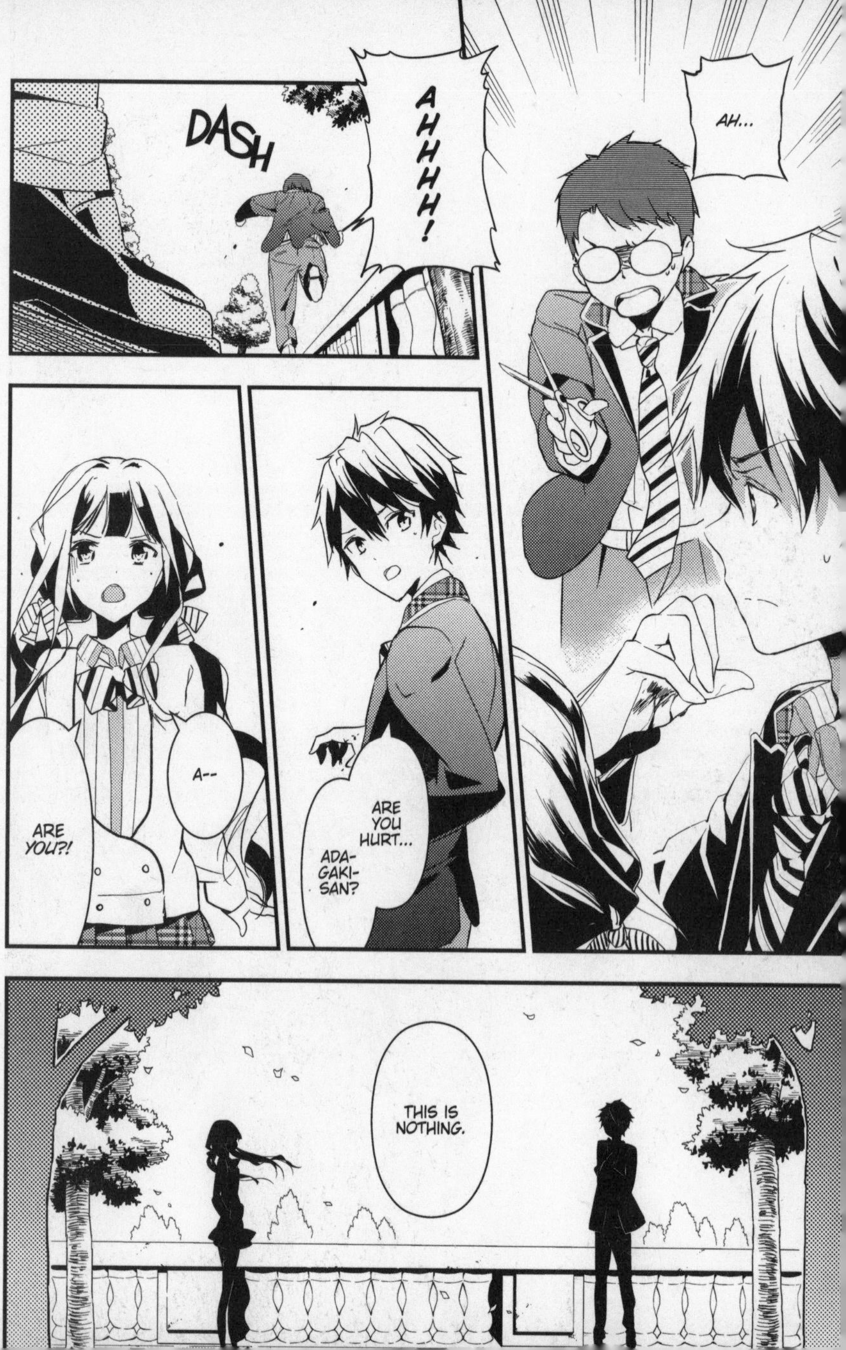
AH...
AHHHHH!
DASH
ARE YOU HURT... ADAGAKI-SAN?
A--
ARE YOU?!
THIS IS NOTHING.

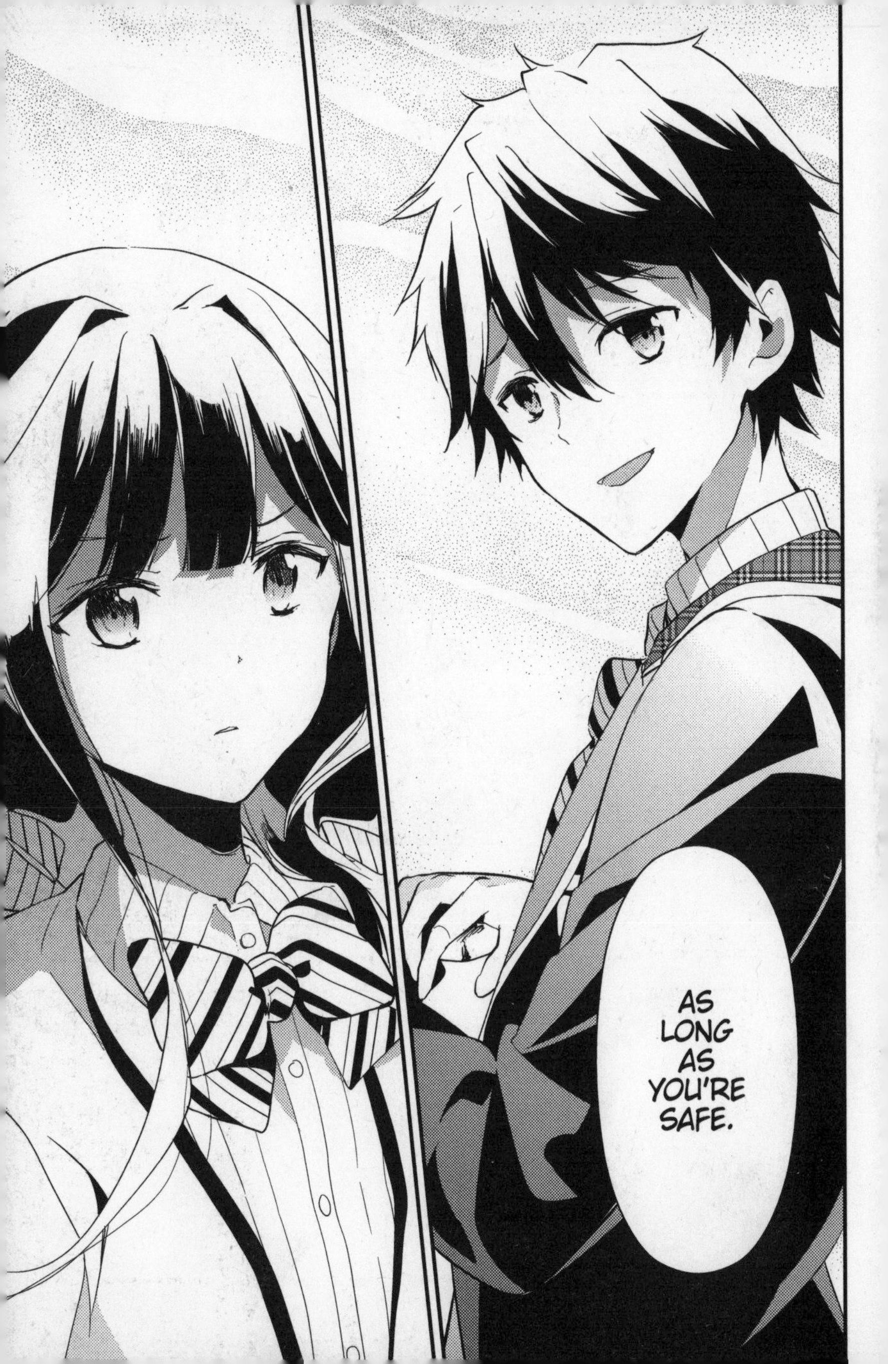
AS LONG AS YOU'RE SAFE.

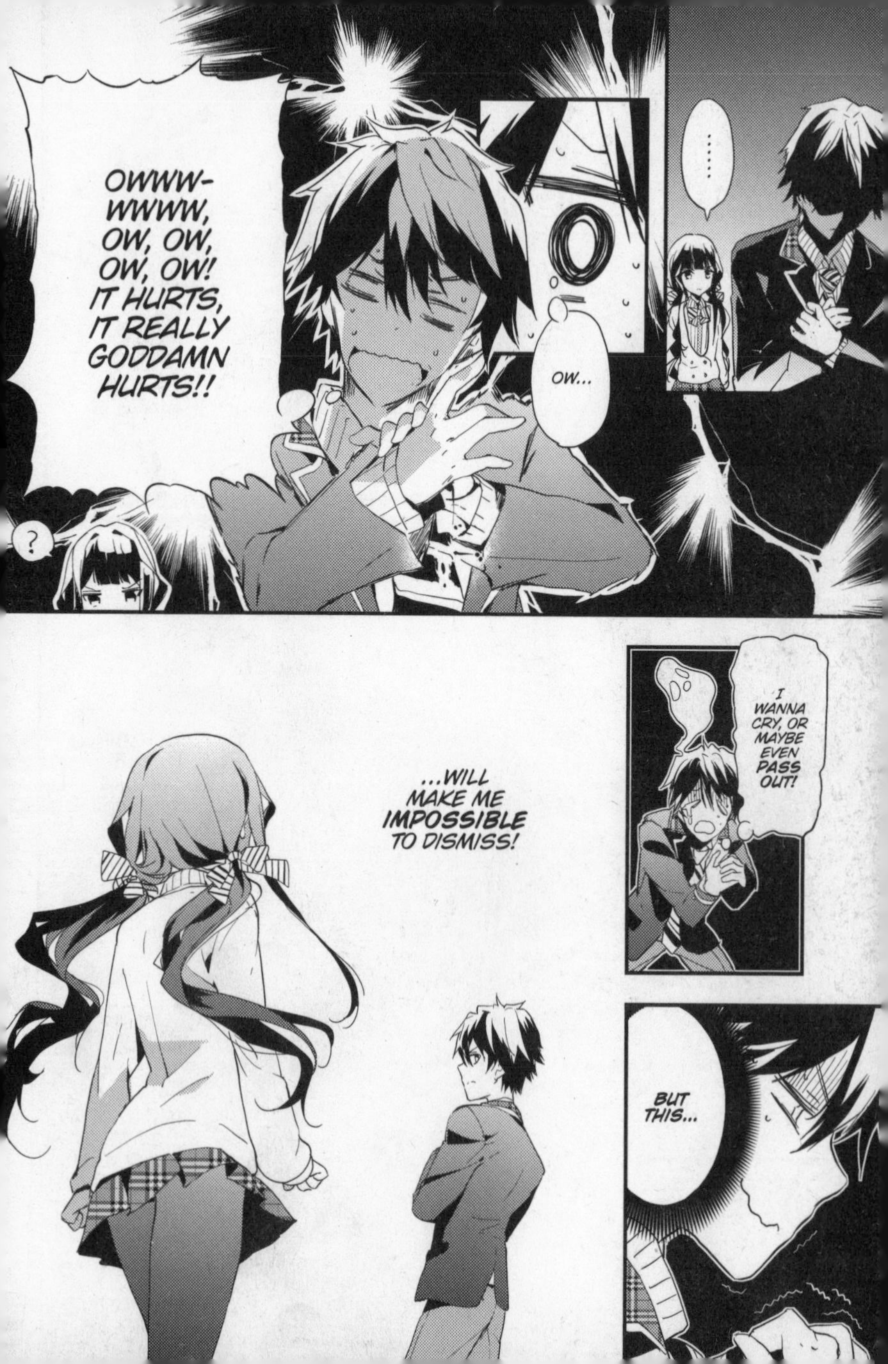
......
OW...
OWWWW-WWWW, OW, OW, OW, OW! IT HURTS, IT REALLY GODDAMN HURTS!!
?
I WANNA CRY, OR MAYBE EVEN PASS OUT!
BUT THIS...
...WILL MAKE ME IMPOSSIBLE TO DISMISS!

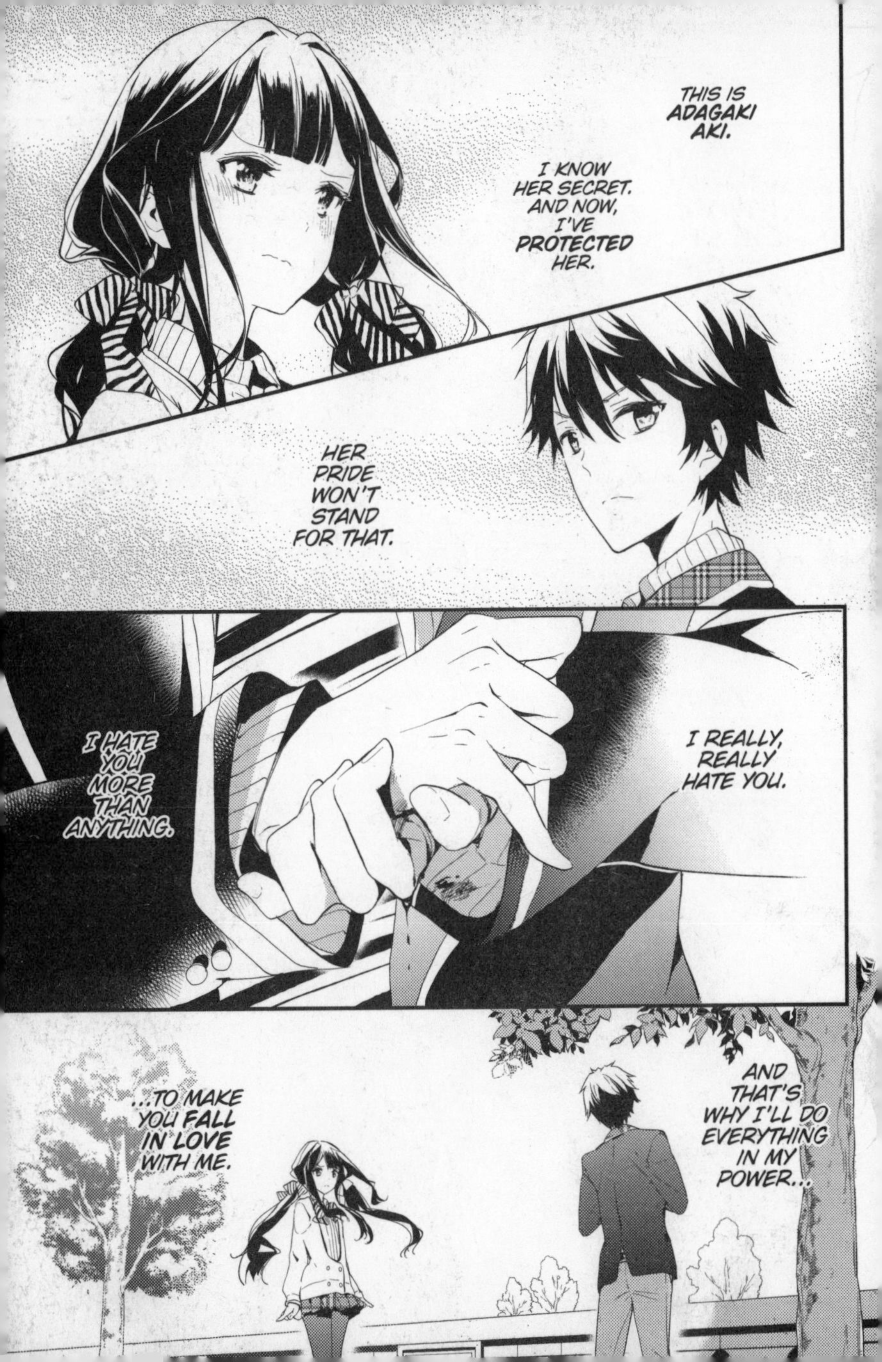
THIS IS ADAGAKI AKI.
I KNOW HER SECRET. AND NOW, I'VE PROTECTED HER.
HER PRIDE WON'T STAND FOR THAT.
I REALLY, REALLY HATE YOU.
I HATE YOU MORE THAN ANYTHING.
AND THAT'S WHY I'LL DO EVERYTHING IN MY POWER...
...TO MAKE YOU FALL IN LOVE WITH ME.

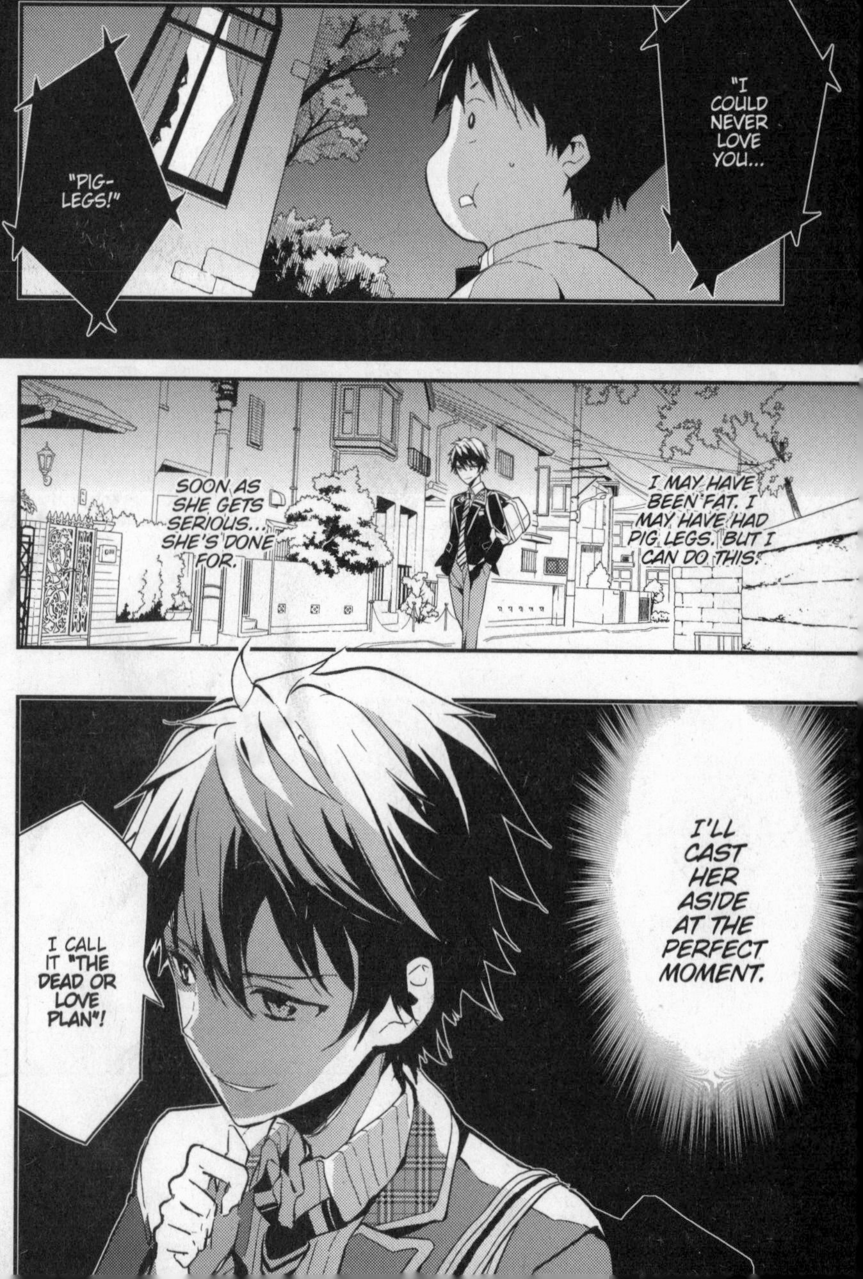
"I COULD NEVER LOVE YOU...
"PIG-LEGS!"
I MAY HAVE BEEN FAT. I MAY HAVE HAD PIG LEGS. BUT I CAN DO THIS.
SOON AS SHE GETS SERIOUS... SHE'S DONE FOR.
I'LL CAST HER ASIDE AT THE PERFECT MOMENT.
I CALL IT "THE DEAD OR LOVE PLAN"!

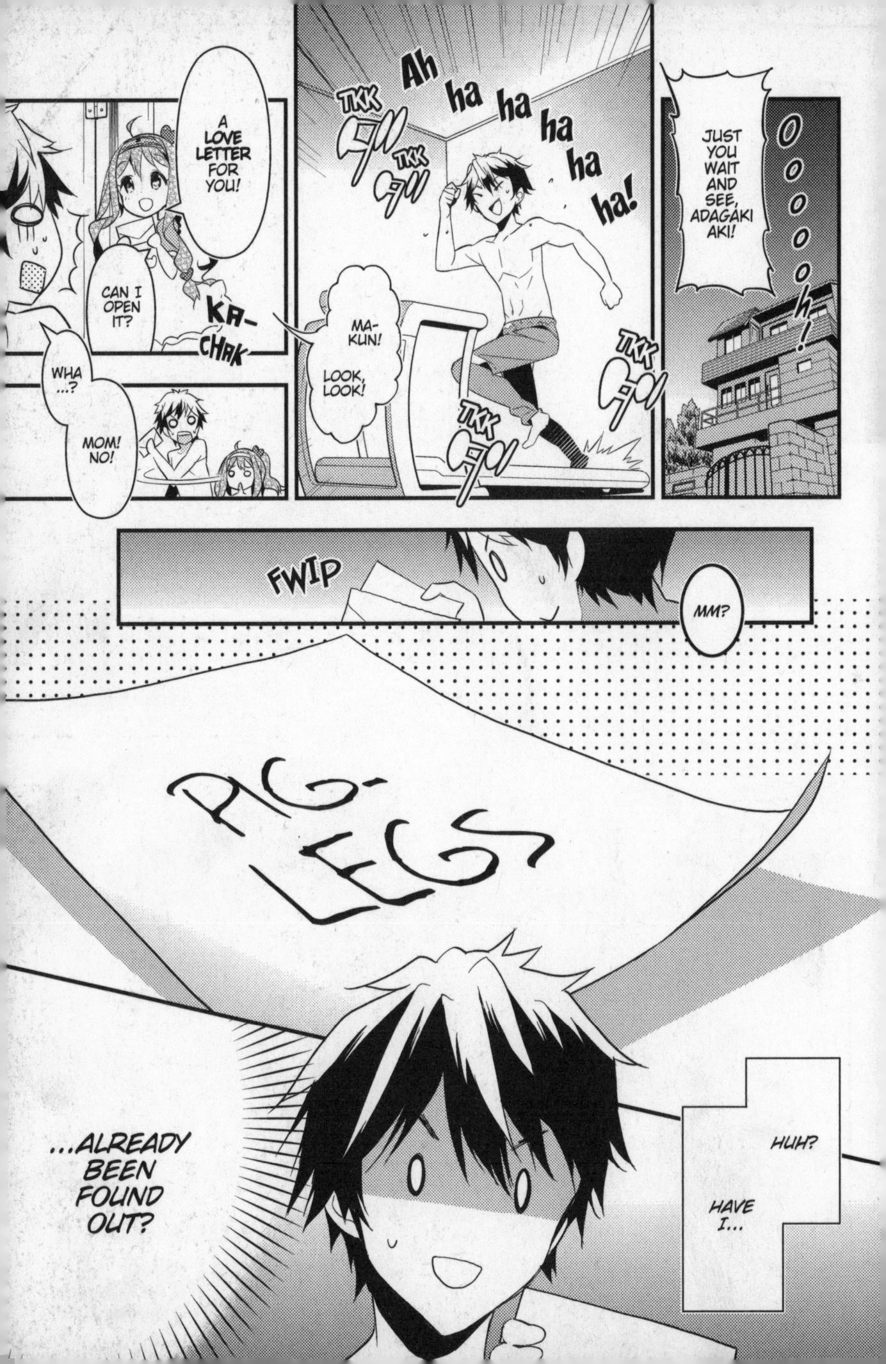
JUST YOU WAIT AND SEE, ADAGAKI AKI!
Ooooooh!
Ah ha ha ha ha ha!
TKK
TKK
TKK
TKK
MA-KUN! LOOK, LOOK!
A LOVE LETTER FOR YOU!
CAN I OPEN IT?
KA-CHAK
WHA...?
MOM! NO!
MM?
FWIP
AG-LEGS
HUH?
HAVE I...
...ALREADY BEEN FOUND OUT?

Masamune-kun's
REVENGE
Presented by Hazuki Takeoka & TIV

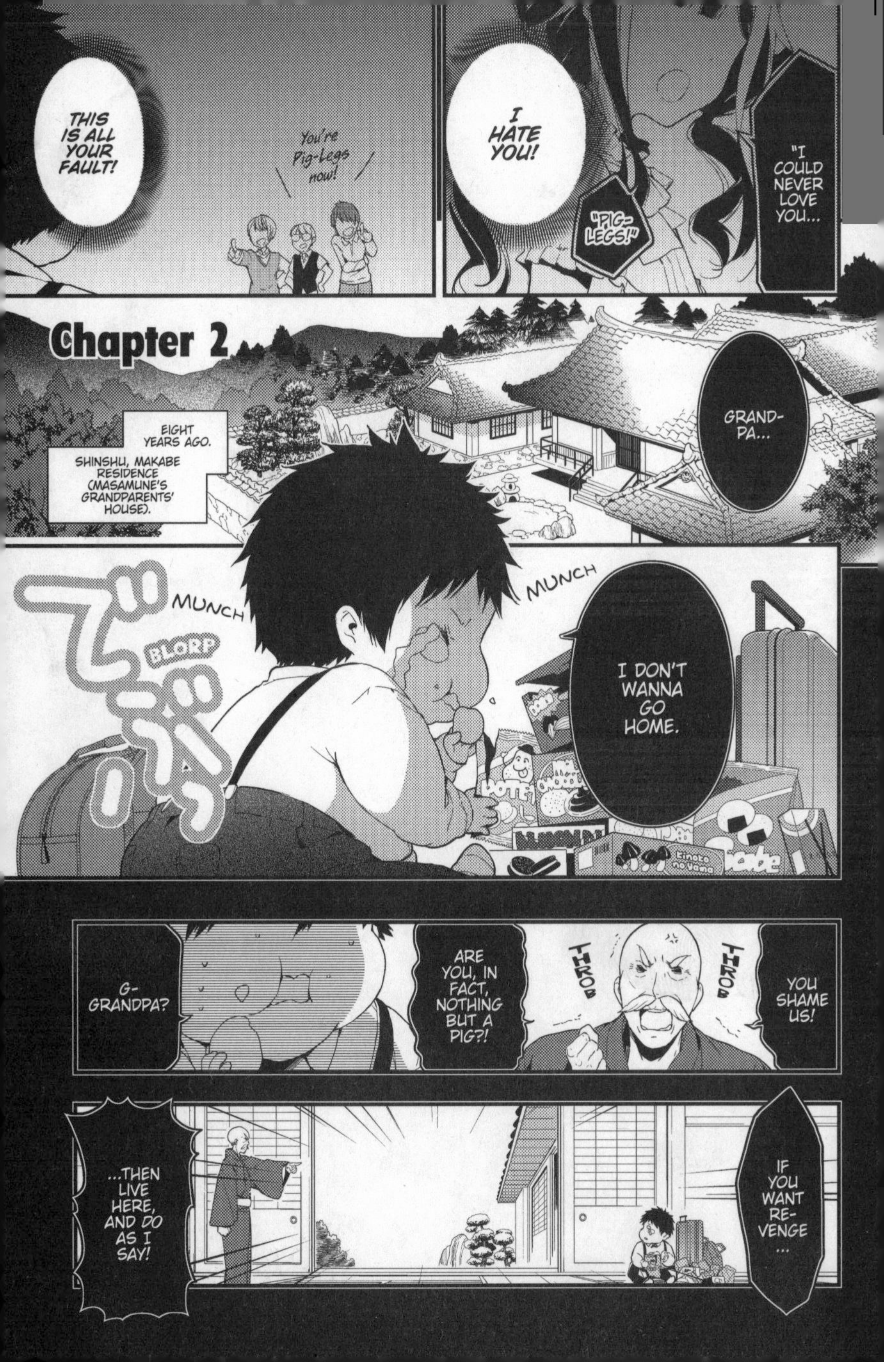
I HATE YOU!
"I COULD NEVER LOVE YOU...
"PIG-LEGS!"
THIS IS ALL YOUR FAULT!
You're Pig-Legs now!
Chapter 2
GRAND-PA...
EIGHT YEARS AGO.
SHINSHU, MAKABE RESIDENCE (MASAMUNE'S GRANDPARENTS' HOUSE).
MUNCH
I DON'T WANNA GO HOME.
MUNCH
BLORP
YOU SHAME US!
THROB
THROB
ARE YOU, IN FACT, NOTHING BUT A PIG?!
G-GRANDPA?
IF YOU WANT RE-VENGE...
...THEN LIVE HERE, AND DO AS I SAY!

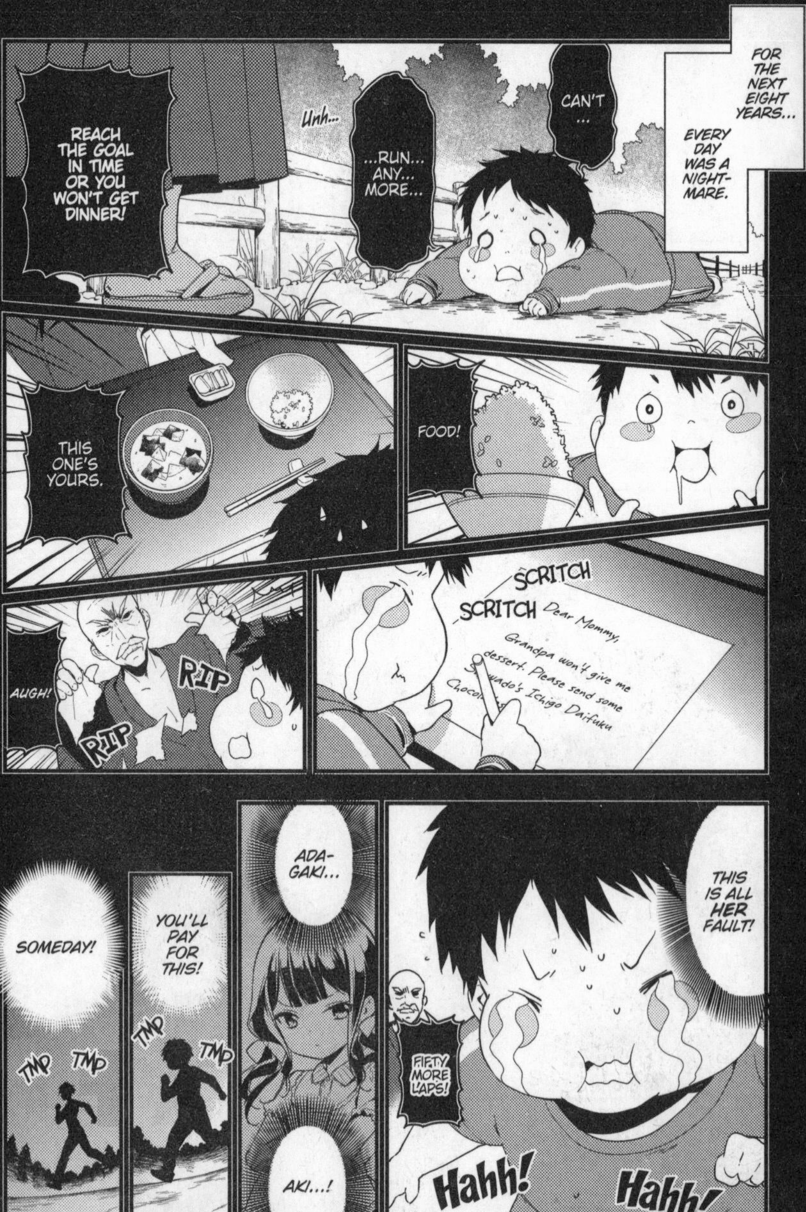
FOR THE NEXT EIGHT YEARS...
EVERY DAY WAS A NIGHTMARE.
CAN'T ...
...RUN... ANY... MORE...
Unh...
REACH THE GOAL IN TIME OR YOU WON'T GET DINNER!
FOOD!
THIS ONE'S YOURS.
SCRITCH
SCRITCH
Dear Mommy,
Grandpa won't give me dessert. Please send some
Ichigo Daifuku
RIP
AUGH!
RIP
THIS IS ALL HER FAULT!
FIFTY MORE LAPS!
Hahh!
Hahh!
ADAGAKI...
AKI...!
YOU'LL PAY FOR THIS!
TMP
TMP
SOMEDAY!
TMP
TMP

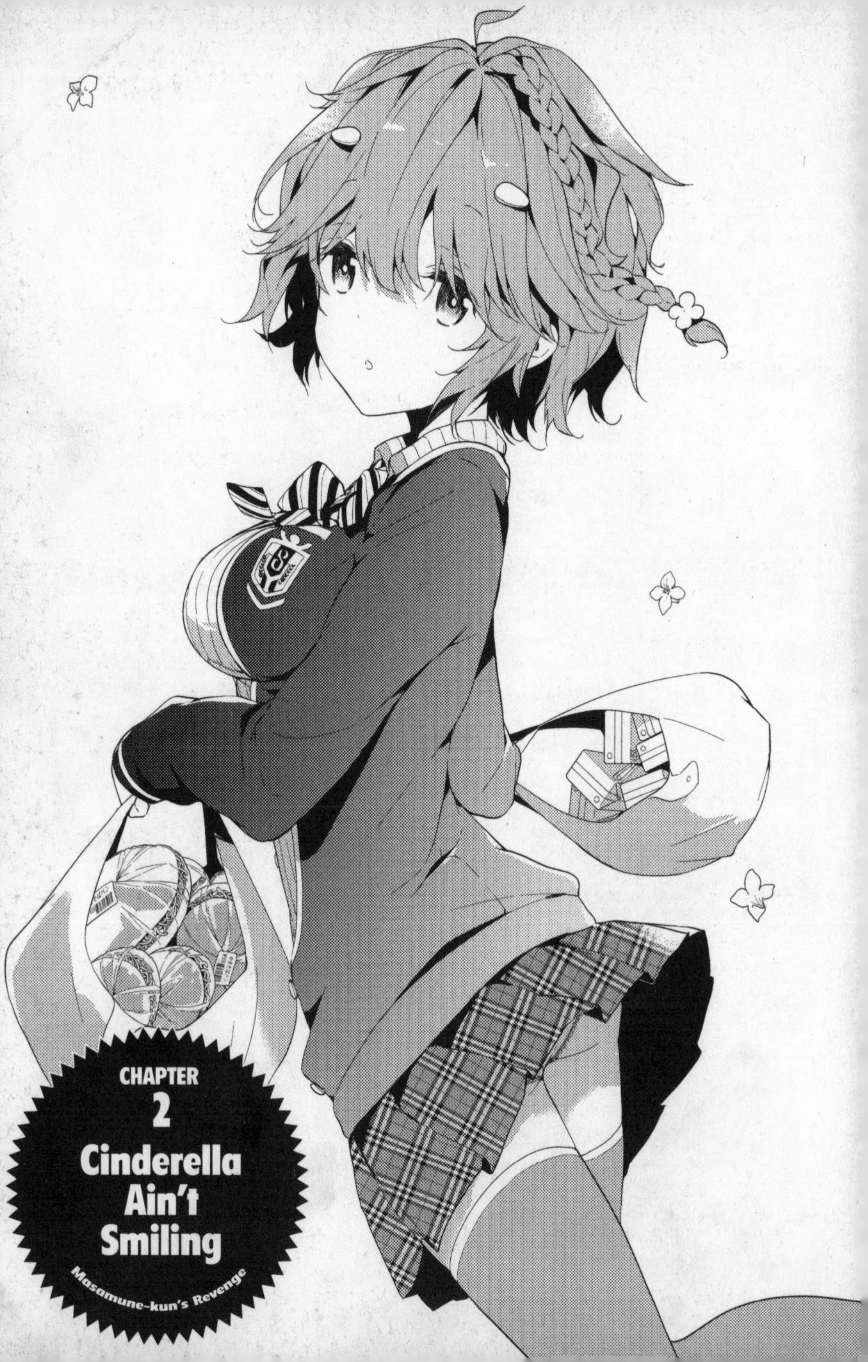
CHAPTER
2
Cinderella Ain't Smiling
Masamune-kun's Revenge

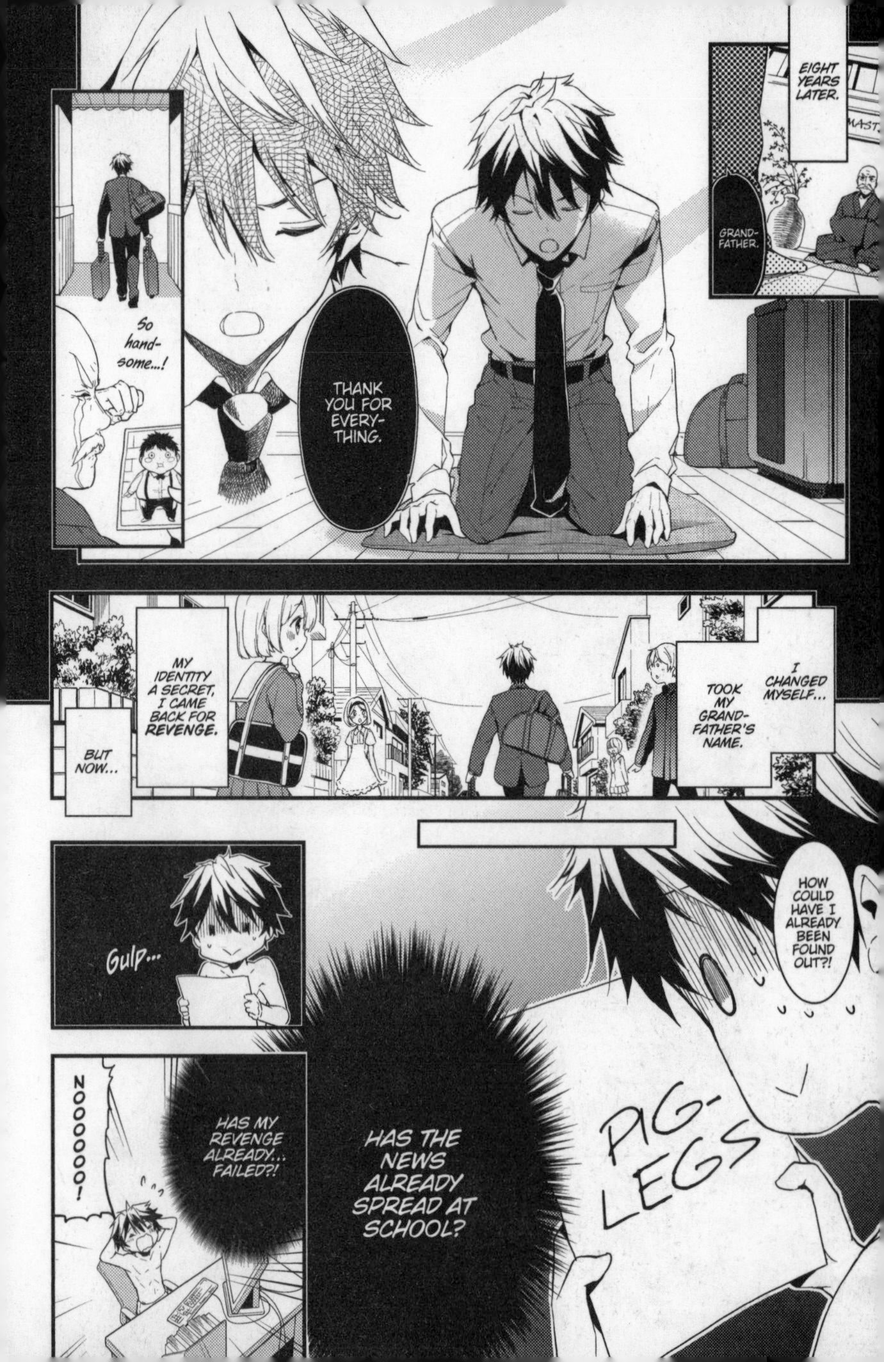

EIGHT YEARS LATER.
MAST.
GRAND-FATHER.
THANK YOU FOR EVERY-THING.
So hand-some...!
I CHANGED MYSELF...
TOOK MY GRAND-FATHER'S NAME.
MY IDENTITY A SECRET, I CAME BACK FOR REVENGE.
BUT NOW...
HOW COULD HAVE I ALREADY BEEN FOUND OUT?!
PIG-LEGS
Gulp...
HAS THE NEWS ALREADY SPREAD AT SCHOOL?
HAS MY REVENGE ALREADY... FAILED?!
NOOOOOOO!

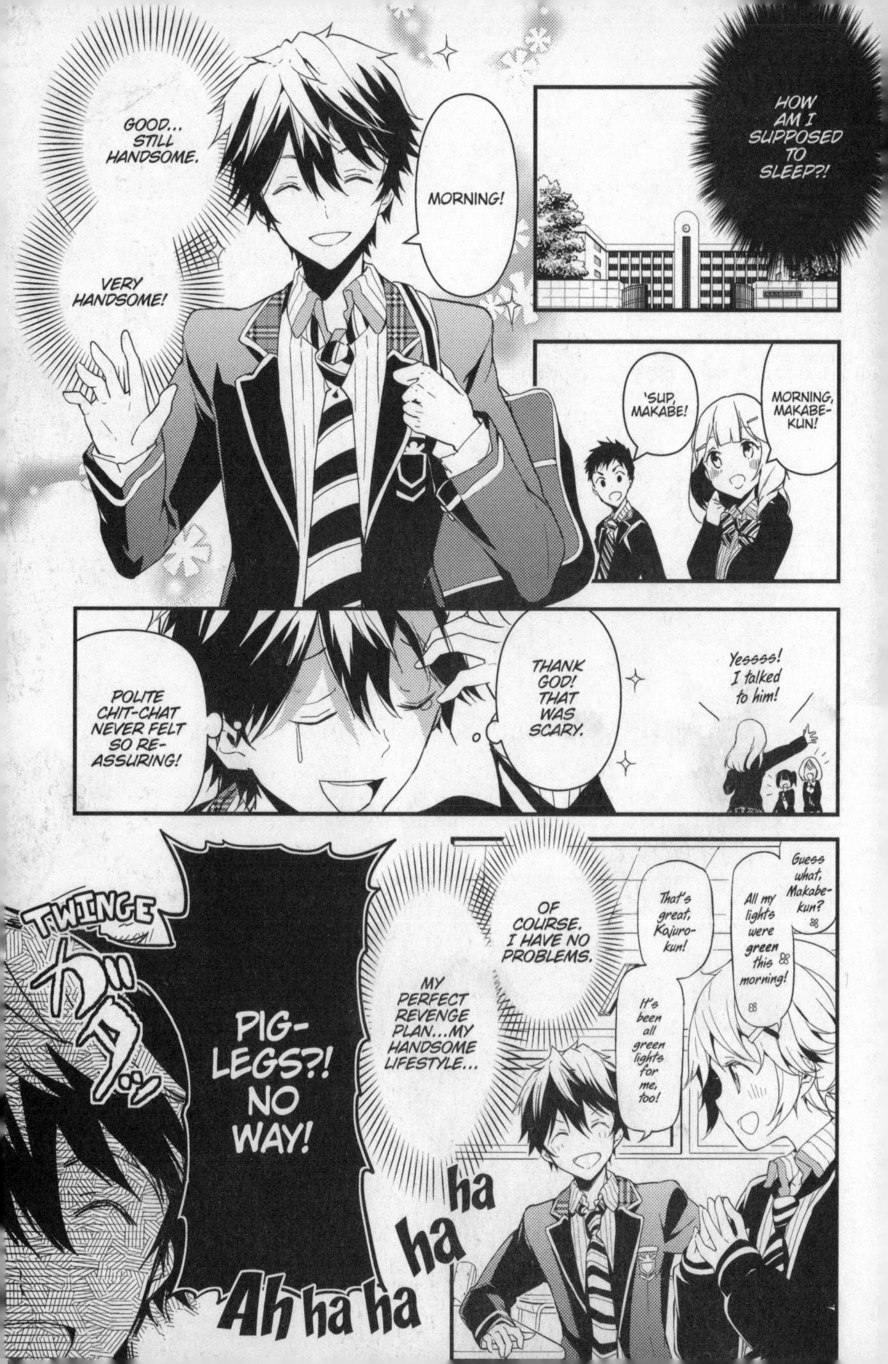
HOW AM I SUPPOSED TO SLEEP?!
MORNING, MAKABE-KUN!
'SUP, MAKABE!
MORNING!
GOOD... STILL HANDSOME.
VERY HANDSOME!
Yessss! I talked to him!
THANK GOD! THAT WAS SCARY.
POLITE CHIT-CHAT NEVER FELT SO RE-ASSURING!
Guess what, Makabe-kun?
All my lights were green this morning!
That's great, Kajuro-kun!
It's been all green lights for me, too!
OF COURSE. I HAVE NO PROBLEMS.
MY PERFECT REVENGE PLAN...MY HANDSOME LIFESTYLE...
Ah ha ha ha ha ha
TWINGE
PIG-LEGS?! NO WAY!

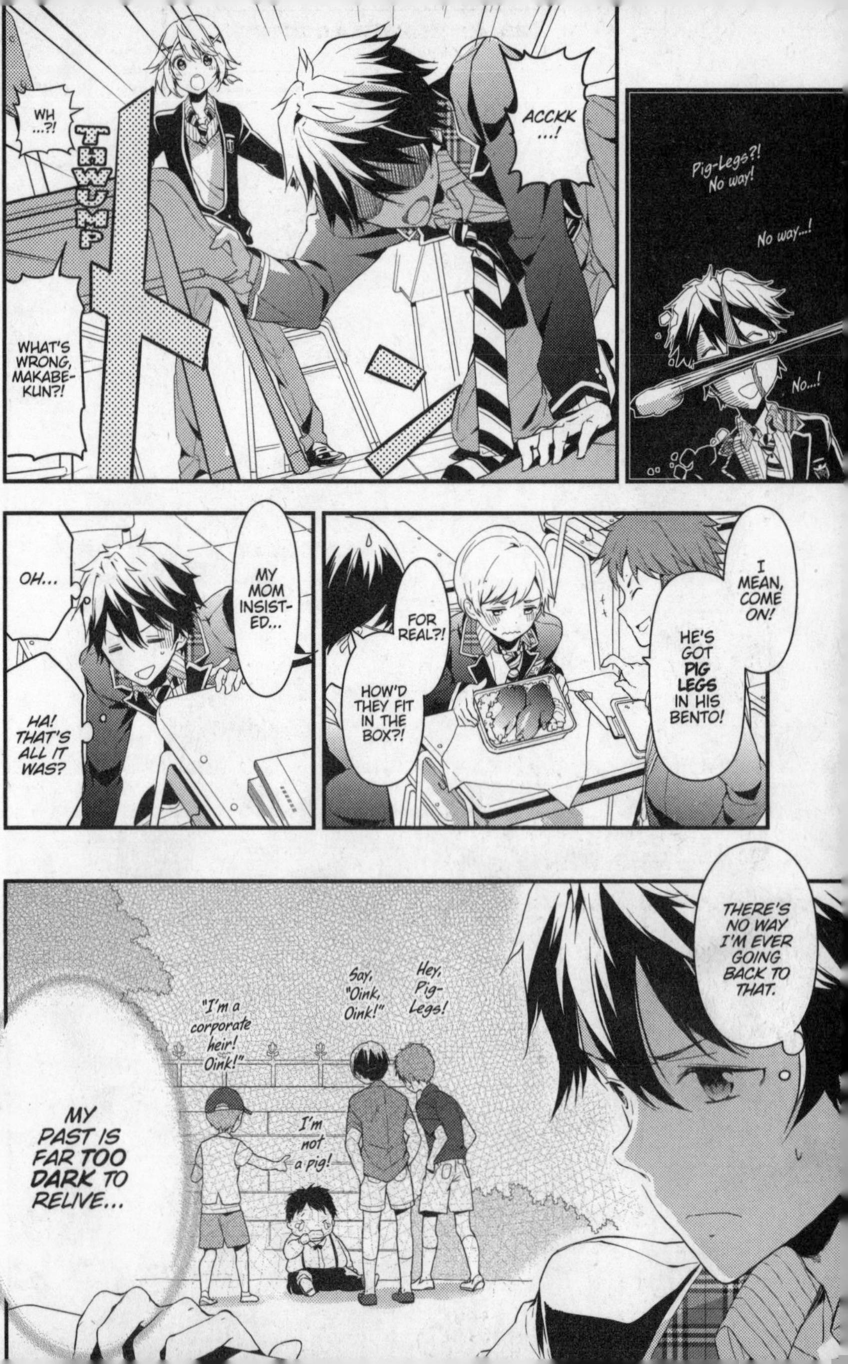

Pig-Legs?! No way!
No way...!
No...!
ACCKK ...!
WH ...?!
THWUMP
WHAT'S WRONG, MAKABE-KUN?!
I MEAN, COME ON!
HE'S GOT PIG LEGS IN HIS BENTO!
FOR REAL?!
HOW'D THEY FIT IN THE BOX?!
MY MOM INSISTED...
OH...
HA! THAT'S ALL IT WAS?
THERE'S NO WAY I'M EVER GOING BACK TO THAT.
Hey, Pig-Legs!
Say, "Oink, Oink!"
"I'm a corporate heir! Oink!"
I'm not a pig!
MY PAST IS FAR TOO DARK TO RELIVE...

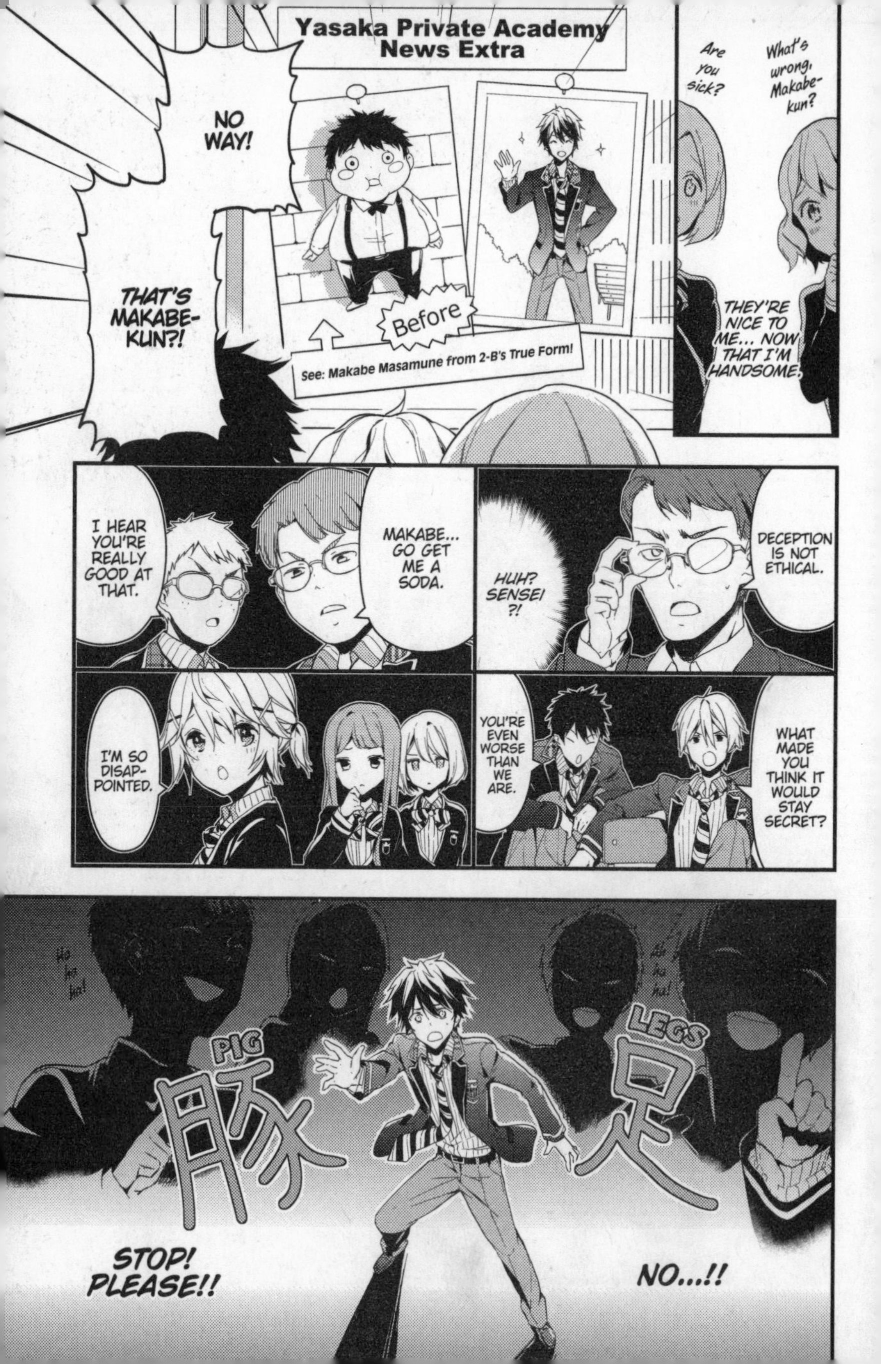
What's wrong, Makabe-kun?
Are you sick?
THEY'RE NICE TO ME... NOW THAT I'M HANDSOME.
Yasaka Private Academy News Extra
NO WAY!
Before
See: Makabe Masamune from 2-B's True Form!
THAT'S MAKABE-KUN?!
DECEPTION IS NOT ETHICAL.
HUH? SENSEI?!
MAKABE... GO GET ME A SODA.
I HEAR YOU'RE REALLY GOOD AT THAT.
WHAT MADE YOU THINK IT WOULD STAY SECRET?
YOU'RE EVEN WORSE THAN WE ARE.
I'M SO DISAPPOINTED.
LEGS
PIG
NO...!!
STOP! PLEASE!!

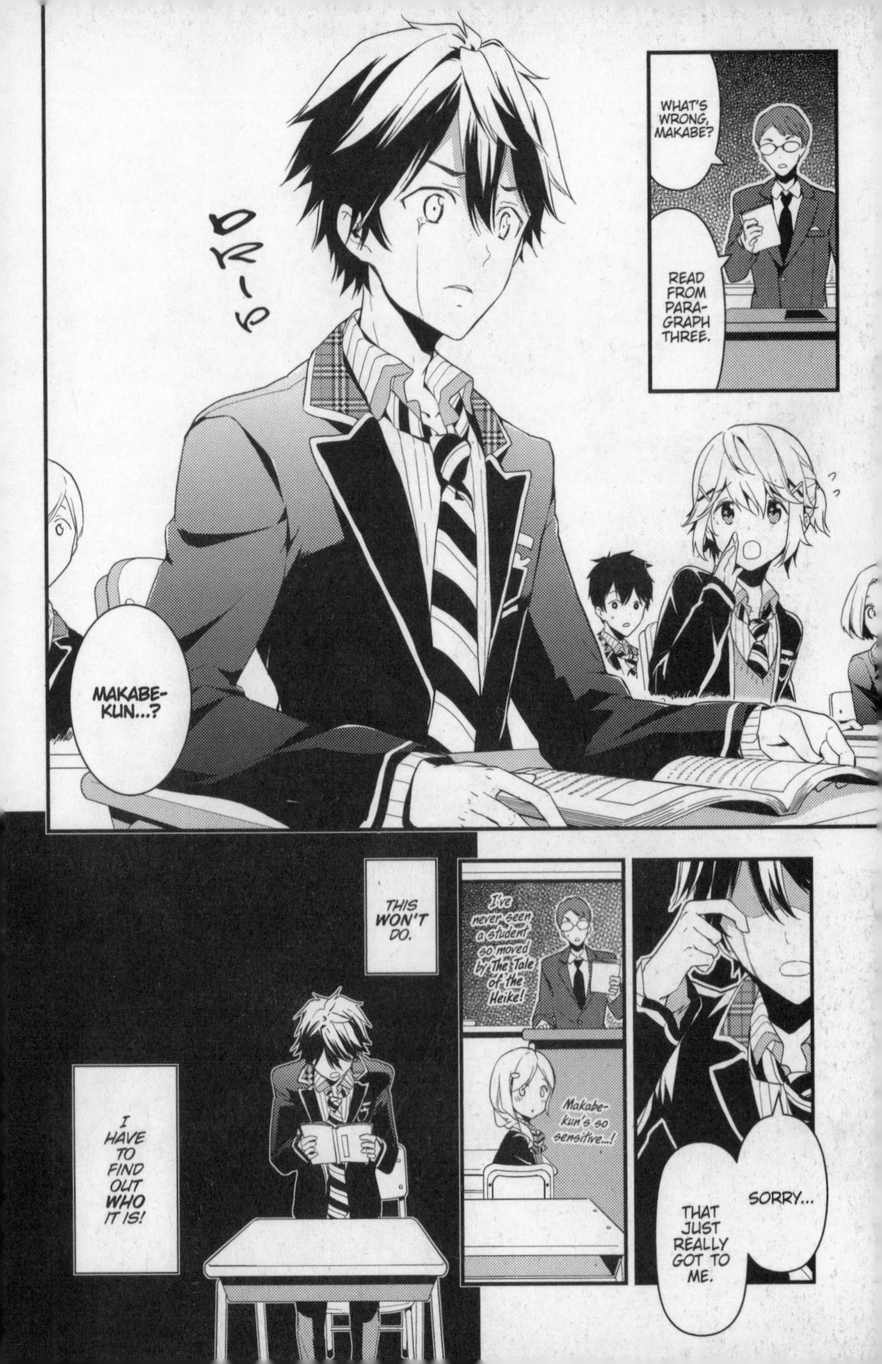
WHAT'S WRONG, MAKABE?
READ FROM PARA-GRAPH THREE.
MAKABE-KUN...?
SORRY...
THAT JUST REALLY GOT TO ME.
I've never seen a student so moved by The Tale of the Heike!
Makabe-kun's so sensitive...!
THIS WON'T DO.
I HAVE TO FIND OUT WHO IT IS!

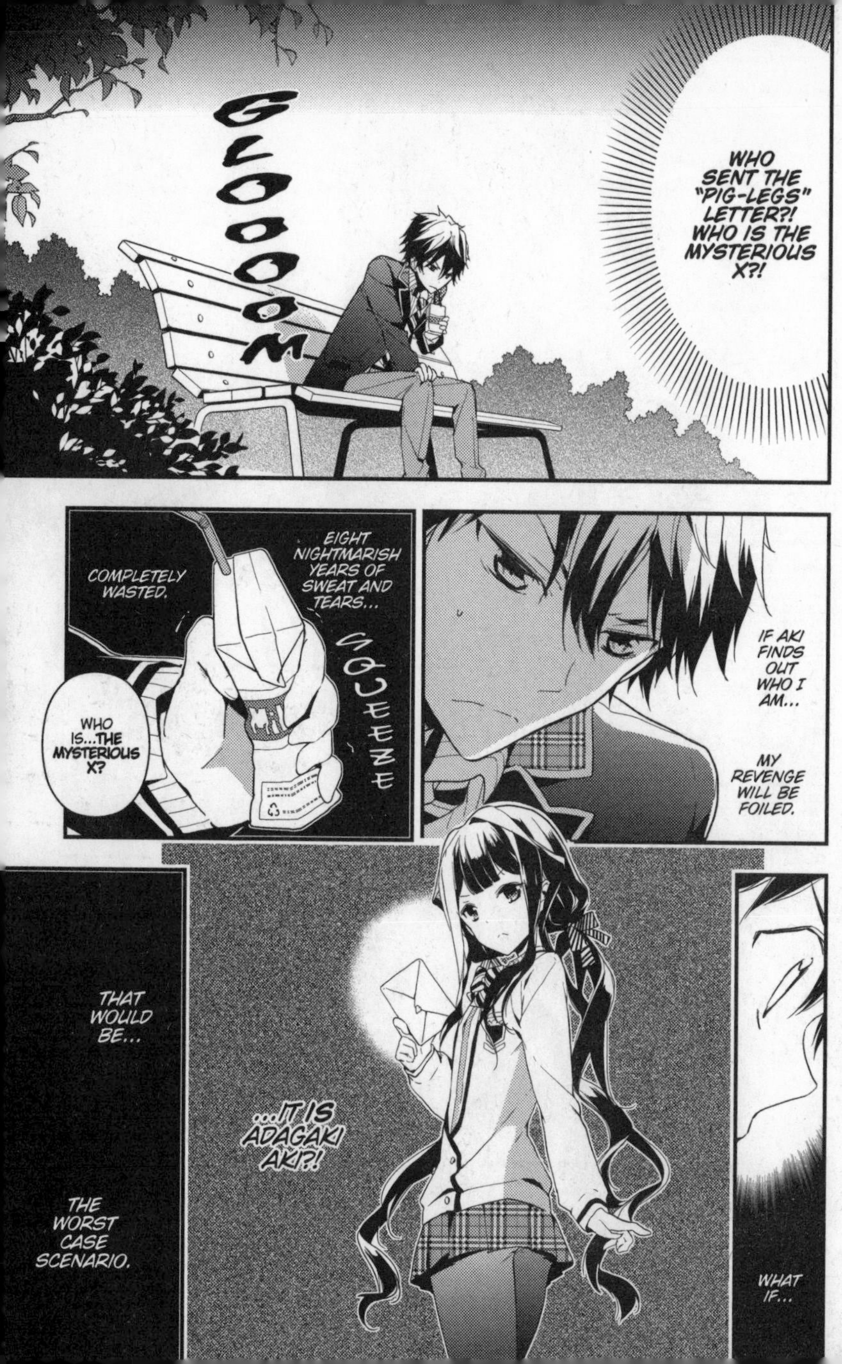
WHO SENT THE "PIG-LEGS" LETTER?! WHO IS THE MYSTERIOUS X?!
GLOOOOOM
IF AKI FINDS OUT WHO I AM...
MY REVENGE WILL BE FOILED.
EIGHT NIGHTMARISH YEARS OF SWEAT AND TEARS...
COMPLETELY WASTED.
SQUEEZE
WHO IS...THE MYSTERIOUS X?
WHAT IF...
...IT IS ADAGAKI AKI?!
THAT WOULD BE...
THE WORST CASE SCENARIO.

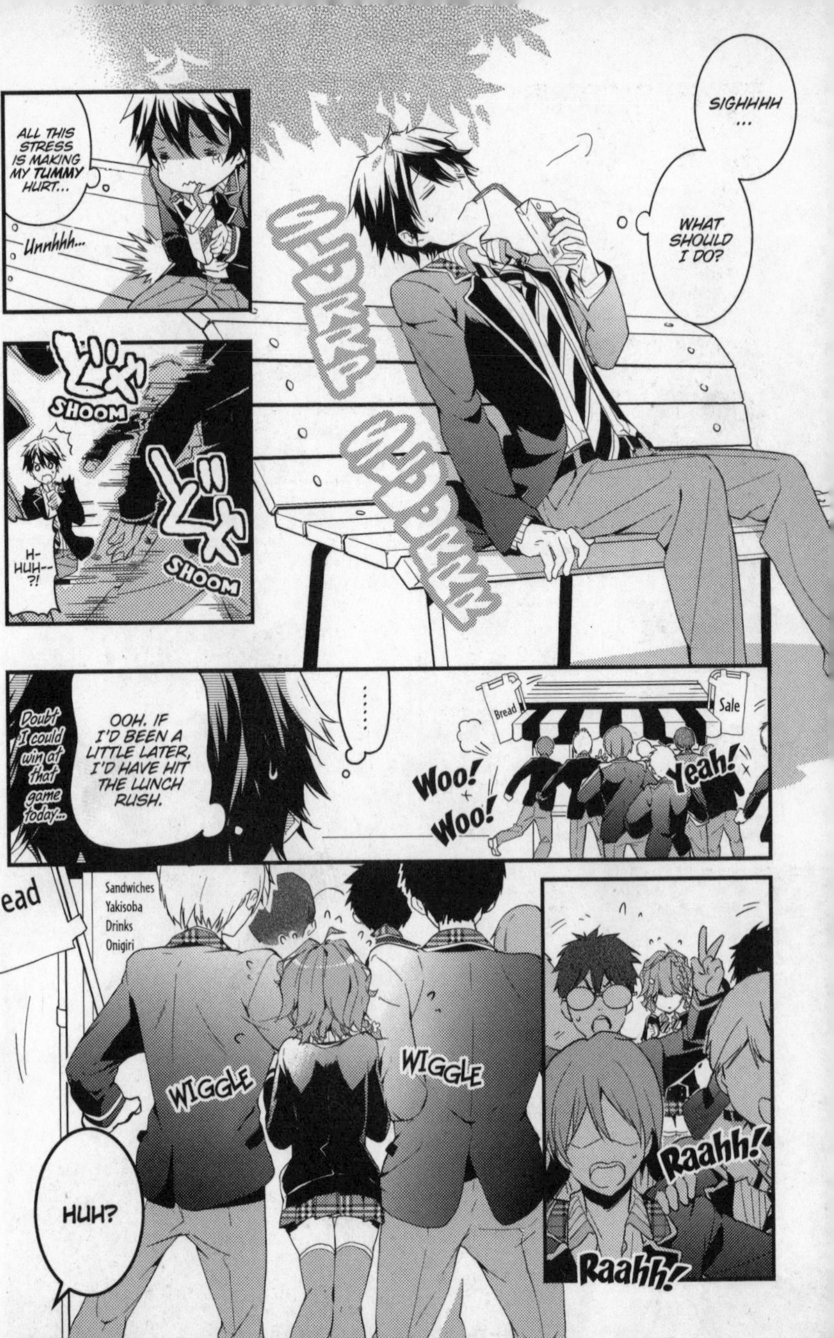
SIGHHHH ...
WHAT SHOULD I DO?
SLURRP
SLURRRR
ALL THIS STRESS IS MAKING MY TUMMY HURT...
Unnhhh...
SHOOM
SHOOM
H-HUH--?!
Bread
Sale
Yeah!
Woo!
Woo!
......
OOH. IF I'D BEEN A LITTLE LATER, I'D HAVE HIT THE LUNCH RUSH.
Doubt I could win at that game today...
Raahh!
Raahh!
Bread
Sandwiches
Yakisoba
Drinks
Onigiri
WIGGLE
WIGGLE
HUH?

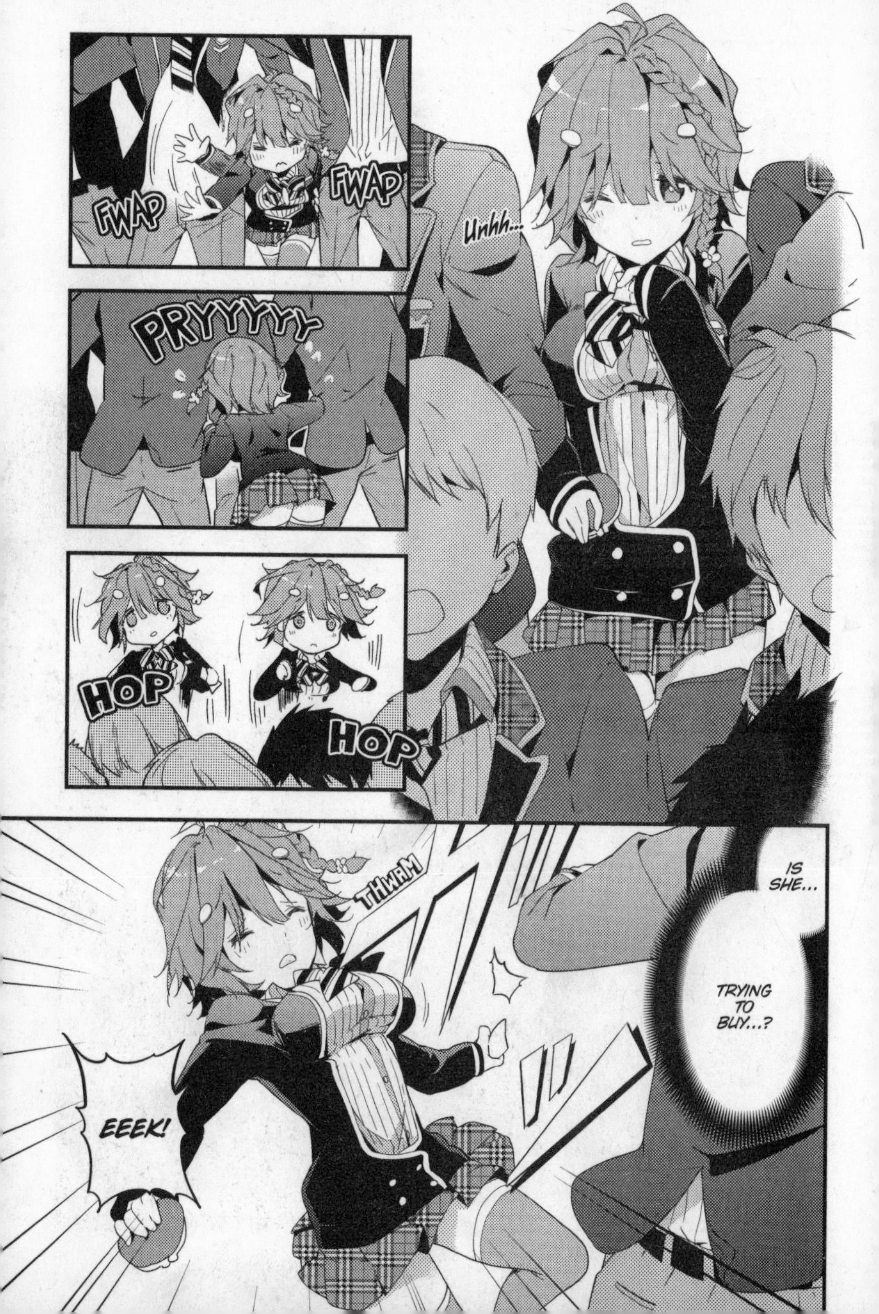
Unhh...
FWAP
FWAP
PRYYYYY
HOP
HOP
IS SHE...
TRYING TO BUY...?
THWAM
EEEK!

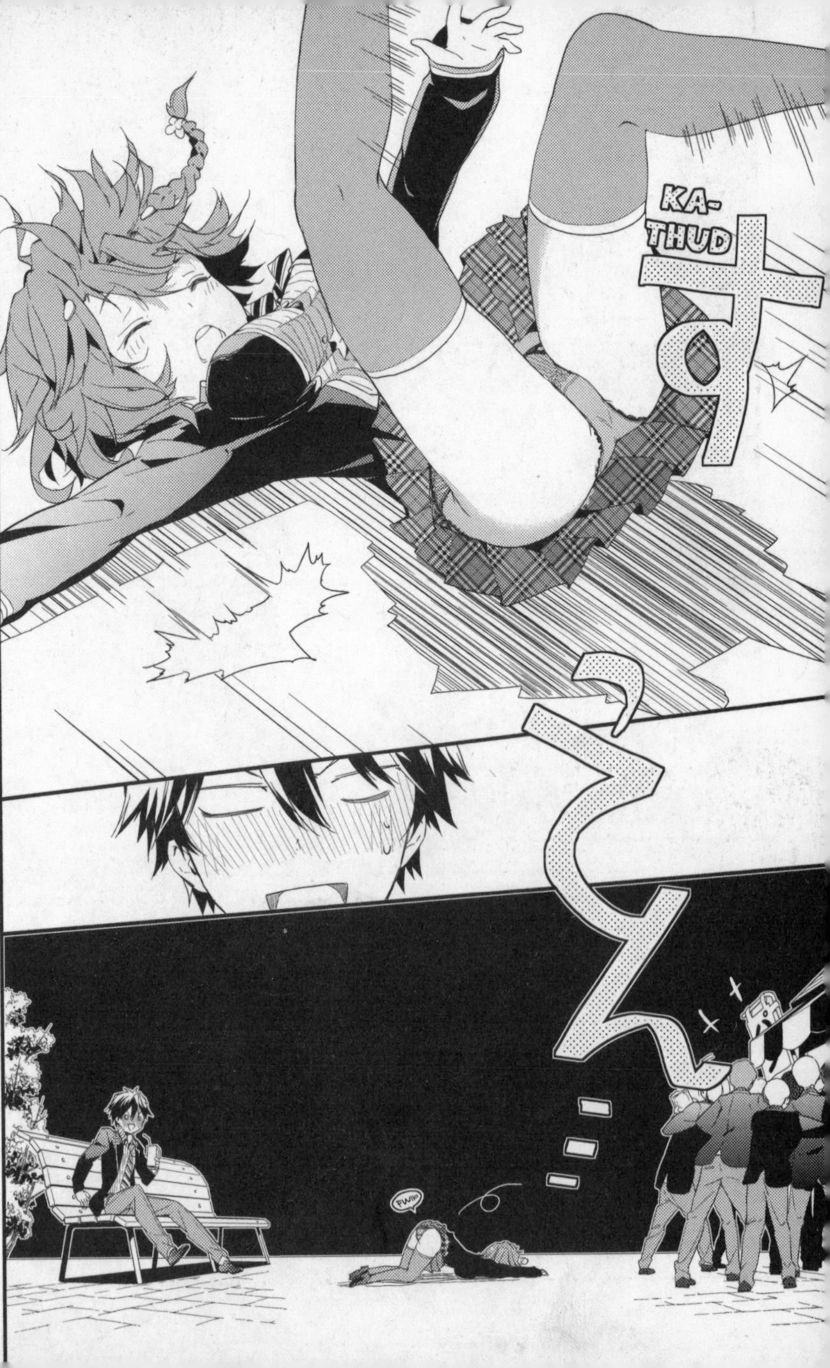
KA-
THUD
FWIP

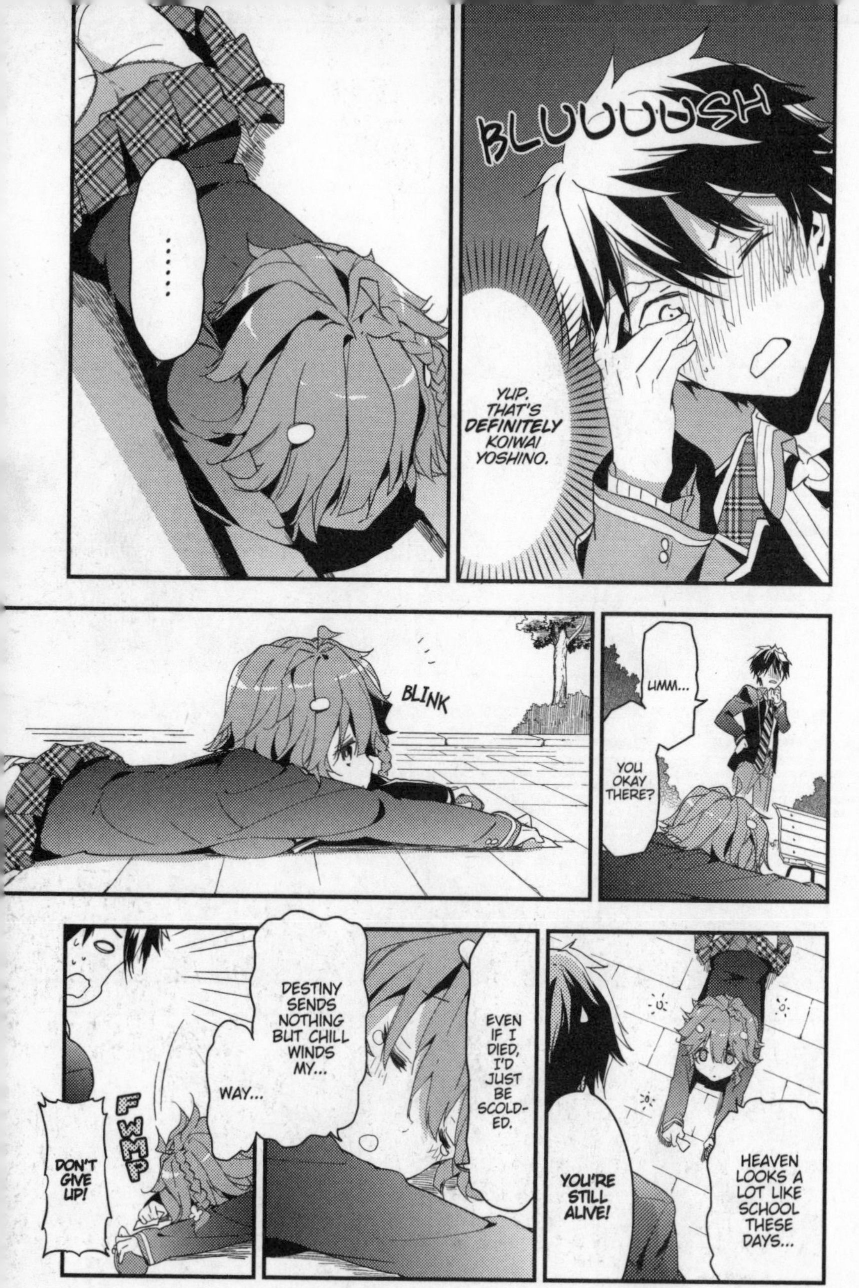
BLUUUUSH
YUP. THAT'S DEFINITELY KOIWAI YOSHINO.
......
UMM...
YOU OKAY THERE?
BLINK
HEAVEN LOOKS A LOT LIKE SCHOOL THESE DAYS...
YOU'RE STILL ALIVE!
EVEN IF I DIED, I'D JUST BE SCOLD-ED.
DESTINY SENDS NOTHING BUT CHILL WINDS MY...
WAY...
FWMP
DON'T GIVE UP!

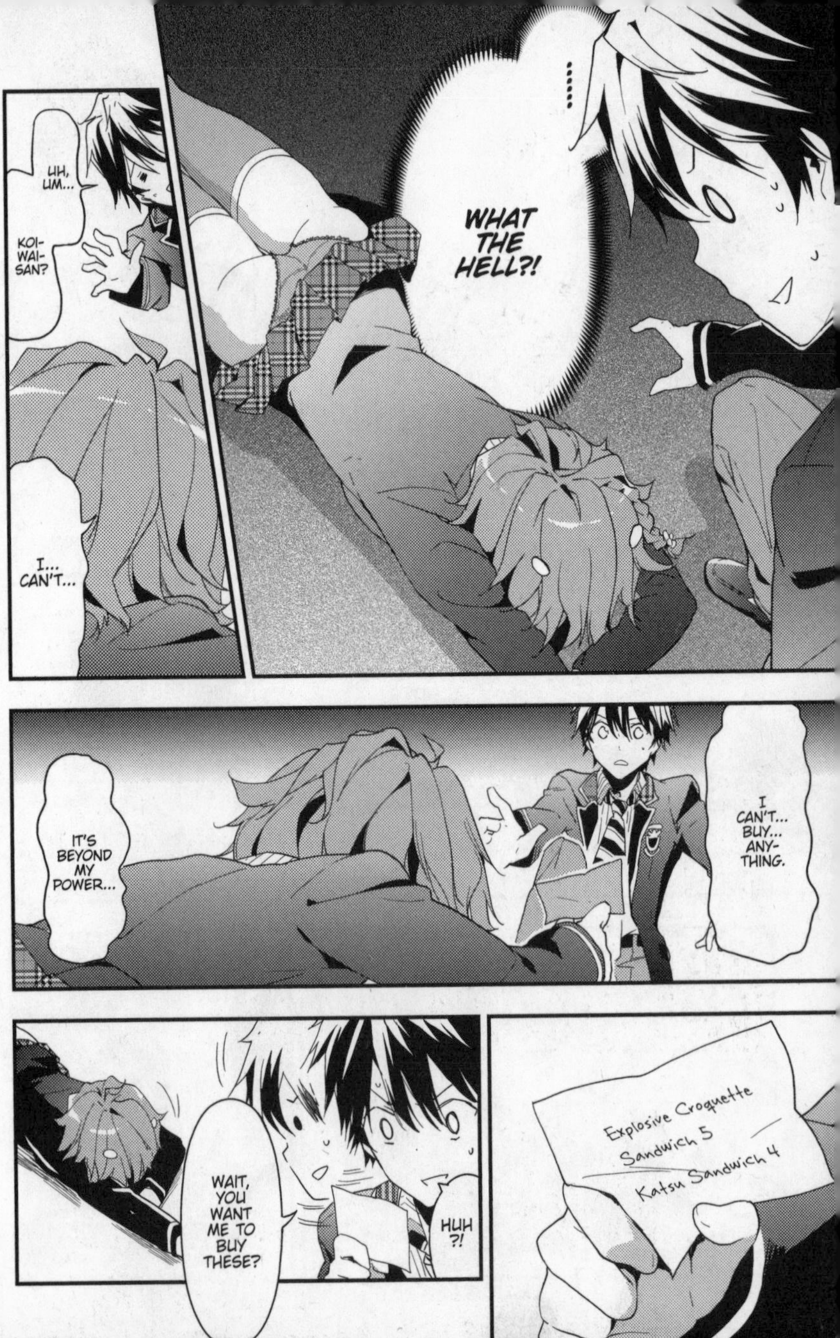
......
WHAT THE HELL?!
UH, UM...
KOI-WAI-SAN?
I... CAN'T...
I CAN'T... BUY... ANY-THING.
IT'S BEYOND MY POWER...
Explosive Croquette Sandwich 5
Katsu Sandwich 4
HUH?!
WAIT, YOU WANT ME TO BUY THESE?

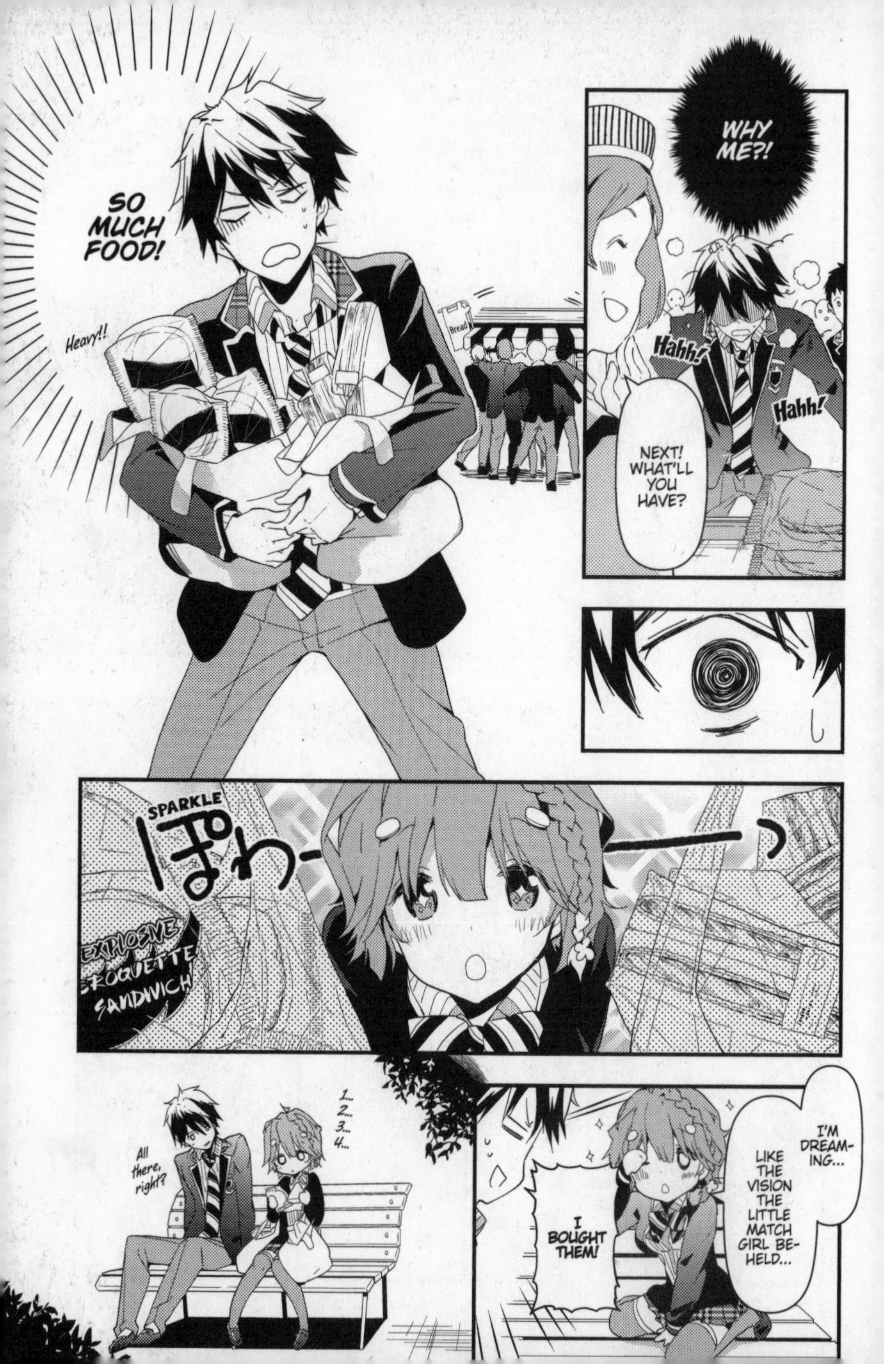
WHY ME?!
Hahh!
Hahh!
NEXT! WHAT'LL YOU HAVE?
SO MUCH FOOD!
Bread
Heavy!!
SPARKLE
ぽわーっ
EXPLOSIVE CROQUETTE SANDWICH
I'M DREAMING... LIKE THE VISION THE LITTLE MATCH GIRL BE-HELD...
I BOUGHT THEM!
1... 2... 3... 4...
All there, right?

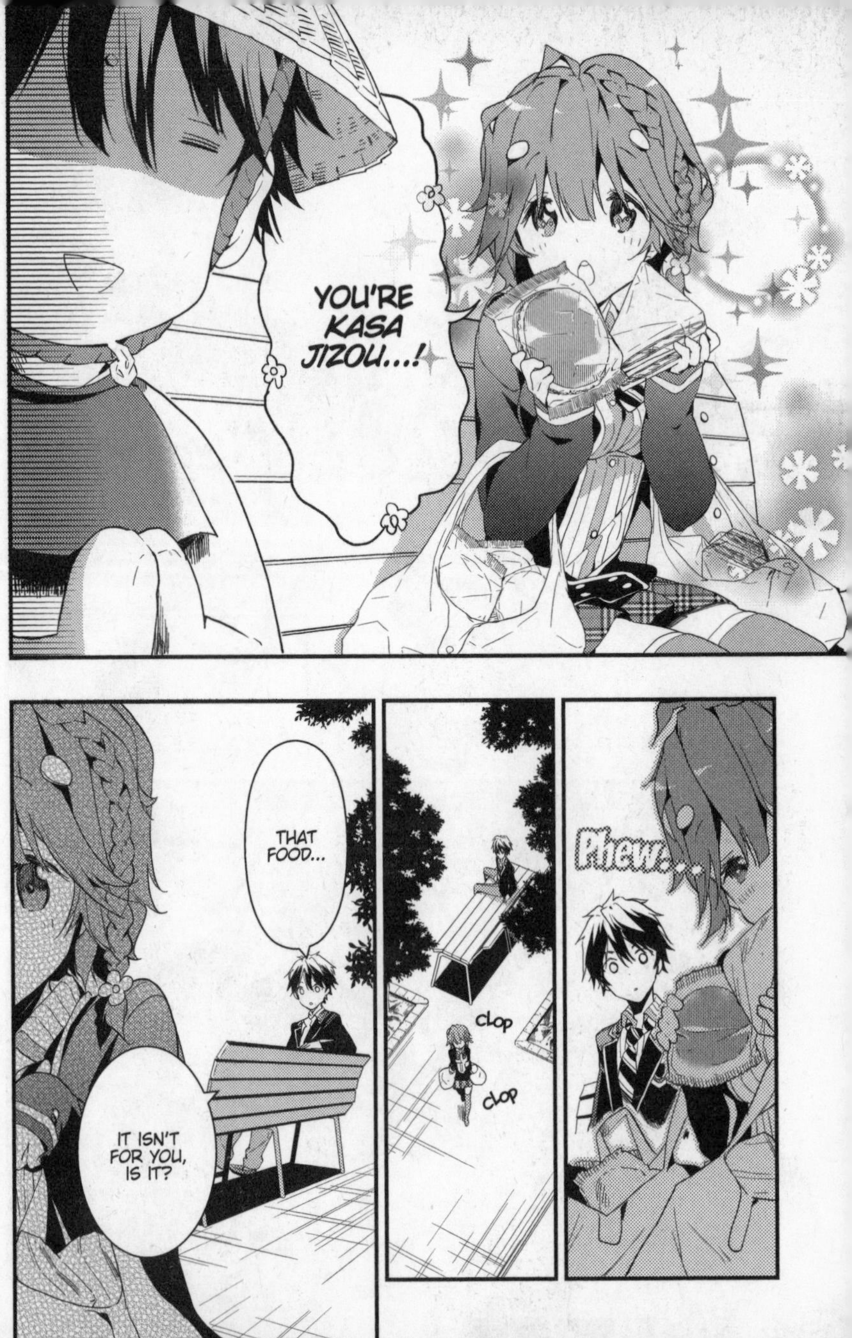
YOU'RE KASA JIZOU...!
Phew...
CLOP
CLOP
THAT FOOD...
IT ISN'T FOR YOU, IS IT?

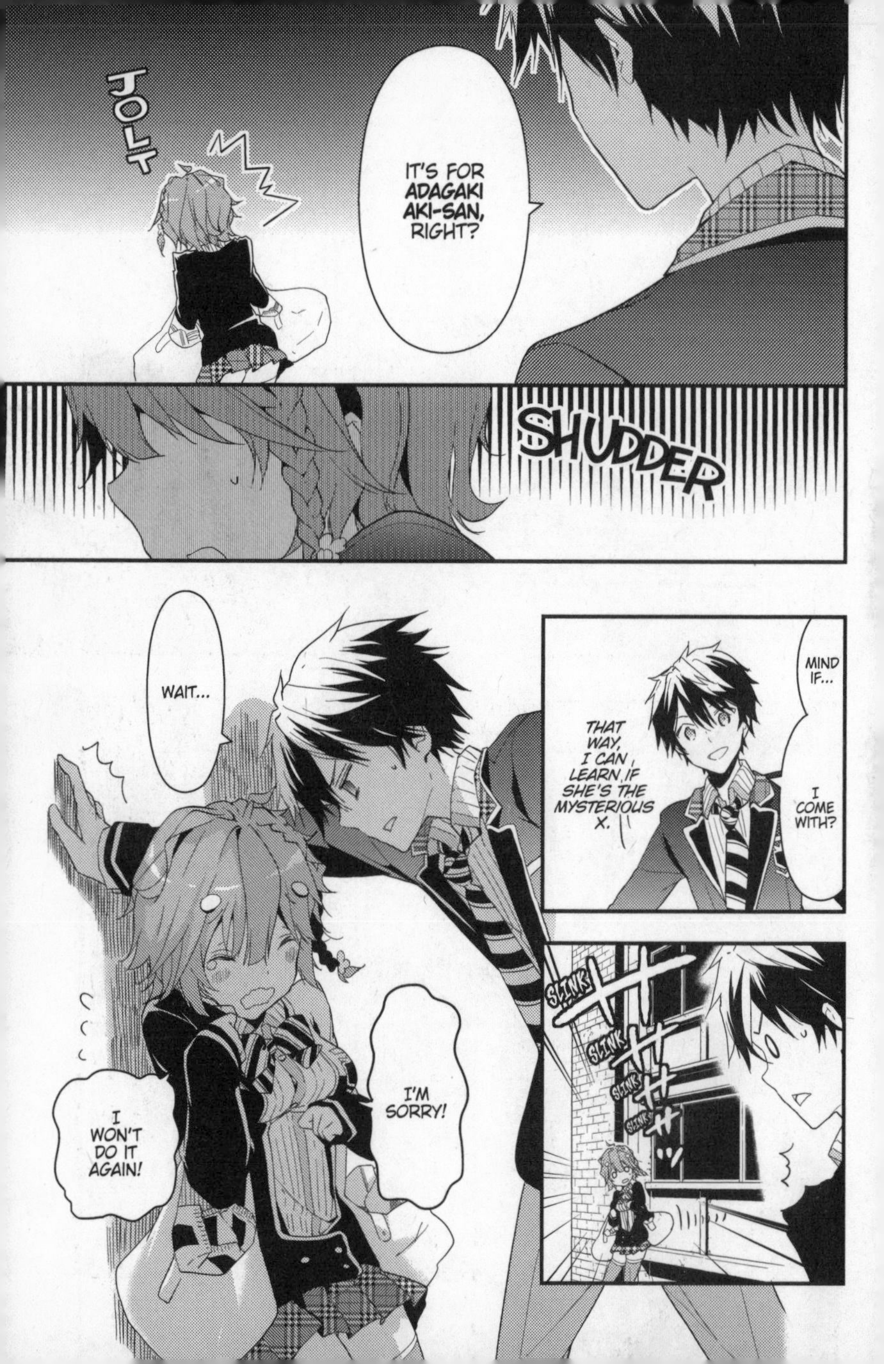
IT'S FOR ADAGAKI AKI-SAN, RIGHT?
JOLT
SHUDDER
MIND IF... I COME WITH?
THAT WAY, I CAN LEARN IF SHE'S THE MYSTERIOUS X.
SLINK
SLINK
SLINK
SLINK
WAIT...
I'M SORRY!
I WON'T DO IT AGAIN!

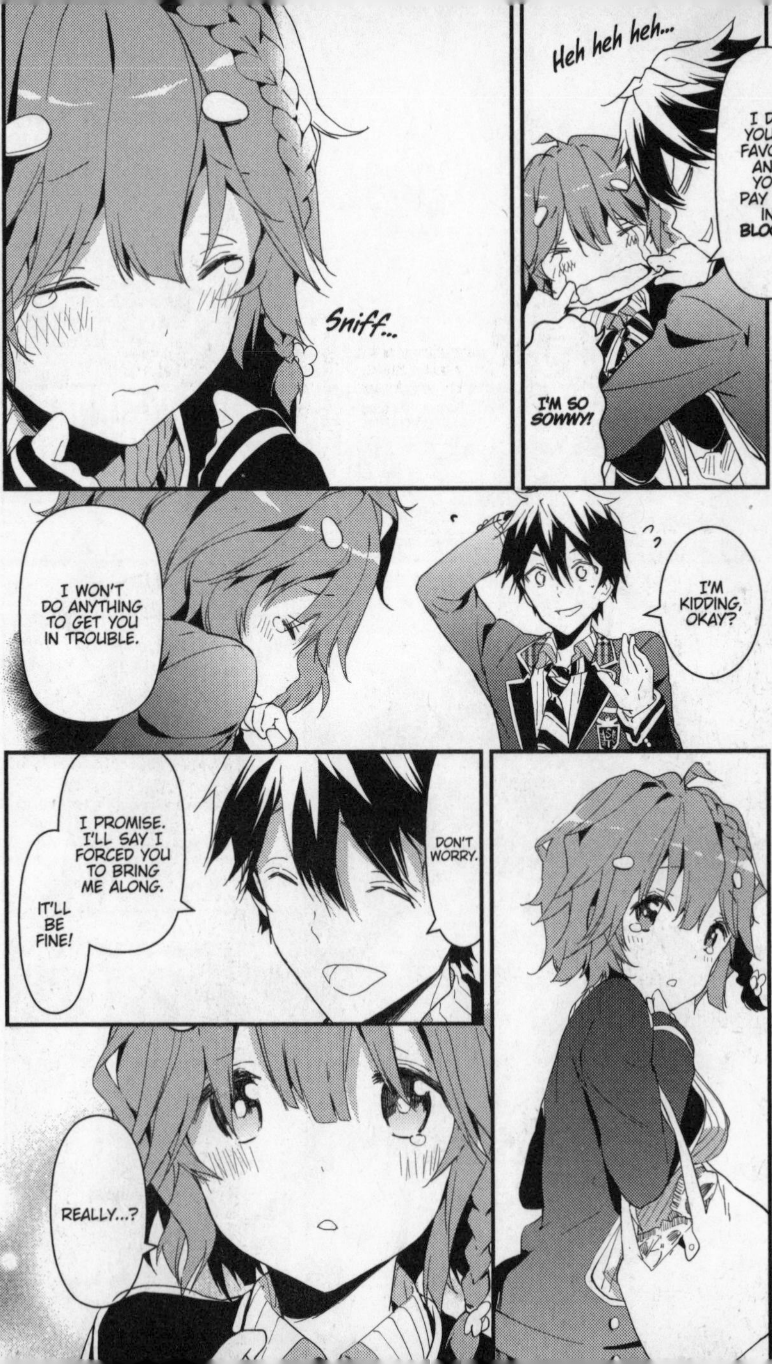
Heh heh heh...
I DO YOU A FAVOR, AND YOU PAY ME IN BLOOD.
I'M SO SOWWY!
Sniff...
I'M KIDDING, OKAY?
I WON'T DO ANYTHING TO GET YOU IN TROUBLE.
DON'T WORRY.
I PROMISE. I'LL SAY I FORCED YOU TO BRING ME ALONG.
IT'LL BE FINE!
REALLY...?

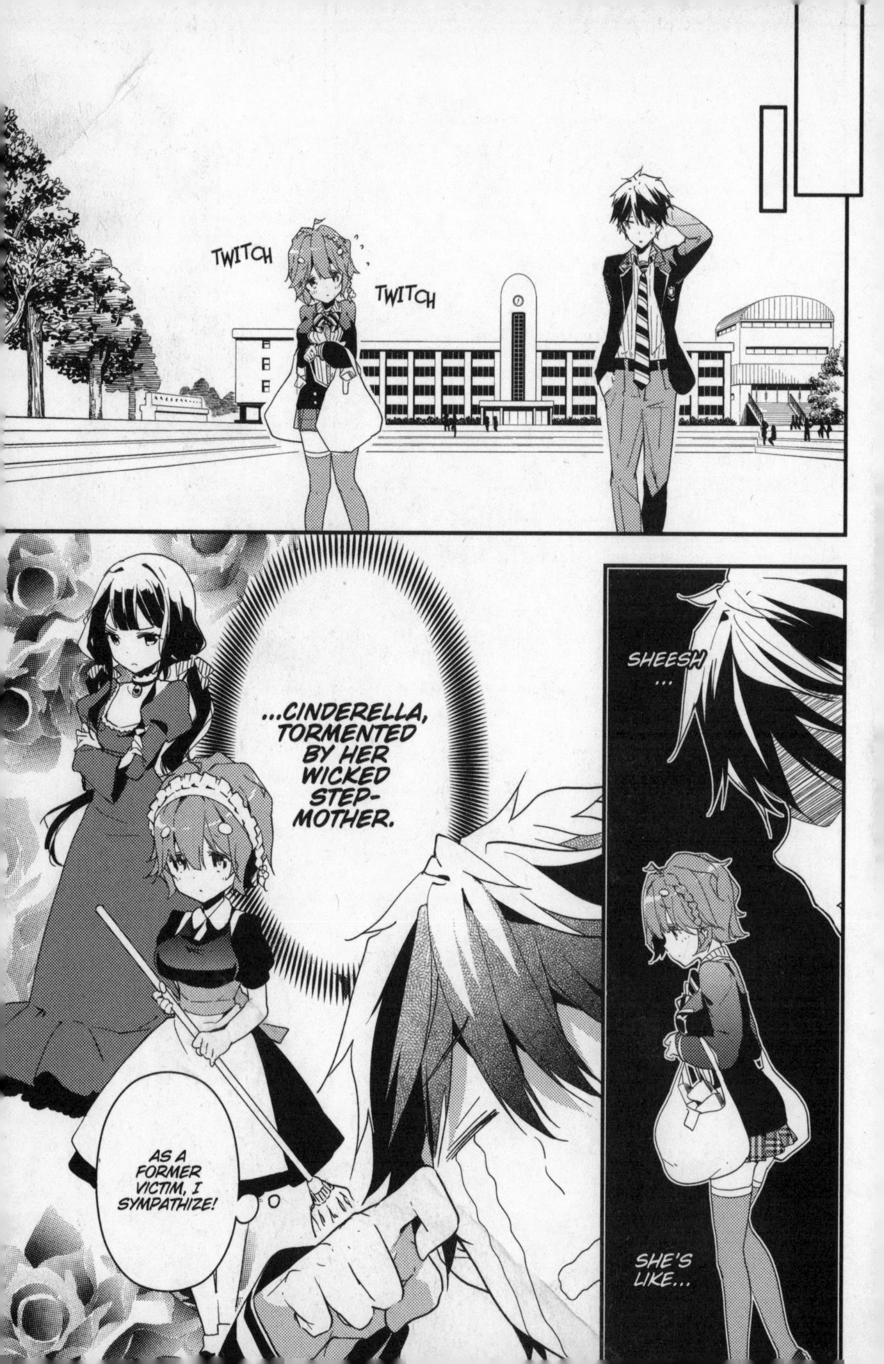
TWITCH
TWITCH
SHEESH...
SHE'S LIKE...
...CINDERELLA, TORMENTED BY HER WICKED STEP-MOTHER.
AS A FORMER VICTIM, I SYMPATHIZE!

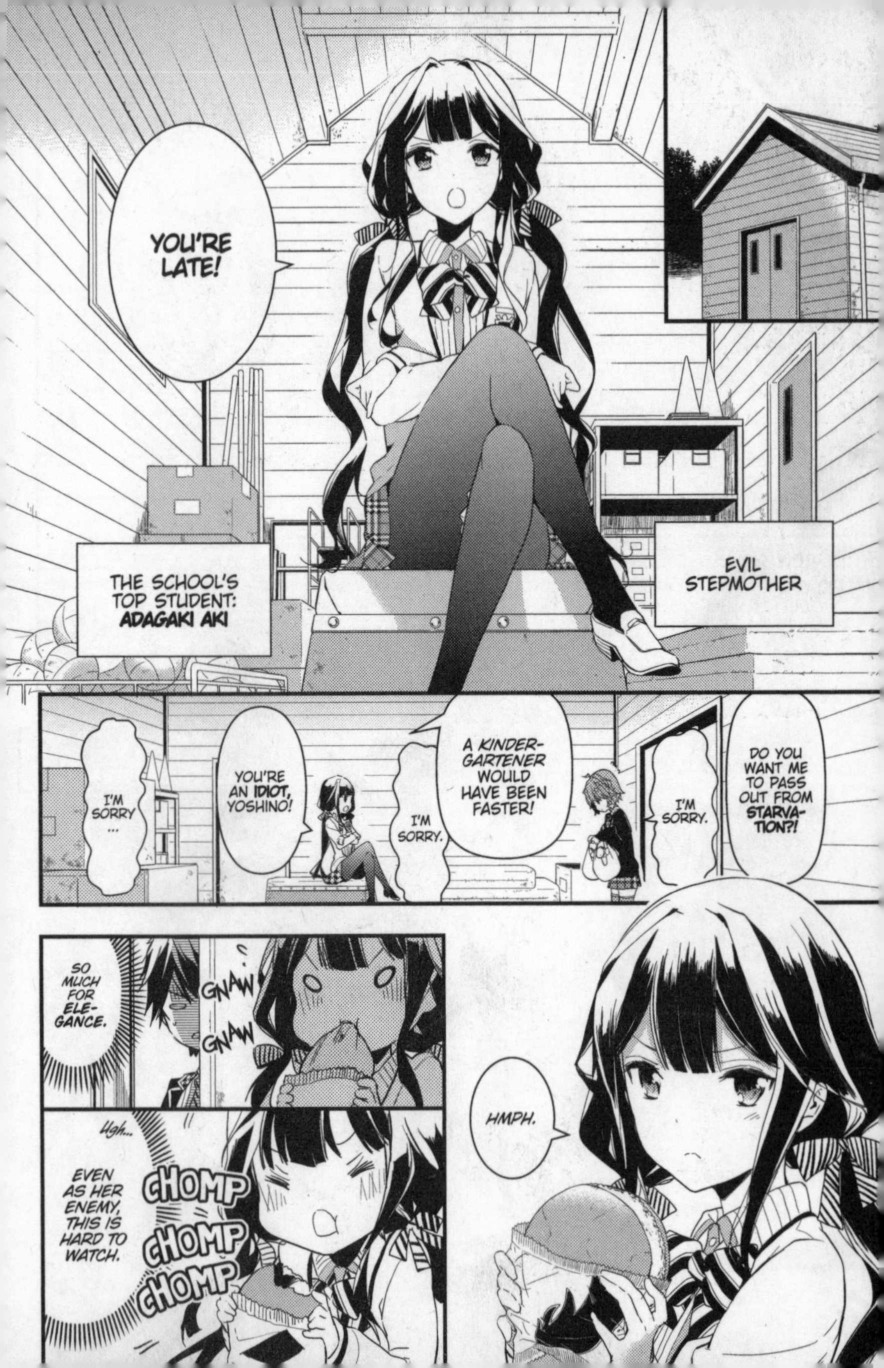
YOU'RE LATE!
EVIL STEPMOTHER
THE SCHOOL'S TOP STUDENT: ADAGAKI AKI
DO YOU WANT ME TO PASS OUT FROM STARVATION?!
I'M SORRY.
A KINDERGARTENER WOULD HAVE BEEN FASTER!
I'M SORRY.
YOU'RE AN IDIOT, YOSHINO!
I'M SORRY...
HMPH.
GNAW
GNAW
SO MUCH FOR ELEGANCE.
Ugh...
CHOMP
CHOMP
CHOMP
EVEN AS HER ENEMY, THIS IS HARD TO WATCH.

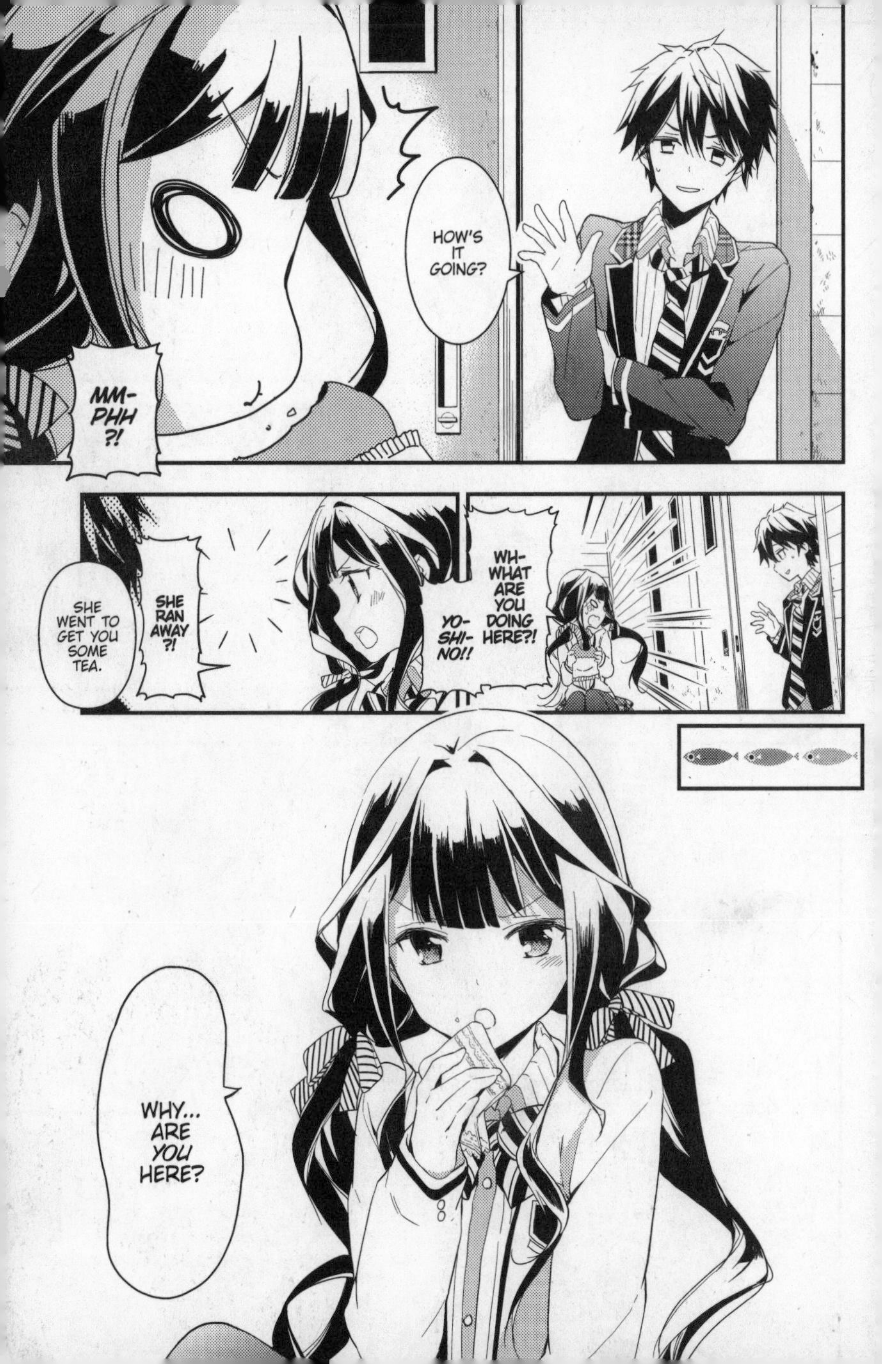
HOW'S IT GOING?
MM-PHH?!
WH-WHAT ARE YOU DOING HERE?!
YO-SHI-NO!!
SHE RAN AWAY?!
SHE WENT TO GET YOU SOME TEA.
WHY... ARE YOU HERE?

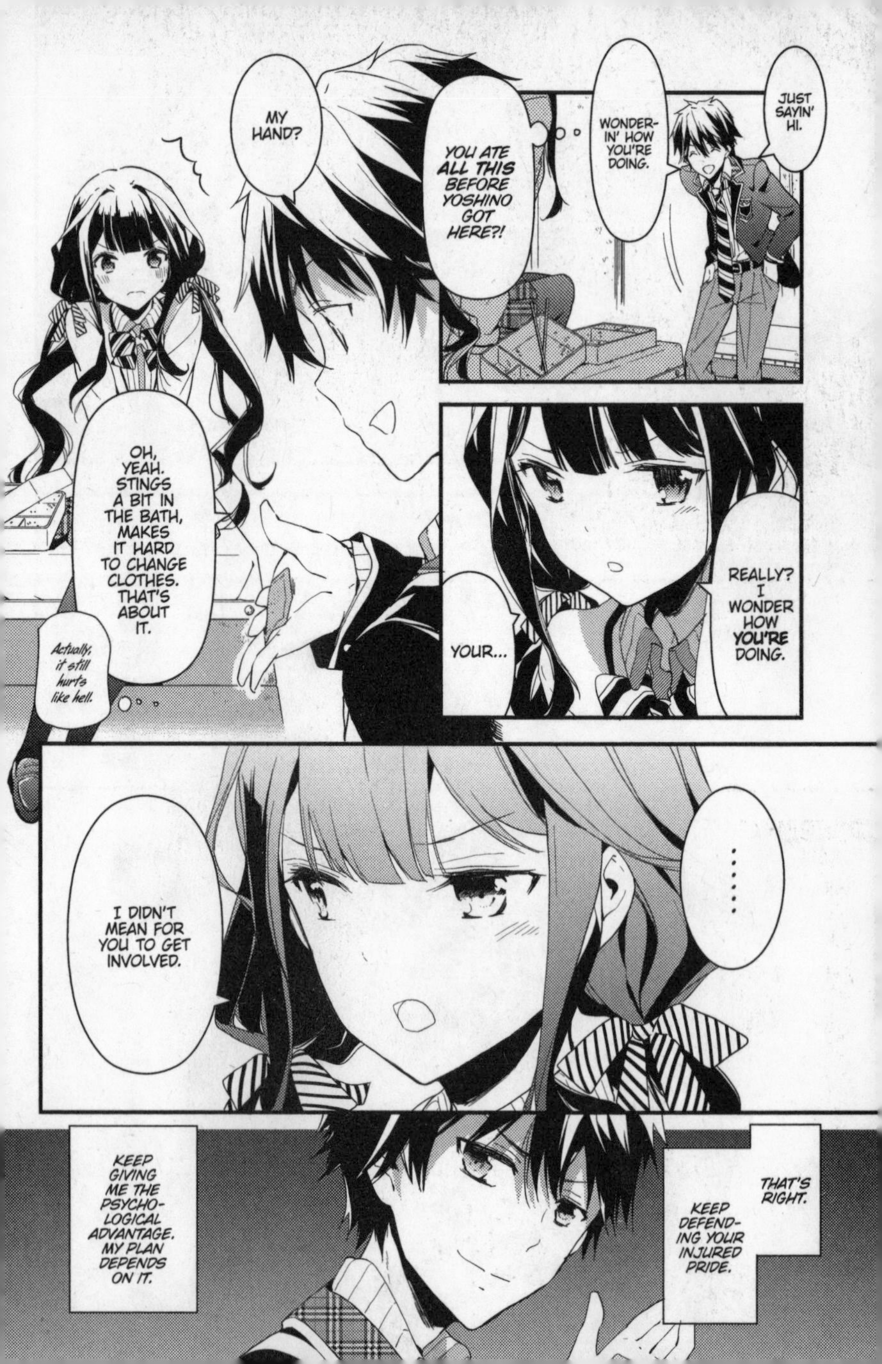
JUST SAYIN' HI.
WONDER-IN' HOW YOU'RE DOING.
YOU ATE ALL THIS BEFORE YOSHINO GOT HERE?!
MY HAND?
REALLY? I WONDER HOW YOU'RE DOING.
YOUR...
OH, YEAH. STINGS A BIT IN THE BATH, MAKES IT HARD TO CHANGE CLOTHES. THAT'S ABOUT IT.
Actually, it still hurts like hell.
......
I DIDN'T MEAN FOR YOU TO GET INVOLVED.
THAT'S RIGHT.
KEEP DEFEND-ING YOUR INJURED PRIDE.
KEEP GIVING ME THE PSYCHO-LOGICAL ADVANTAGE. MY PLAN DEPENDS ON IT.

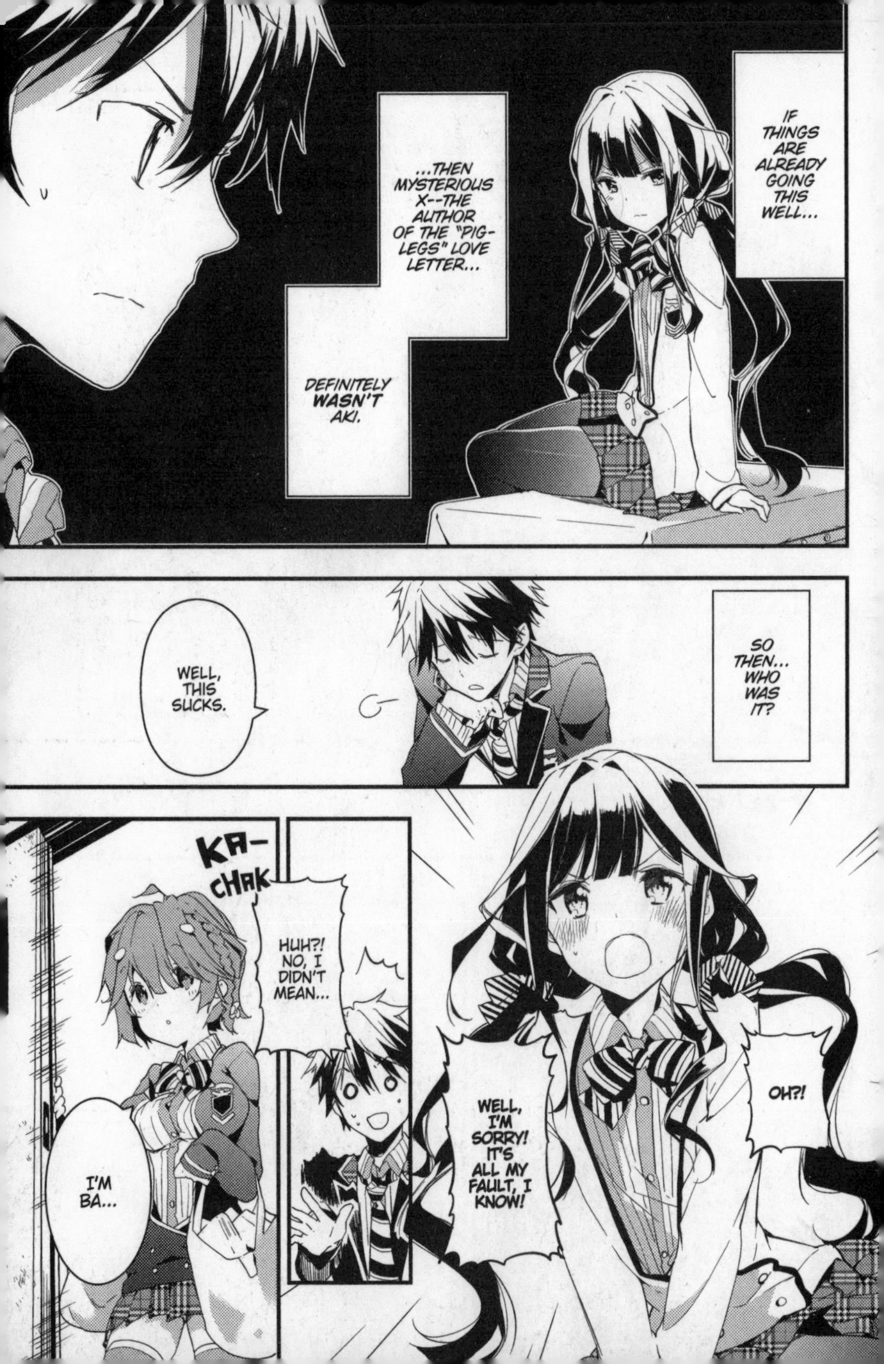
IF THINGS ARE ALREADY GOING THIS WELL...
...THEN MYSTERIOUS X--THE AUTHOR OF THE "PIG-LEGS" LOVE LETTER...
DEFINITELY WASN'T AKI.
SO THEN... WHO WAS IT?
WELL, THIS SUCKS.
OH?!
WELL, I'M SORRY! IT'S ALL MY FAULT, I KNOW!
HUH?! NO, I DIDN'T MEAN...
KA-CHAK
I'M BA...

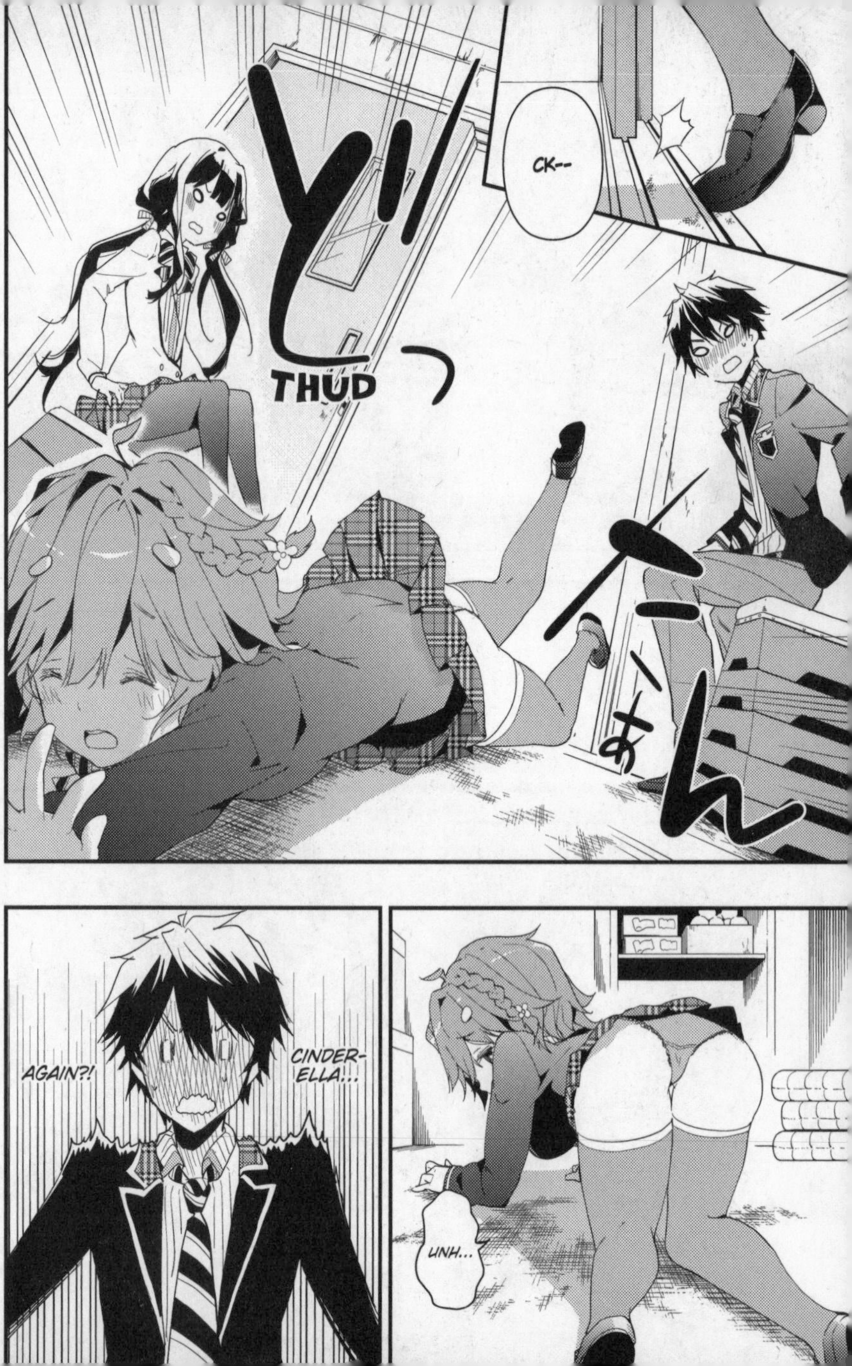
CK--
THUD
UNH...
CINDER-ELLA...
AGAIN?!

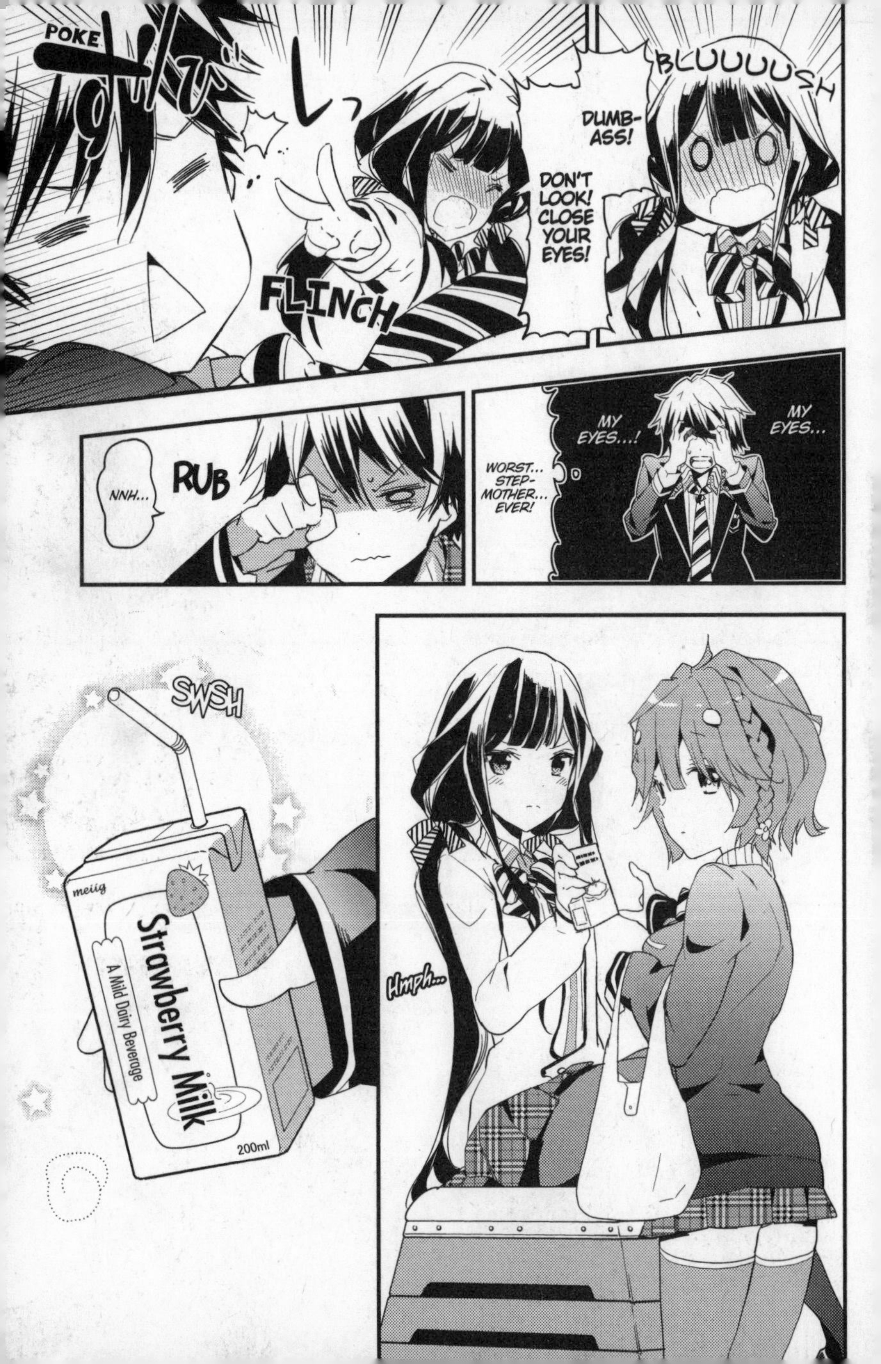
BLUUUUSH
DUMB-ASS!
DON'T LOOK! CLOSE YOUR EYES!
POKE
FLINCH
MY EYES...
MY EYES...!
WORST... STEP-MOTHER... EVER!
RUB
NNH...
Hmph...
SWSH
meiig
Strawberry Milk
A Mild Dairy Beverage
200ml

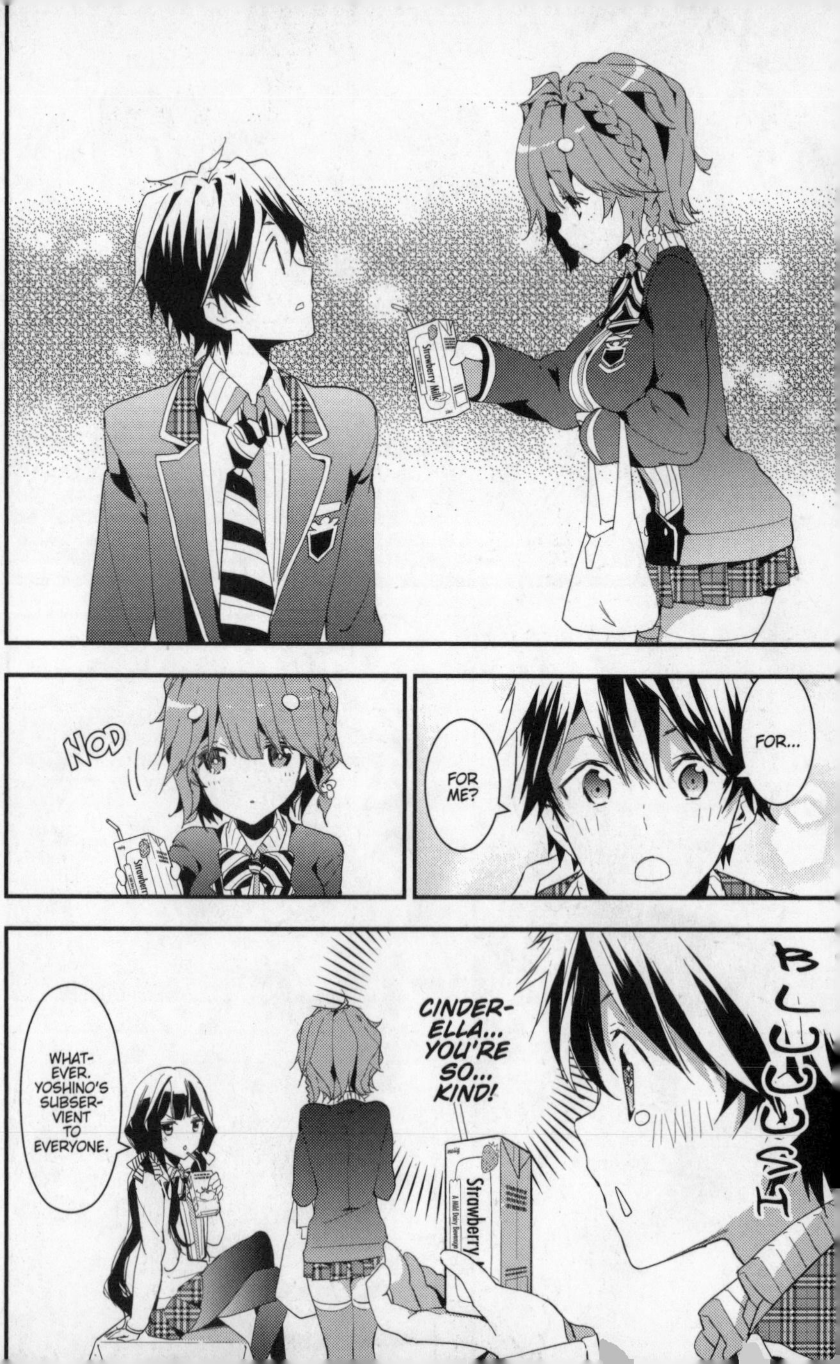
Strawberry Milk
FOR...
FOR ME?
NOD
Strawberry
BLUUUSH
CINDER-ELLA... YOU'RE SO... KIND!
A Mild Dairy Beverage
WHAT-EVER. YOSHINO'S SUBSER-VIENT TO EVERYONE.

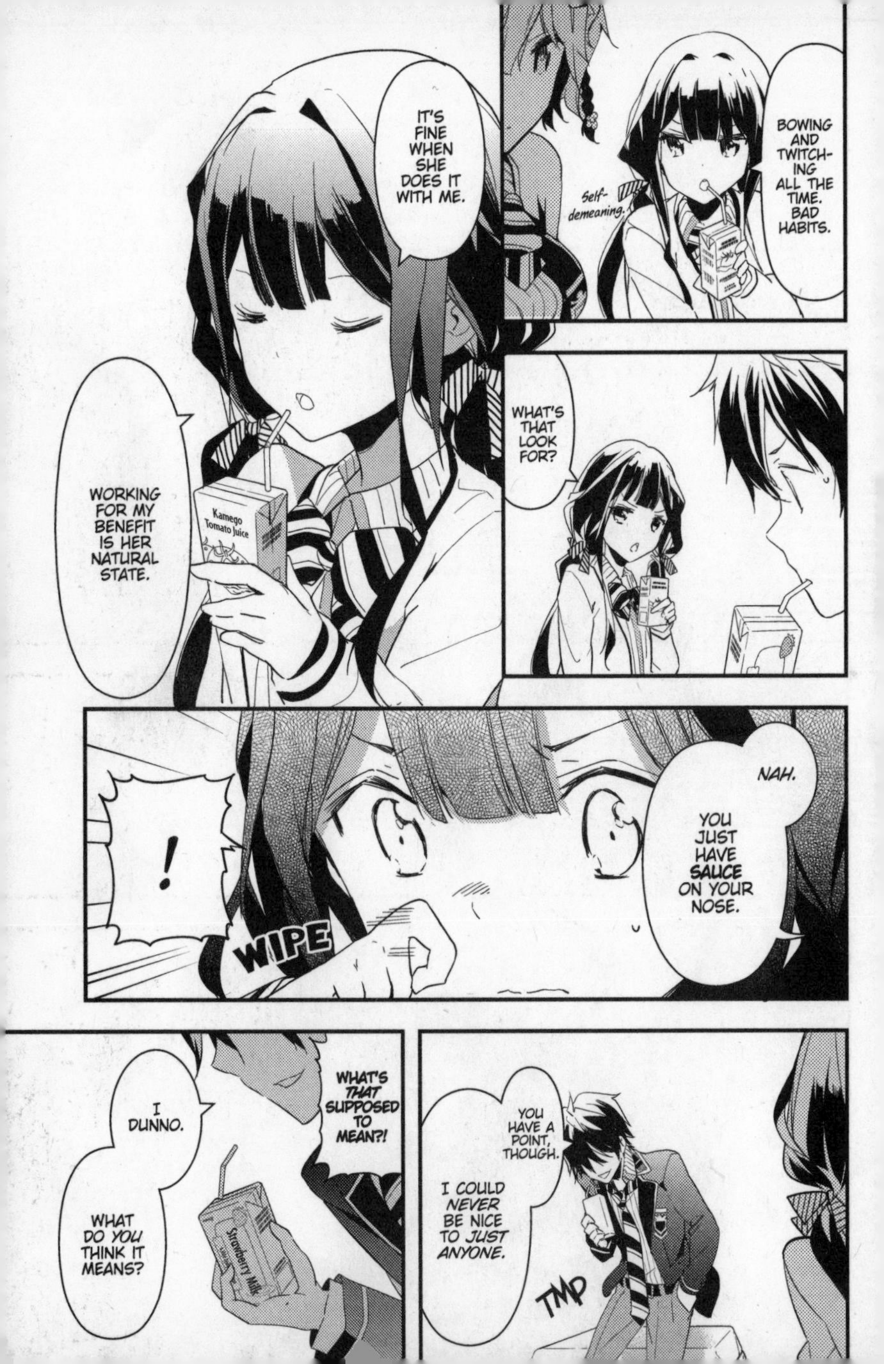
BOWING AND TWITCHING ALL THE TIME. BAD HABITS.
Self-demeaning.
WHAT'S THAT LOOK FOR?
IT'S FINE WHEN SHE DOES IT WITH ME.
WORKING FOR MY BENEFIT IS HER NATURAL STATE.
Kamego Tomato Juice
NAH.
YOU JUST HAVE SAUCE ON YOUR NOSE.
!
WIPE
YOU HAVE A POINT, THOUGH.
I COULD NEVER BE NICE TO JUST ANYONE.
TMP
WHAT'S THAT SUPPOSED TO MEAN?!
I DUNNO.
WHAT DO YOU THINK IT MEANS?
Strawberry Milk

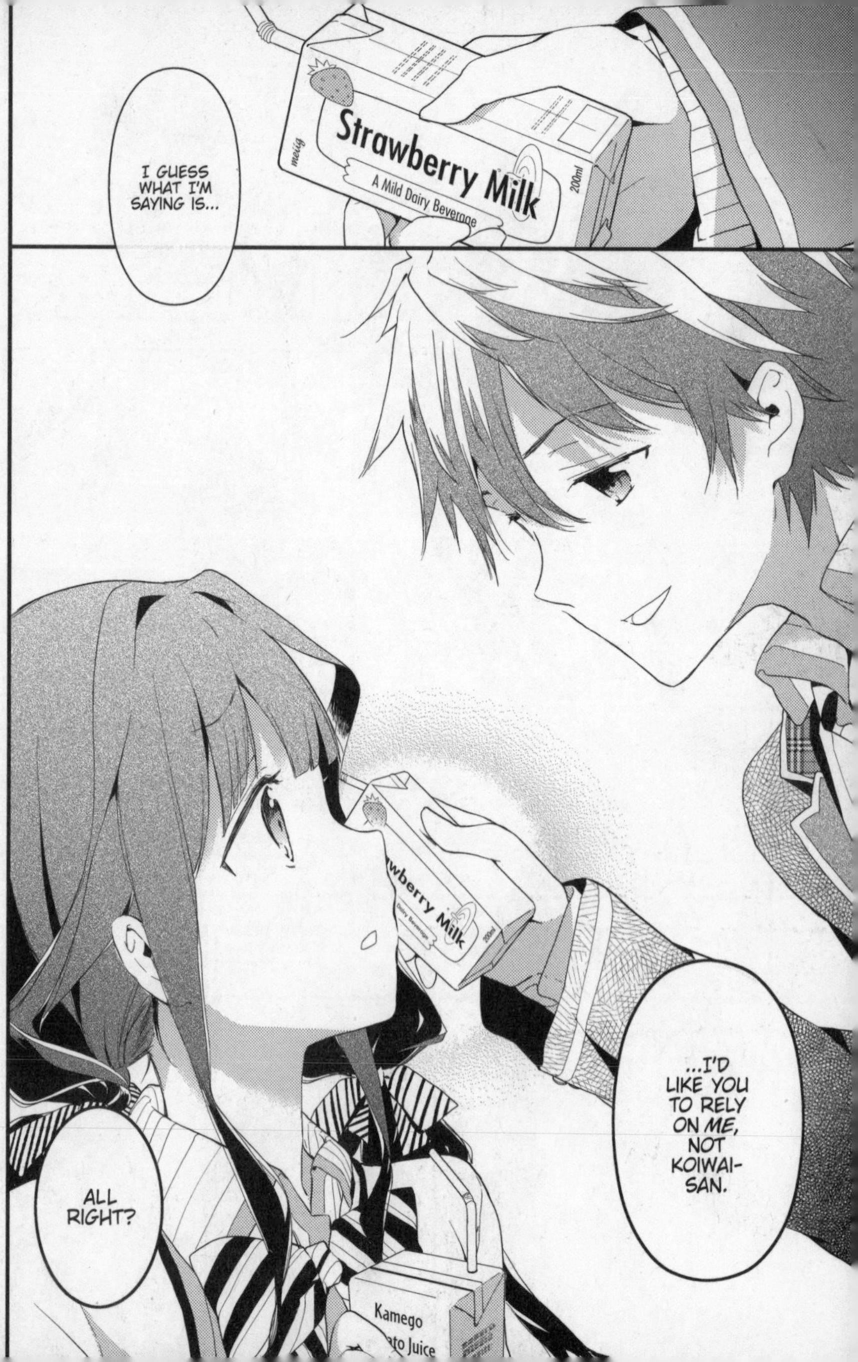
Strawberry Milk
A Mild Dairy Beverage
200ml
I GUESS WHAT I'M SAYING IS...
...I'D LIKE YOU TO RELY ON *ME*, NOT KOIWAI-SAN.
ALL RIGHT?

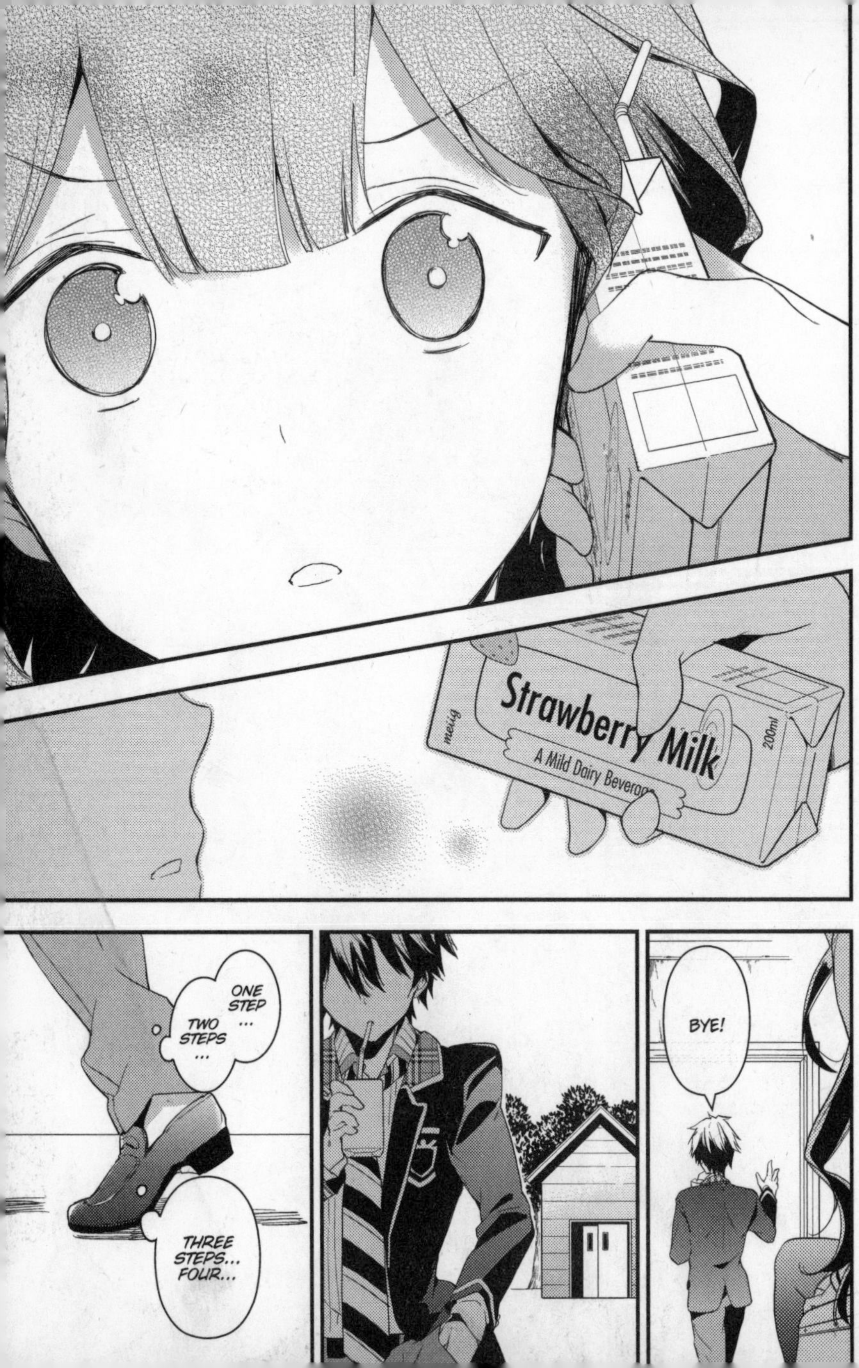
Strawberry Milk
200ml
BYE!
ONE STEP ... TWO STEPS ...
THREE STEPS... FOUR...

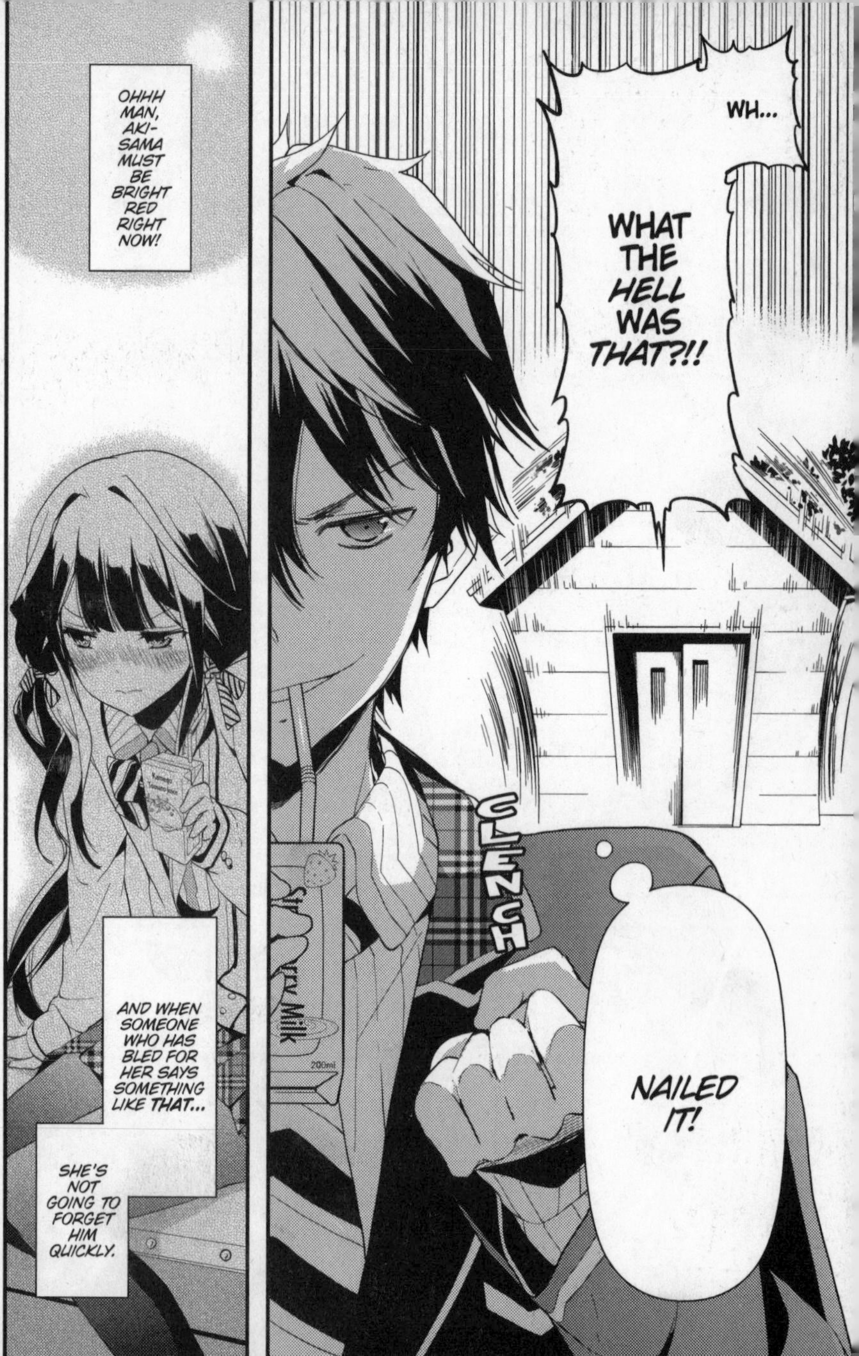
WH...
WHAT THE HELL WAS THAT?!!
CLENCH
NAILED IT!
OHHH MAN, AKI-SAMA MUST BE BRIGHT RED RIGHT NOW!
AND WHEN SOMEONE WHO HAS BLED FOR HER SAYS SOMETHING LIKE THAT...
SHE'S NOT GOING TO FORGET HIM QUICKLY.

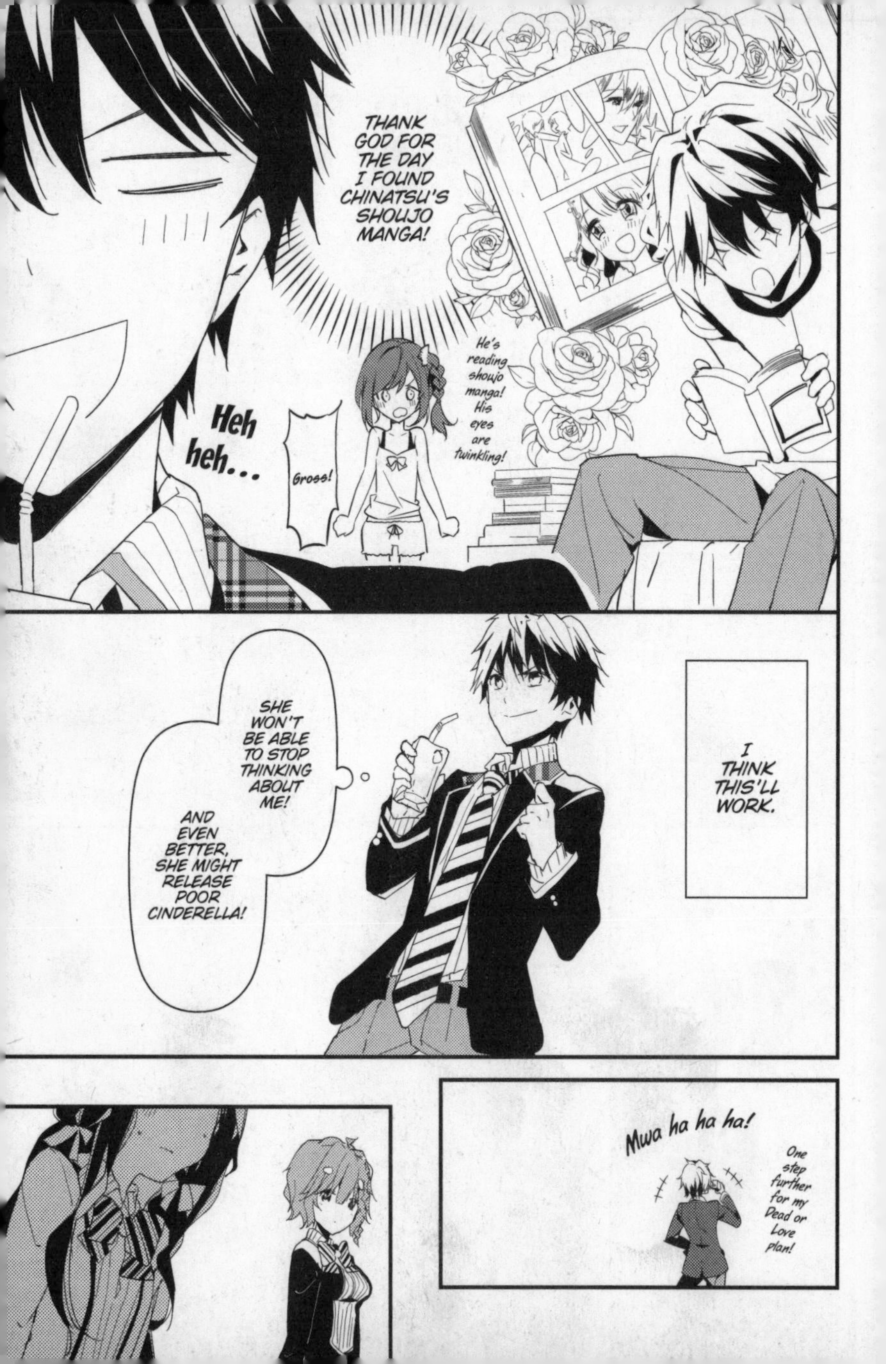
THANK GOD FOR THE DAY I FOUND CHINATSU'S SHOUJO MANGA!
He's reading shoujo manga! His eyes are twinkling!
Gross!
Heh heh...
I THINK THIS'LL WORK.
SHE WON'T BE ABLE TO STOP THINKING ABOUT ME!
AND EVEN BETTER, SHE MIGHT RELEASE POOR CINDERELLA!
Mwa ha ha ha!
One step further for my Dead or Love plan!

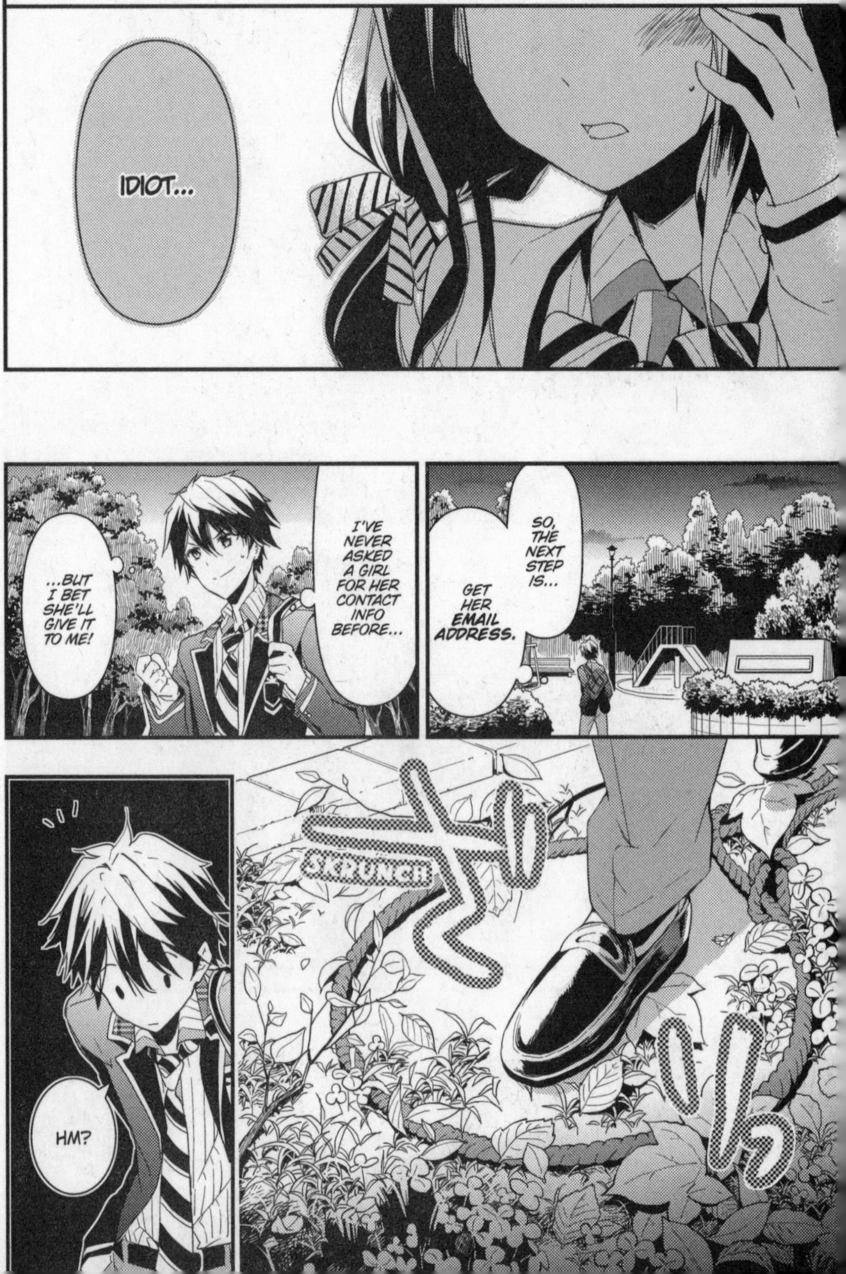
IDIOT...
SO, THE NEXT STEP IS...
GET HER EMAIL ADDRESS.
I'VE NEVER ASKED A GIRL FOR HER CONTACT INFO BEFORE...
...BUT I BET SHE'LL GIVE IT TO ME!
SKPUNCH
HM?

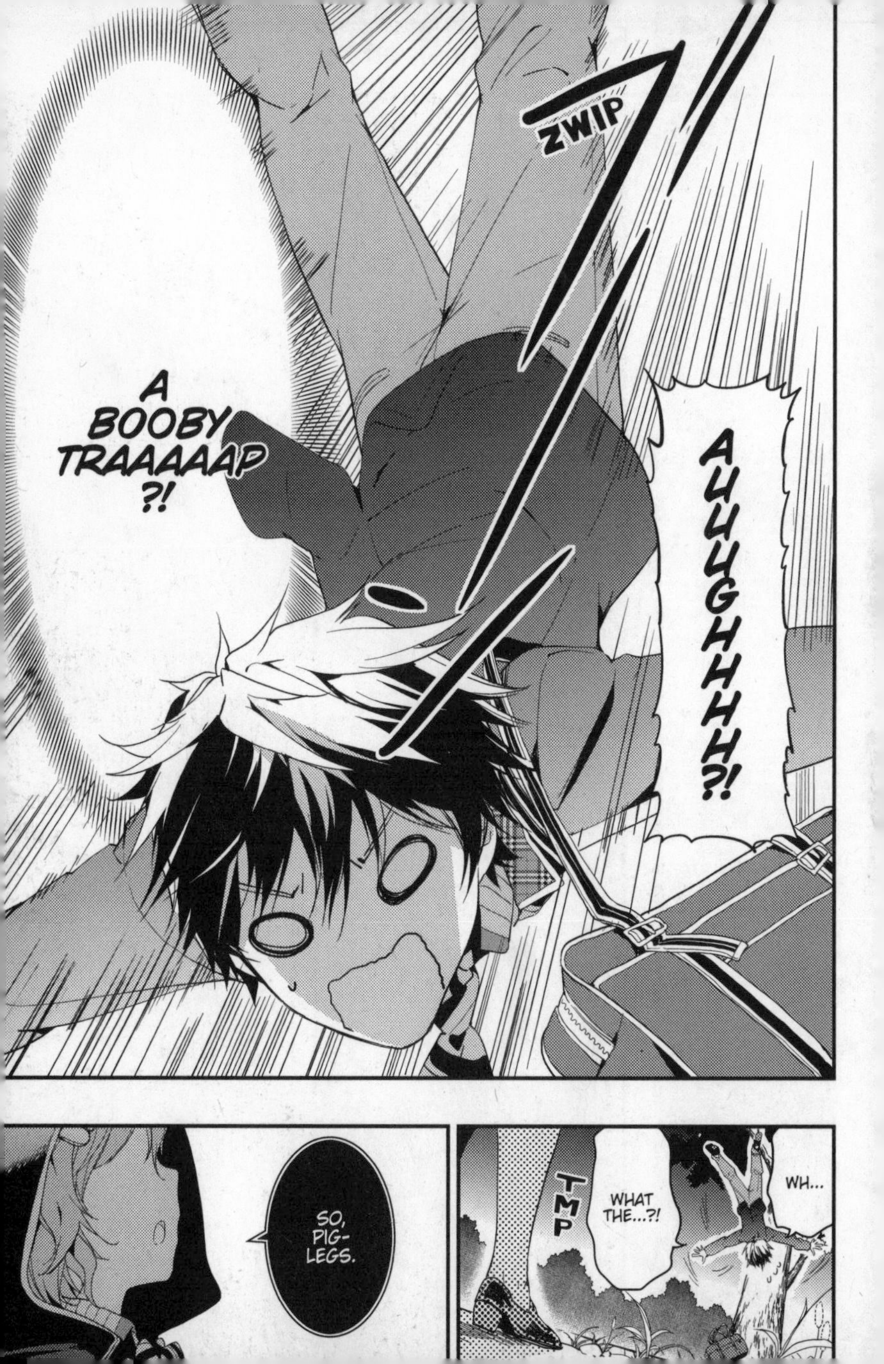
ZWIP
AUUUGHHHHH?!
A BOOBY TRAAAAAP?!
WH...
WHAT THE...?!
TMP
SO, PIG-LEGS.

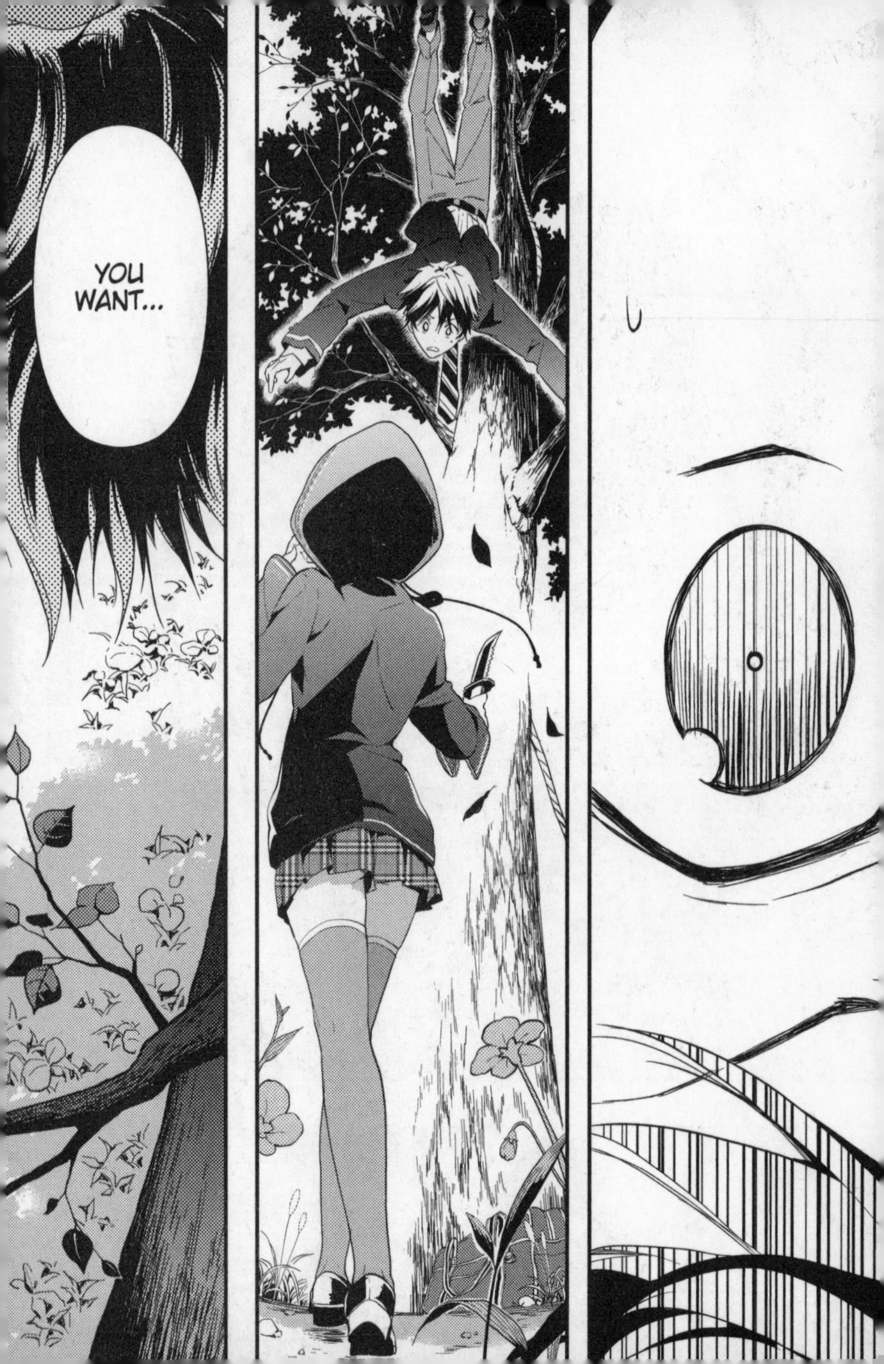
YOU WANT...

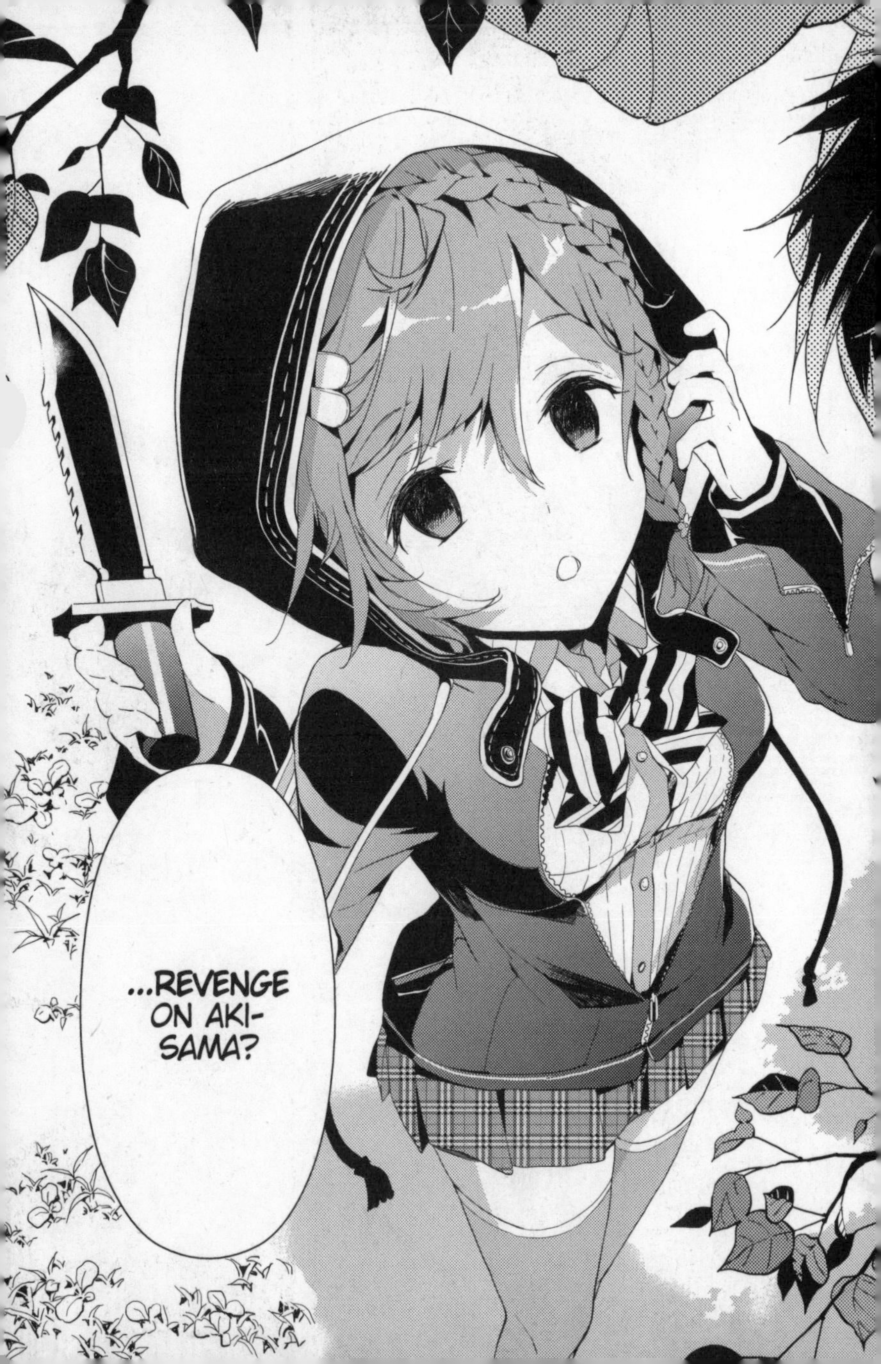
...REVENGE ON AKI-SAMA?

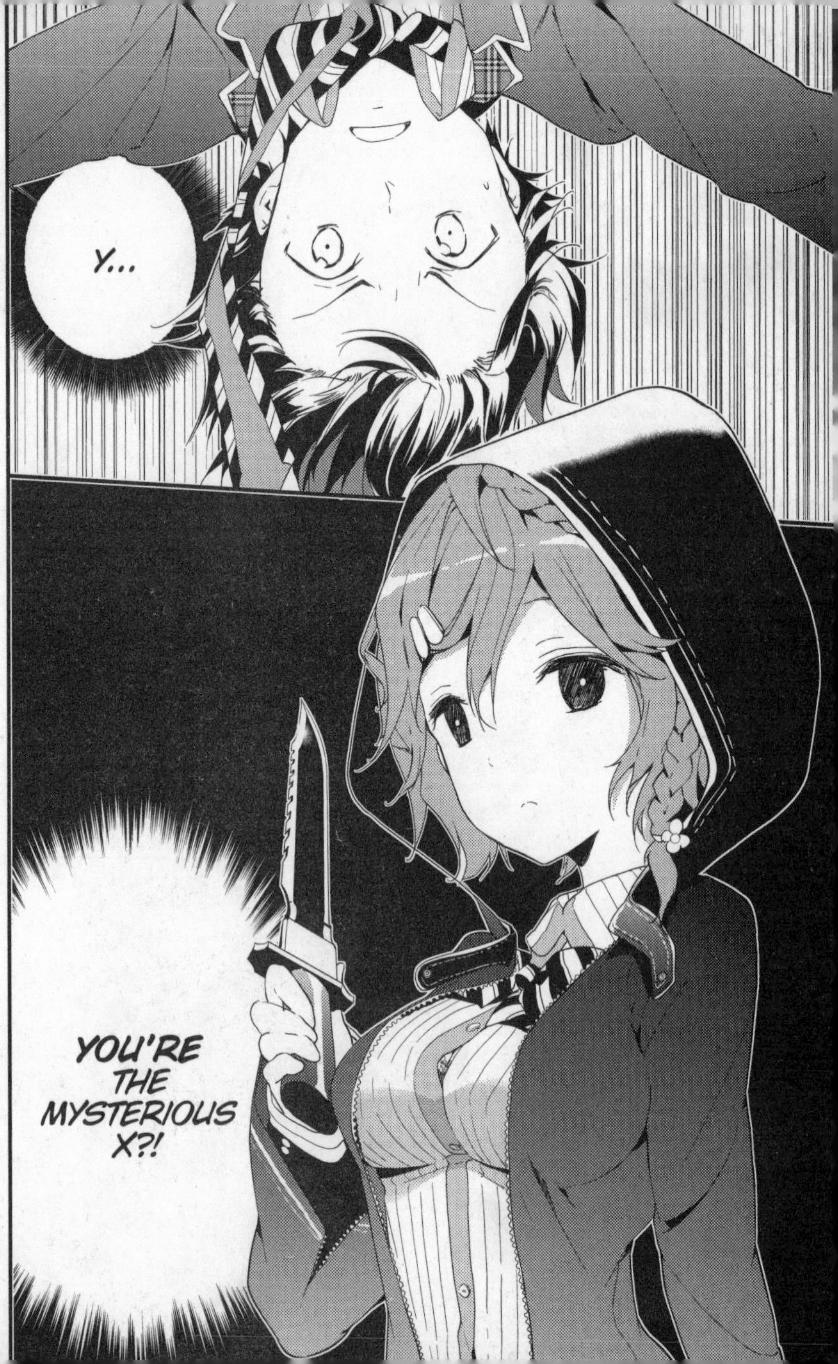
Y...
YOU'RE THE MYSTERIOUS X?!

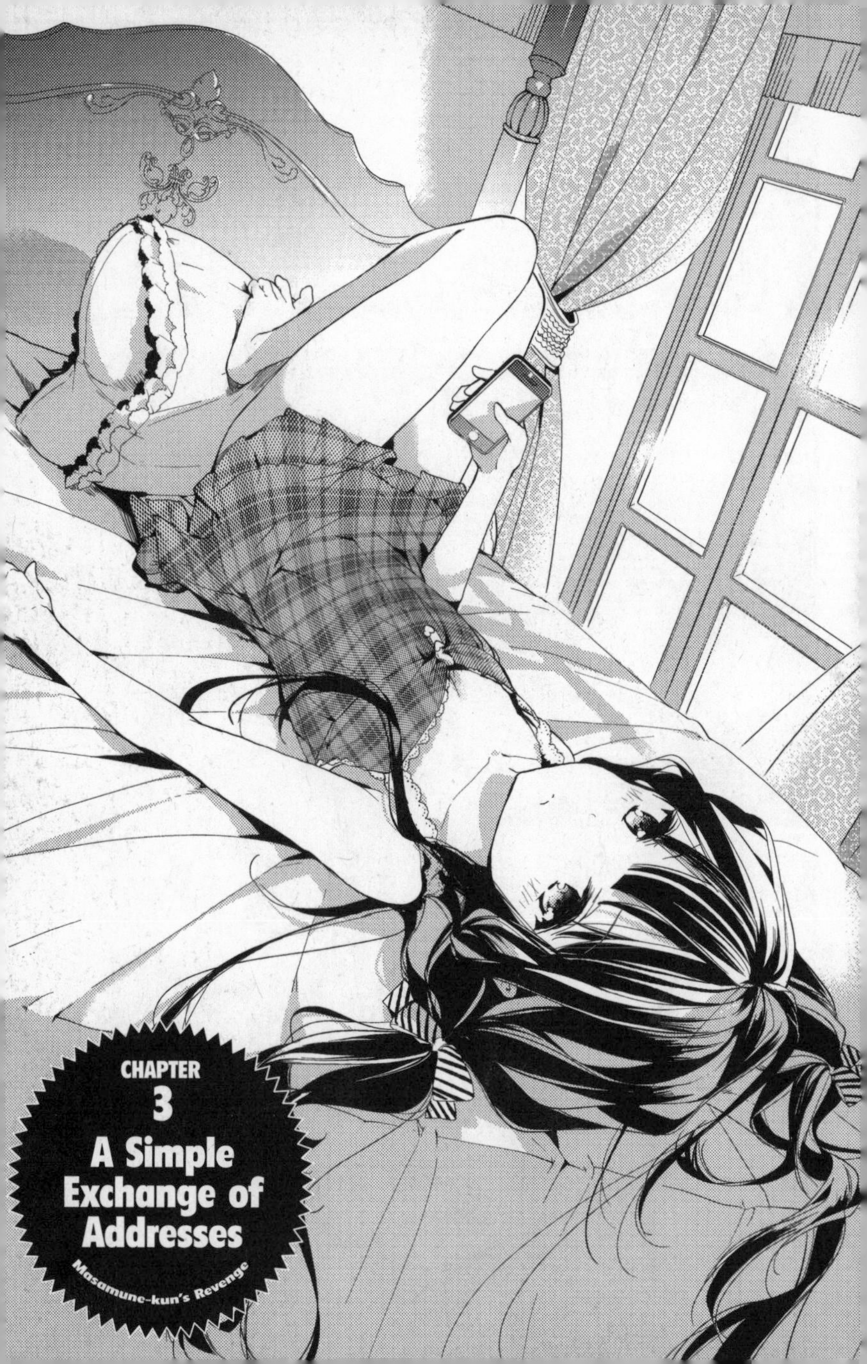
CHAPTER
3
A Simple
Exchange of
Addresses
Masamune-kun's Revenge

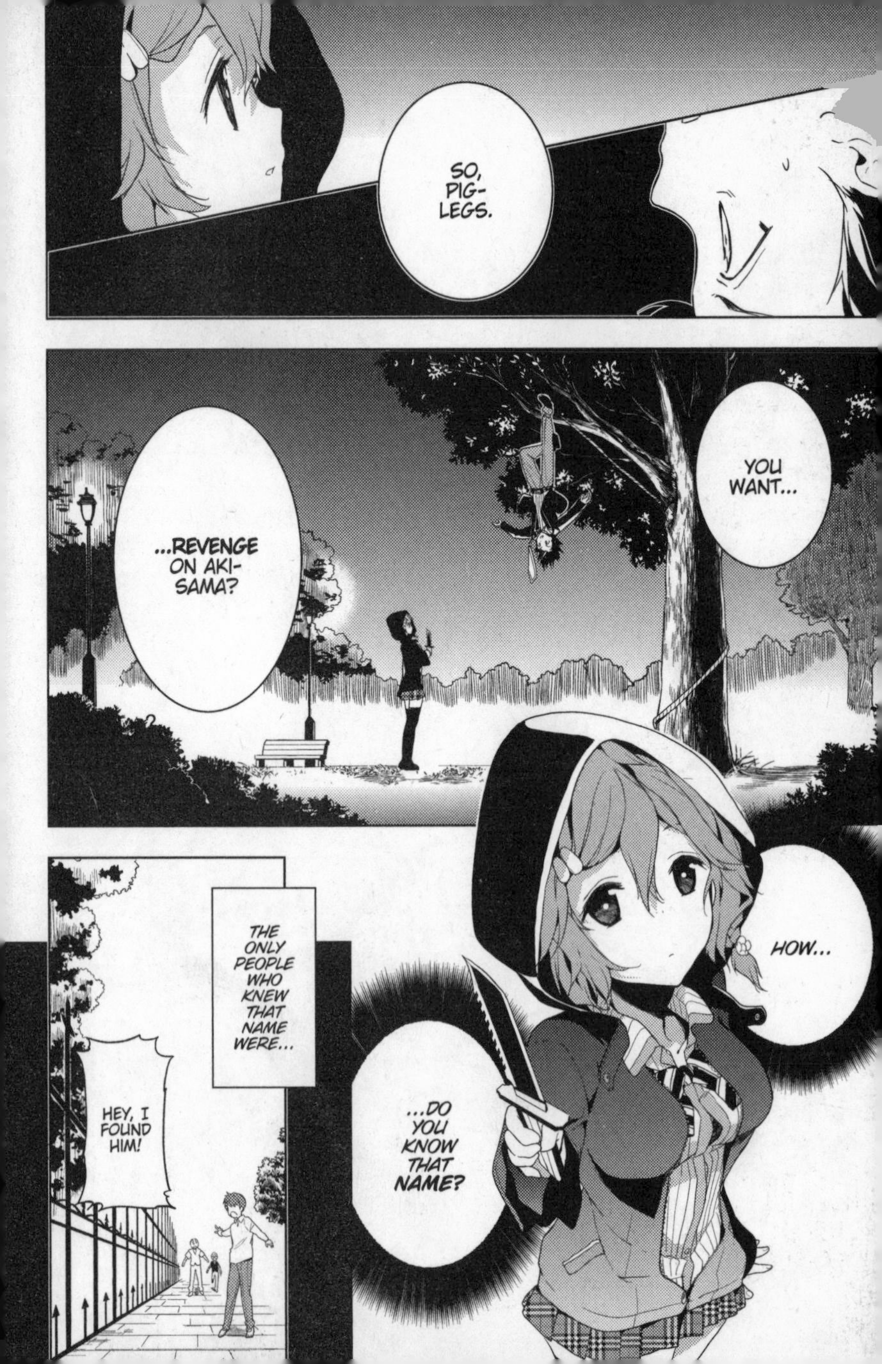
SO, PIG-LEGS.
YOU WANT...
...REVENGE ON AKI-SAMA?
HOW...
...DO YOU KNOW THAT NAME?
THE ONLY PEOPLE WHO KNEW THAT NAME WERE...
HEY, I FOUND HIM!

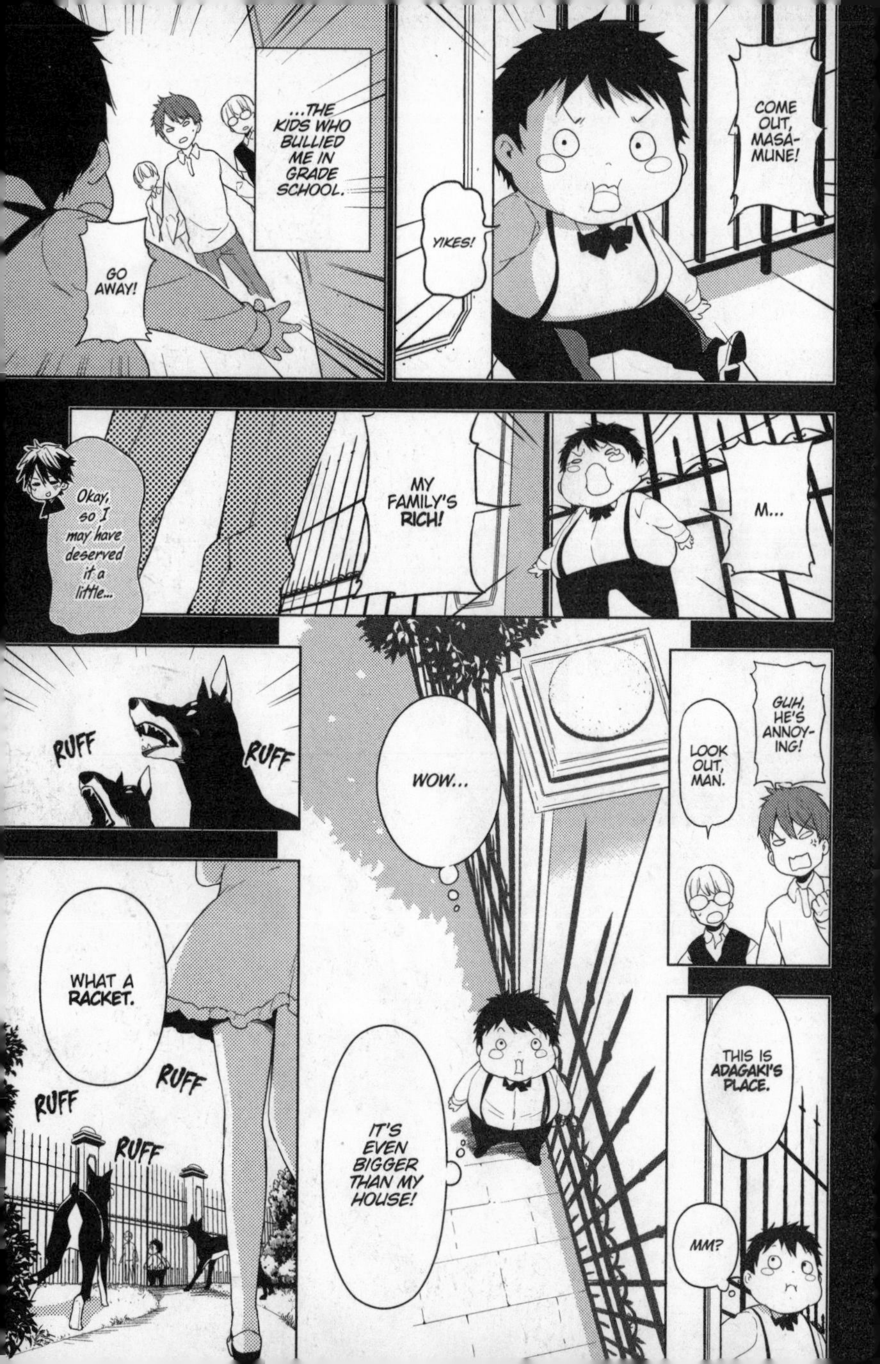
COME OUT, MASAMUNE!
YIKES!
...THE KIDS WHO BULLIED ME IN GRADE SCHOOL.
GO AWAY!
M...
MY FAMILY'S RICH!
Okay, so I may have deserved it a little...
GUH, HE'S ANNOYING!
LOOK OUT, MAN.
THIS IS ADAGAKI'S PLACE.
MM?
WOW...
IT'S EVEN BIGGER THAN MY HOUSE!
RUFF
RUFF
WHAT A RACKET.
RUFF
RUFF
RUFF

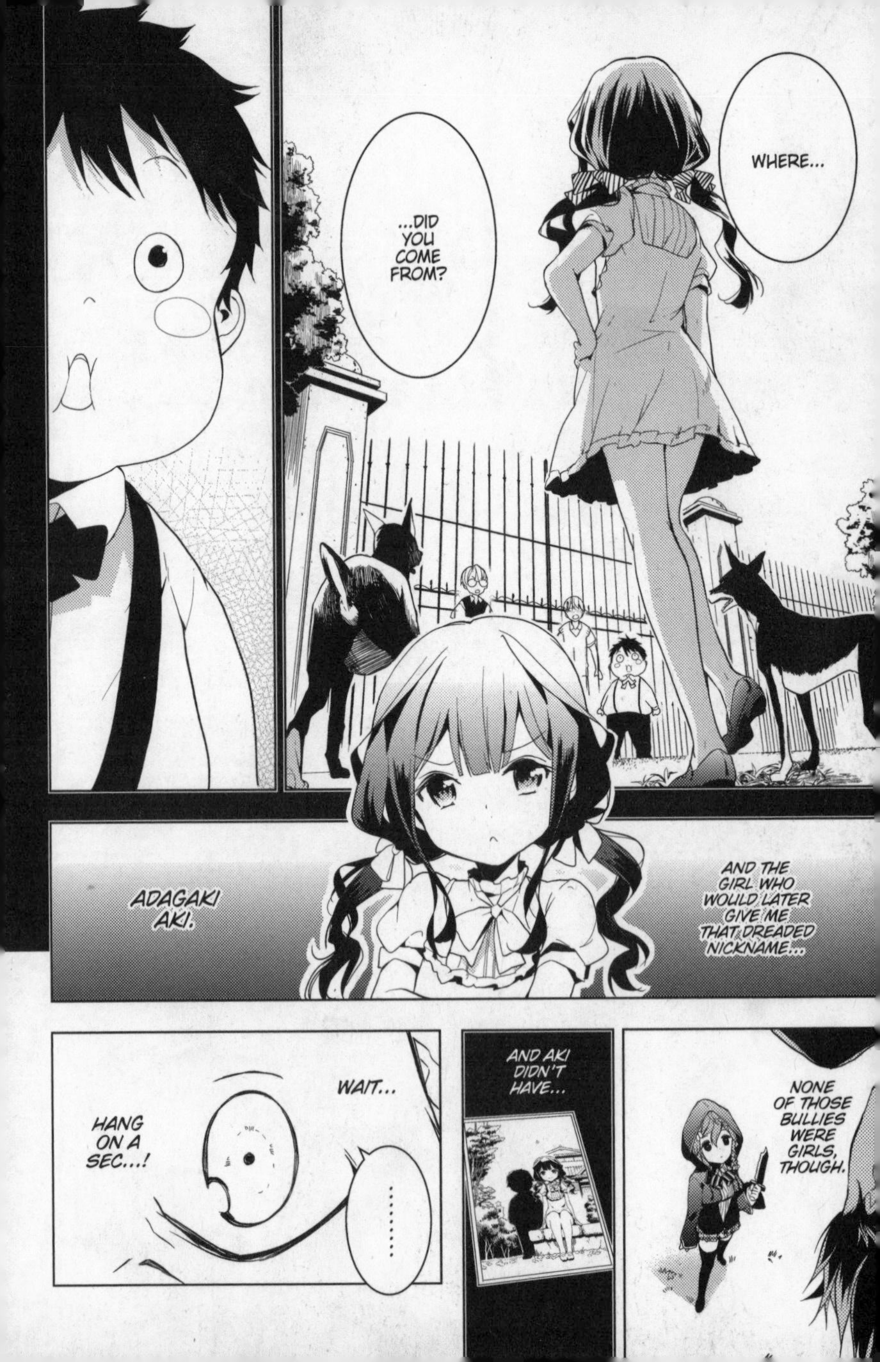
WHERE...
...DID YOU COME FROM?
AND THE GIRL WHO WOULD LATER GIVE ME THAT DREADED NICKNAME...
ADAGAKI AKI.
NONE OF THOSE BULLIES WERE GIRLS, THOUGH.
AND AKI DIDN'T HAVE...
......
WAIT...
HANG ON A SEC...!

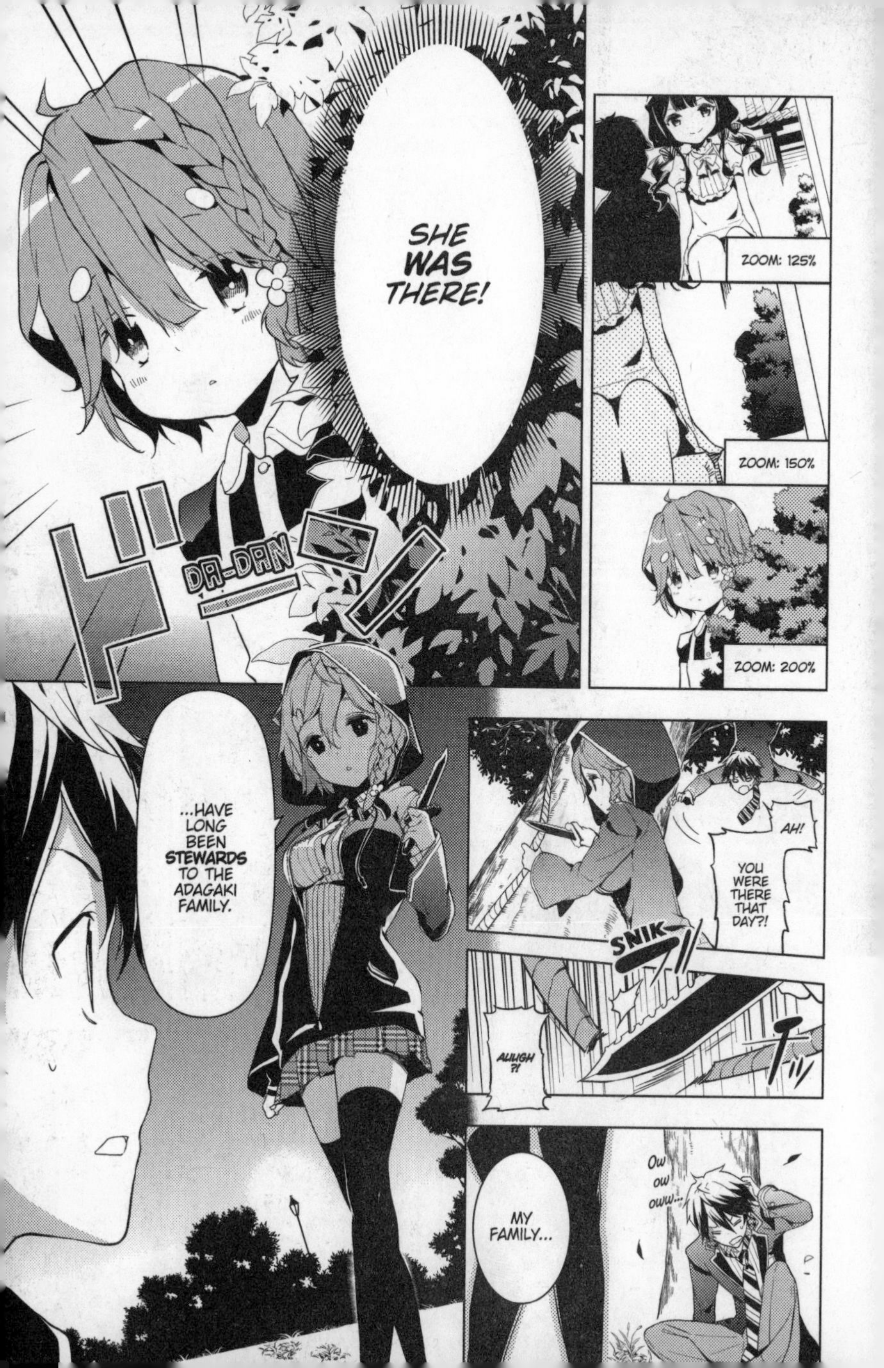
ZOOM: 125%
ZOOM: 150%
ZOOM: 200%
SHE WAS THERE!
DR-DAN
AH!
YOU WERE THERE THAT DAY?!
SNIK
AUGH ?!
Ow ow oww...
MY FAMILY...
...HAVE LONG BEEN STEWARDS TO THE ADAGAKI FAMILY.

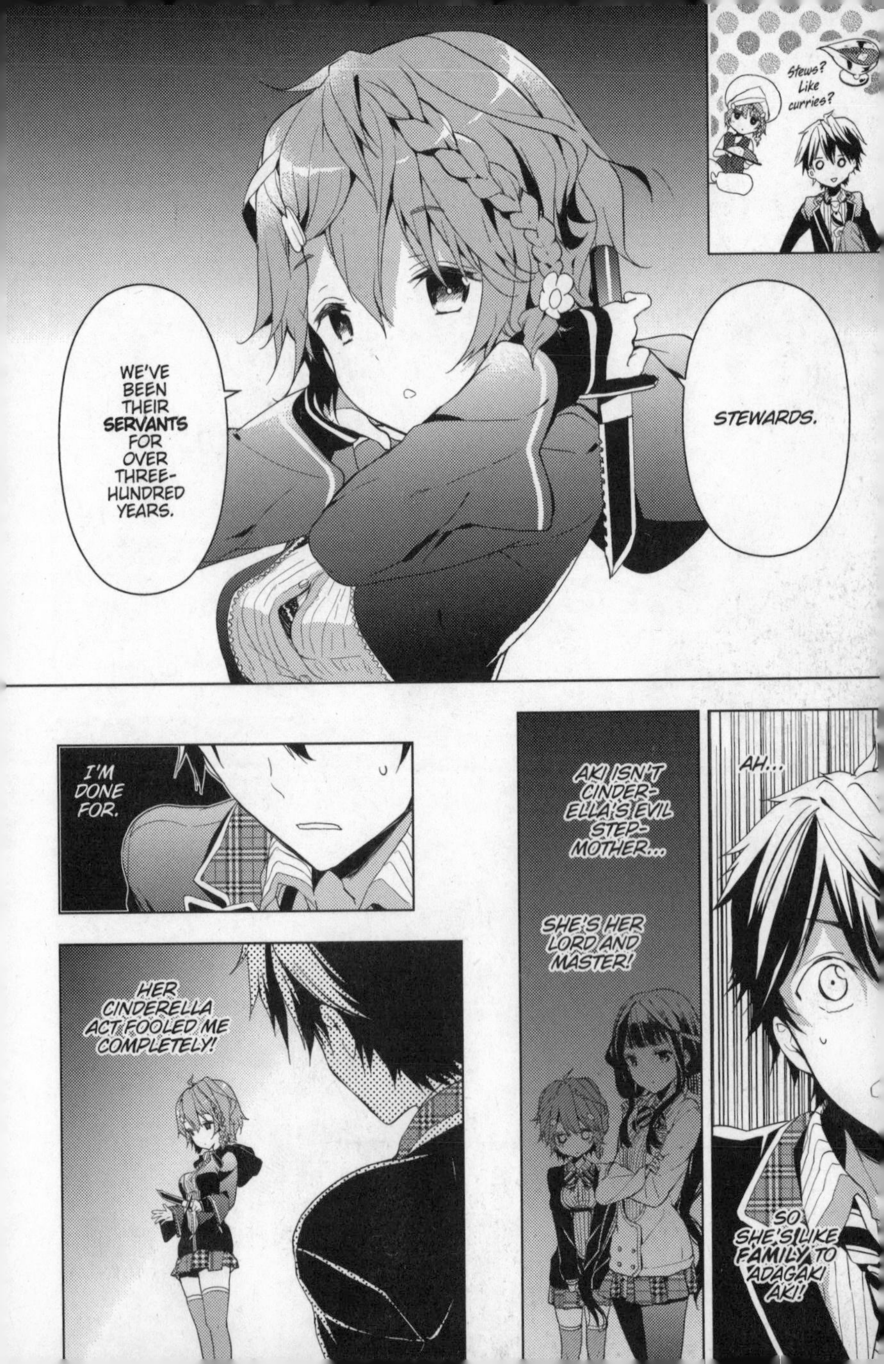
STEWARDS.
WE'VE BEEN THEIR SERVANTS FOR OVER THREE-HUNDRED YEARS.
Stews? Like curries?
AH...
SO SHE'S LIKE FAMILY TO ADAGAKI AKI!
AKI ISN'T CINDER-ELLA'S EVIL STEP-MOTHER...
SHE'S HER LORD AND MASTER!
I'M DONE FOR.
HER CINDERELLA ACT FOOLED ME COMPLETELY!

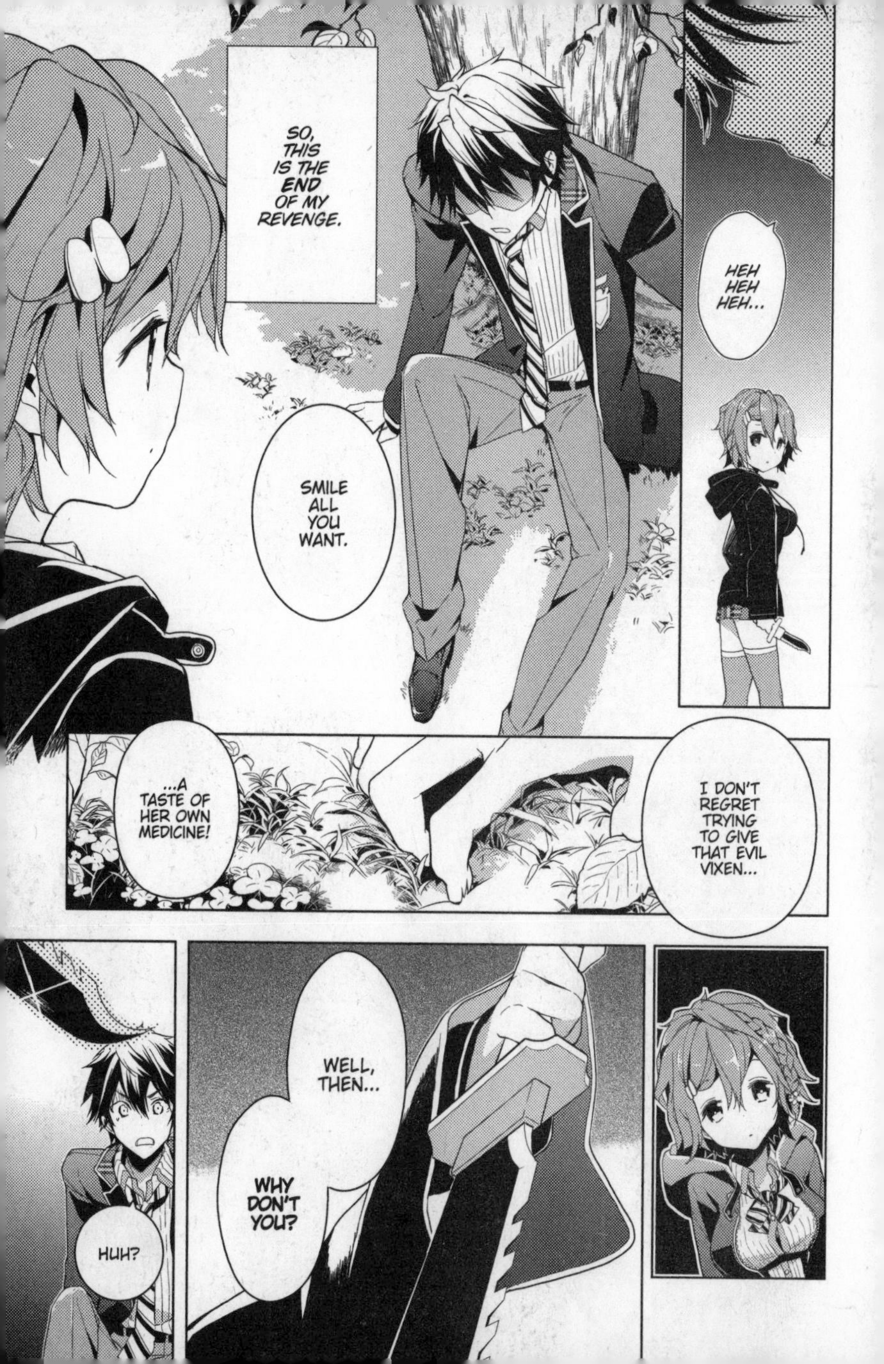
HEH HEH HEH...
SO, THIS IS THE END OF MY REVENGE.
SMILE ALL YOU WANT.
I DON'T REGRET TRYING TO GIVE THAT EVIL VIXEN...
...A TASTE OF HER OWN MEDICINE!
WELL, THEN...
WHY DON'T YOU?
HUH?

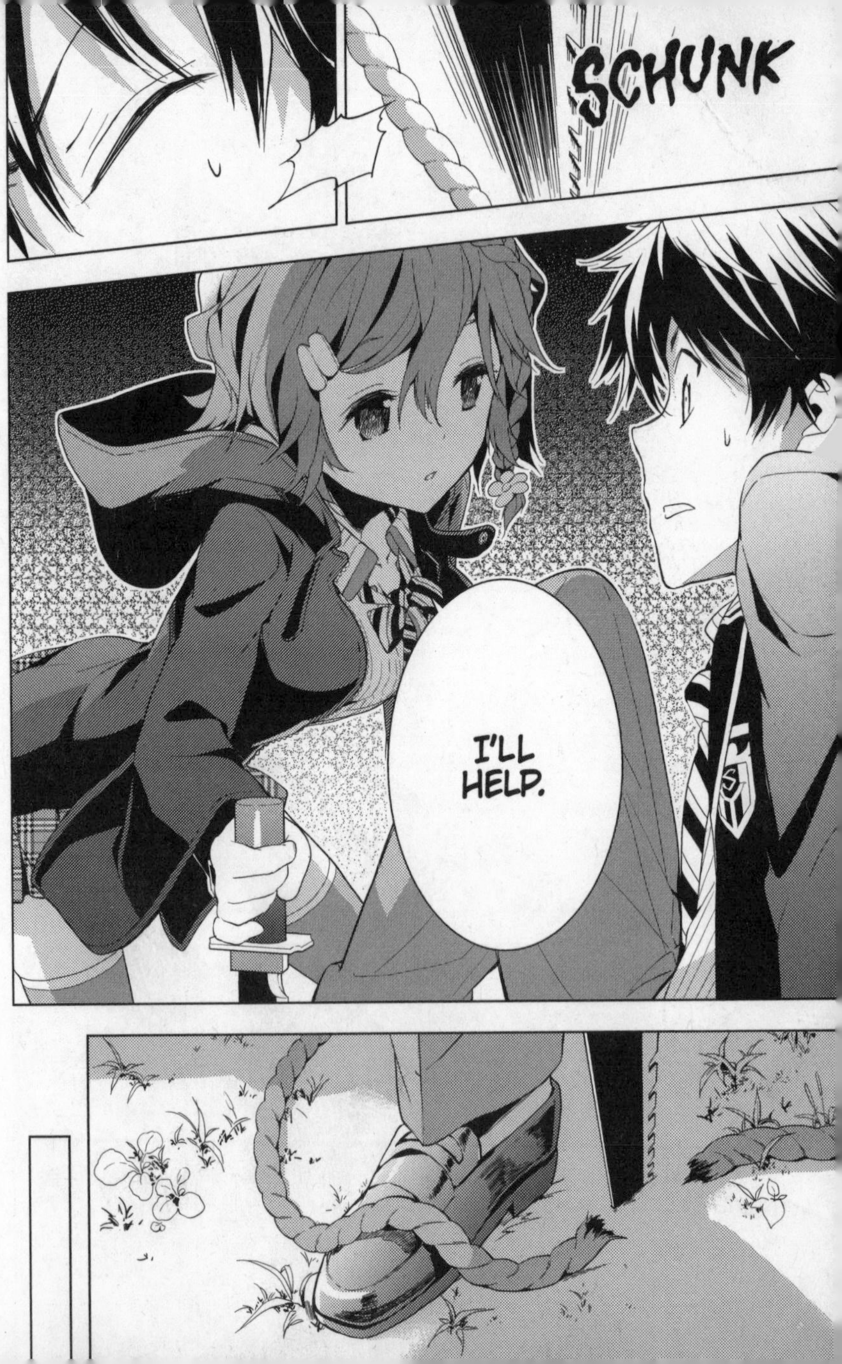
SCHUNK
I'LL HELP.

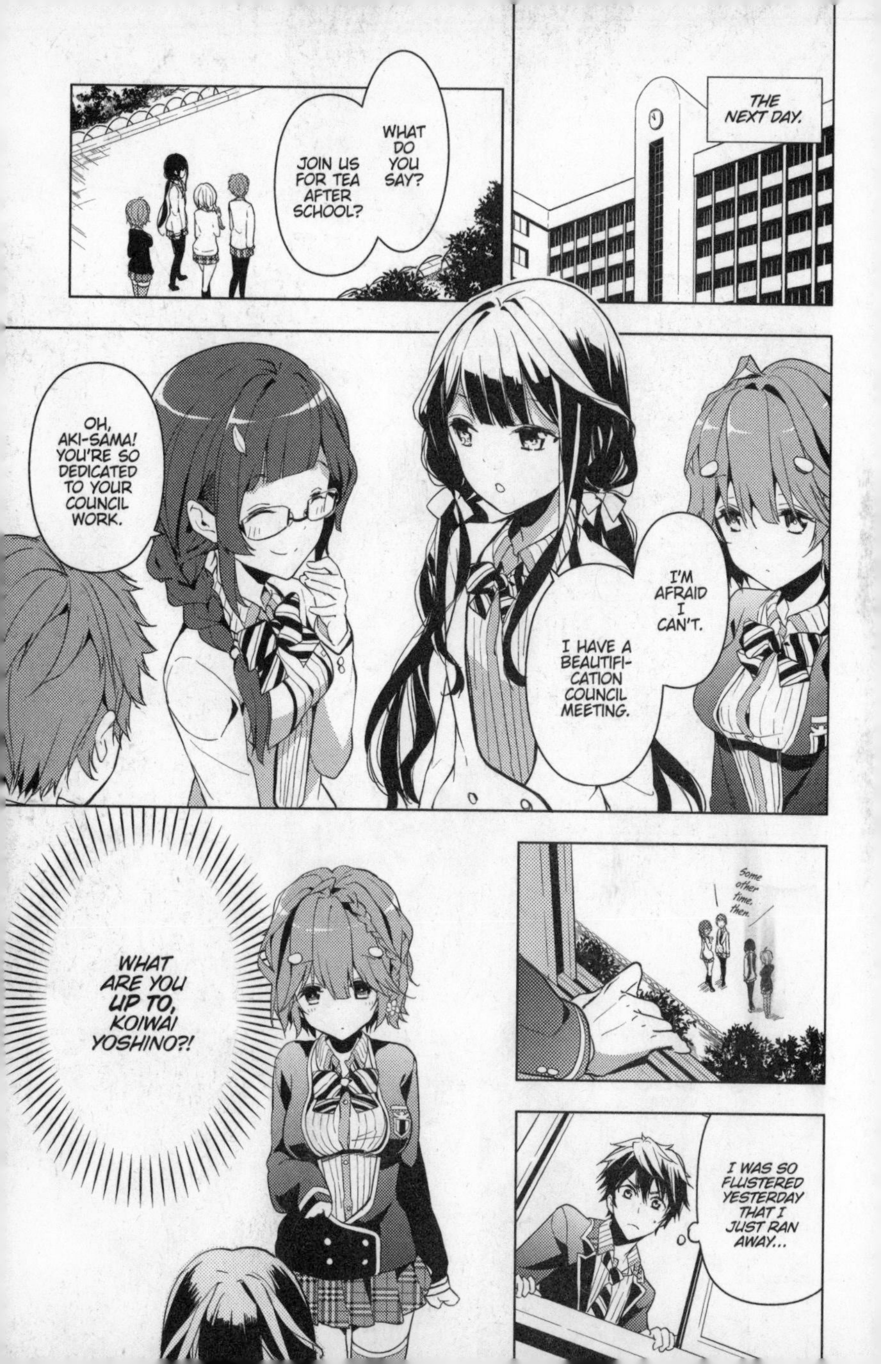
THE NEXT DAY.
WHAT DO YOU SAY?
JOIN US FOR TEA AFTER SCHOOL?
I'M AFRAID I CAN'T.
I HAVE A BEAUTIFICATION COUNCIL MEETING.
OH, AKI-SAMA! YOU'RE SO DEDICATED TO YOUR COUNCIL WORK.
Some other time, then.
I WAS SO FLUSTERED YESTERDAY THAT I JUST RAN AWAY...
WHAT ARE YOU UP TO, KOIWAI YOSHINO?!

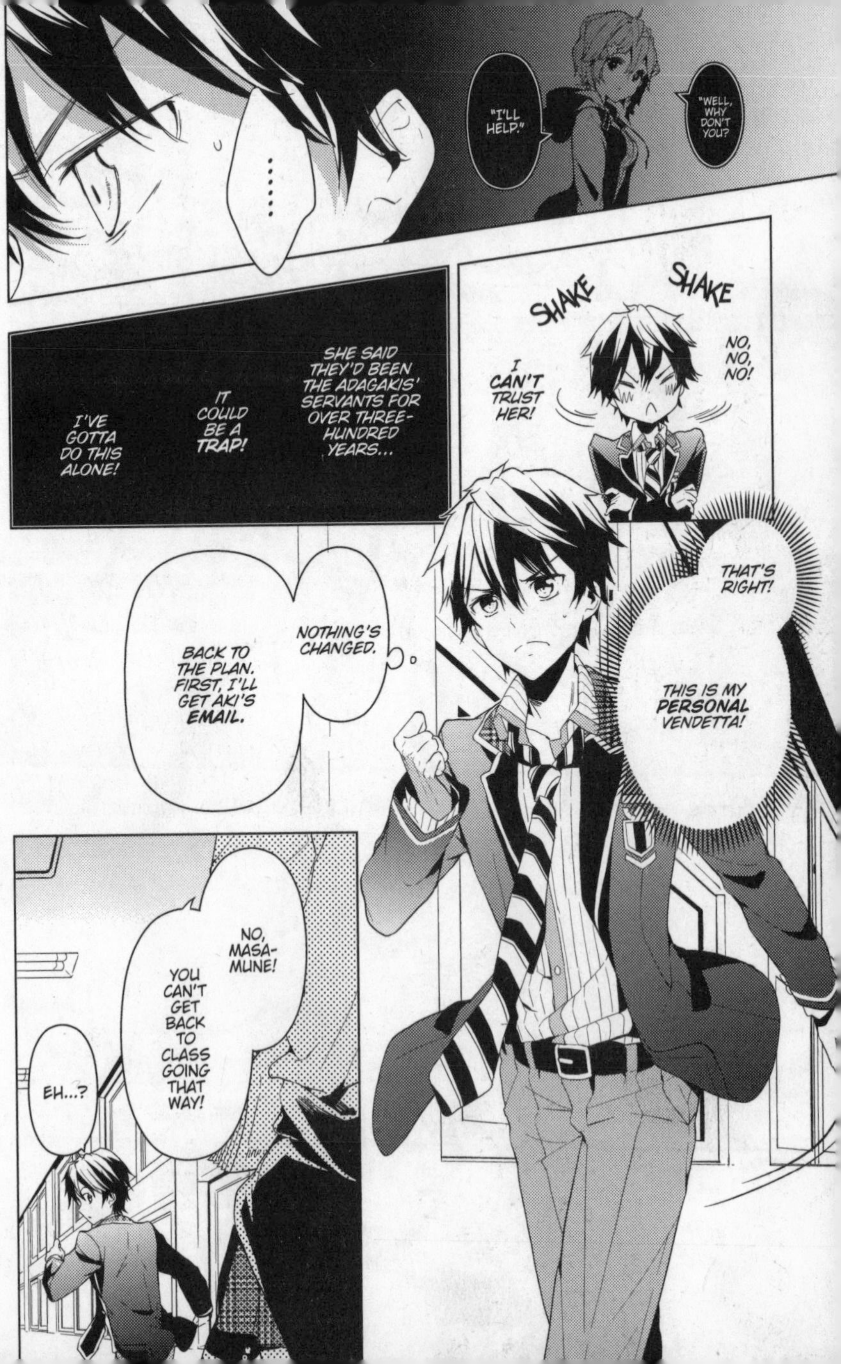
"WELL, WHY DON'T YOU?
"I'LL HELP."
......
SHAKE SHAKE
NO, NO, NO!
I CAN'T TRUST HER!
SHE SAID THEY'D BEEN THE ADAGAKIS' SERVANTS FOR OVER THREE-HUNDRED YEARS...
IT COULD BE A TRAP!
I'VE GOTTA DO THIS ALONE!
THAT'S RIGHT!
THIS IS MY PERSONAL VENDETTA!
NOTHING'S CHANGED.
BACK TO THE PLAN. FIRST, I'LL GET AKI'S EMAIL.
NO, MASA-MUNE!
YOU CAN'T GET BACK TO CLASS GOING THAT WAY!
EH...?

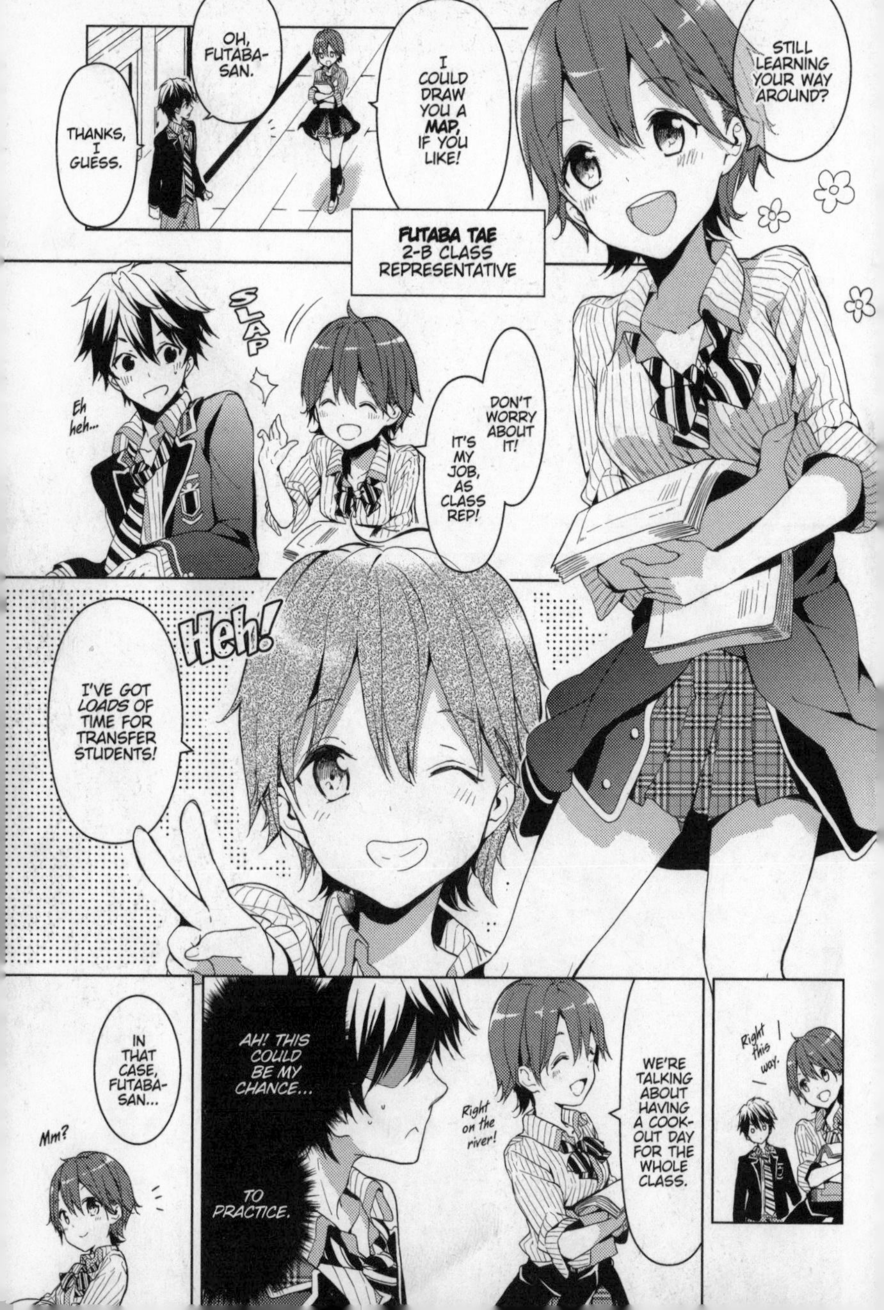
STILL LEARNING YOUR WAY AROUND?
I COULD DRAW YOU A MAP, IF YOU LIKE!
FUTABA TAE
2-B CLASS REPRESENTATIVE
OH, FUTABA-SAN.
THANKS, I GUESS.
DON'T WORRY ABOUT IT!
IT'S MY JOB, AS CLASS REP!
SLAP
Eh heh...
Heh!
I'VE GOT LOADS OF TIME FOR TRANSFER STUDENTS!
Right this way.
WE'RE TALKING ABOUT HAVING A COOK-OUT DAY FOR THE WHOLE CLASS.
Right on the river!
AH! THIS COULD BE MY CHANCE...
TO PRACTICE.
IN THAT CASE, FUTABA-SAN...
Mm?

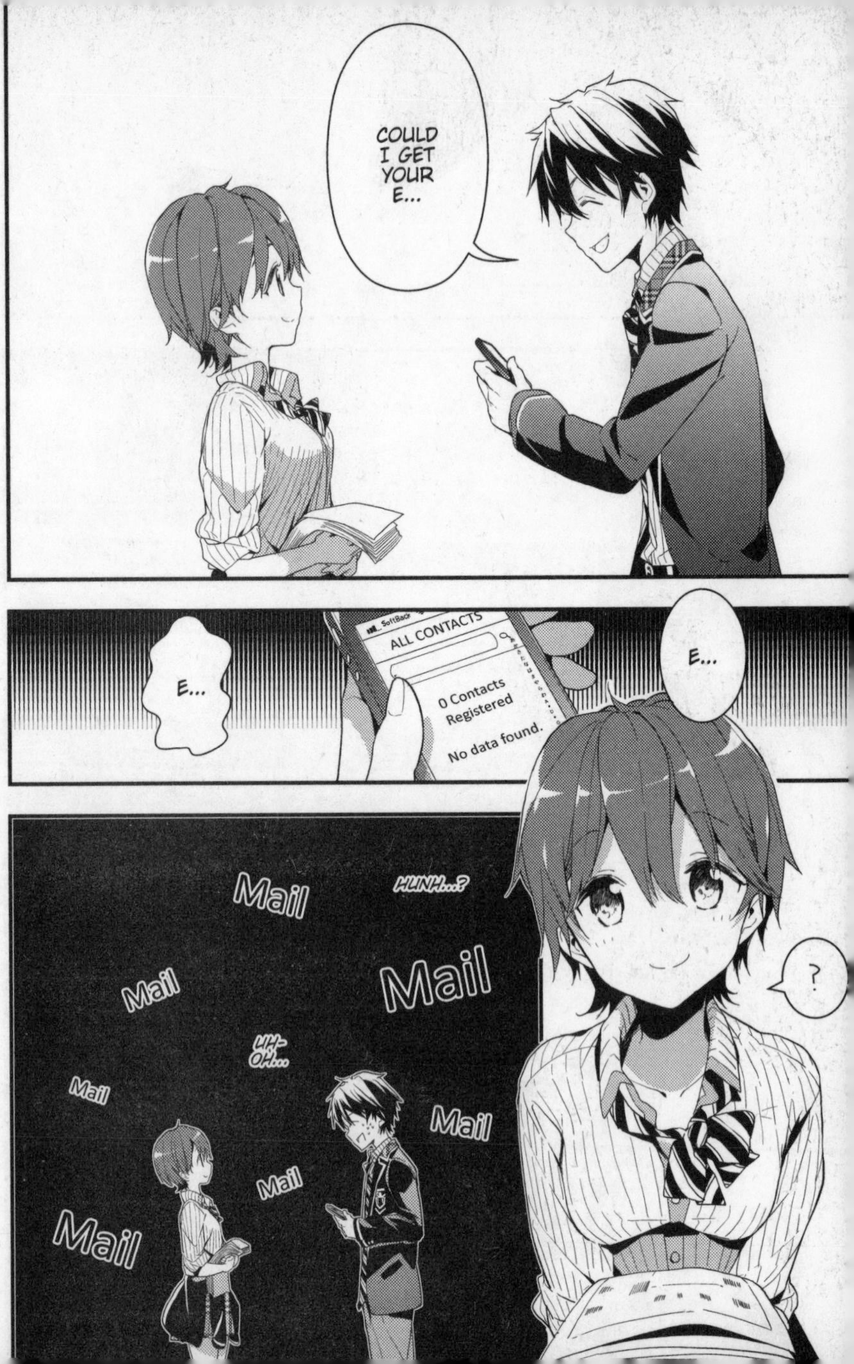
COULD I GET YOUR E...
E...
?
E...
SoftBank
ALL CONTACTS
0 Contacts Registered
No data found.
HUNH...?
Mail
Mail
Mail
UH-OH...
Mail
Mail
Mail
Mail

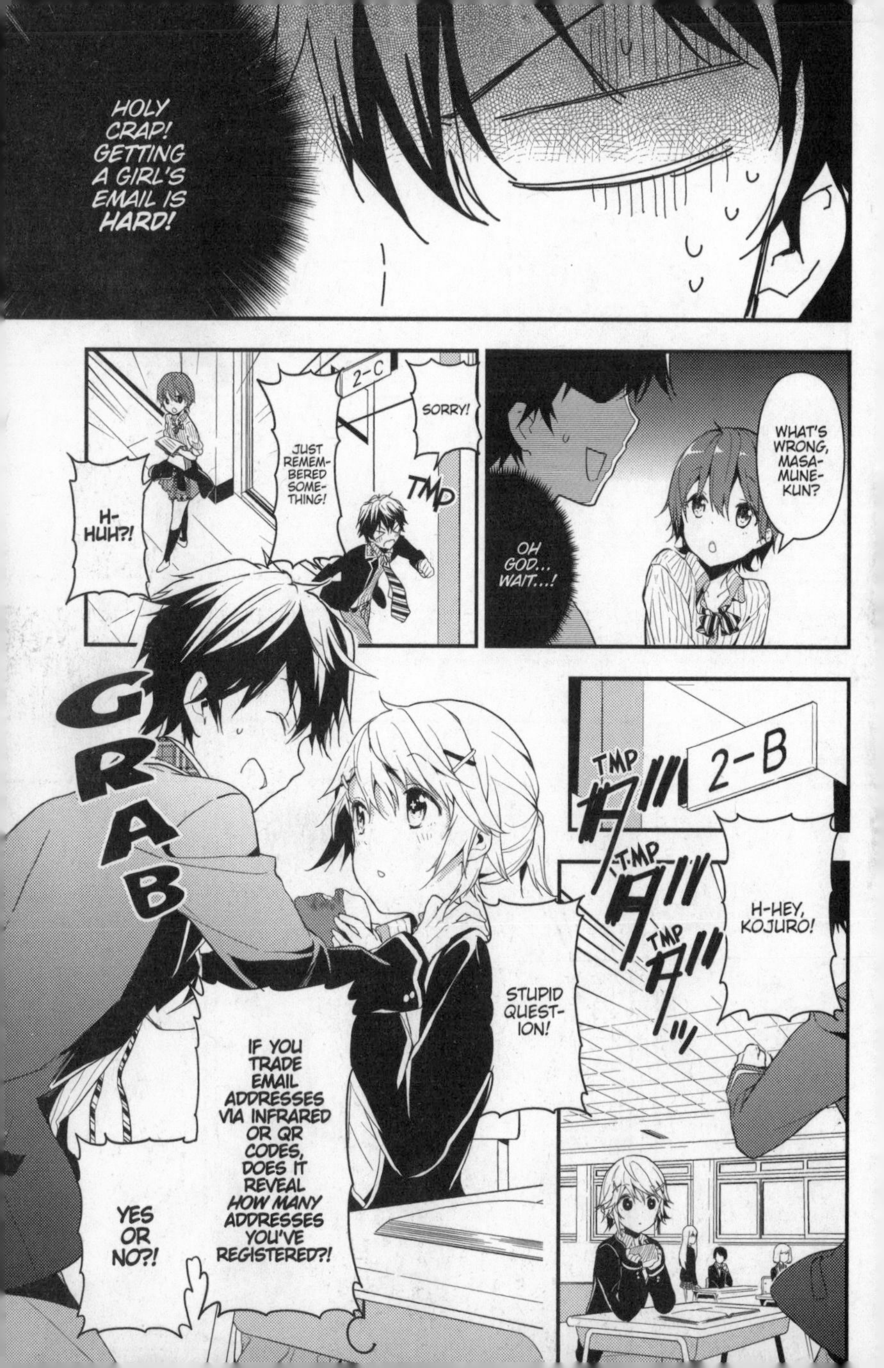
HOLY CRAP! GETTING A GIRL'S EMAIL IS HARD!
WHAT'S WRONG, MASAMUNE-KUN?
OH GOD... WAIT...!
2-C
SORRY!
JUST REMEMBERED SOMETHING!
TMP
H-HUH?!
2-B
TMP
TMP
TMP
H-HEY, KOJURO!
STUPID QUESTION!
GRAB
IF YOU TRADE EMAIL ADDRESSES VIA INFRARED OR QR CODES, DOES IT REVEAL *HOW MANY* ADDRESSES YOU'VE REGISTERED?!
YES OR NO?!

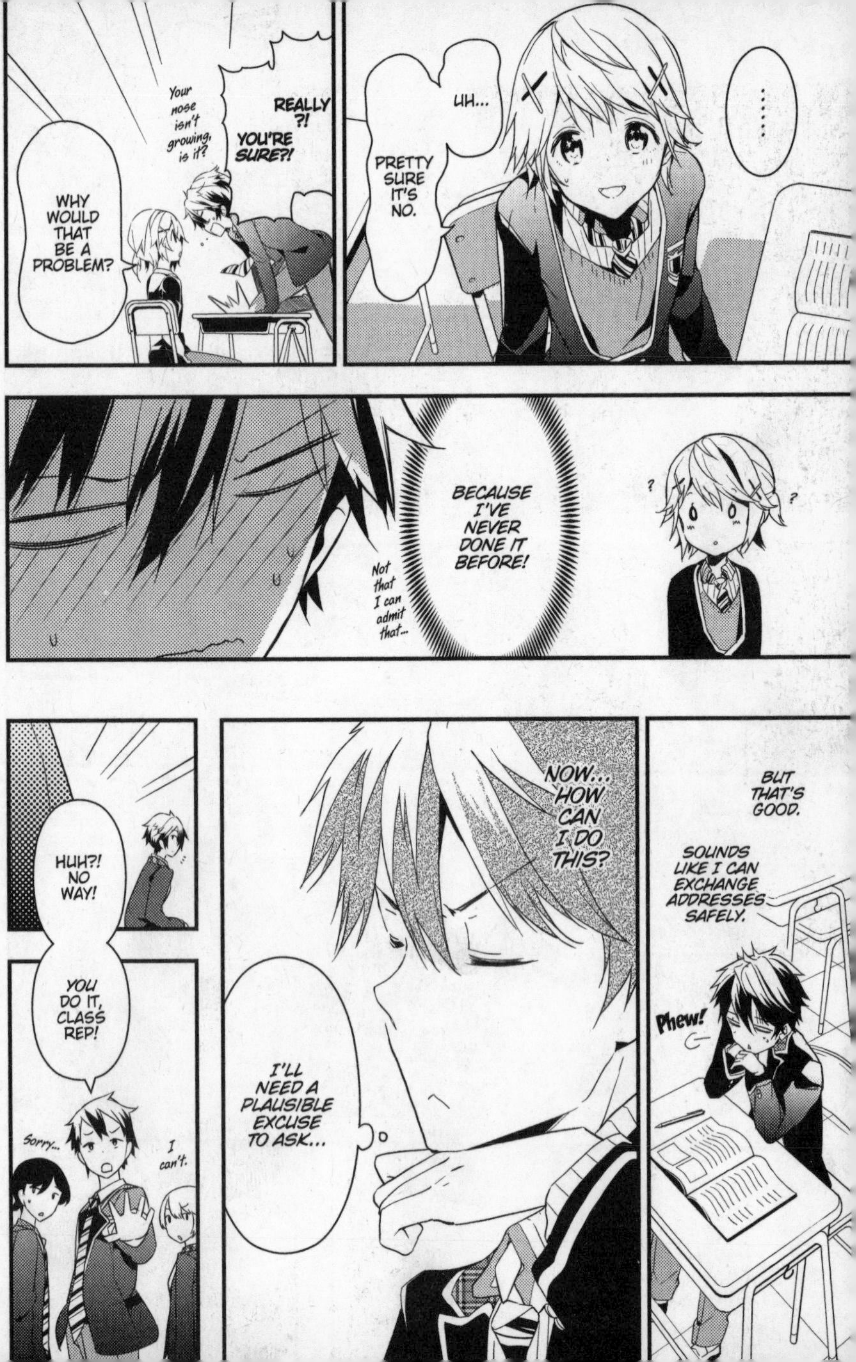
......
UH...
PRETTY SURE IT'S NO.
REALLY?! YOU'RE SURE?!
Your nose isn't growing, is it?
WHY WOULD THAT BE A PROBLEM?
?
?
BECAUSE I'VE NEVER DONE IT BEFORE!
Not that I can admit that...
BUT THAT'S GOOD.
SOUNDS LIKE I CAN EXCHANGE ADDRESSES SAFELY.
Phew!
NOW... HOW CAN I DO THIS?
I'LL NEED A PLAUSIBLE EXCUSE TO ASK...
HUH?! NO WAY!
YOU DO IT, CLASS REP!
I can't.
Sorry...

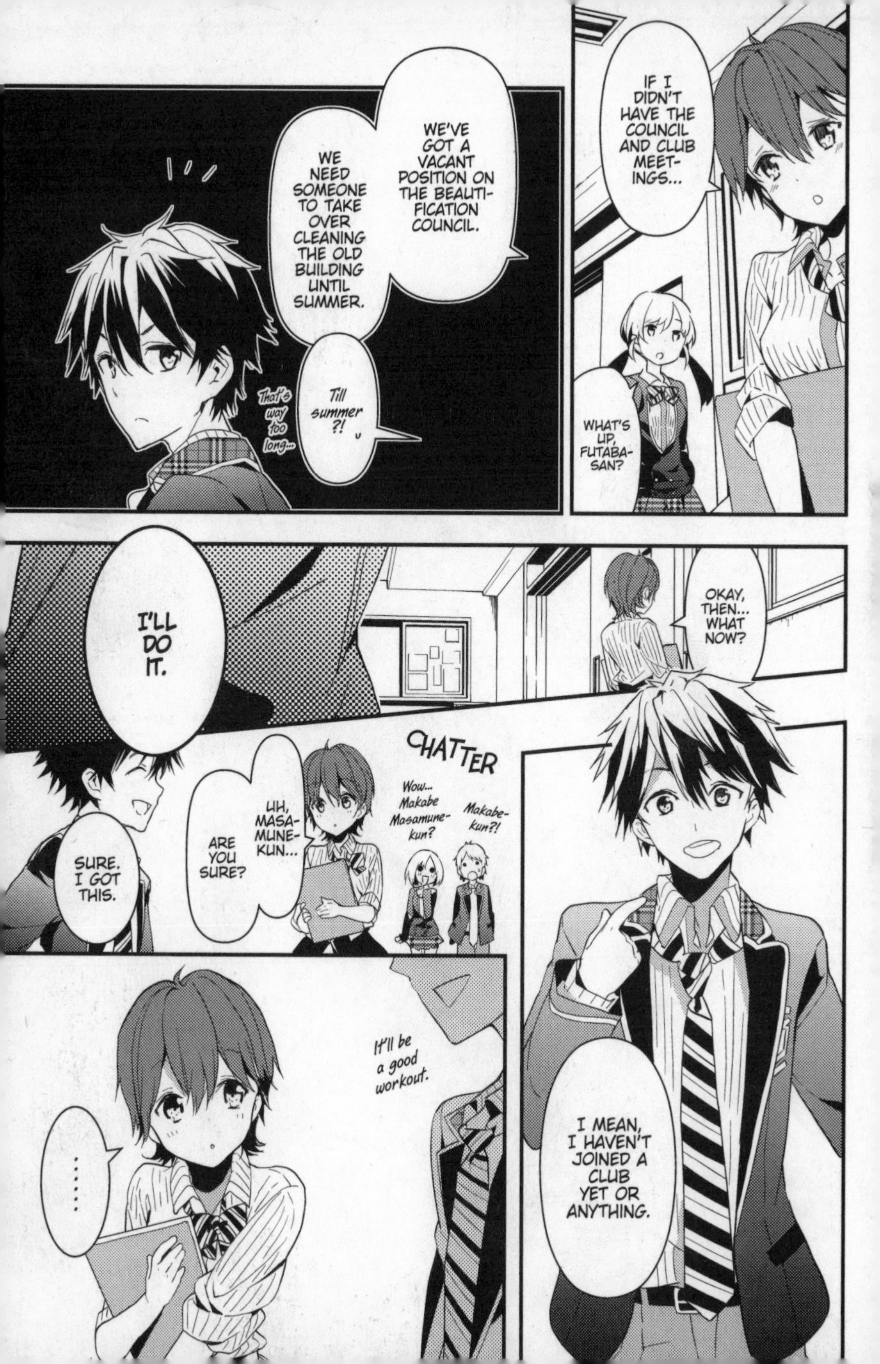
IF I DIDN'T HAVE THE COUNCIL AND CLUB MEET-INGS...
WHAT'S UP, FUTABA-SAN?
WE'VE GOT A VACANT POSITION ON THE BEAUTI-FICATION COUNCIL.
WE NEED SOMEONE TO TAKE OVER CLEANING THE OLD BUILDING UNTIL SUMMER.
Till summer?!
That's way too long...
OKAY, THEN... WHAT NOW?
I'LL DO IT.
I MEAN, I HAVEN'T JOINED A CLUB YET OR ANYTHING.
CHATTER
Makabe-kun?!
Wow... Makabe Masamune-kun?
UH, MASA-MUNE-KUN...
ARE YOU SURE?
SURE. I GOT THIS.
It'll be a good workout.
......

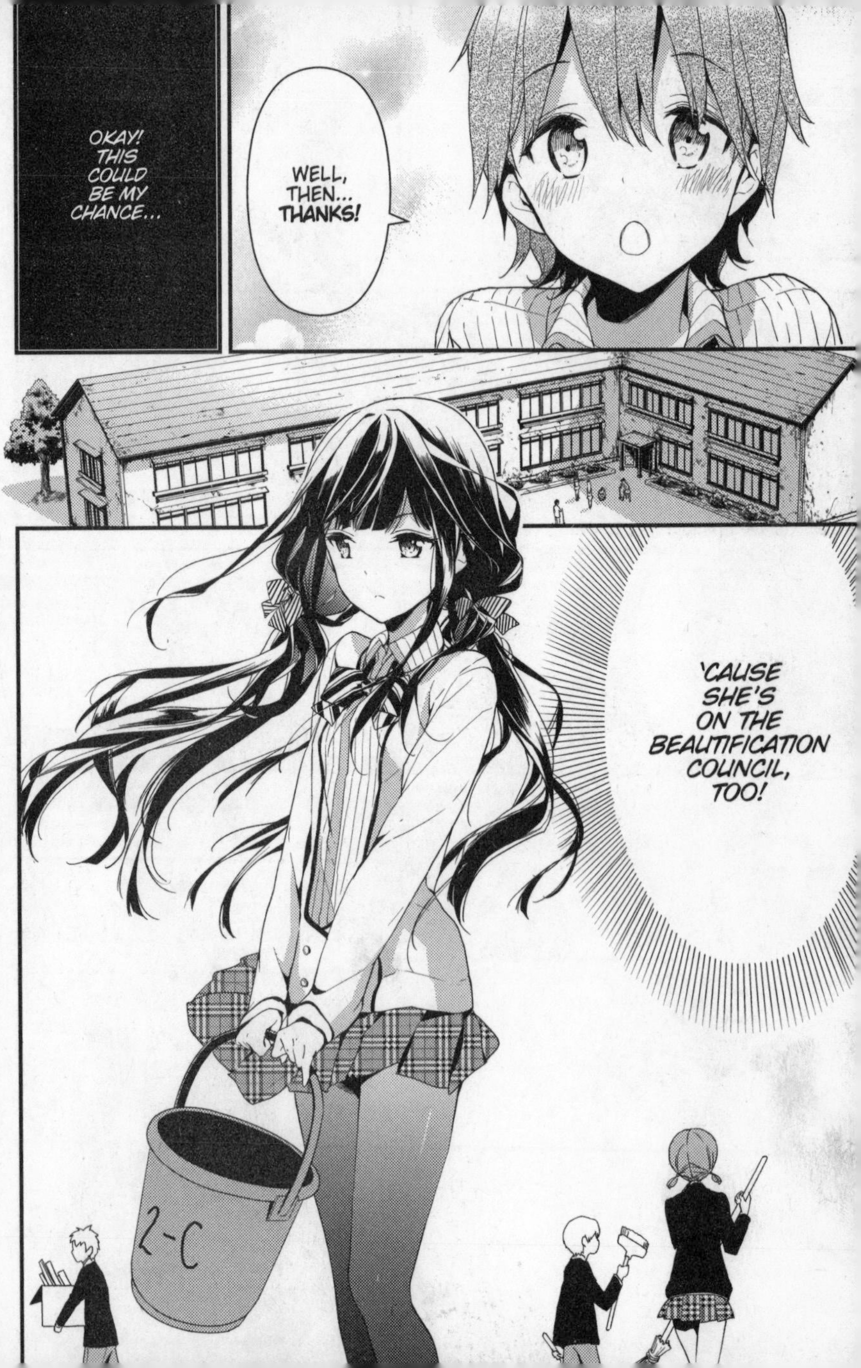
WELL, THEN... THANKS!
OKAY! THIS COULD BE MY CHANCE...
'CAUSE SHE'S ON THE BEAUTIFICATION COUNCIL, TOO!
2-C

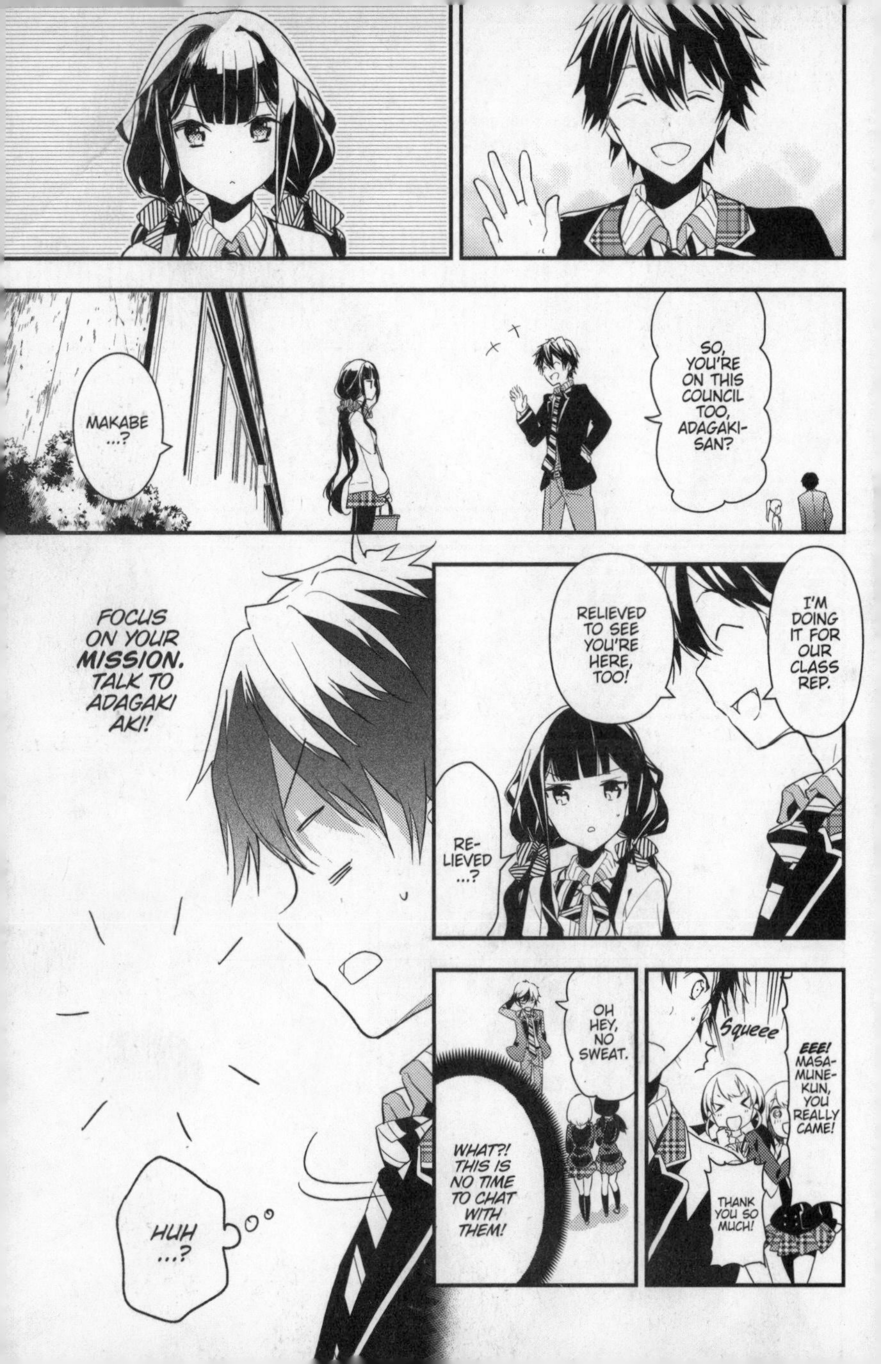
SO, YOU'RE ON THIS COUNCIL TOO, ADAGAKI-SAN?
MAKABE ...?
I'M DOING IT FOR OUR CLASS REP.
RELIEVED TO SEE YOU'RE HERE, TOO!
RE-LIEVED ...?
FOCUS ON YOUR MISSION. TALK TO ADAGAKI AKI!
Squeee
EEE! MASA-MUNE-KUN, YOU REALLY CAME!
THANK YOU SO MUCH!
OH HEY, NO SWEAT.
WHAT?! THIS IS NO TIME TO CHAT WITH THEM!
HUH ...?

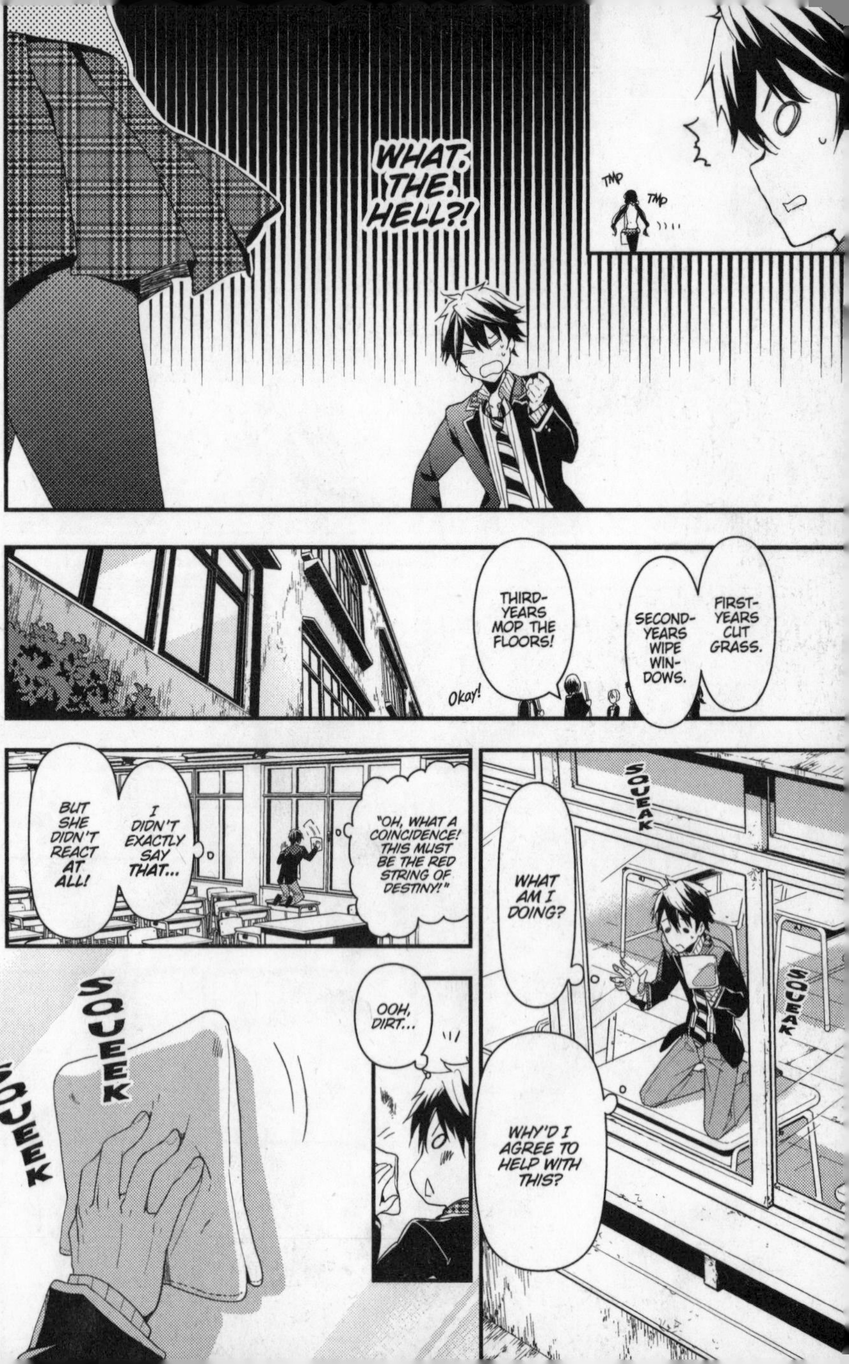
TMP
TMP
WHAT. THE. HELL?!
FIRST-YEARS CUT GRASS.
SECOND-YEARS WIPE WIN-DOWS.
THIRD-YEARS MOP THE FLOORS!
Okay!
SQUEAK
WHAT AM I DOING?
SQUEAK
WHY'D I AGREE TO HELP WITH THIS?
"OH, WHAT A COINCIDENCE! THIS MUST BE THE RED STRING OF DESTINY!"
I DIDN'T EXACTLY SAY THAT...
BUT SHE DIDN'T REACT AT ALL!
OOH, DIRT...
SQUEEK
SQUEEK

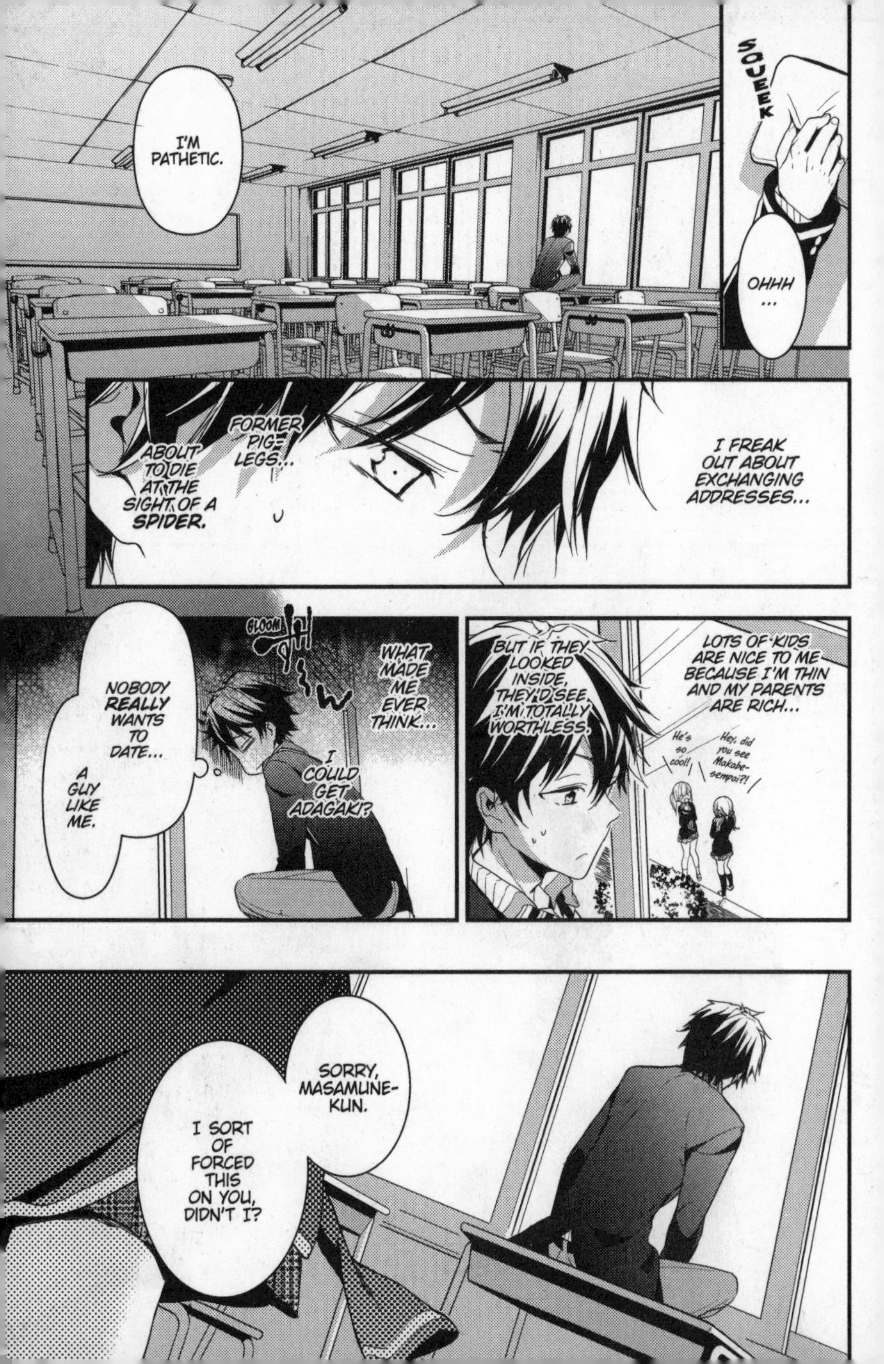
SQUEEK
OHHH...
I'M PATHETIC.
I FREAK OUT ABOUT EXCHANGING ADDRESSES...
FORMER PIG-LEGS...
ABOUT TO DIE AT THE SIGHT OF A SPIDER.
LOTS OF KIDS ARE NICE TO ME BECAUSE I'M THIN AND MY PARENTS ARE RICH...
Hey, did you see Makabe-sempai?!
He's so cool!
BUT IF THEY LOOKED INSIDE, THEY'D SEE I'M TOTALLY WORTHLESS.
WHAT MADE ME EVER THINK...
I COULD GET ADAGAKI?
GLOOM
NOBODY REALLY WANTS TO DATE...
A GUY LIKE ME.
SORRY, MASAMUNE-KUN.
I SORT OF FORCED THIS ON YOU, DIDN'T I?

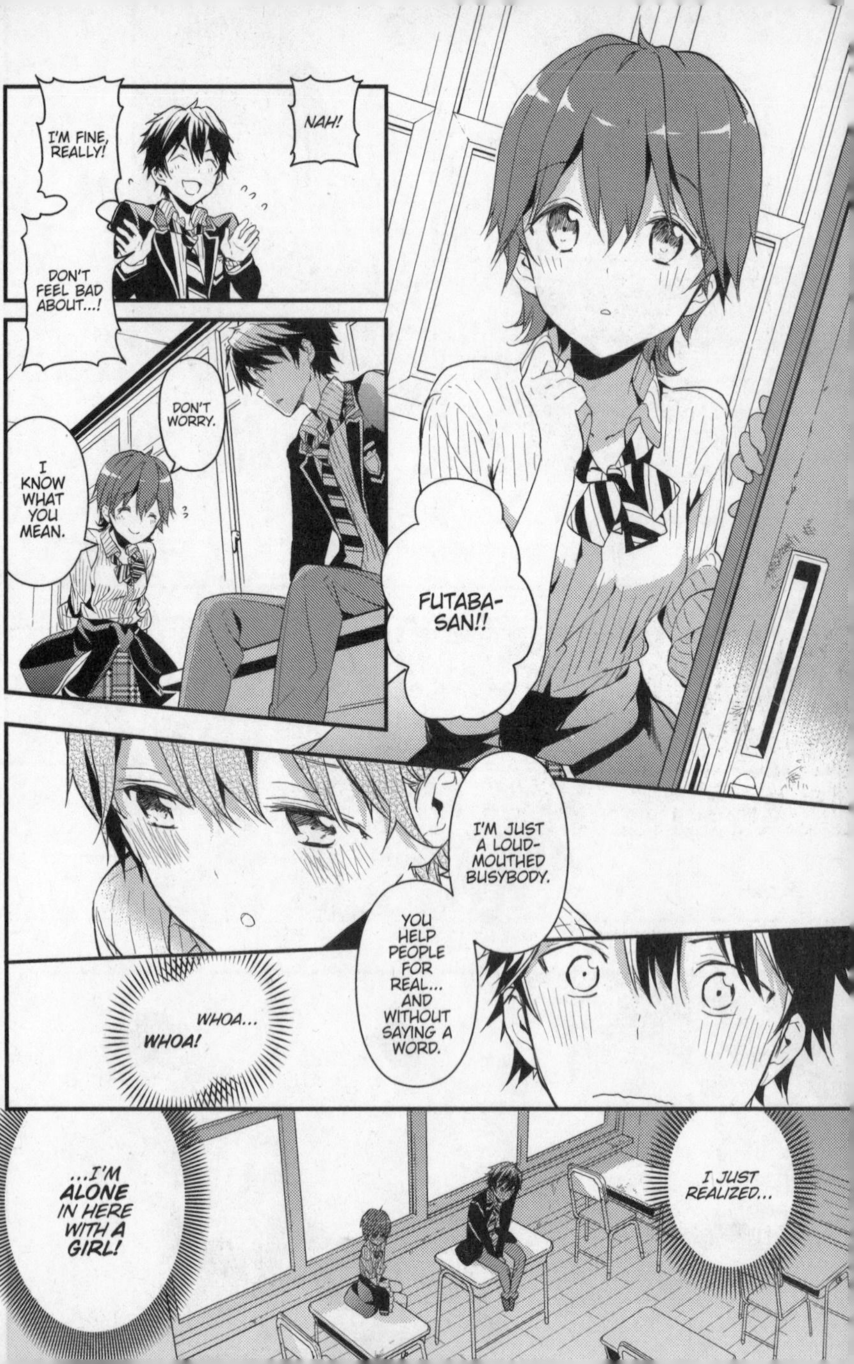
FUTABA-SAN!!
NAH!
I'M FINE, REALLY!
DON'T FEEL BAD ABOUT...!
DON'T WORRY.
I KNOW WHAT YOU MEAN.
I'M JUST A LOUD-MOUTHED BUSYBODY.
YOU HELP PEOPLE FOR REAL... AND WITHOUT SAYING A WORD.
WHOA... WHOA!
I JUST REALIZED...
...I'M ALONE IN HERE WITH A GIRL!

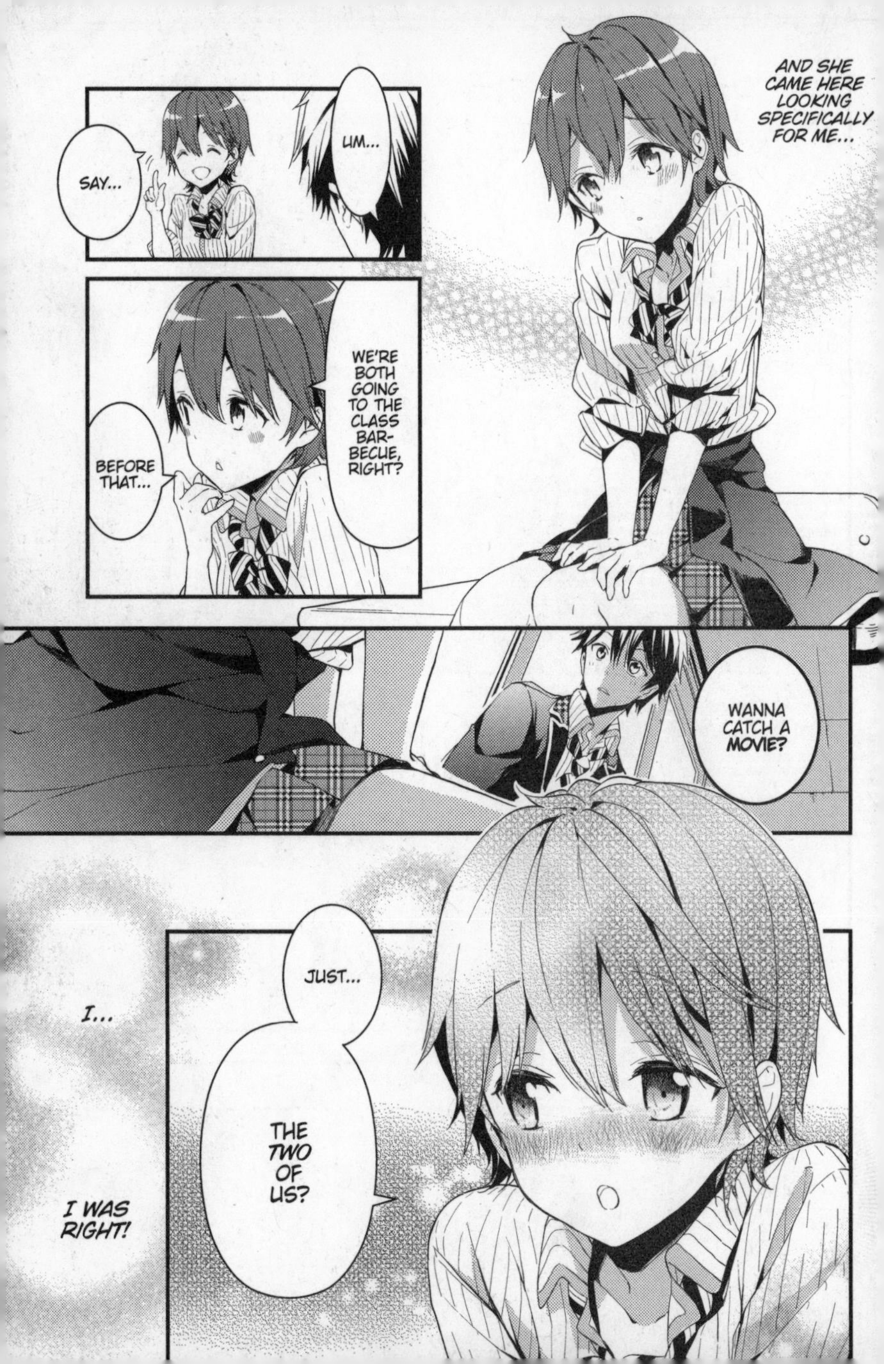
AND SHE CAME HERE LOOKING SPECIFICALLY FOR ME...
UM...
SAY...
WE'RE BOTH GOING TO THE CLASS BAR-BECUE, RIGHT?
BEFORE THAT...
WANNA CATCH A MOVIE?
JUST...
THE TWO OF US?
I...
I WAS RIGHT!

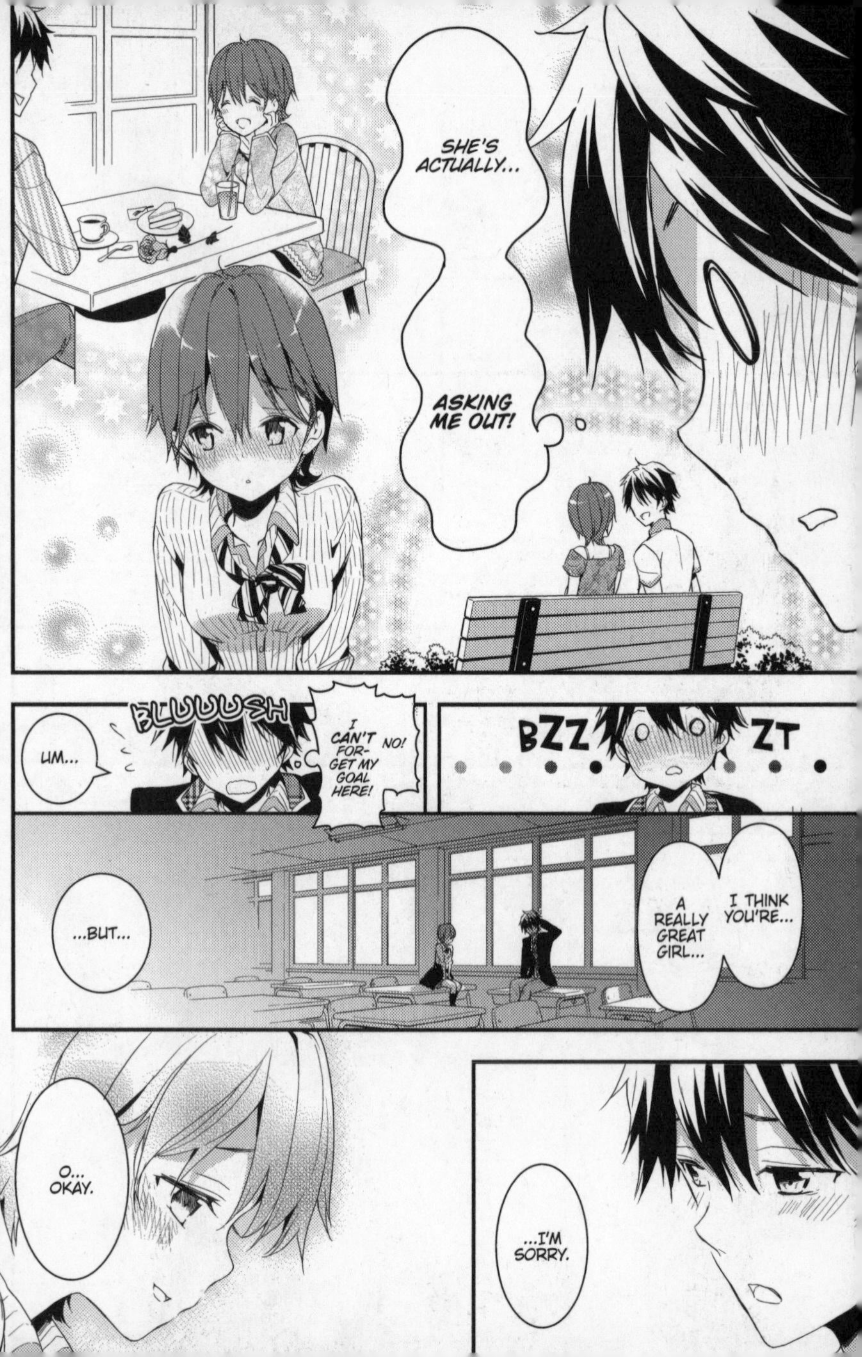
SHE'S ACTUALLY...
ASKING ME OUT!
BZZ
ZT
NO!
I CAN'T FOR-GET MY GOAL HERE!
BLUUUSH
UM...
I THINK YOU'RE...
A REALLY GREAT GIRL...
...BUT...
...I'M SORRY.
O... OKAY.

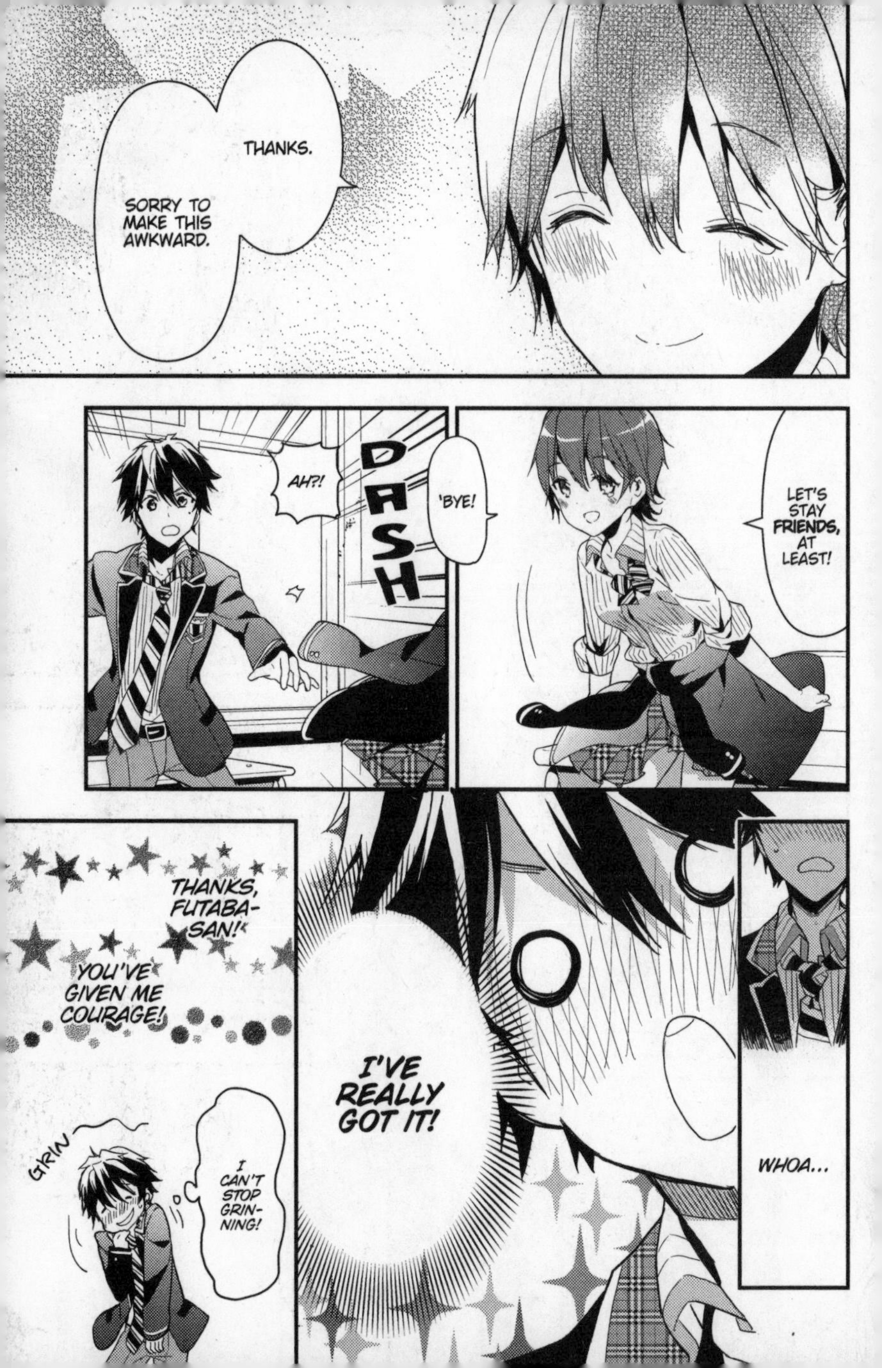
THANKS.
SORRY TO MAKE THIS AWKWARD.
LET'S STAY FRIENDS, AT LEAST!
'BYE!
DASH
AH?!
WHOA...
I'VE REALLY GOT IT!
THANKS, FUTABA-SAN!
YOU'VE GIVEN ME COURAGE!
I CAN'T STOP GRIN-NING!
GRIN

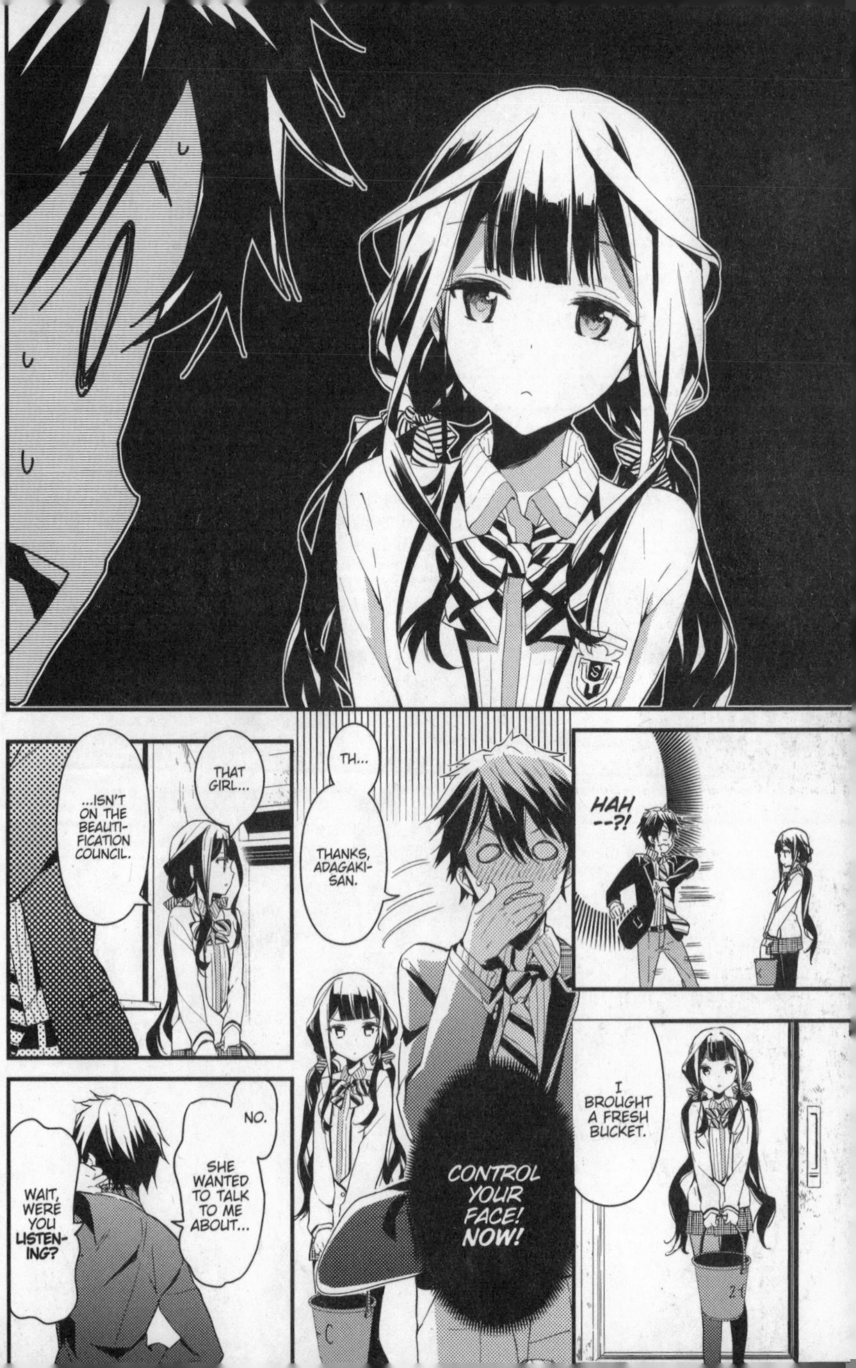
HAH --?!
I BROUGHT A FRESH BUCKET.
TH...
THANKS, ADAGAKI-SAN.
CONTROL YOUR FACE! NOW!
THAT GIRL...
...ISN'T ON THE BEAUTIFICATION COUNCIL.
NO.
SHE WANTED TO TALK TO ME ABOUT...
WAIT, WERE YOU LISTENING?

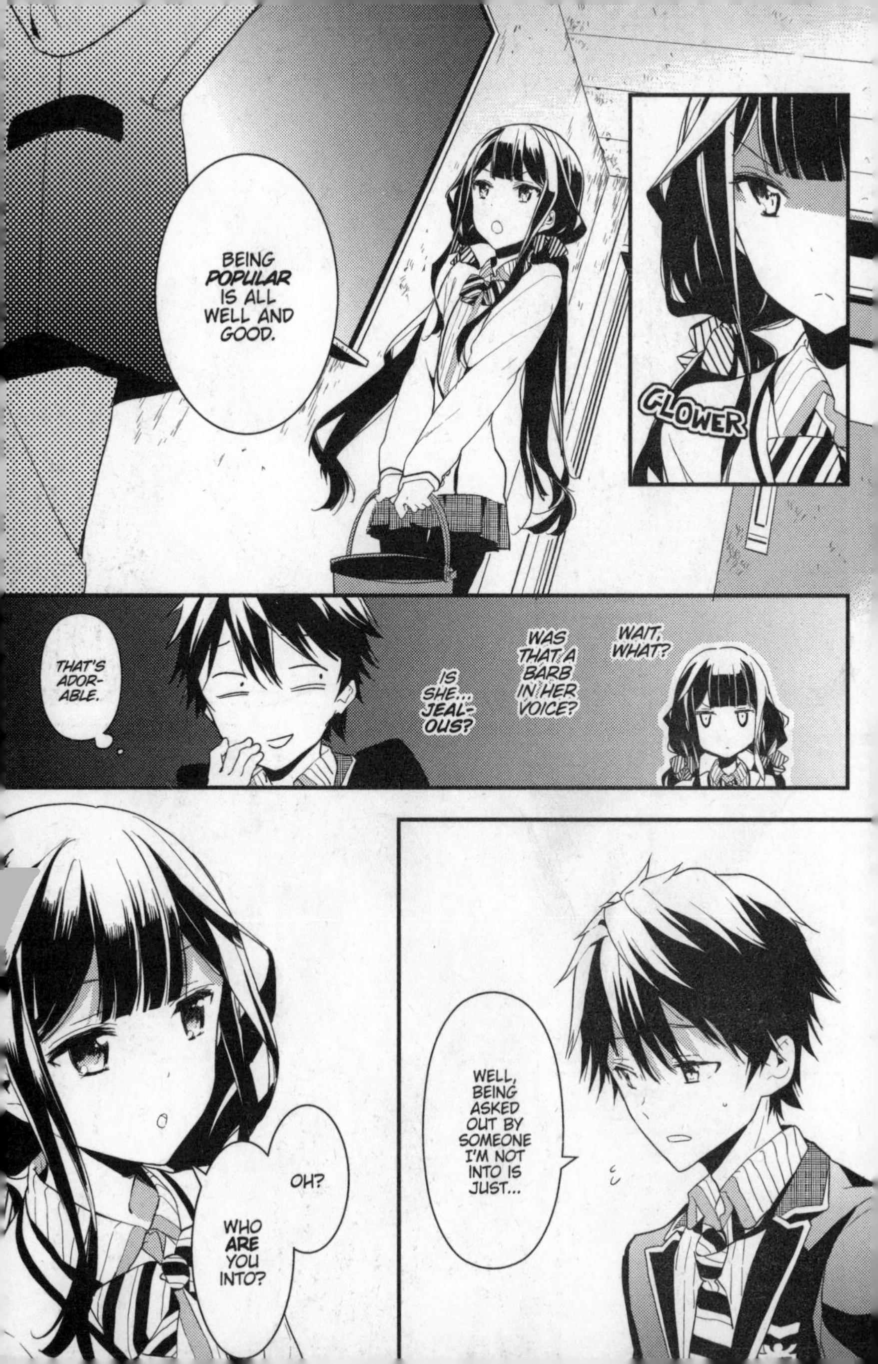
BEING POPULAR IS ALL WELL AND GOOD.
GLOWER
WAIT, WHAT?
WAS THAT A BARB IN HER VOICE?
IS SHE... JEAL-OUS?
THAT'S ADOR-ABLE.
WELL, BEING ASKED OUT BY SOMEONE I'M NOT INTO IS JUST...
OH?
WHO ARE YOU INTO?

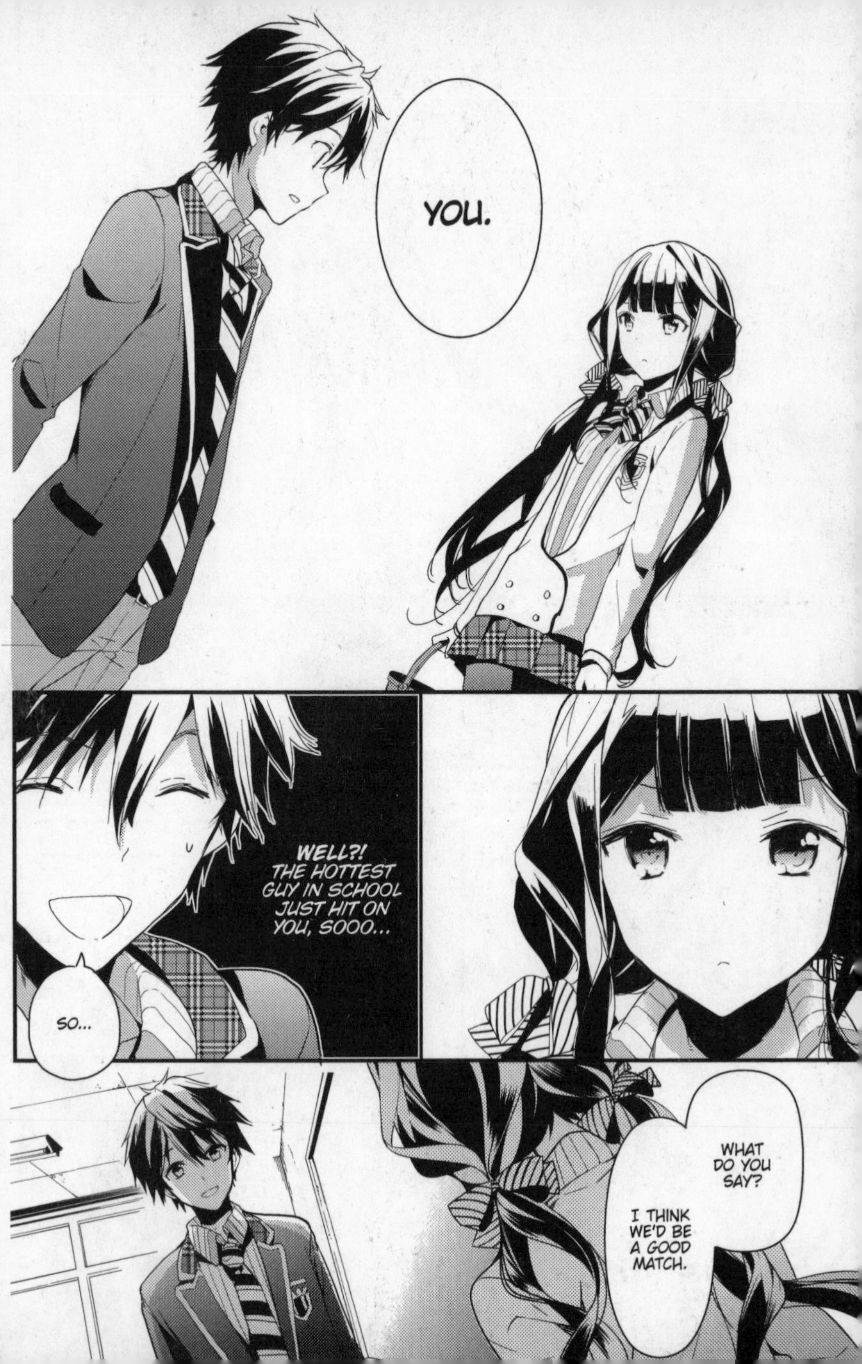
YOU.
WELL?! THE HOTTEST GUY IN SCHOOL JUST HIT ON YOU, SOOO...
SO...
WHAT DO YOU SAY?
I THINK WE'D BE A GOOD MATCH.

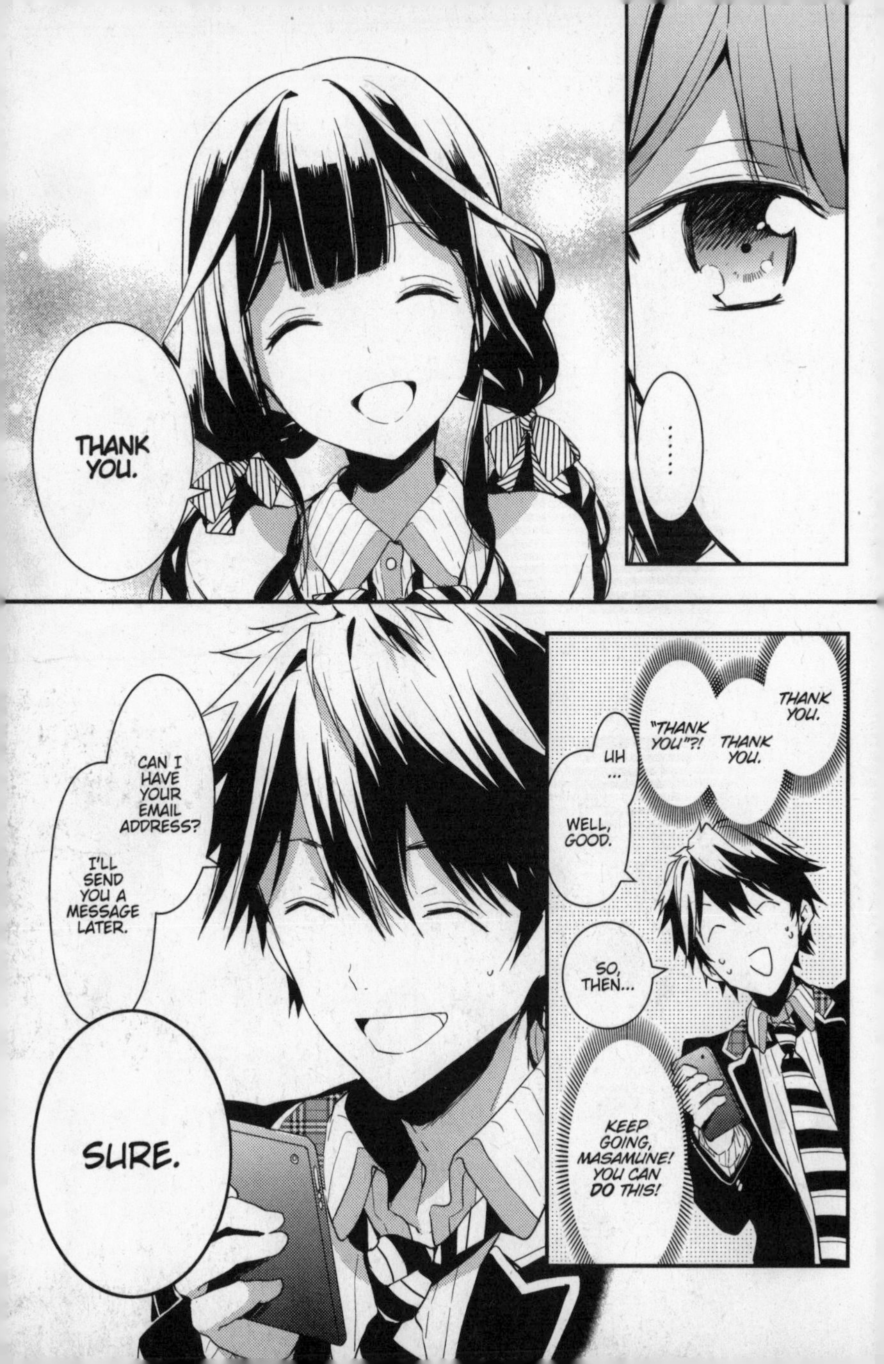
……
THANK YOU.
THANK YOU.
THANK YOU.
"THANK YOU"?!
UH ...
WELL, GOOD.
SO, THEN...
KEEP GOING, MASAMUNE! YOU CAN DO THIS!
CAN I HAVE YOUR EMAIL ADDRESS?
I'LL SEND YOU A MESSAGE LATER.
SURE.

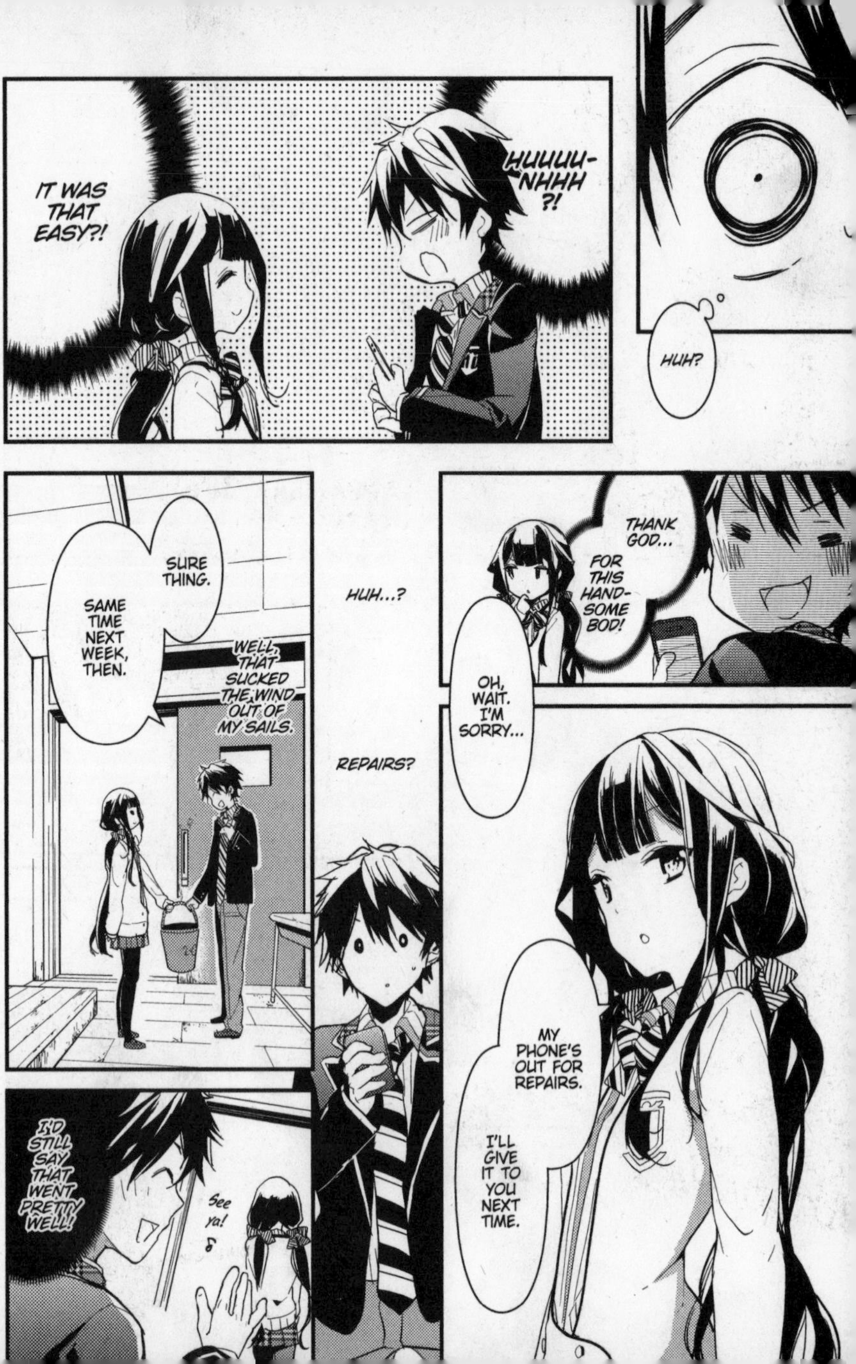
HUH?
HUUUU-NHHH ?!
IT WAS THAT EASY?!
THANK GOD... FOR THIS HAND-SOME BOD!
OH, WAIT. I'M SORRY...
MY PHONE'S OUT FOR REPAIRS.
I'LL GIVE IT TO YOU NEXT TIME.
HUH...?
REPAIRS?
SURE THING.
SAME TIME NEXT WEEK, THEN.
WELL, THAT SUCKED THE WIND OUT OF MY SAILS.
See ya! ♪
I'D STILL SAY THAT WENT PRETTY WELL!

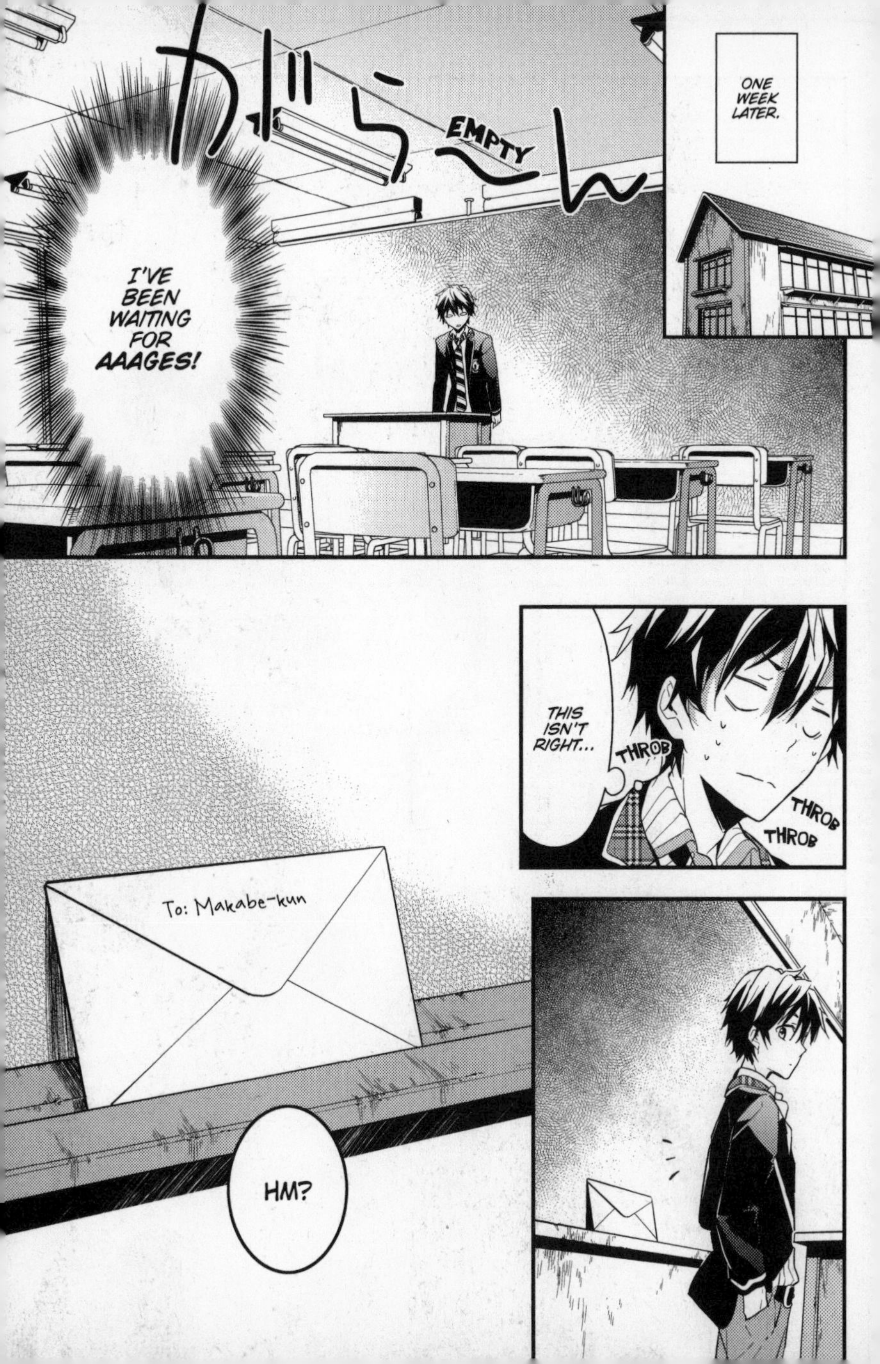
ONE WEEK LATER.
がら〜ん
EMPTY
I'VE BEEN WAITING FOR AAAGES!
THIS ISN'T RIGHT...
THROB
THROB
THROB
To: Makabe-kun
HM?

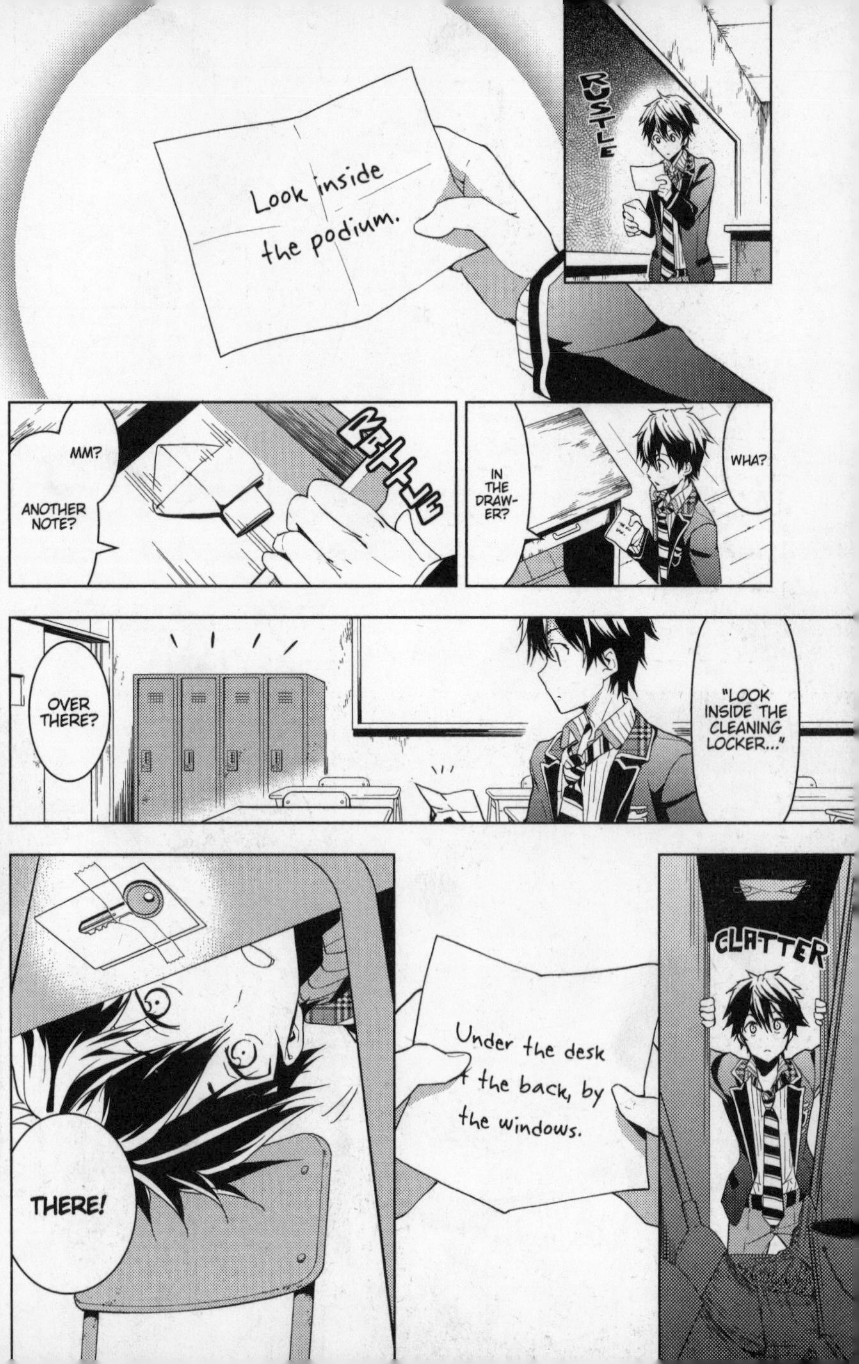
RUSTLE
Look inside the podium.
WHA?
IN THE DRAWER?
MM?
ANOTHER NOTE?
"LOOK INSIDE THE CLEANING LOCKER..."
OVER THERE?
CLATTER
Under the desk
t the back, by
the windows.
THERE!

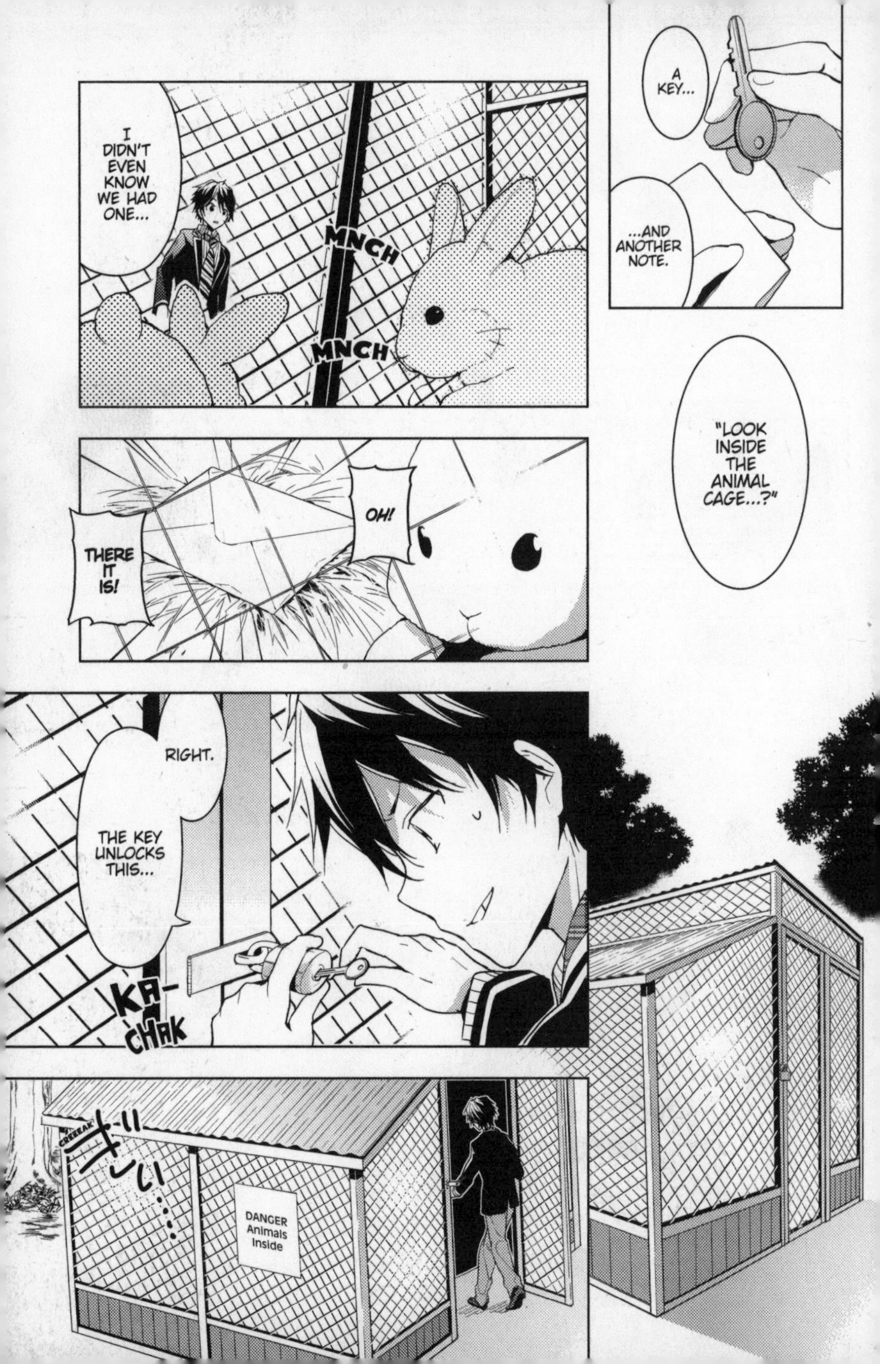
A KEY...
...AND ANOTHER NOTE.
"LOOK INSIDE THE ANIMAL CAGE...?"
I DIDN'T EVEN KNOW WE HAD ONE...
MNCH
MNCH
OH!
THERE IT IS!
RIGHT.
THE KEY UNLOCKS THIS...
KA-CHAK
CREEEAK
DANGER Animals Inside

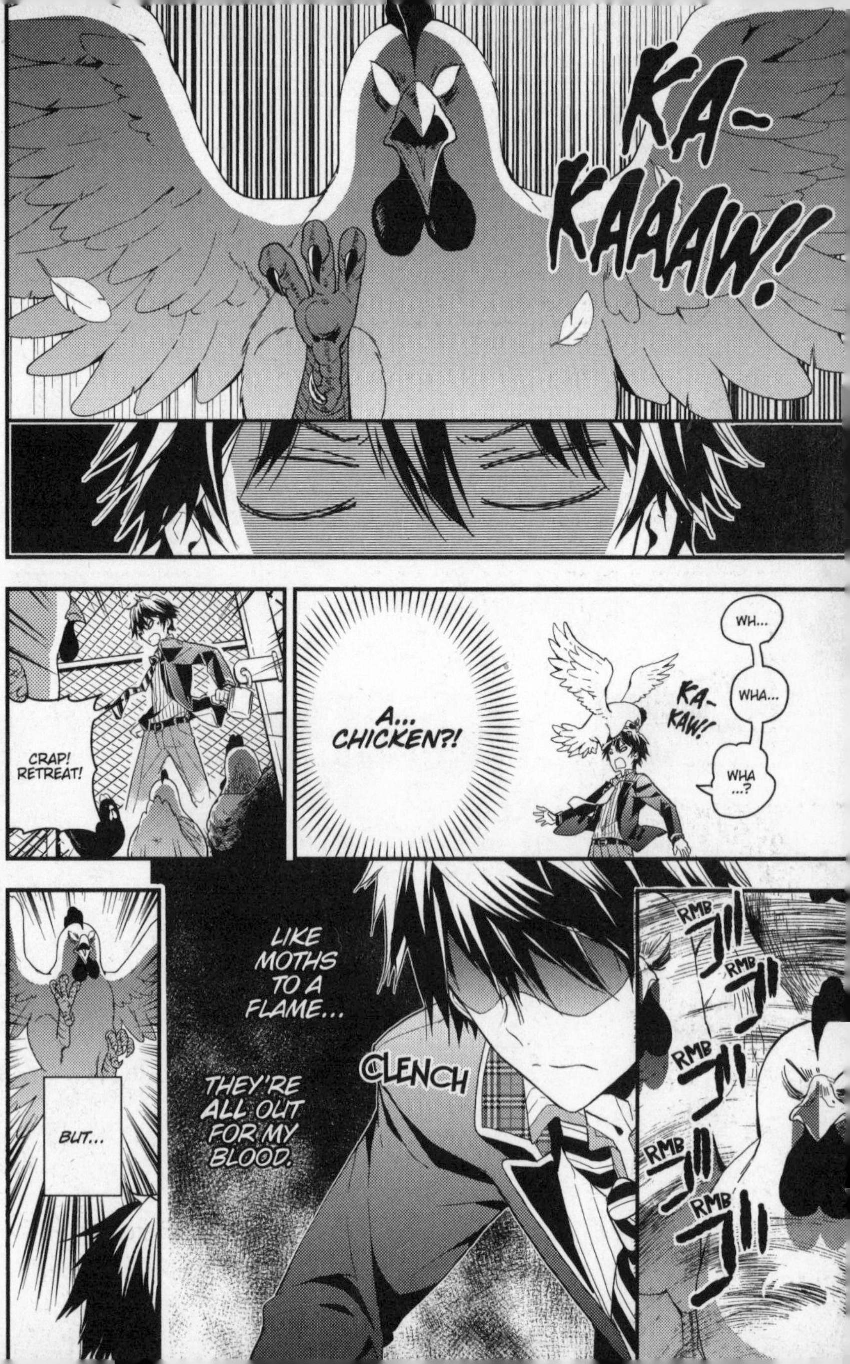
KA-KAAAW!
WH...
WHA...
WHA...?
KA-KAW!
A... CHICKEN?!
CRAP! RETREAT!
RMB RMB RMB RMB RMB
LIKE MOTHS TO A FLAME...
CLENCH
THEY'RE ALL OUT FOR MY BLOOD.
BUT...

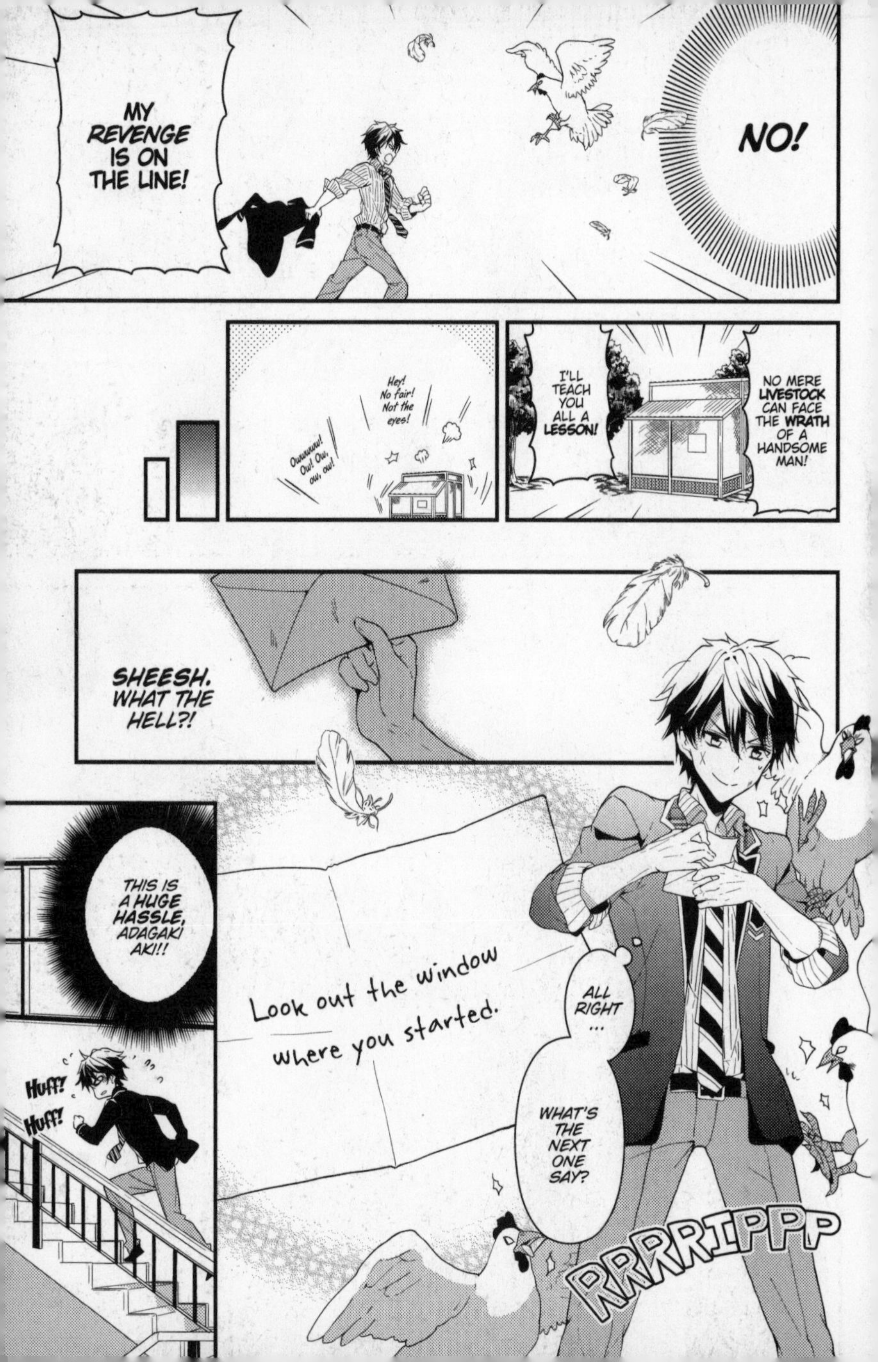
NO!
MY REVENGE IS ON THE LINE!
NO MERE LIVESTOCK CAN FACE THE WRATH OF A HANDSOME MAN!
I'LL TEACH YOU ALL A LESSON!
Hey! No fair! Not the eyes!
Owwwww! Ow! Ow, ow, ow!
SHEESH. WHAT THE HELL?!
ALL RIGHT...
WHAT'S THE NEXT ONE SAY?
RRRRIPPP
Look out the window where you started.
THIS IS A HUGE HASSLE, ADAGAKI AKI!!
Huff! Huff!

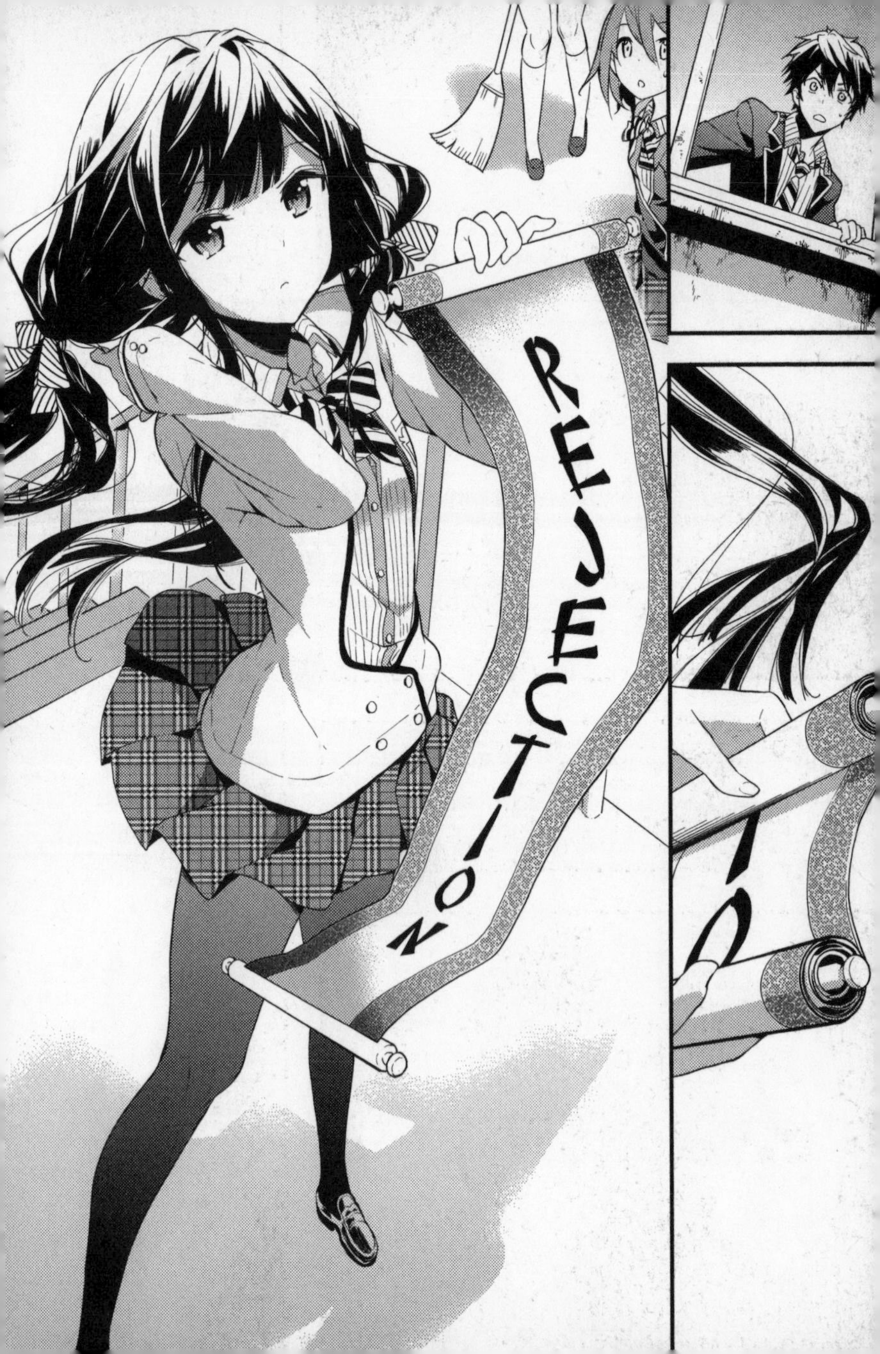
REJECTION

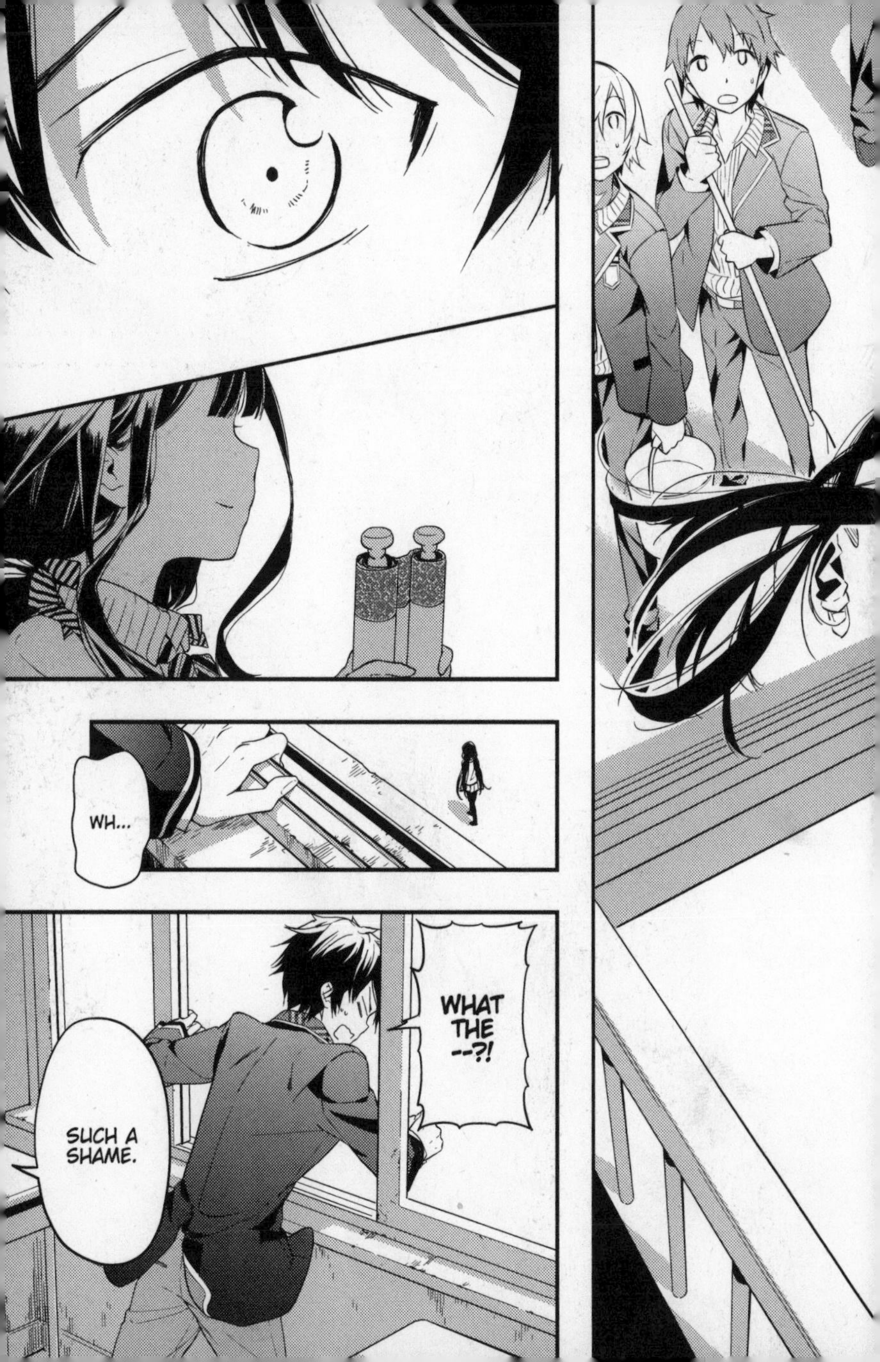
WH...
WHAT THE --?!
SUCH A SHAME.

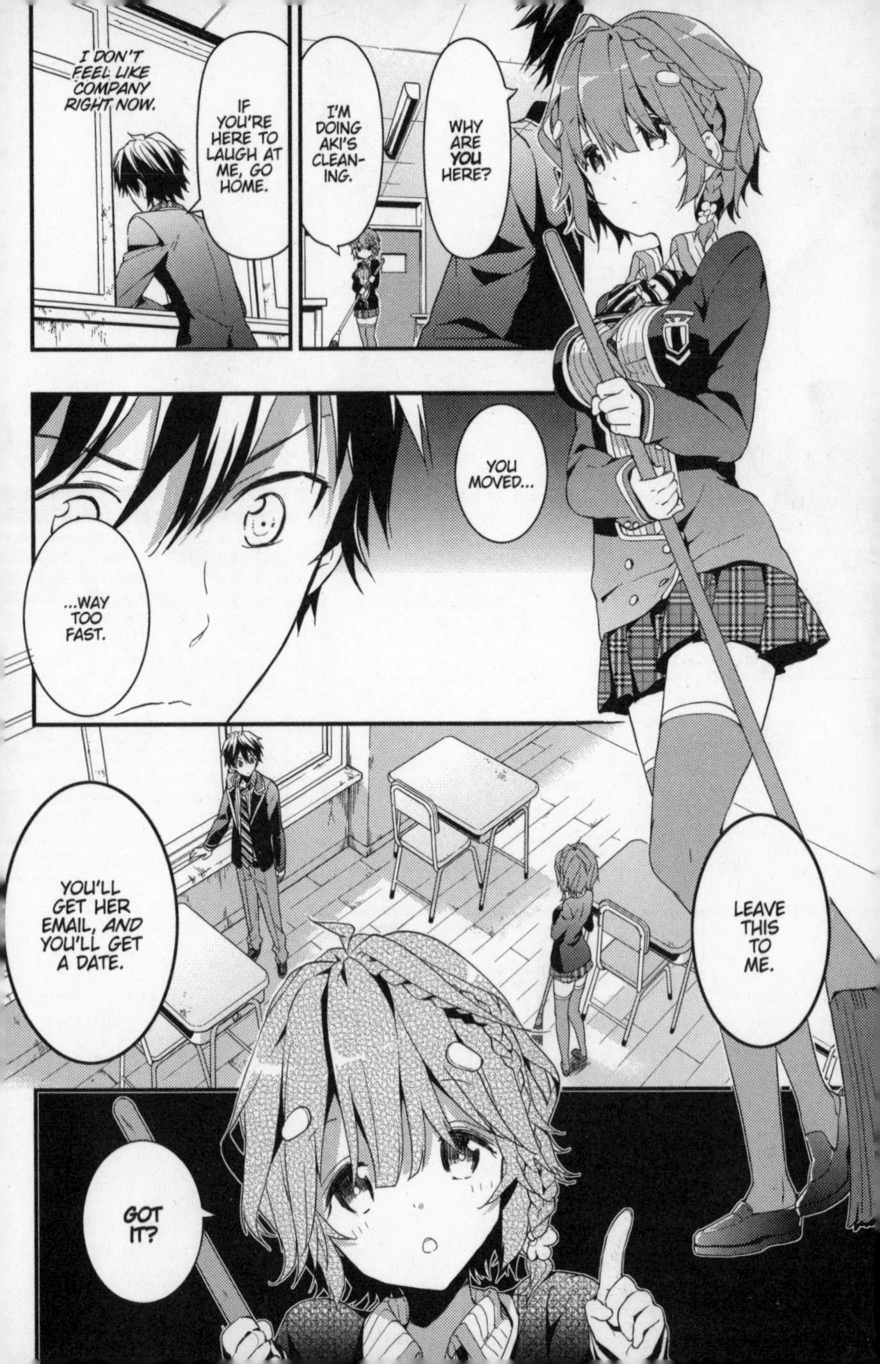
WHY ARE YOU HERE?
I'M DOING AKI'S CLEAN-ING.
IF YOU'RE HERE TO LAUGH AT ME, GO HOME.
I DON'T FEEL LIKE COMPANY RIGHT NOW.
YOU MOVED...
...WAY TOO FAST.
LEAVE THIS TO ME.
YOU'LL GET HER EMAIL, AND YOU'LL GET A DATE.
GOT IT?

1

Masamune-kun's
REVENGE

Presented by Hazuki Takeoka & TIV

Masamune-kun's REVENGE
Presented by Hazuki Takeoka & TIV

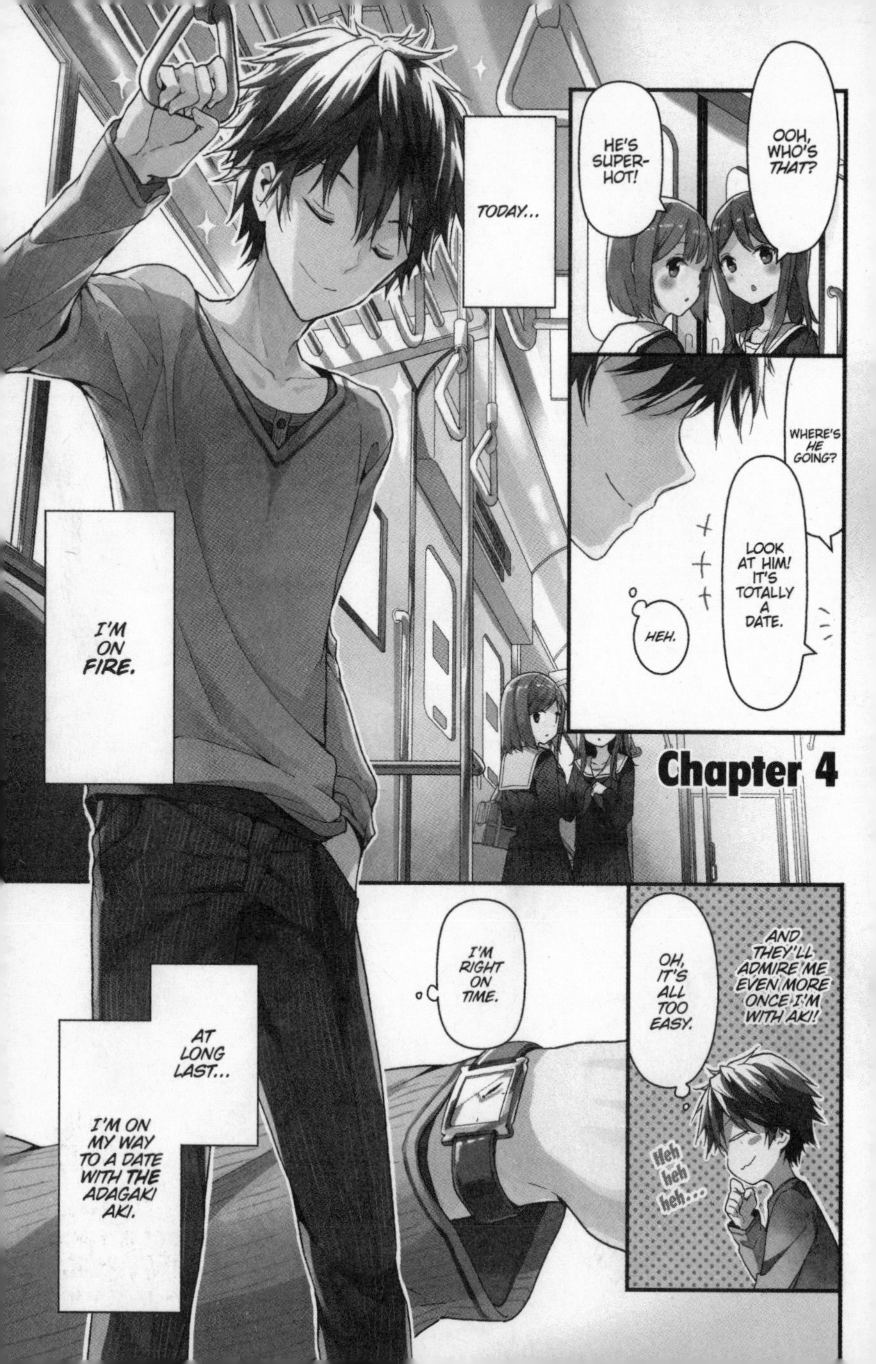

OOH, WHO'S THAT?
HE'S SUPER-HOT!
WHERE'S HE GOING?
LOOK AT HIM! IT'S TOTALLY A DATE.
HEH.
Chapter 4
TODAY...
I'M ON FIRE.
AND THEY'LL ADMIRE ME EVEN MORE ONCE I'M WITH AKI!
OH, IT'S ALL TOO EASY.
Heh heh heh...
I'M RIGHT ON TIME.
AT LONG LAST...
I'M ON MY WAY TO A DATE WITH THE ADAGAKI AKI.

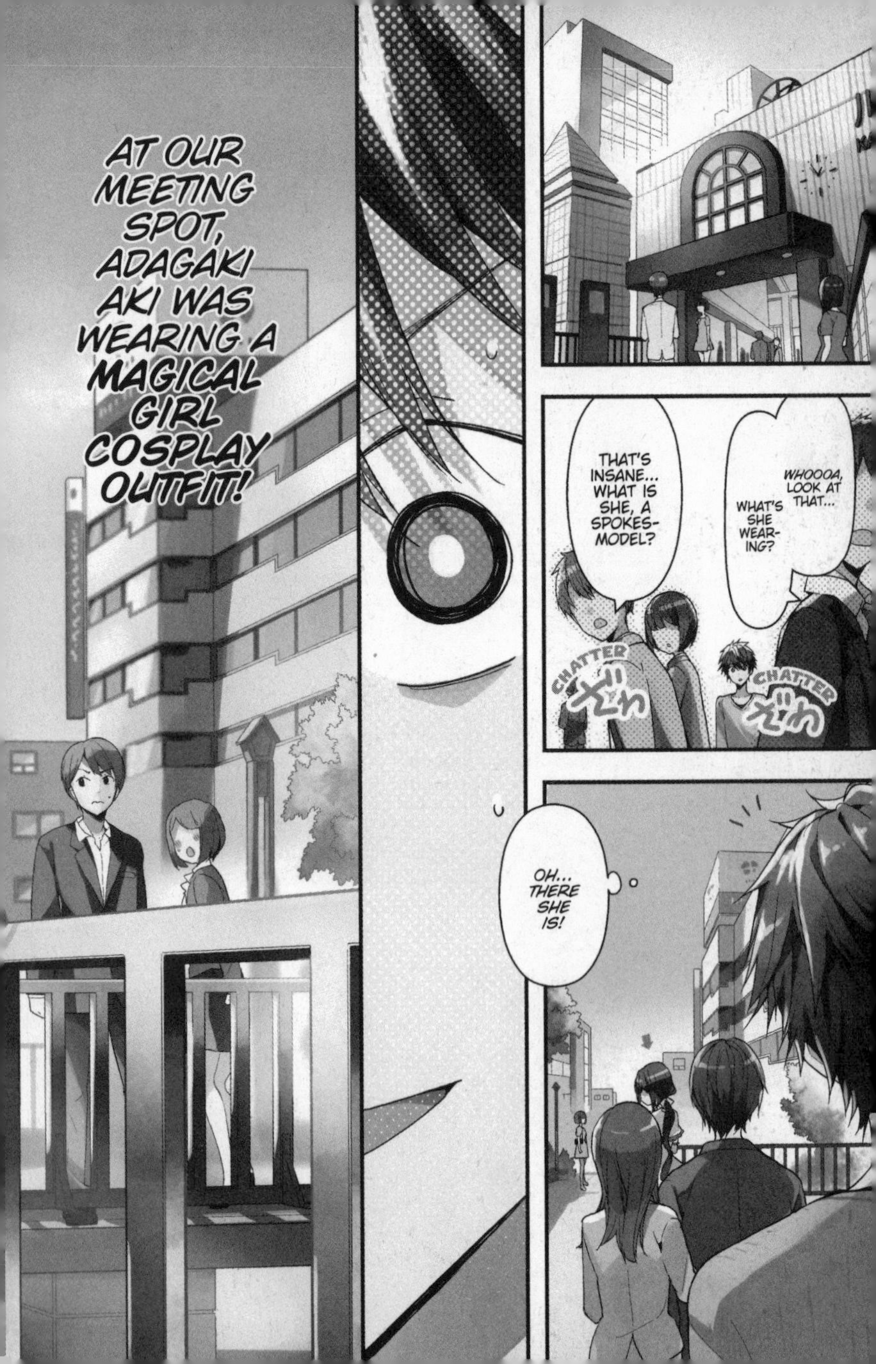
WHOOOA, LOOK AT THAT...
WHAT'S SHE WEAR-ING?
THAT'S INSANE... WHAT IS SHE, A SPOKES-MODEL?
CHATTER ざわ
CHATTER ざわ
OH... THERE SHE IS!
AT OUR MEETING SPOT, ADAGAKI AKI WAS WEARING A MAGICAL GIRL COSPLAY OUTFIT!

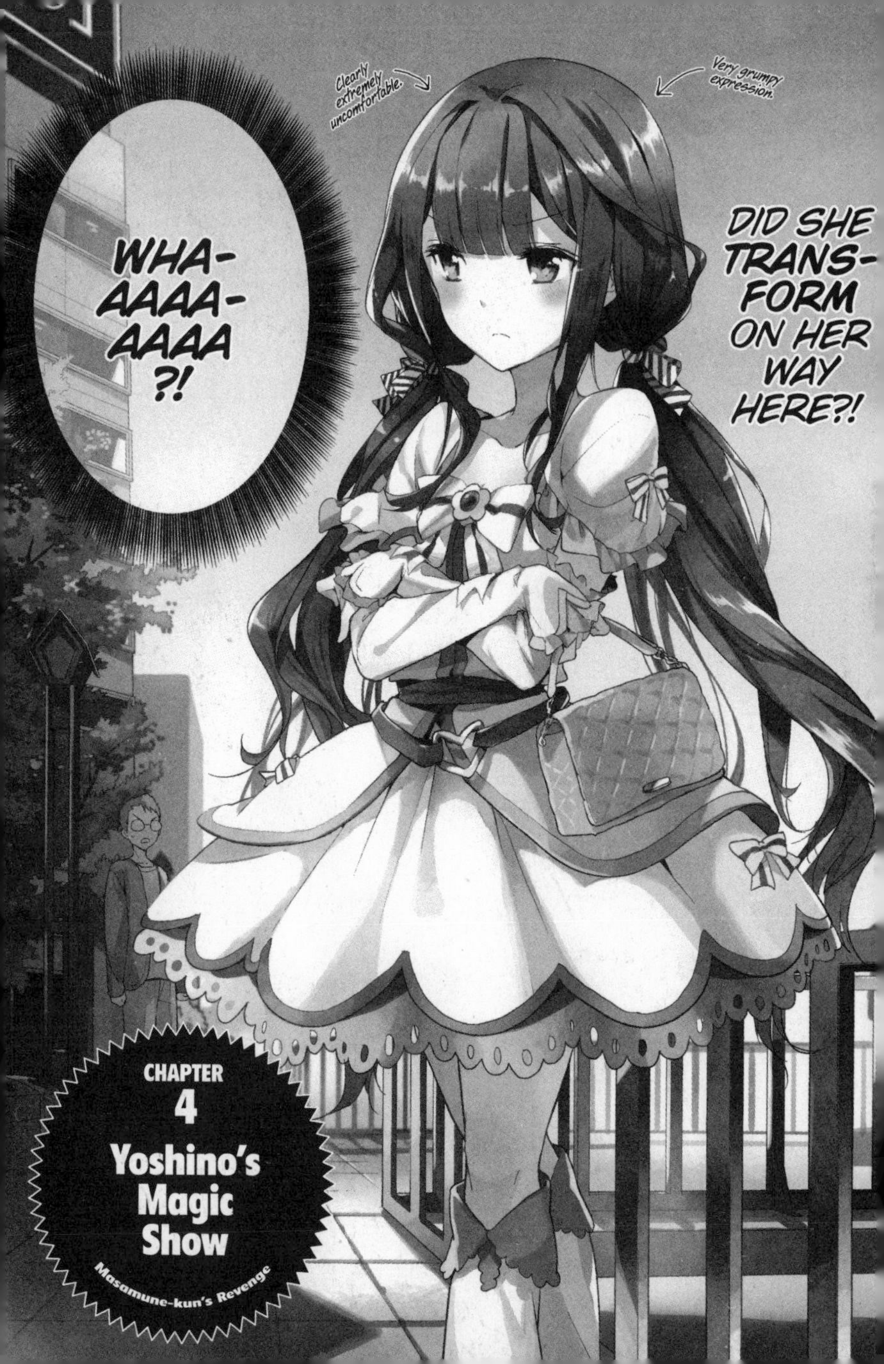
Very grumpy expression.
Clearly extremely uncomfortable.
DID SHE TRANS-FORM ON HER WAY HERE?!
WHA-AAAA-AAAA?!
CHAPTER 4
Yoshino's Magic Show
Masamune-kun's Revenge

Masamune-kun's
REVENGE
Presented by Hazuki Takeoka & TIV

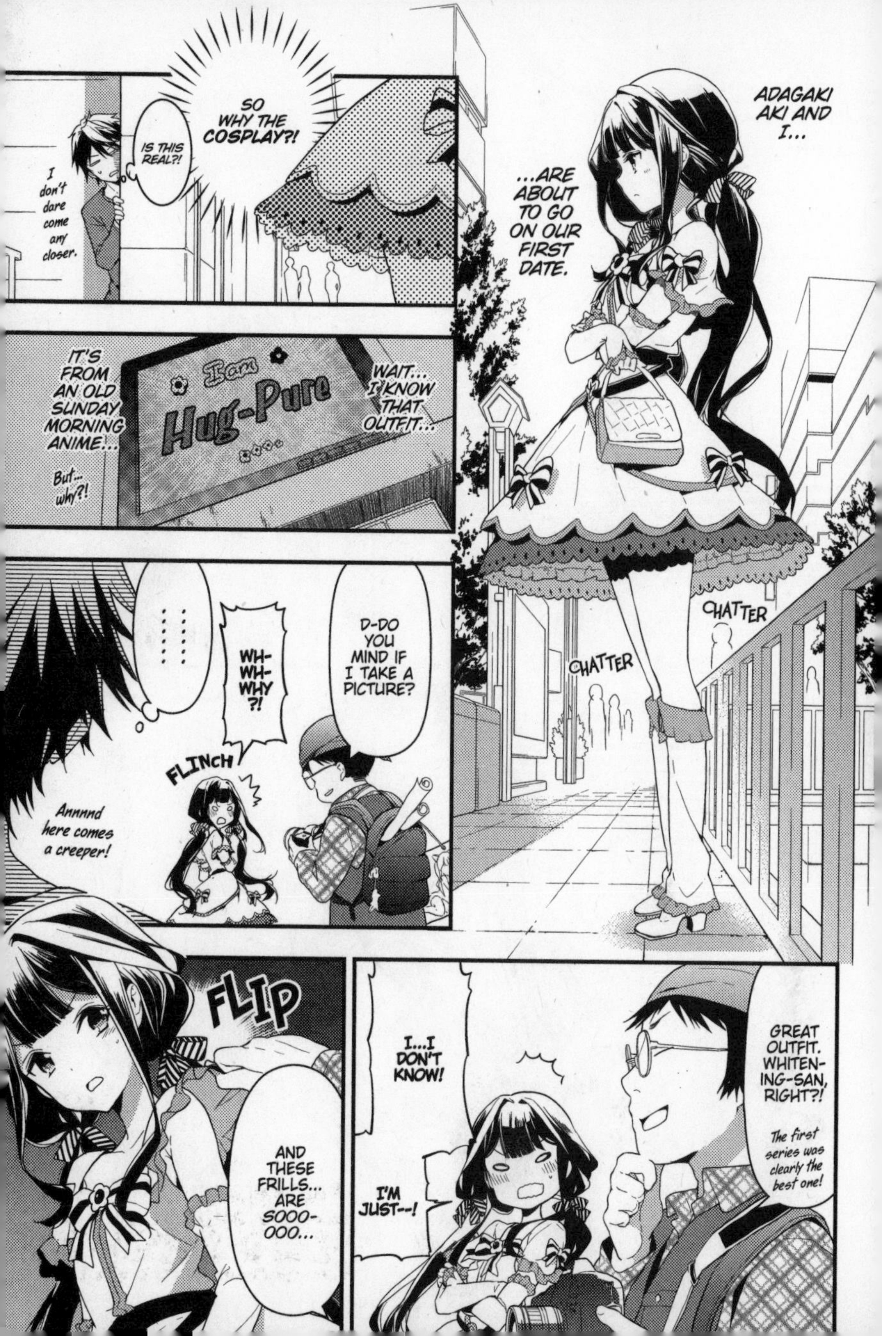
ADAGAKI AKI AND I...
...ARE ABOUT TO GO ON OUR FIRST DATE.
CHATTER
CHATTER
SO WHY THE COSPLAY?!
IS THIS REAL?!
I don't dare come any closer.
WAIT... I KNOW THAT OUTFIT...
I am Hug-Pure
IT'S FROM AN OLD SUNDAY MORNING ANIME...
But... why?!
D-DO YOU MIND IF I TAKE A PICTURE?
WH-WH-WHY?!
......
FLINCH
Annnnd here comes a creeper!
GREAT OUTFIT. WHITENING-SAN, RIGHT?!
The first series was clearly the best one!
I...I DON'T KNOW!
I'M JUST--!
FLIP
AND THESE FRILLS... ARE SOOO-OOO...

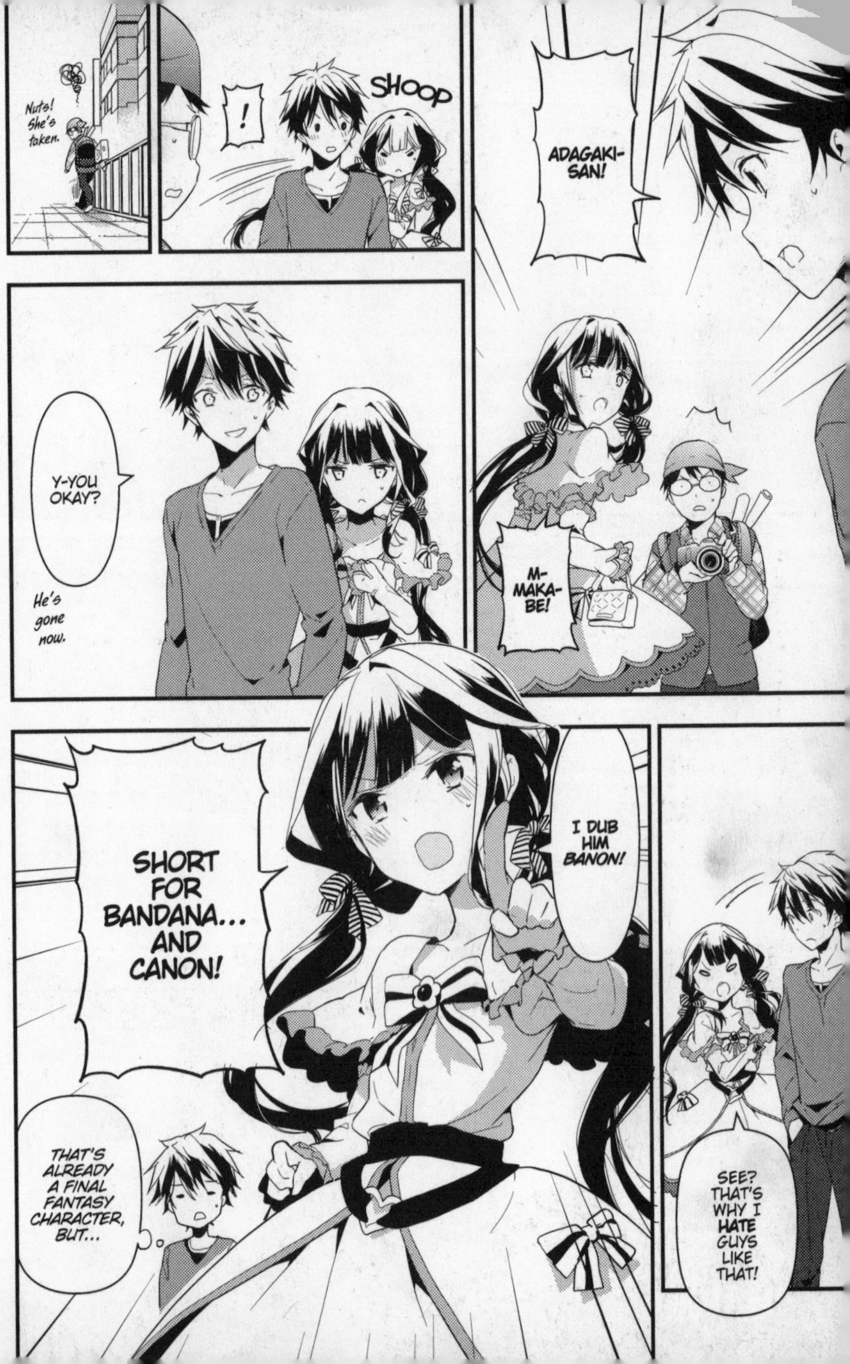
ADAGAKI-SAN!
M-MAKABE!
SHOOP
!
Nuts! She's taken.
Y-YOU OKAY?
He's gone now.
SEE? THAT'S WHY I HATE GUYS LIKE THAT!
I DUB HIM BANON!
SHORT FOR BANDANA... AND CANON!
THAT'S ALREADY A FINAL FANTASY CHARACTER, BUT...

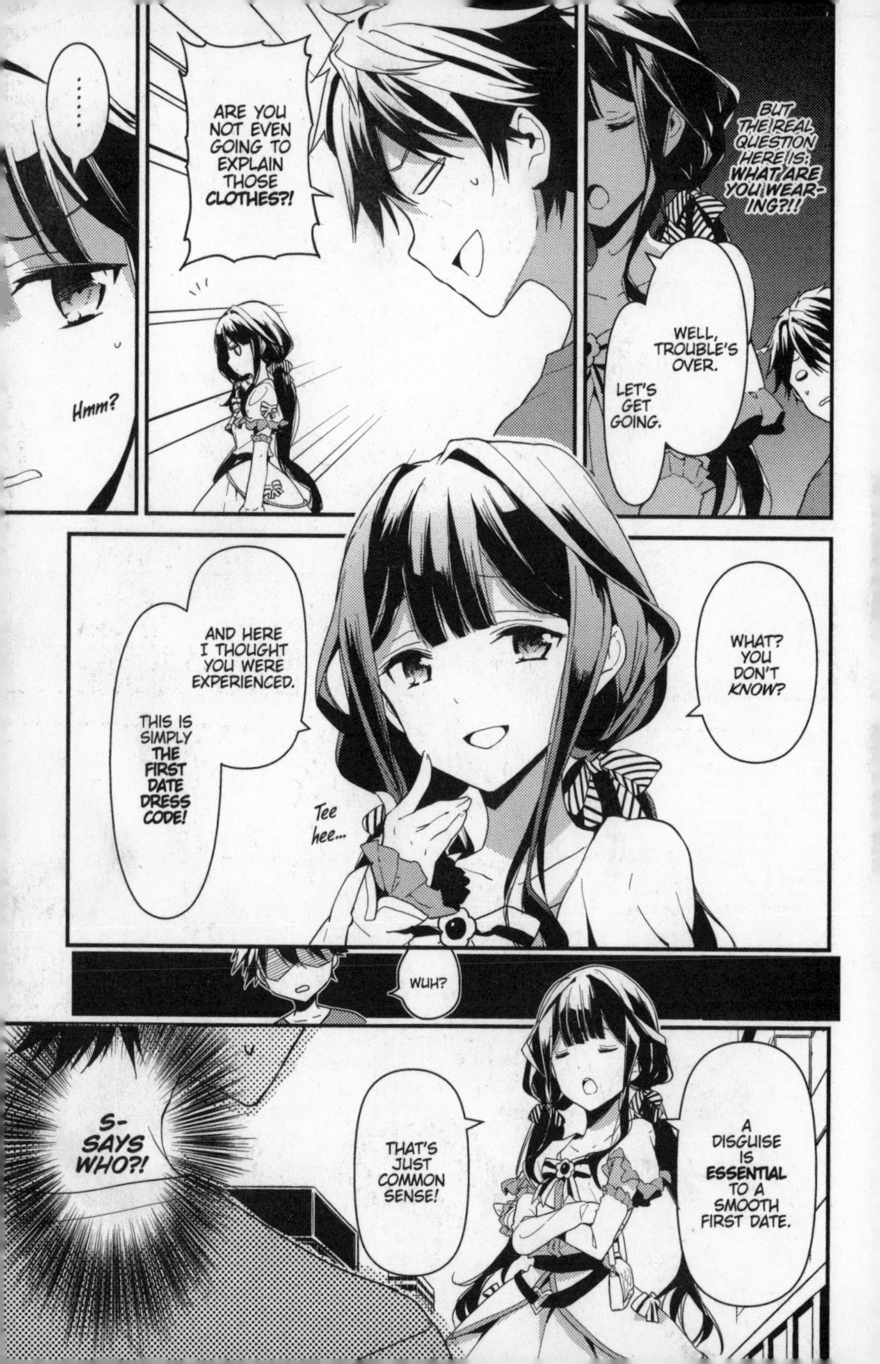
BUT THE REAL QUESTION HERE IS: WHAT ARE YOU WEARING?!!
WELL, TROUBLE'S OVER.
LET'S GET GOING.
ARE YOU NOT EVEN GOING TO EXPLAIN THOSE CLOTHES?!
......
Hmm?
WHAT? YOU DON'T KNOW?
AND HERE I THOUGHT YOU WERE EXPERIENCED.
THIS IS SIMPLY THE FIRST DATE DRESS CODE!
Tee hee...
WUH?
A DISGUISE IS ESSENTIAL TO A SMOOTH FIRST DATE.
THAT'S JUST COMMON SENSE!
S-SAYS WHO?!

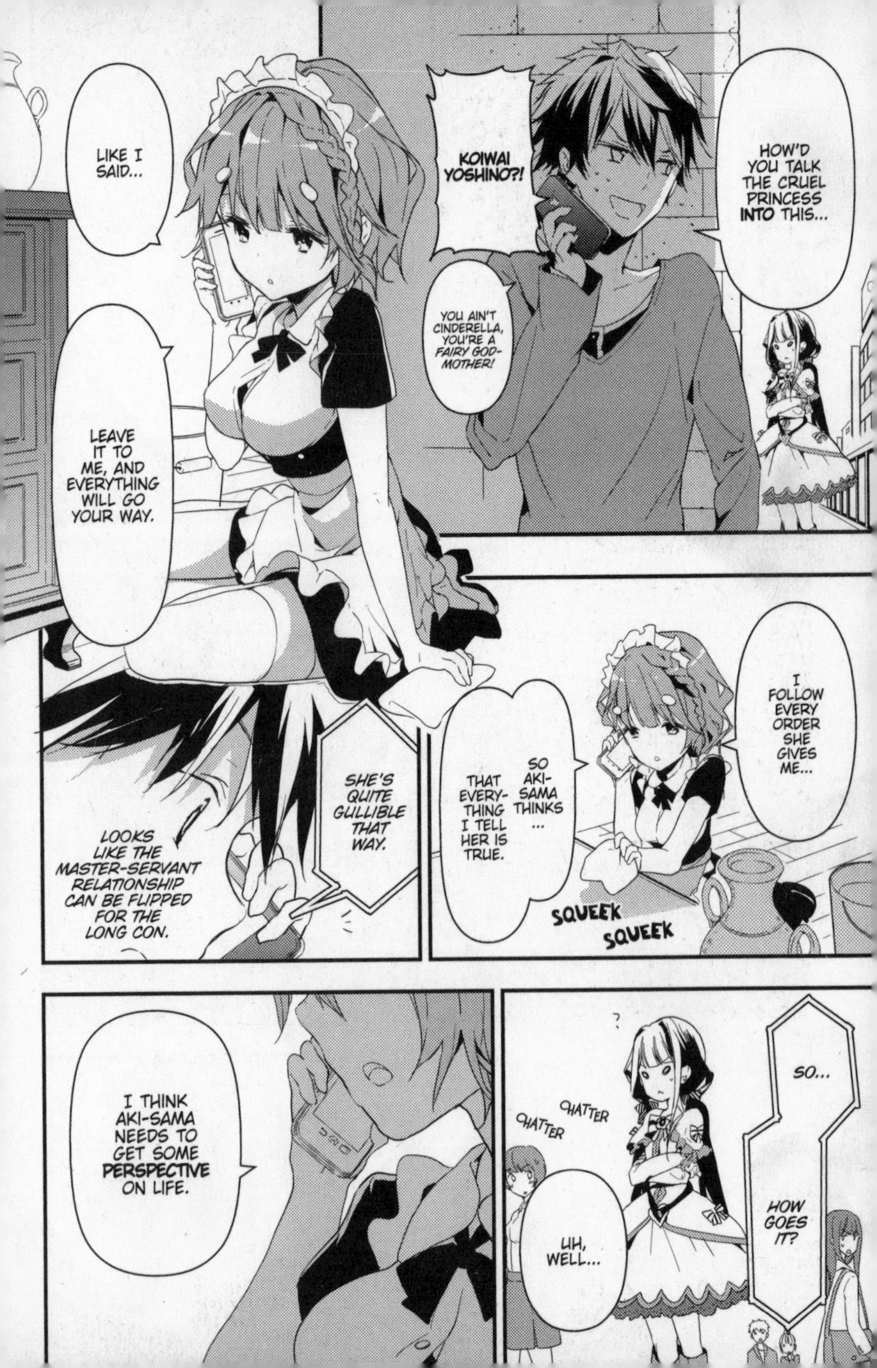
HOW'D YOU TALK THE CRUEL PRINCESS INTO THIS...
KOIWAI YOSHINO?!
YOU AIN'T CINDERELLA, YOU'RE A FAIRY GOD-MOTHER!
LIKE I SAID...
LEAVE IT TO ME, AND EVERYTHING WILL GO YOUR WAY.
I FOLLOW EVERY ORDER SHE GIVES ME...
SO AKI-SAMA THINKS...
THAT EVERYTHING I TELL HER IS TRUE.
SQUEEK
SQUEEK
SHE'S QUITE GULLIBLE THAT WAY.
LOOKS LIKE THE MASTER-SERVANT RELATIONSHIP CAN BE FLIPPED FOR THE LONG CON.
SO...
HOW GOES IT?
CHATTER
CHATTER
UH, WELL...
I THINK AKI-SAMA NEEDS TO GET SOME PERSPECTIVE ON LIFE.

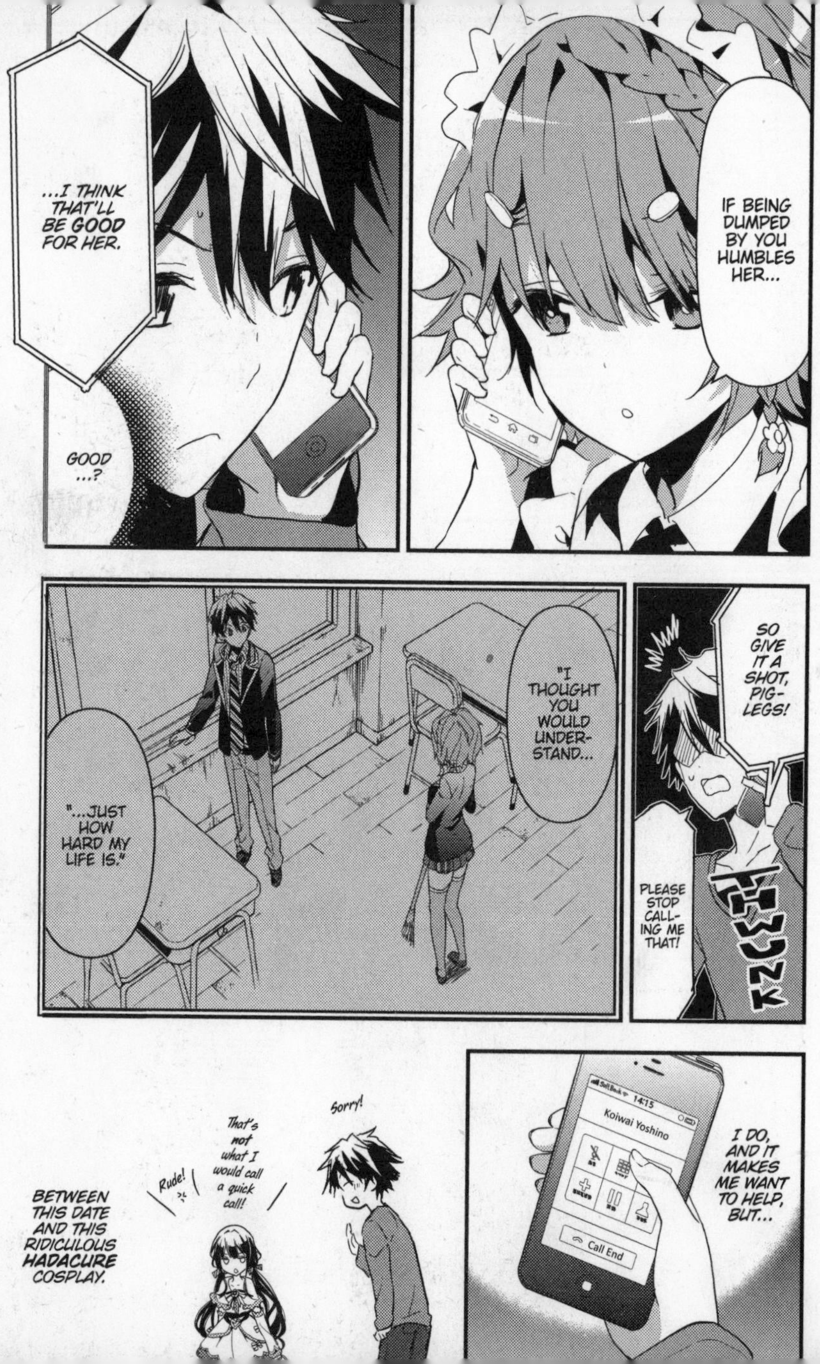
IF BEING DUMPED BY YOU HUMBLES HER...
...I THINK THAT'LL BE GOOD FOR HER.
GOOD ...?
SO GIVE IT A SHOT, PIG-LEGS!
THWUNK
PLEASE STOP CALLING ME THAT!
"I THOUGHT YOU WOULD UNDERSTAND...
"...JUST HOW HARD MY LIFE IS."
14:15
Koiwai Yoshino
Call End
I DO, AND IT MAKES ME WANT TO HELP, BUT...
Sorry!
That's not what I would call a quick call!
Rude!
BETWEEN THIS DATE AND THIS RIDICULOUS HADACURE COSPLAY.

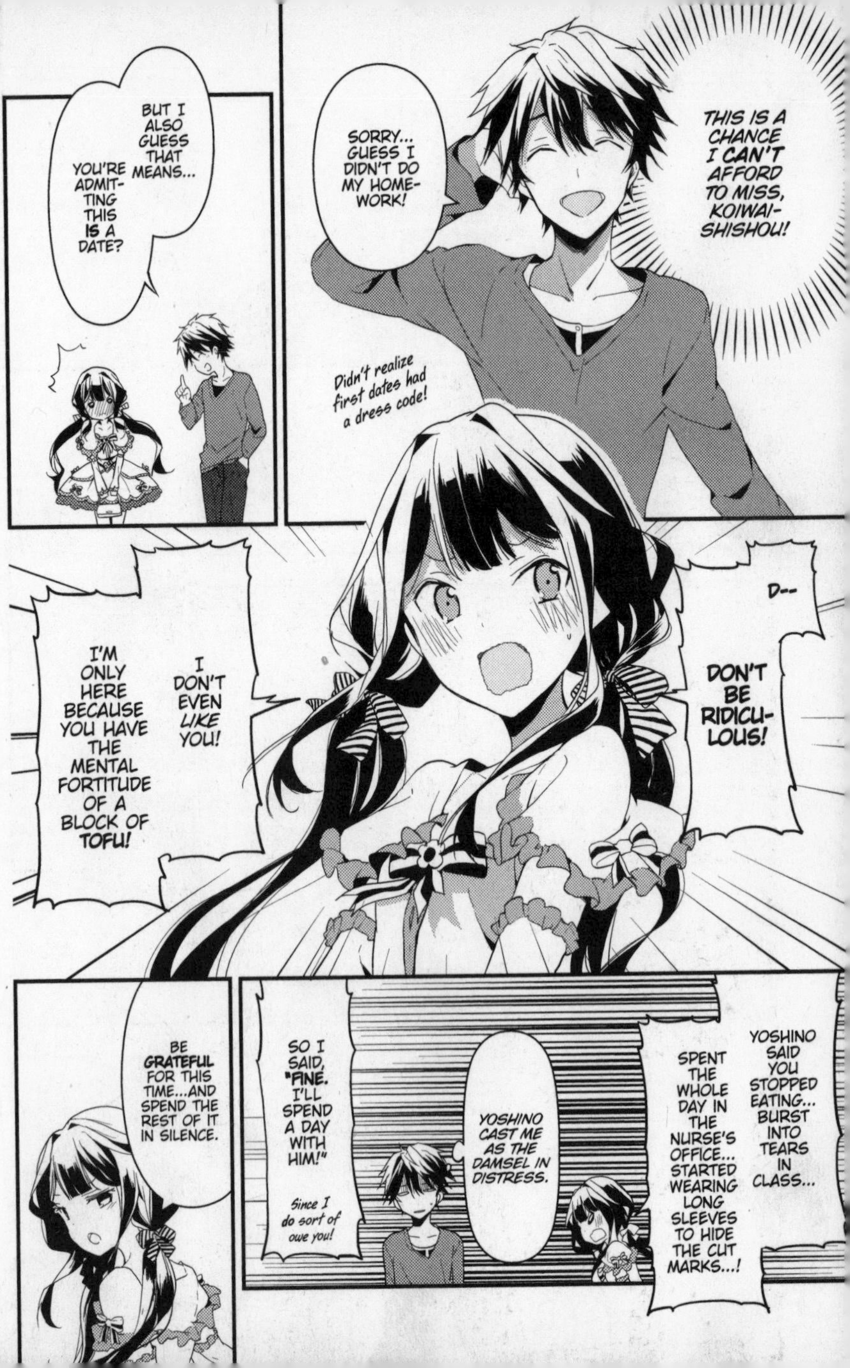
THIS IS A CHANCE I CAN'T AFFORD TO MISS, KOIWAI-SHISHOU!
SORRY... GUESS I DIDN'T DO MY HOME-WORK!
Didn't realize first dates had a dress code!
BUT I ALSO GUESS THAT MEANS... YOU'RE ADMIT-TING THIS IS A DATE?
D--
DON'T BE RIDICU-LOUS!
I DON'T EVEN LIKE YOU!
I'M ONLY HERE BECAUSE YOU HAVE THE MENTAL FORTITUDE OF A BLOCK OF TOFU!
YOSHINO SAID YOU STOPPED EATING... BURST INTO TEARS IN CLASS...
SPENT THE WHOLE DAY IN THE NURSE'S OFFICE... STARTED WEARING LONG SLEEVES TO HIDE THE CUT MARKS...!
YOSHINO CAST ME AS THE DAMSEL IN DISTRESS.
SO I SAID, "FINE. I'LL SPEND A DAY WITH HIM!"
Since I do sort of owe you!
BE GRATEFUL FOR THIS TIME...AND SPEND THE REST OF IT IN SILENCE.

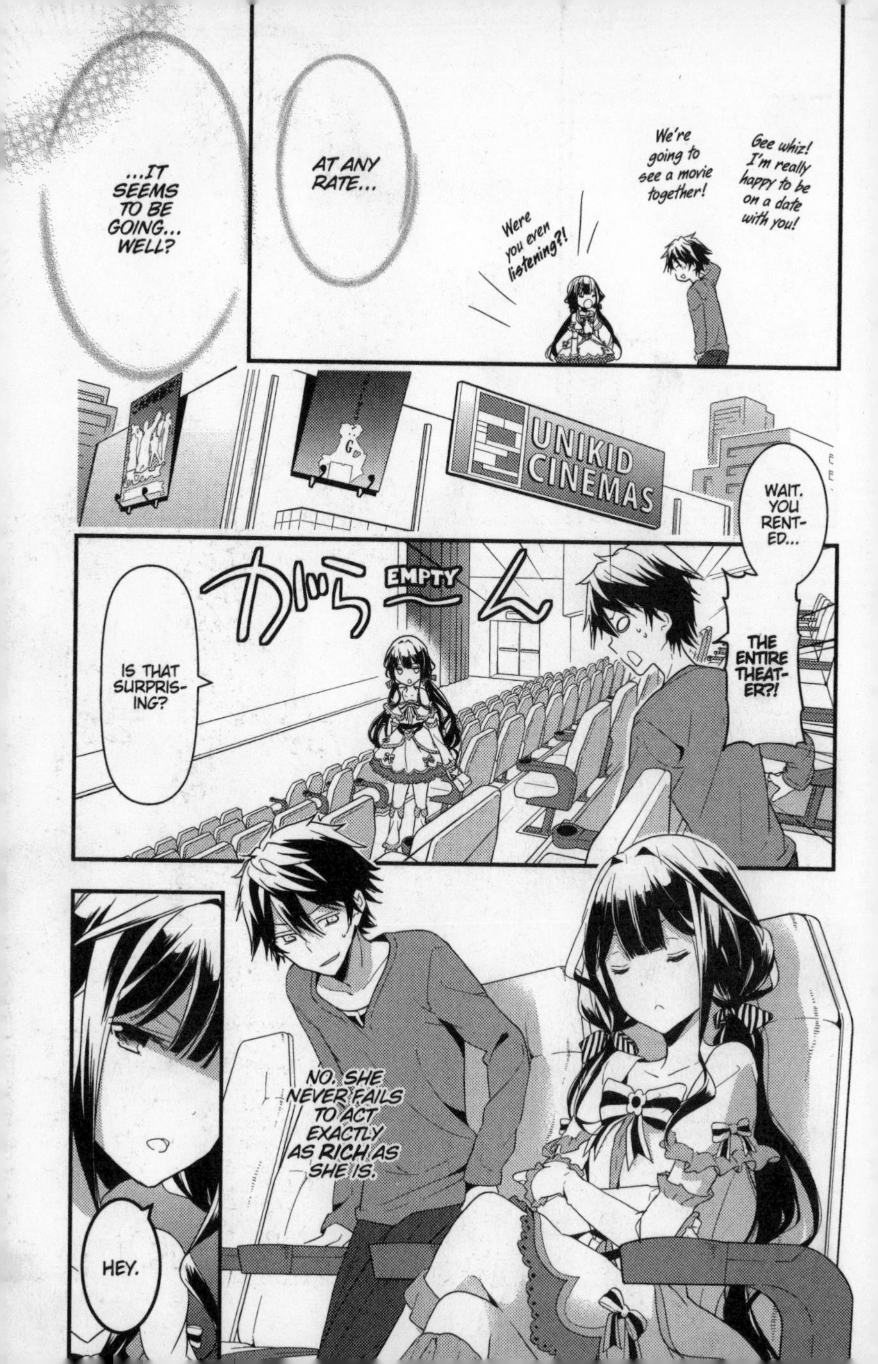
Gee whiz! I'm really happy to be on a date with you!
We're going to see a movie together!
Were you even listening?!
AT ANY RATE...
...IT SEEMS TO BE GOING... WELL?
UNIKID CINEMAS
WAIT. YOU RENTED...
THE ENTIRE THEATER?!
がら～ん
EMPTY
IS THAT SURPRISING?
NO. SHE NEVER FAILS TO ACT EXACTLY AS RICH AS SHE IS.
HEY.

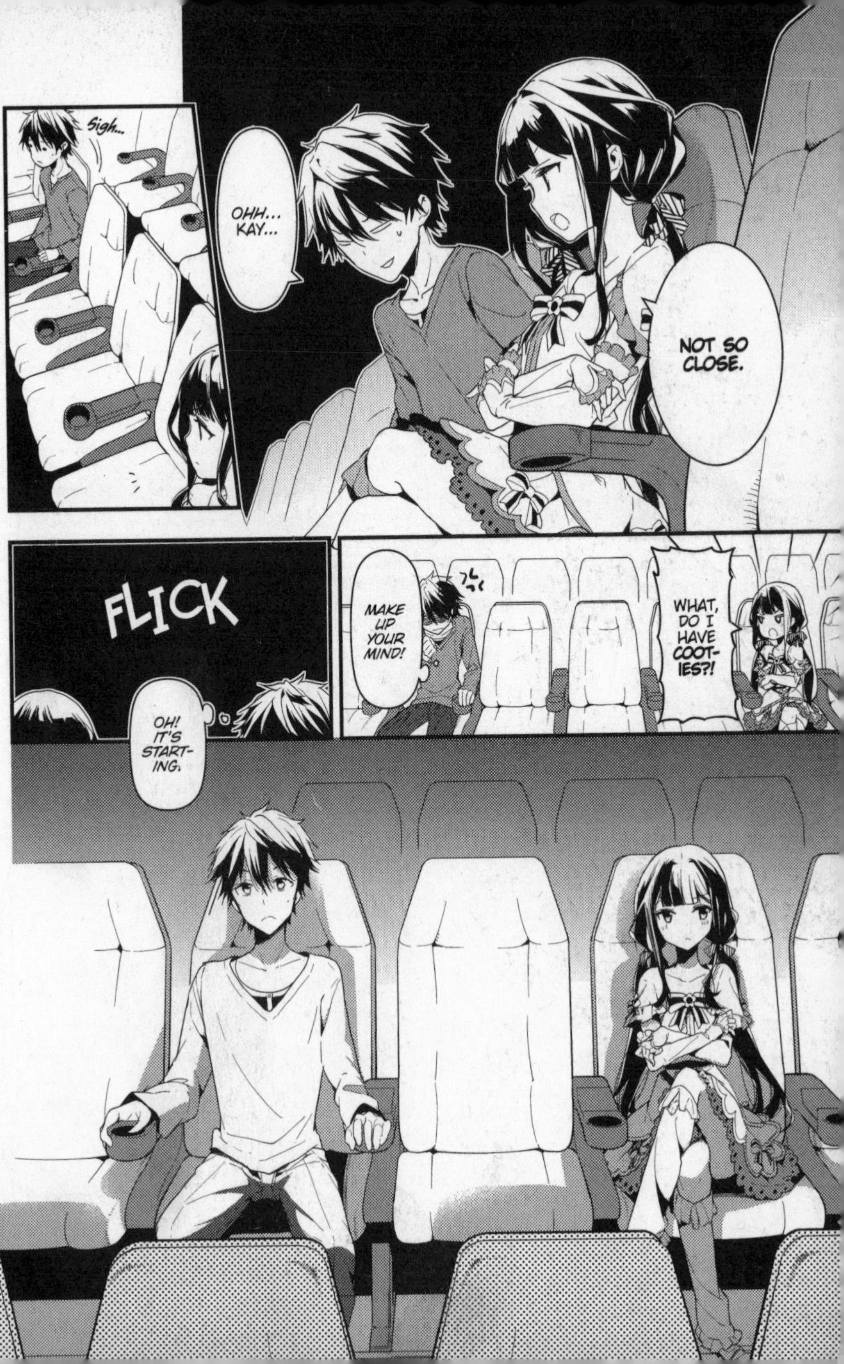
NOT SO CLOSE.
OHH... KAY...
Sigh...
WHAT, DO I HAVE COOTIES?!
MAKE UP YOUR MIND!
FLICK
OH! IT'S STARTING.

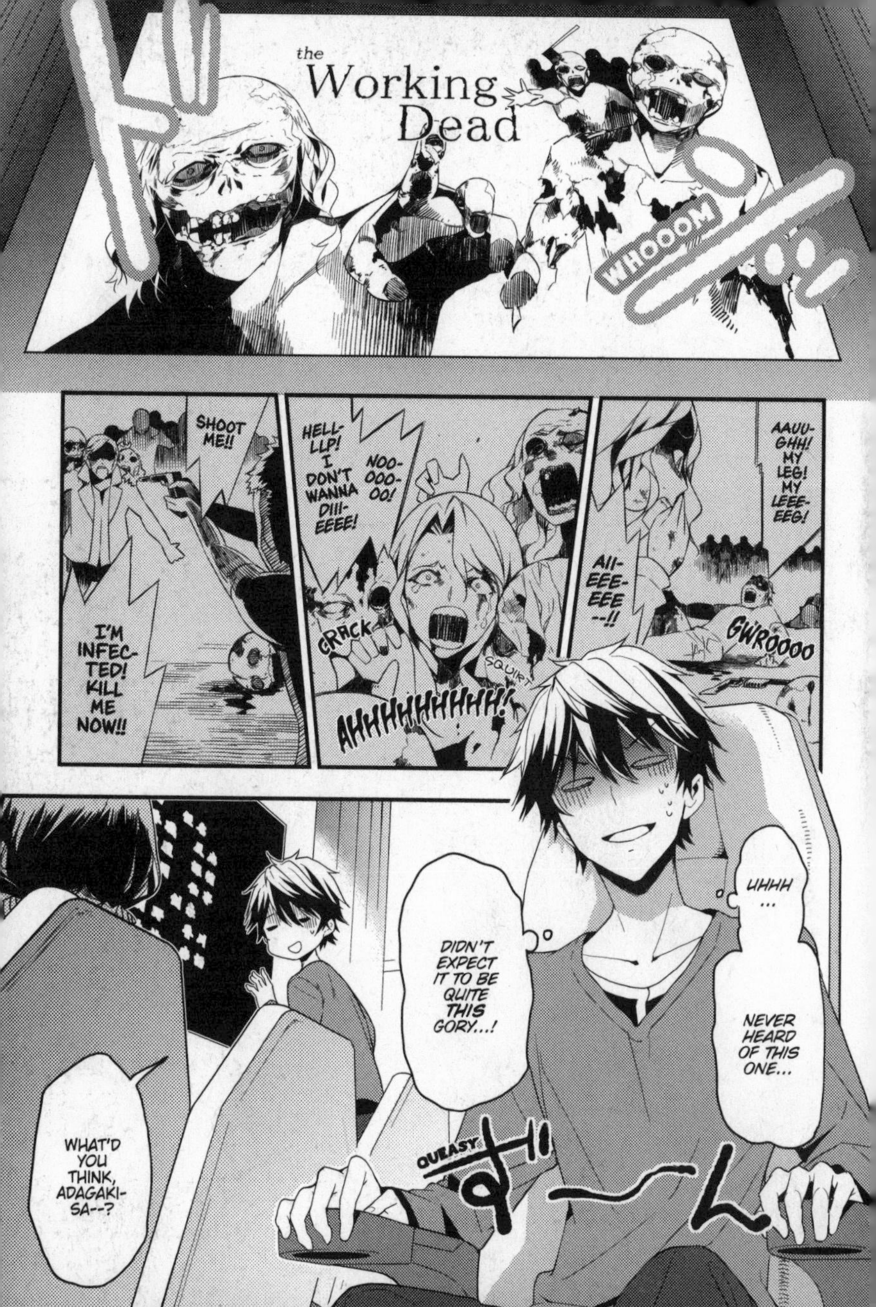
the Working Dead
WHOOOM
AAUU-GHH! MY LEG! MY LEEE-EEG!
AII-EEE-EEE--!!
GWROOOO
NOO-OOO-OO!
HELL-LLP! I DON'T WANNA DIII-EEEE!
CRACK
SQUIRT
AHHHHHHHHH!
SHOOT ME!!
I'M INFECTED! KILL ME NOW!!
UHHH ...
NEVER HEARD OF THIS ONE...
DIDN'T EXPECT IT TO BE QUITE THIS GORY...!
QUEASY
WHAT'D YOU THINK, ADAGAKI-SA--?

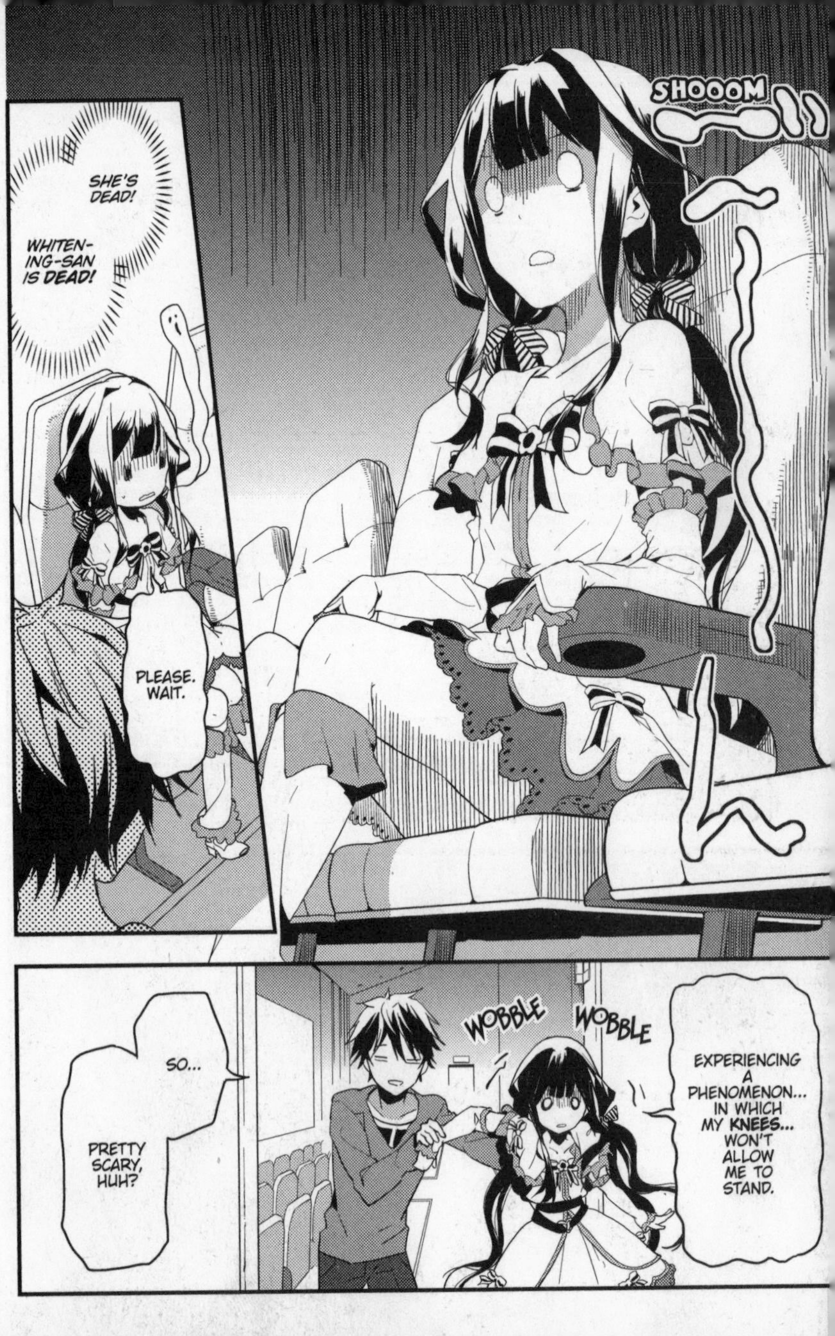
SHOOOM
SHE'S DEAD!
WHITEN-ING-SAN IS DEAD!
PLEASE. WAIT.
WOBBLE WOBBLE
EXPERIENCING A PHENOMENON... IN WHICH MY KNEES... WON'T ALLOW ME TO STAND.
SO...
PRETTY SCARY, HUH?

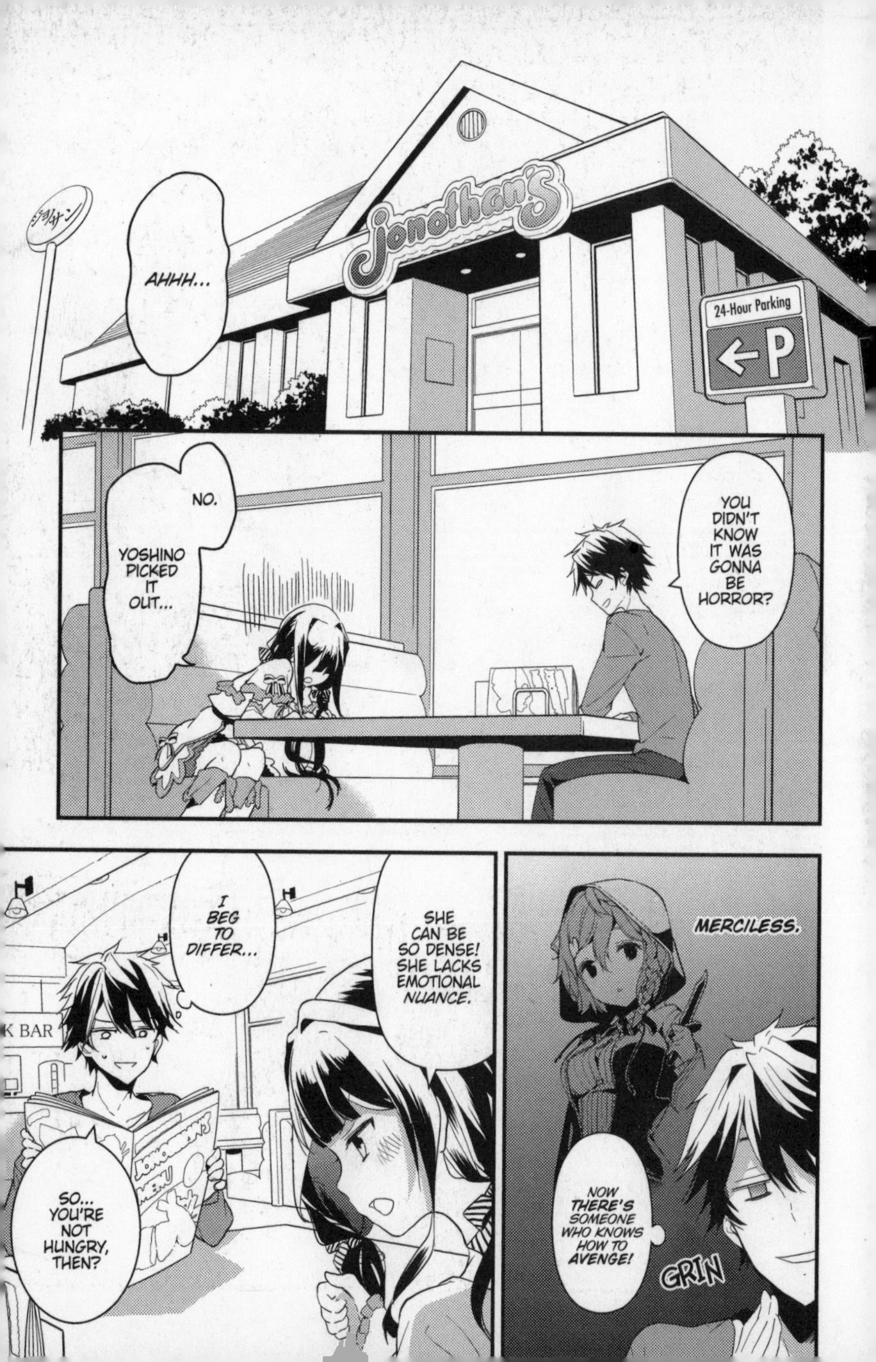
jonathan's
24-Hour Parking
P
AHHH...
YOU DIDN'T KNOW IT WAS GONNA BE HORROR?
NO.
YOSHINO PICKED IT OUT...
MERCILESS.
NOW THERE'S SOMEONE WHO KNOWS HOW TO AVENGE!
GRIN
SHE CAN BE SO DENSE! SHE LACKS EMOTIONAL NUANCE.
I BEG TO DIFFER...
K BAR
SO... YOU'RE NOT HUNGRY, THEN?

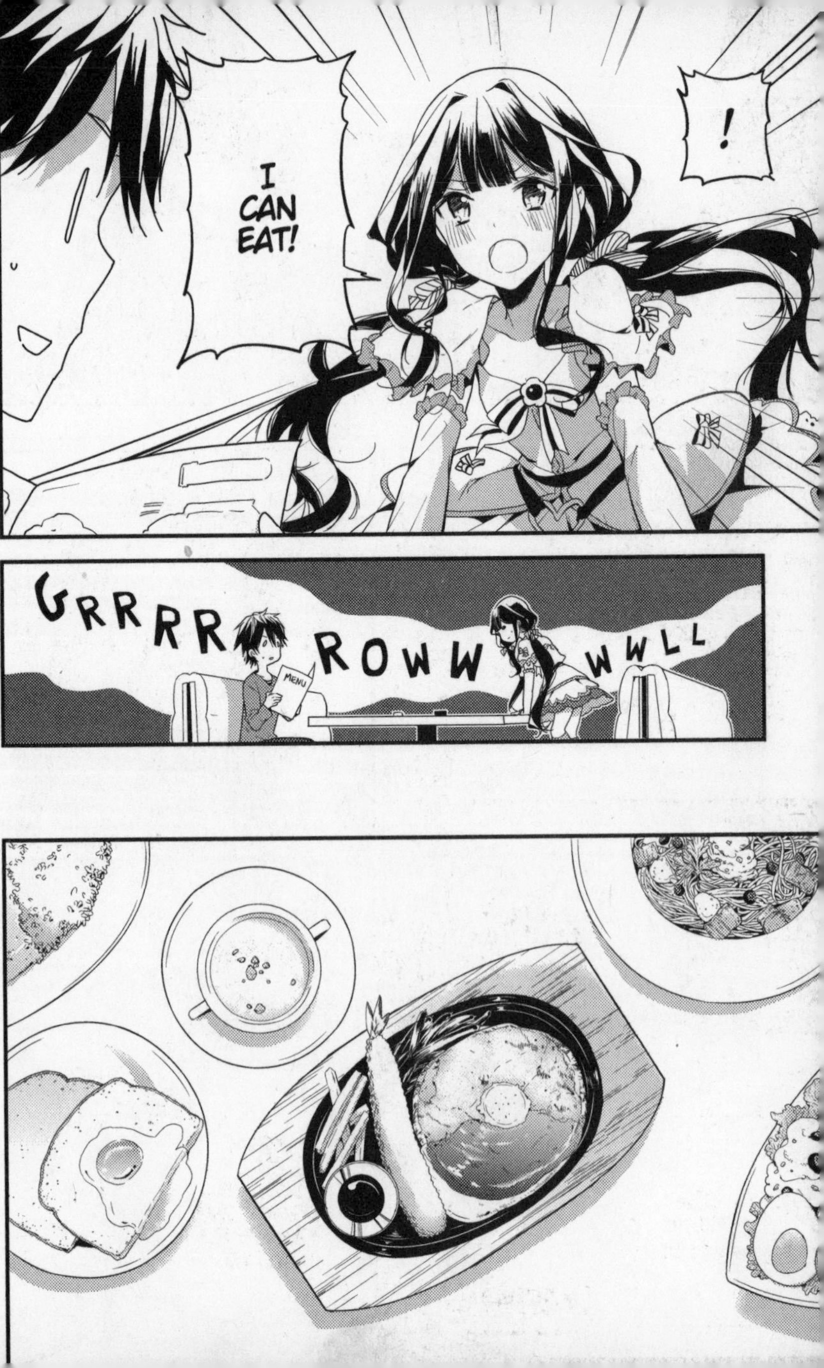
!
I CAN EAT!
GRRRRROWW WWLL
MENU

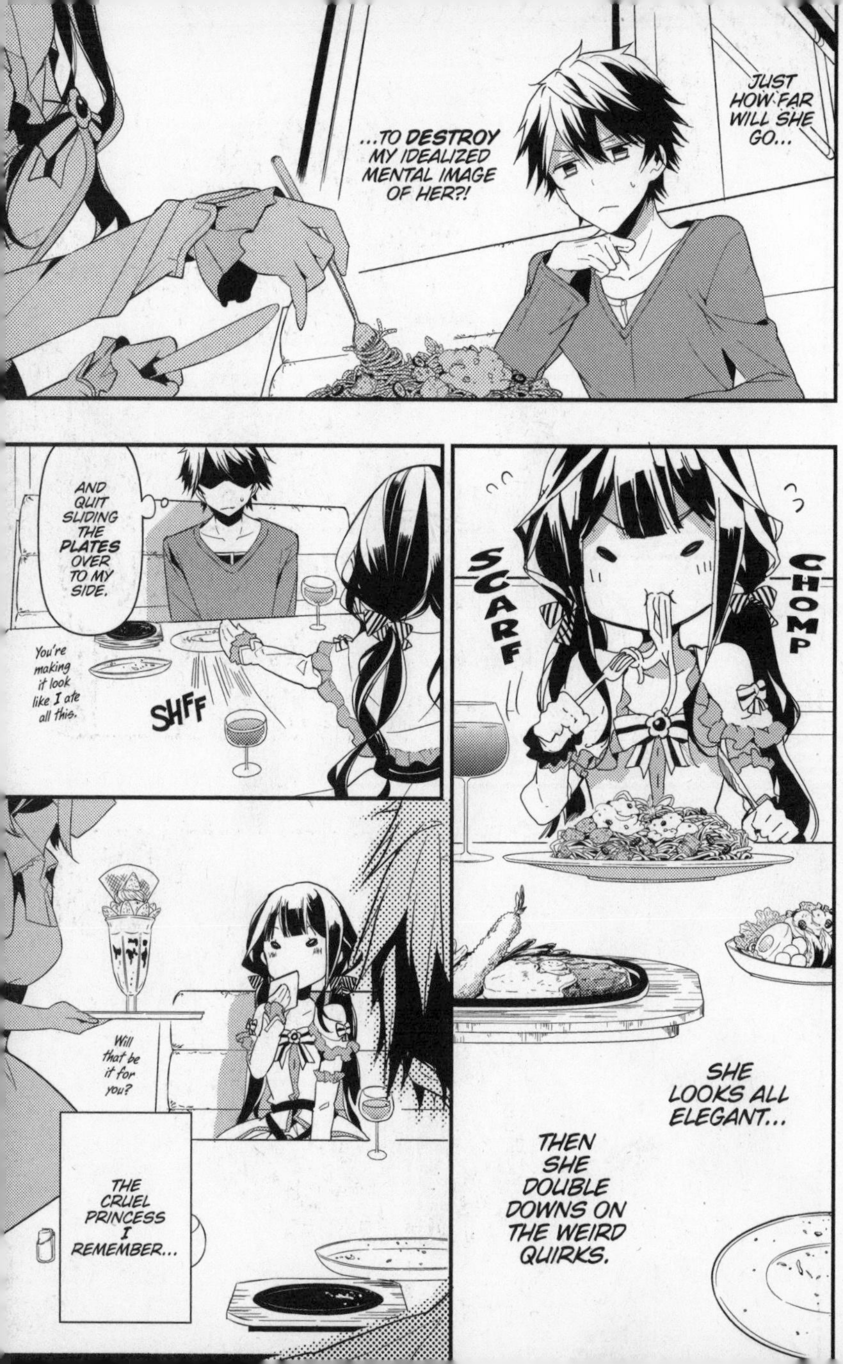
JUST HOW FAR WILL SHE GO...
...TO DESTROY MY IDEALIZED MENTAL IMAGE OF HER?!
CHOMP
SCARF
SHE LOOKS ALL ELEGANT...
THEN SHE DOUBLE DOWNS ON THE WEIRD QUIRKS.
AND QUIT SLIDING THE PLATES OVER TO MY SIDE.
You're making it look like I ate all this.
SHFF
Will that be it for you?
THE CRUEL PRINCESS I REMEMBER...

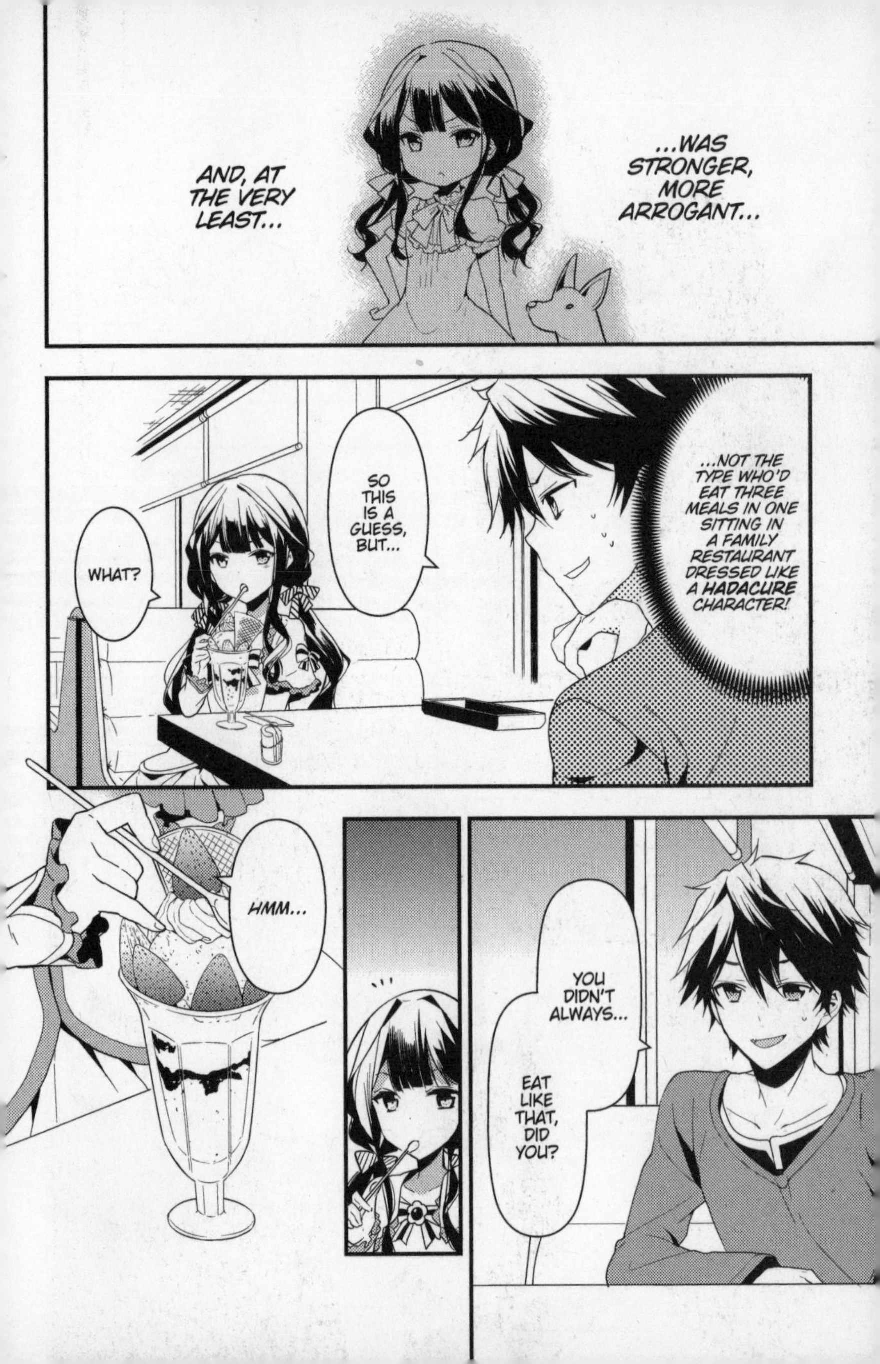
...WAS STRONGER, MORE ARROGANT...
AND, AT THE VERY LEAST...
...NOT THE TYPE WHO'D EAT THREE MEALS IN ONE SITTING IN A FAMILY RESTAURANT DRESSED LIKE A *HADACURE* CHARACTER!
SO THIS IS A GUESS, BUT...
WHAT?
YOU DIDN'T ALWAYS...
EAT LIKE THAT, DID YOU?
HMM...

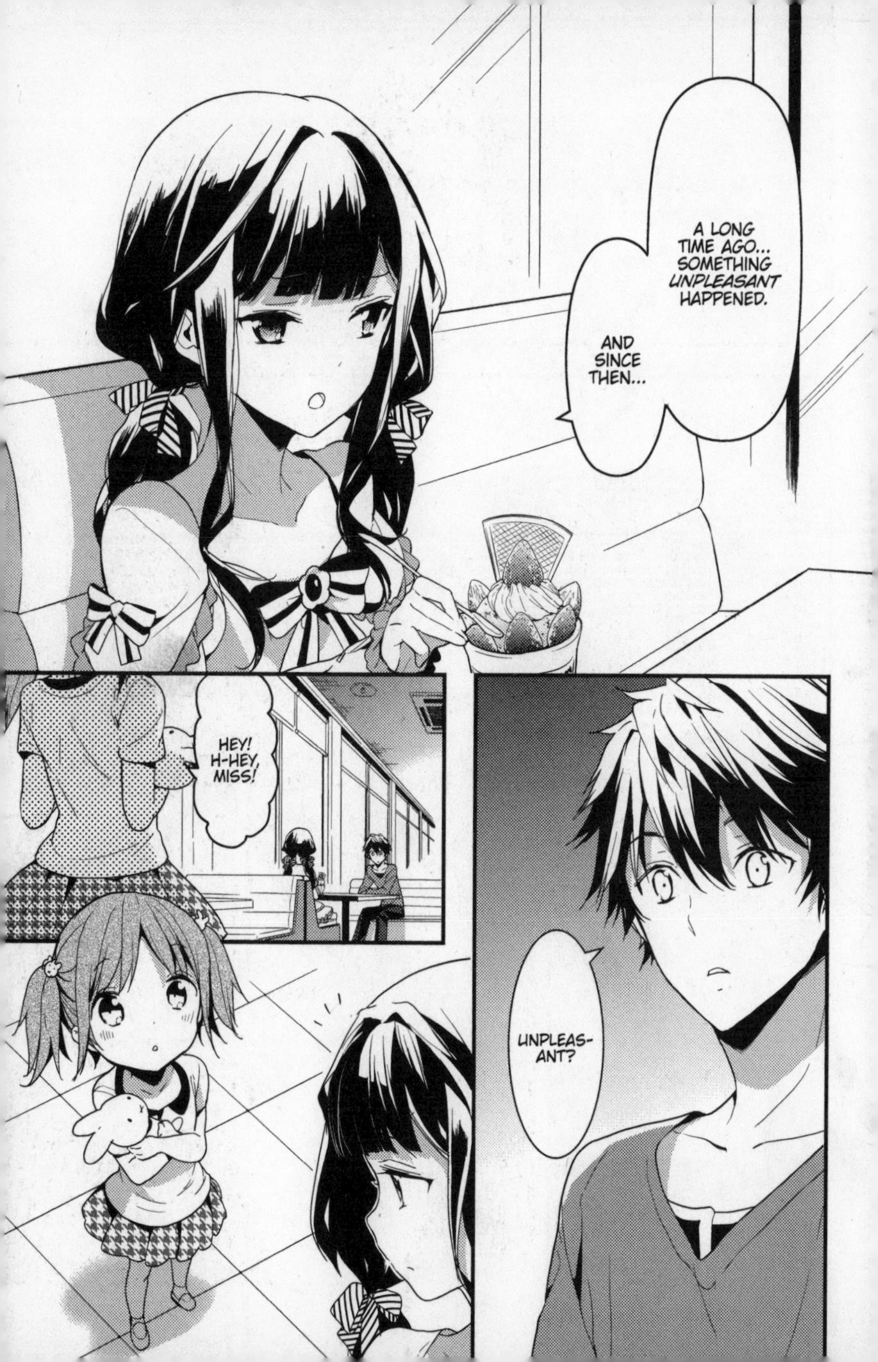
A LONG TIME AGO... SOMETHING UNPLEASANT HAPPENED.
AND SINCE THEN...
UNPLEAS-ANT?
HEY! H-HEY, MISS!

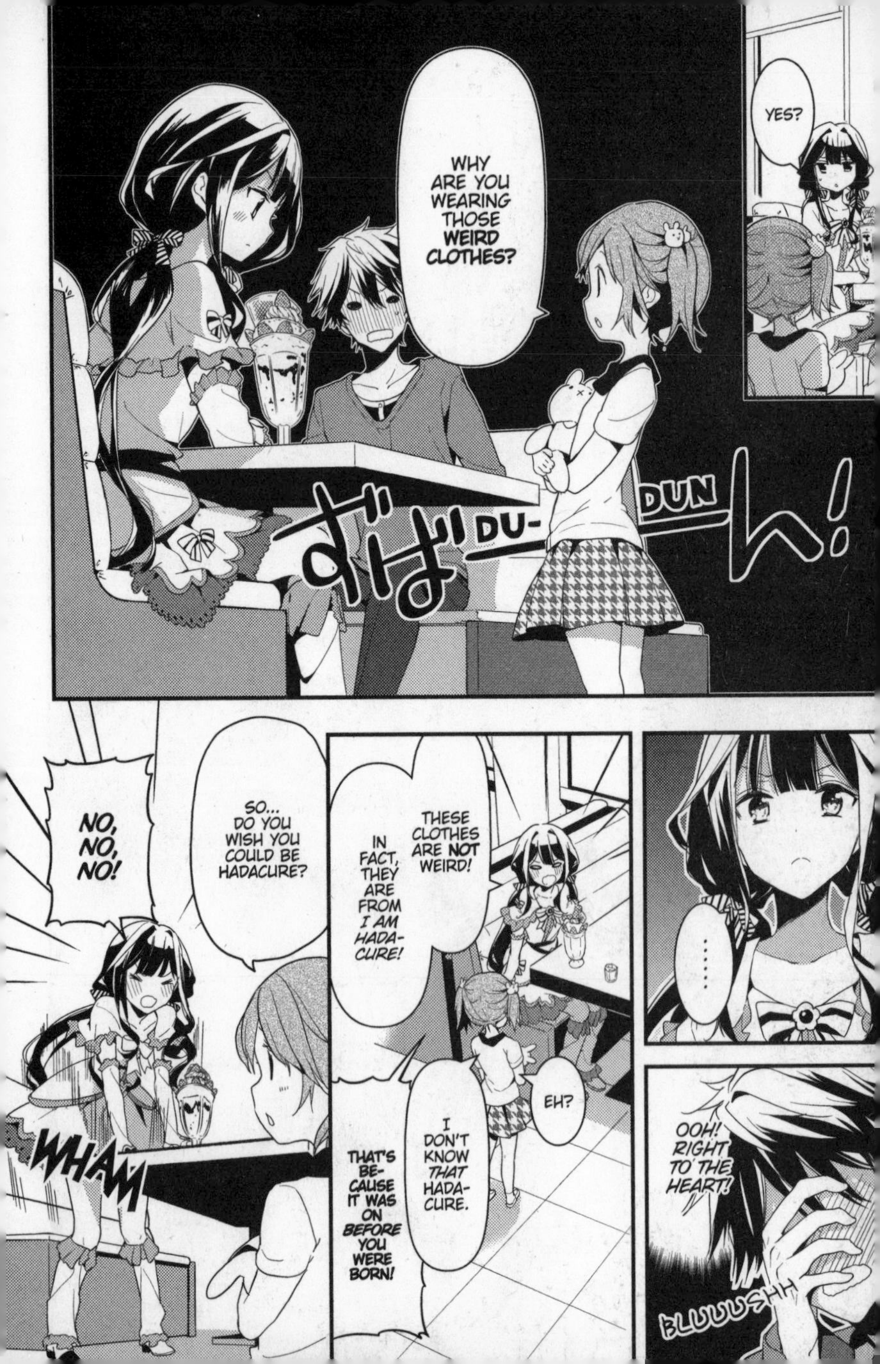
YES?
WHY ARE YOU WEARING THOSE WEIRD CLOTHES?
ずば
DU-
DUN
ん!
......
OOH! RIGHT TO THE HEART!
BLUUUSHH
THESE CLOTHES ARE NOT WEIRD!
IN FACT, THEY ARE FROM *I AM HADACURE!*
EH?
I DON'T KNOW *THAT* HADACURE.
THAT'S BECAUSE IT WAS ON *BEFORE* YOU WERE BORN!
SO... DO YOU WISH YOU COULD BE HADACURE?
NO, NO, NO!
WHAM

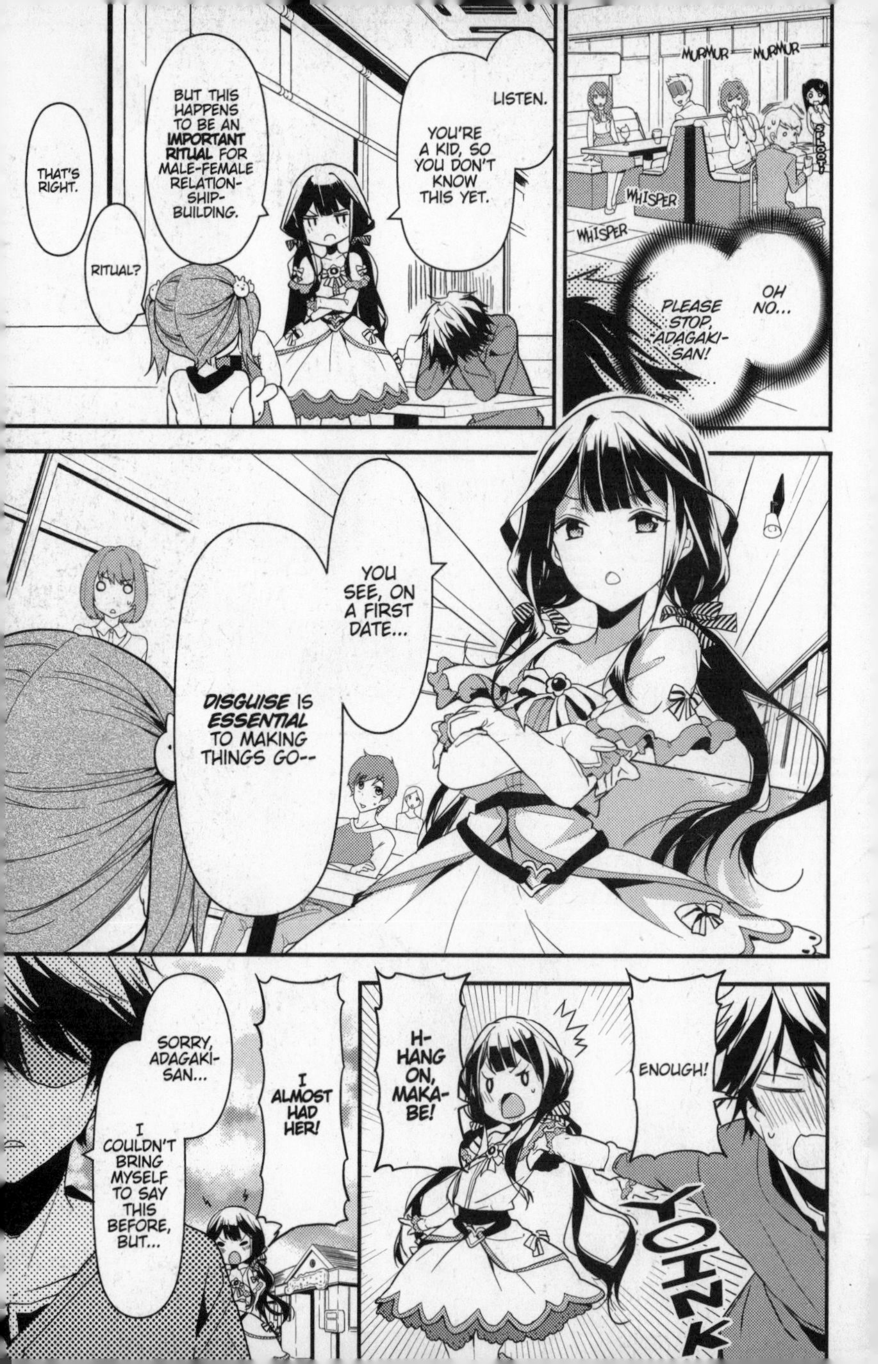
MURMUR
MURMUR
SPLOOT!
WHISPER
WHISPER
OH NO...
PLEASE STOP, ADAGAKI-SAN!
LISTEN.
YOU'RE A KID, SO YOU DON'T KNOW THIS YET.
BUT THIS HAPPENS TO BE AN **IMPORTANT RITUAL** FOR MALE-FEMALE RELATIONSHIP-BUILDING.
THAT'S RIGHT.
RITUAL?
YOU SEE, ON A FIRST DATE...
DISGUISE IS ***ESSENTIAL*** TO MAKING THINGS GO--
ENOUGH!
H-HANG ON, MAKABE!
YOINK
I ALMOST HAD HER!
SORRY, ADAGAKI-SAN...
I COULDN'T BRING MYSELF TO SAY THIS BEFORE, BUT...

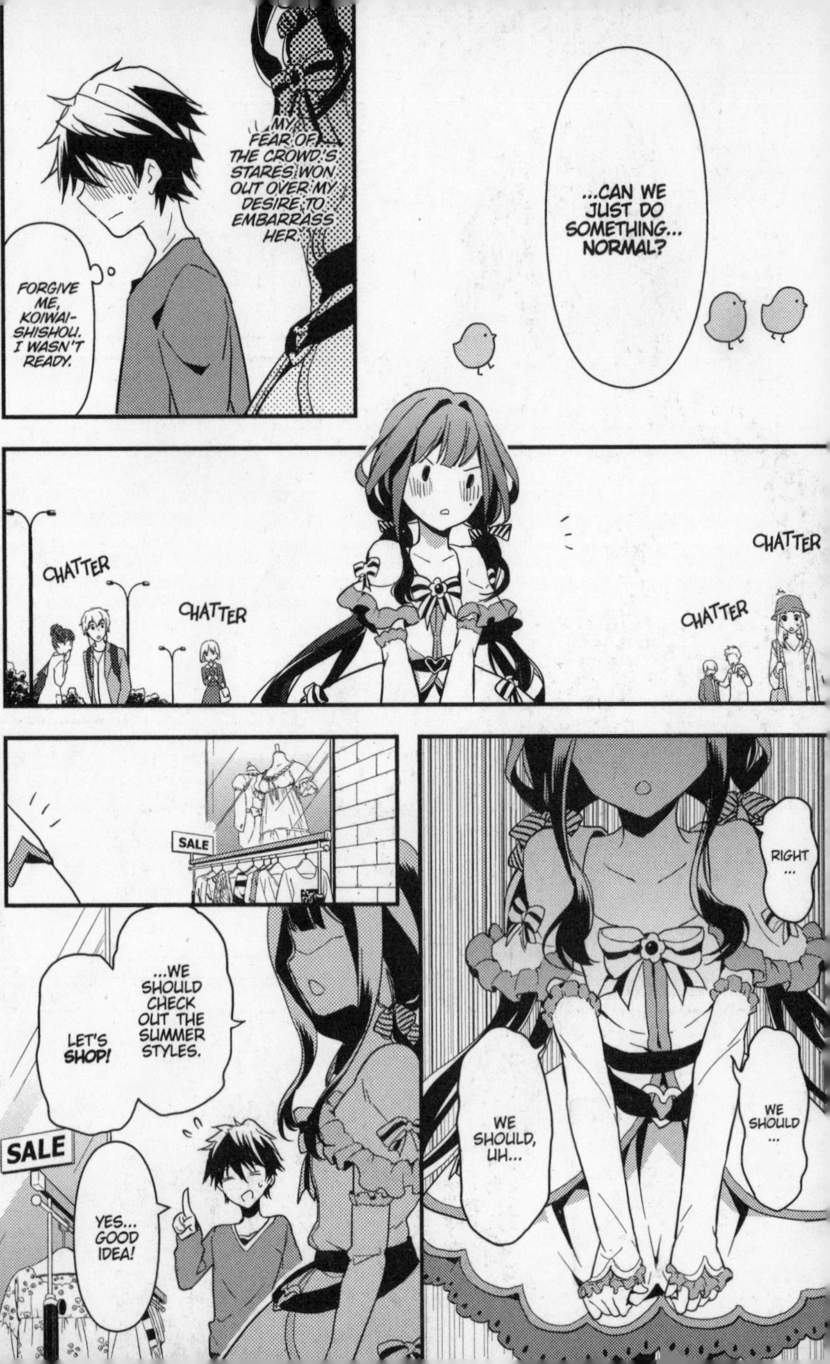
...CAN WE JUST DO SOMETHING... NORMAL?
MY FEAR OF THE CROWD'S STARES WON OUT OVER MY DESIRE TO EMBARRASS HER
FORGIVE ME, KOIWAI-SHISHOU. I WASN'T READY.
CHATTER
CHATTER
CHATTER
CHATTER
RIGHT...
WE SHOULD...
WE SHOULD, UH...
SALE
...WE SHOULD CHECK OUT THE SUMMER STYLES.
LET'S SHOP!
SALE
YES... GOOD IDEA!

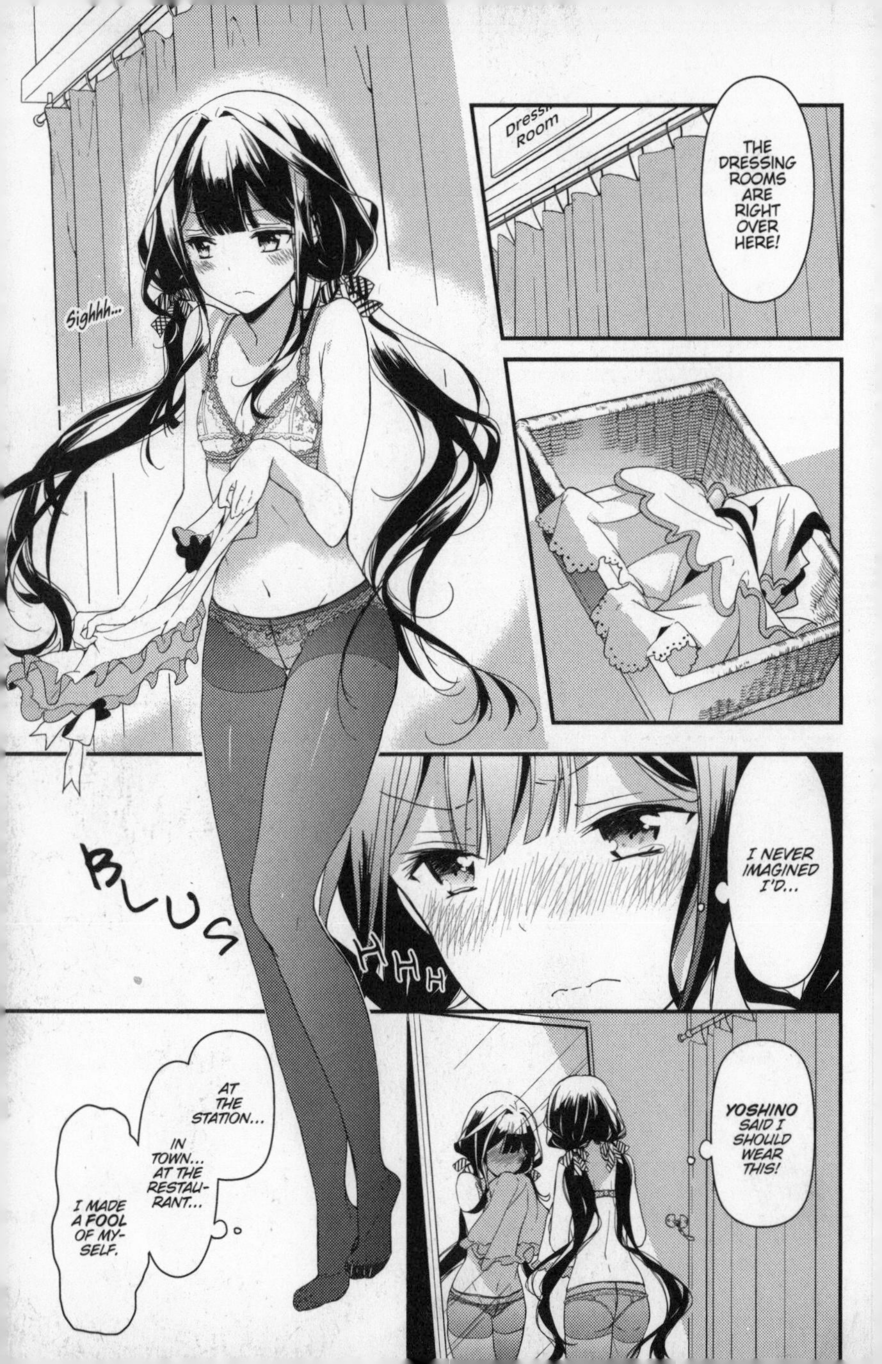
Dressing Room
THE DRESSING ROOMS ARE RIGHT OVER HERE!
I NEVER IMAGINED I'D...
BLUSHHH
YOSHINO SAID I SHOULD WEAR THIS!
Sighhh...
AT THE STATION... IN TOWN... AT THE RESTAURANT...
I MADE A FOOL OF MYSELF.

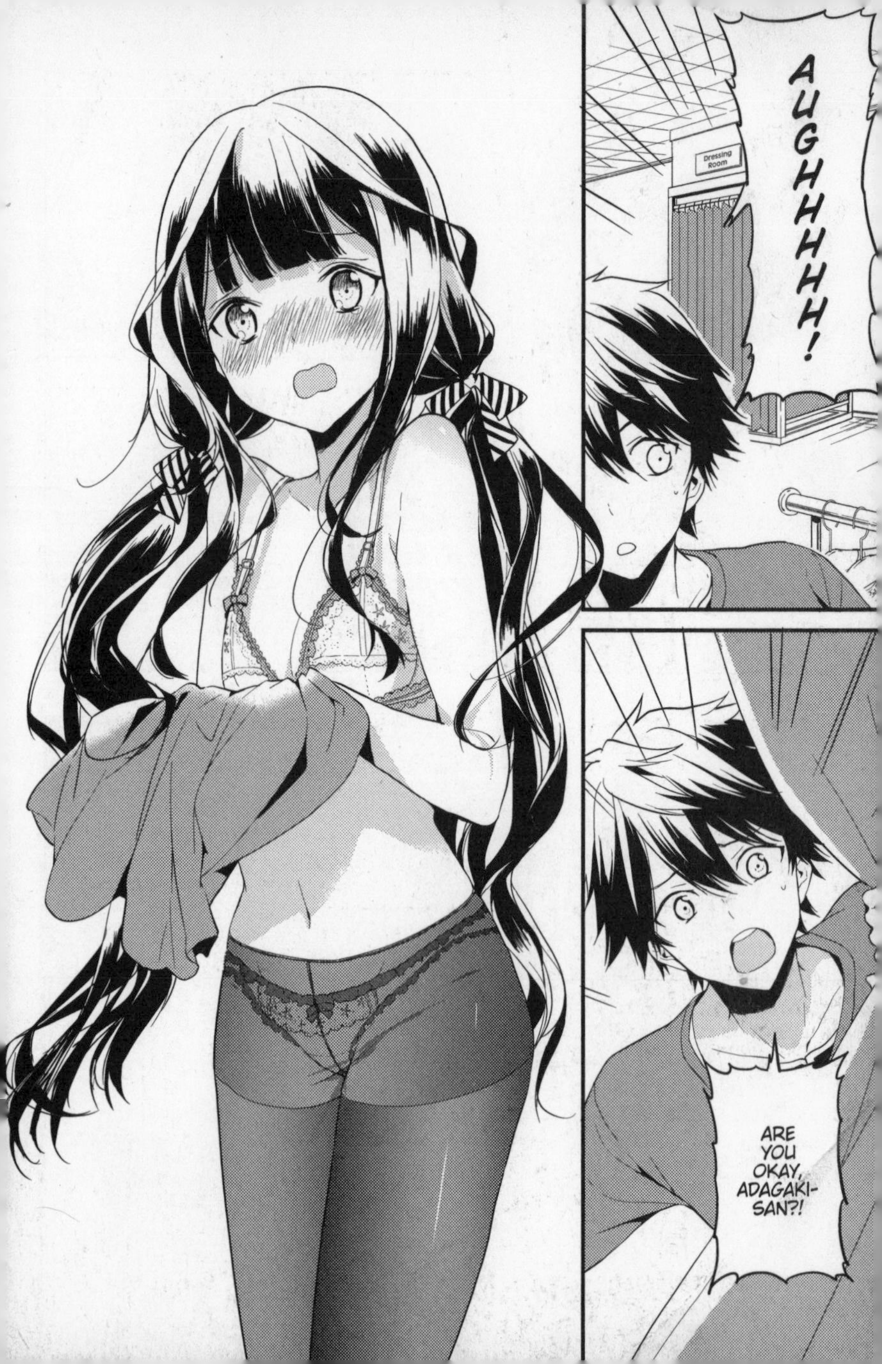
AUGHHHHHH!
Dressing Room
ARE YOU OKAY, ADAGAKI-SAN?!

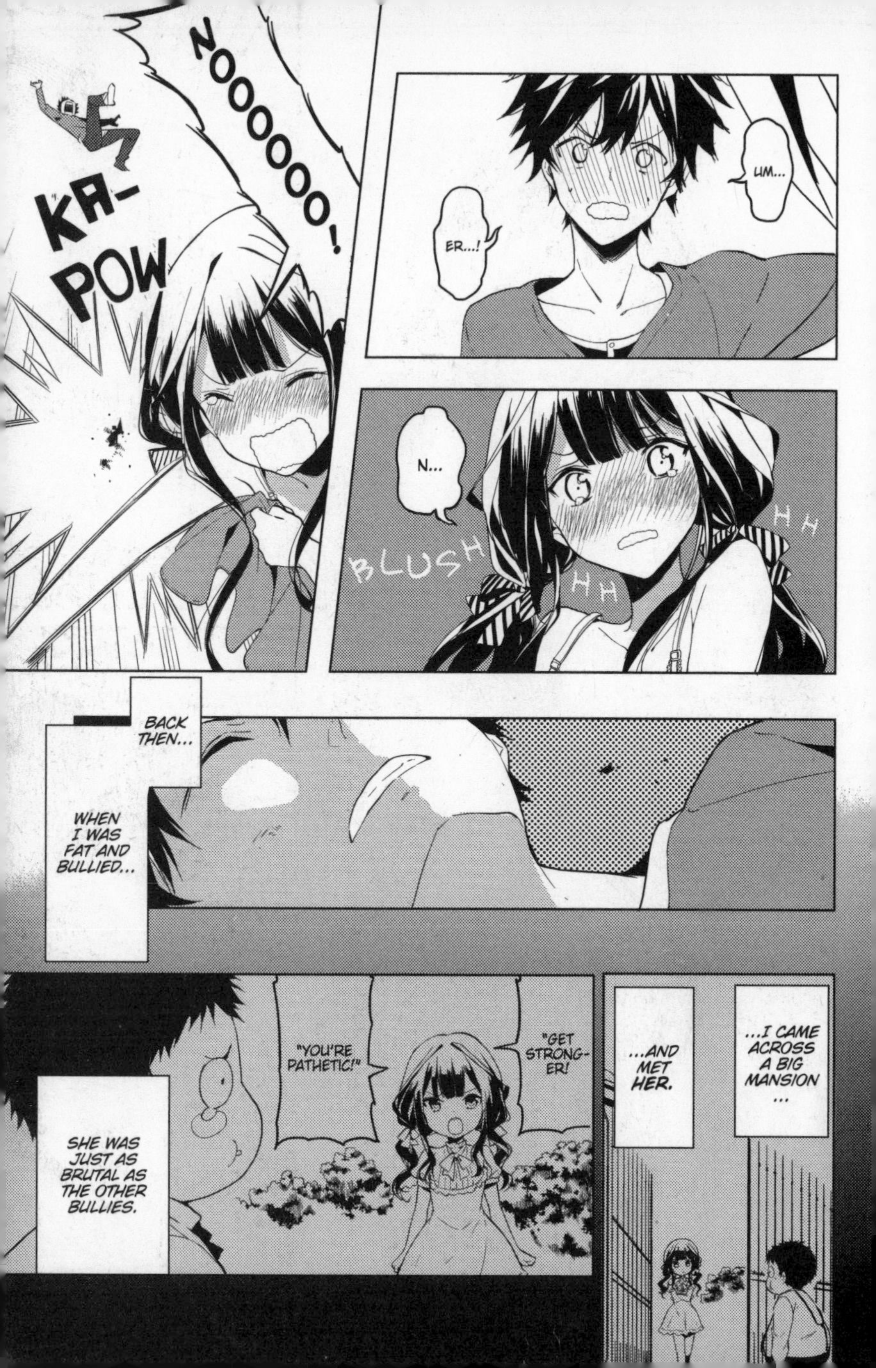
UM...
ER...!
N...
BLUSH
HH
HH
NOOOOOO!
KA-POW
BACK THEN...
WHEN I WAS FAT AND BULLIED...
...I CAME ACROSS A BIG MANSION...
...AND MET HER.
"GET STRONGER!
"YOU'RE PATHETIC!"
SHE WAS JUST AS BRUTAL AS THE OTHER BULLIES.

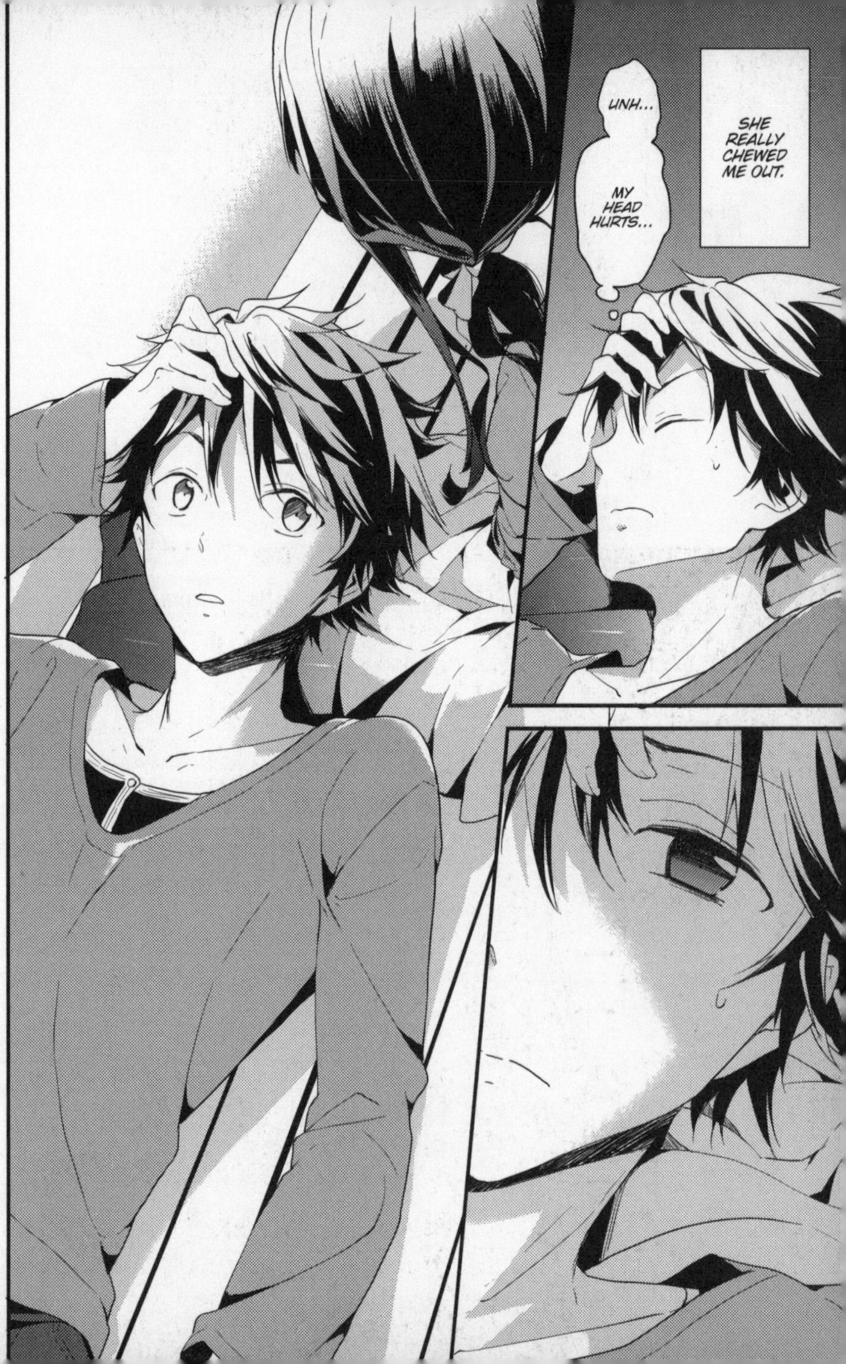
SHE REALLY CHEWED ME OUT.
UNH... MY HEAD HURTS...

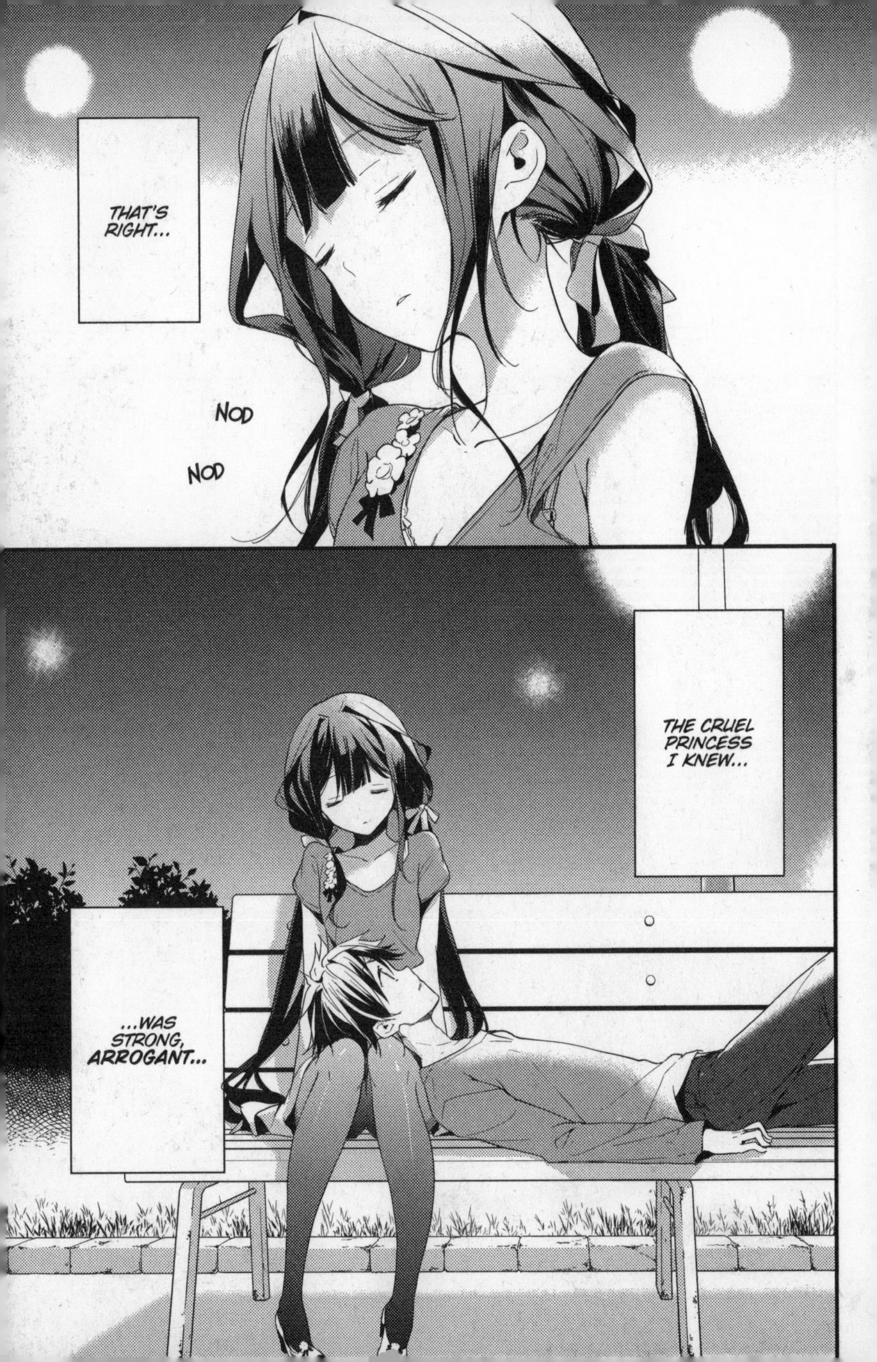
THAT'S RIGHT...
NOD
NOD
THE CRUEL PRINCESS I KNEW...
...WAS STRONG, ARROGANT...

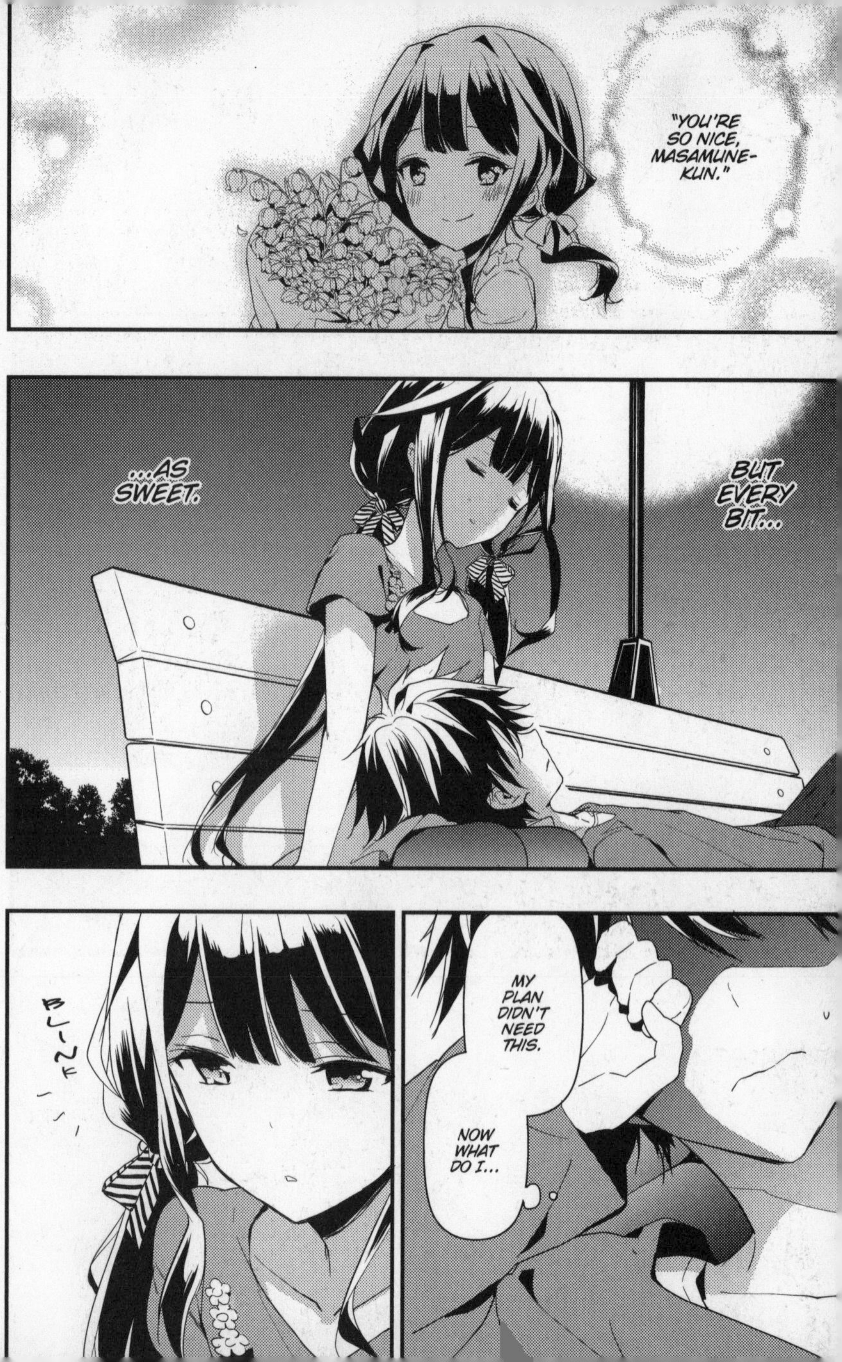
"YOU'RE SO NICE, MASAMUNE-KUN."
BUT EVERY BIT...
...AS SWEET.
MY PLAN DIDN'T NEED THIS.
NOW WHAT DO I...
BLINK

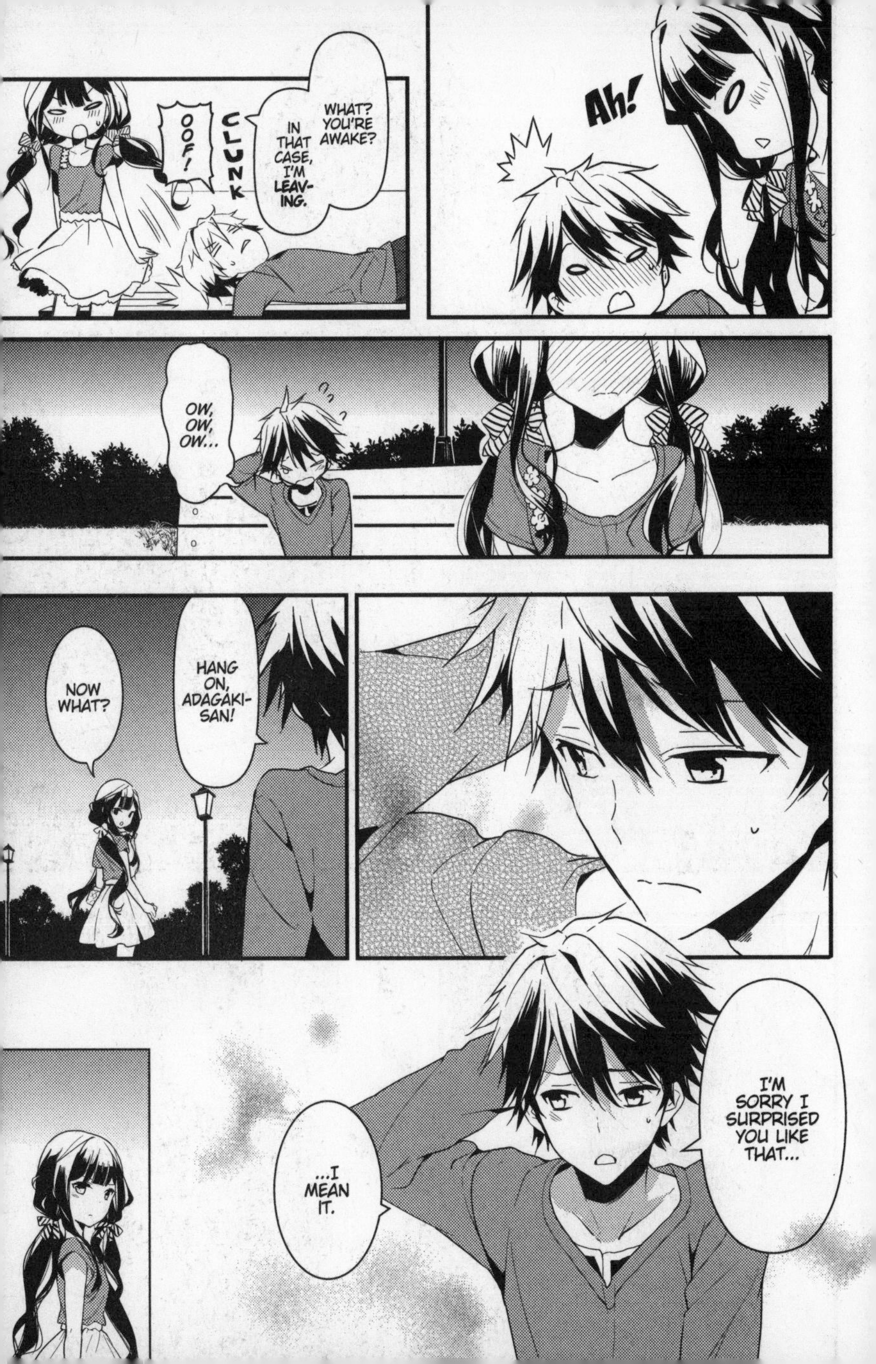
Ah!
WHAT? YOU'RE AWAKE?
IN THAT CASE, I'M LEAVING.
CLUNK
OOF!
OW, OW, OW...
HANG ON, ADAGAKI-SAN!
NOW WHAT?
I'M SORRY I SURPRISED YOU LIKE THAT...
...I MEAN IT.

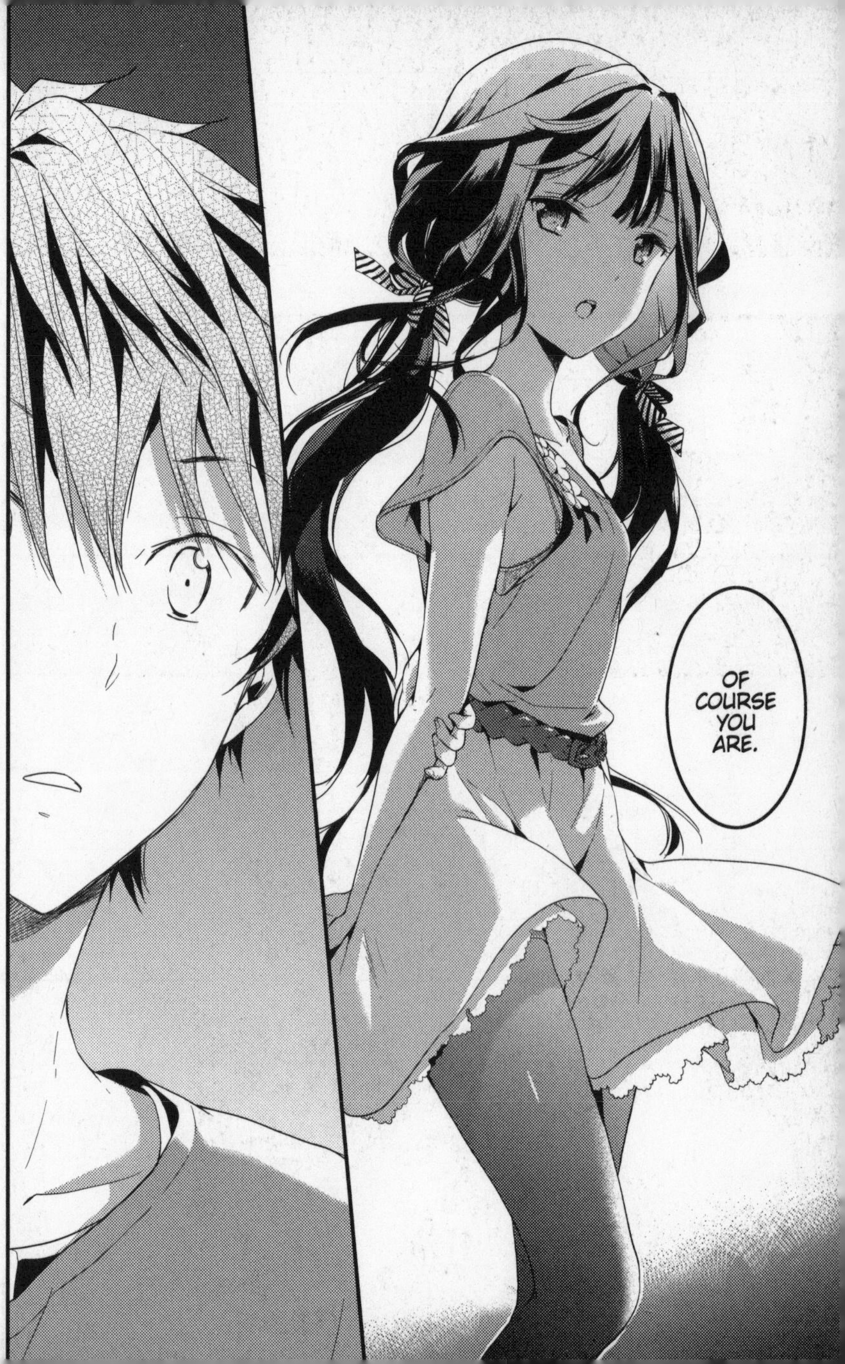
OF COURSE YOU ARE.

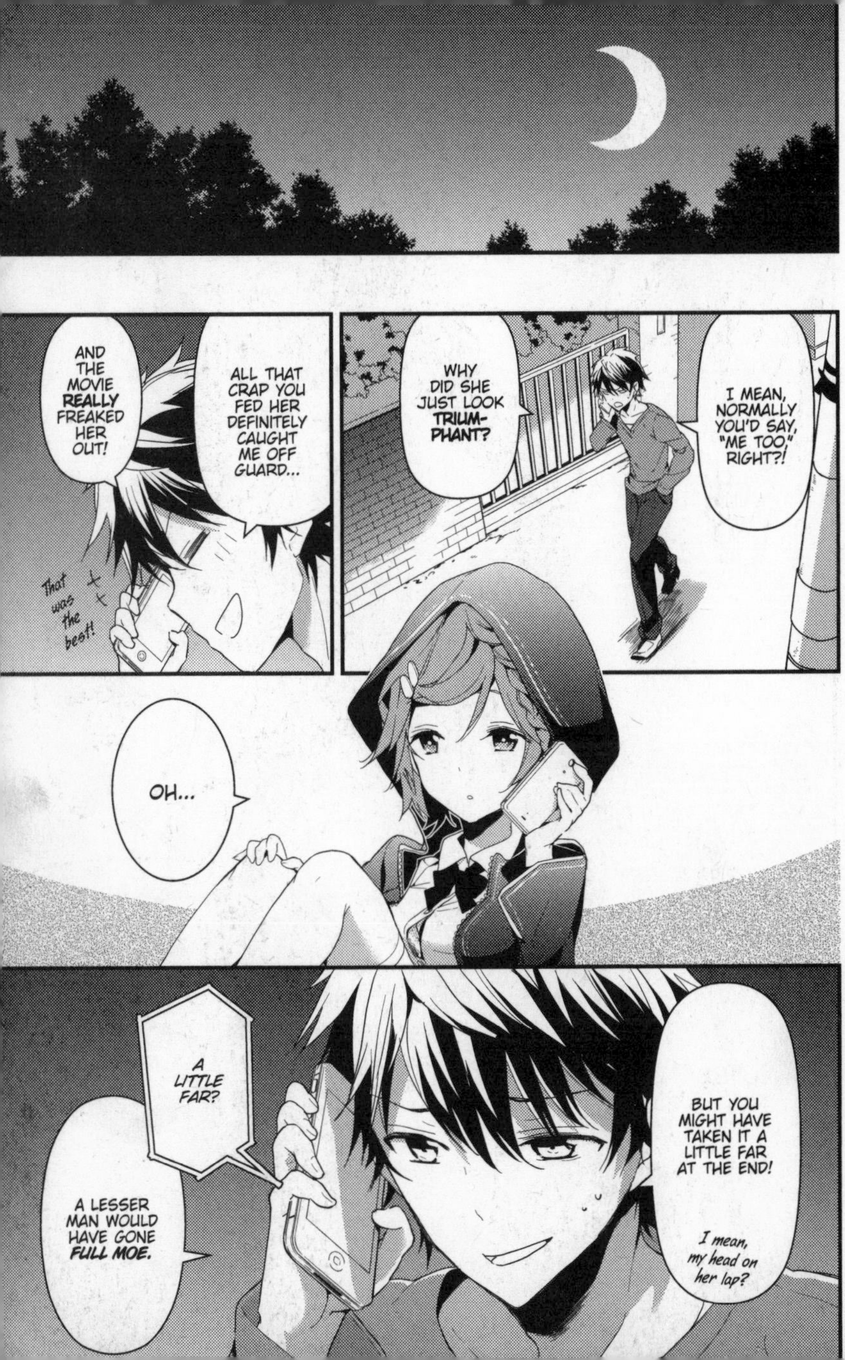
I MEAN, NORMALLY YOU'D SAY, "ME TOO," RIGHT?!
WHY DID SHE JUST LOOK TRIUMPHANT?
ALL THAT CRAP YOU FED HER DEFINITELY CAUGHT ME OFF GUARD...
AND THE MOVIE REALLY FREAKED HER OUT!
That was the best!
OH...
BUT YOU MIGHT HAVE TAKEN IT A LITTLE FAR AT THE END!
I mean, my head on her lap?
A LITTLE FAR?
A LESSER MAN WOULD HAVE GONE FULL MOE.

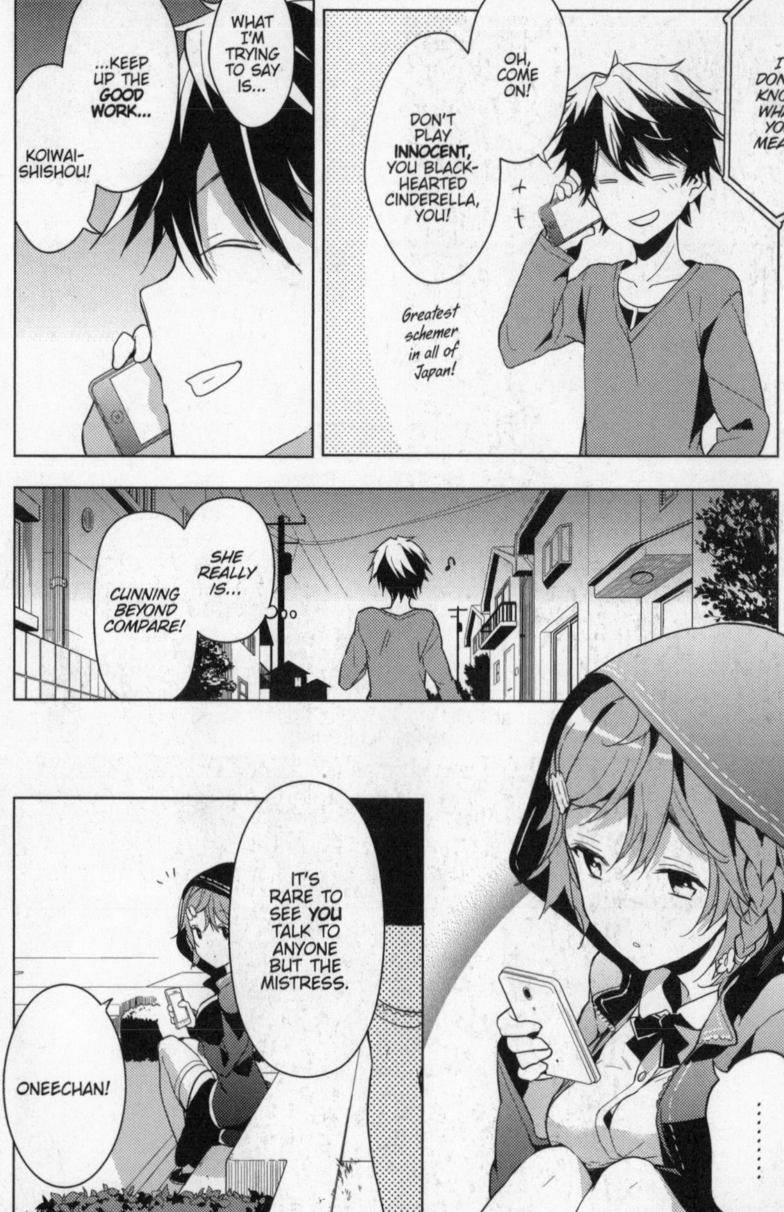

I DON'T KNOW WHAT YOU MEAN.
OH, COME ON!
DON'T PLAY INNOCENT, YOU BLACK-HEARTED CINDERELLA, YOU!
Greatest schemer in all of Japan!
WHAT I'M TRYING TO SAY IS...
...KEEP UP THE GOOD WORK...
KOIWAI-SHISHOU!
SHE REALLY IS...
CUNNING BEYOND COMPARE!
......
IT'S RARE TO SEE YOU TALK TO ANYONE BUT THE MISTRESS.
ONEECHAN!

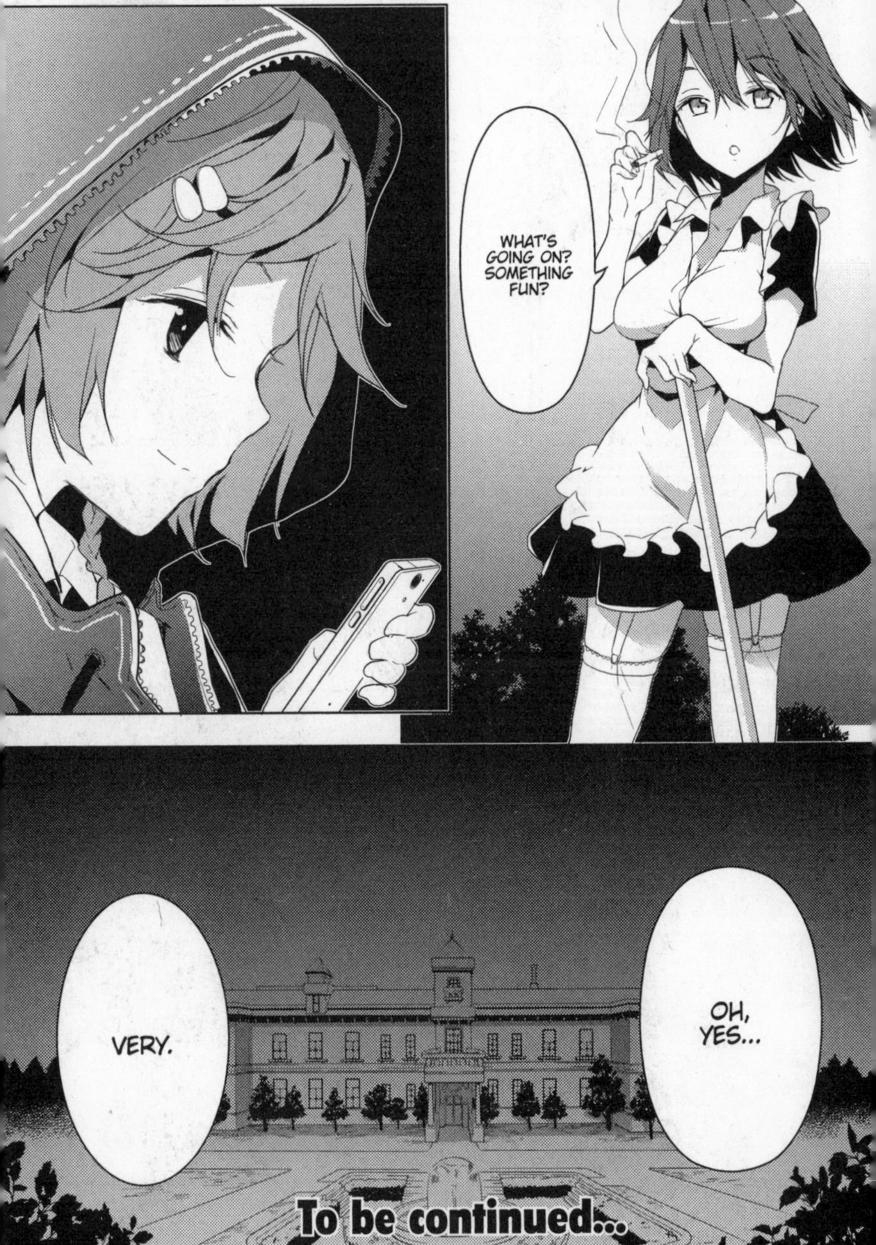
WHAT'S GOING ON? SOMETHING FUN?
OH, YES...
VERY.
To be continued...

4-Koma Theatre 1

Masamune's Mother

"MOM"

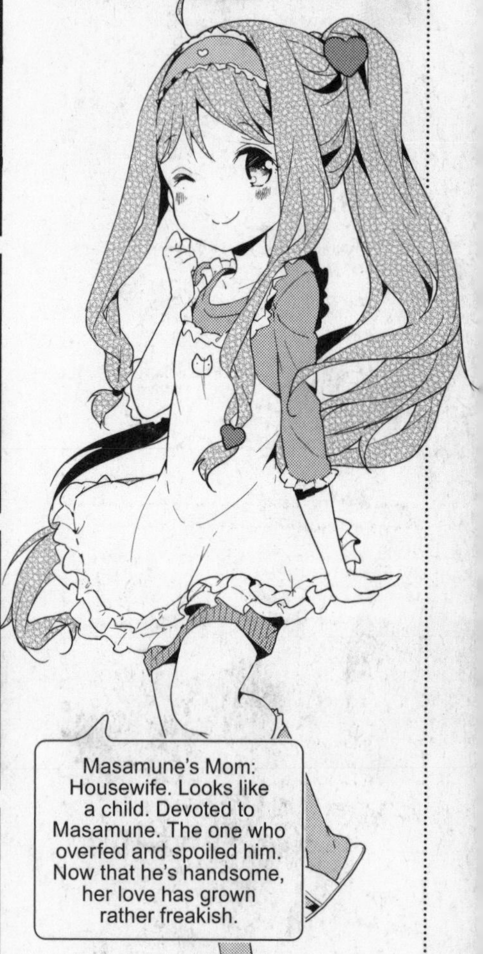
Masamune's Mom: Housewife. Looks like a child. Devoted to Masamune. The one who overfed and spoiled him. Now that he's handsome, her love has grown rather freakish.

Hayase Kinue (42)

I Knew It! My Mom Is Wrong!

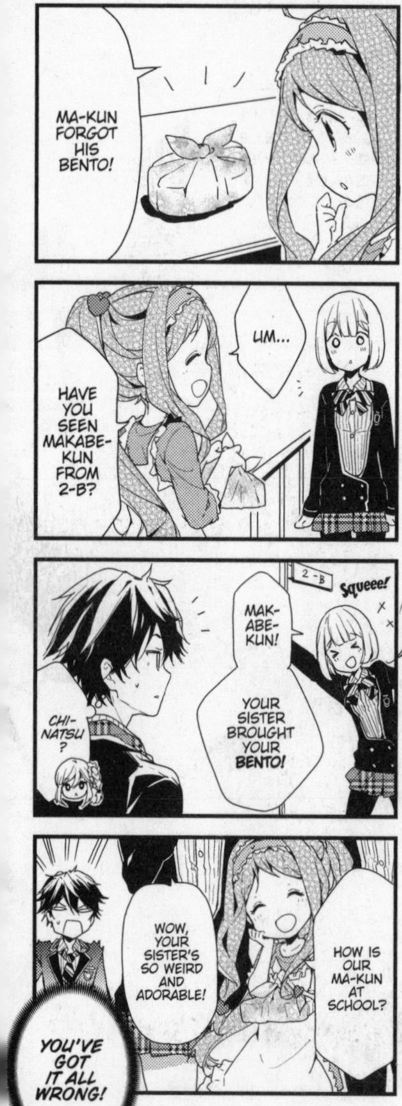
MA-KUN FORGOT HIS BENTO!
UM...
HAVE YOU SEEN MAKABE-KUN FROM 2-B?
2-B
Squeee!
MAK-ABE-KUN!
YOUR SISTER BROUGHT YOUR BENTO!
CHI-NATSU?
HOW IS OUR MA-KUN AT SCHOOL?
WOW, YOUR SISTER'S SO WEIRD AND ADORABLE!
YOU'VE GOT IT ALL WRONG!

4-Koma Theatre 2

Masamune's Sister
"SIS"

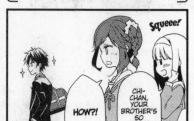

Masamune's little sister. 8th grade. Model figure. Never gains weight, or boobs. Likes eating in front of her brother, since he gets fat easily.

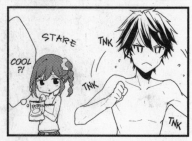

Hayase Chinatsu (14)

My Older Brother Can't Possibly Be Cool

Squeee!
CHI-CHAN, YOUR BROTHER'S SO COOL!
HOW?!
TNK
TNK
TNK
STARE
COOL ?!
SHFF
STARE
IS HE?
My hand... my hand...!
Auughhhhh!
Owwwwww...
NOPE, NOPE, NOPE.

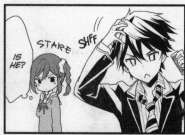

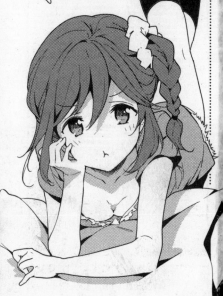

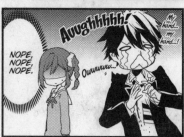

SEVEN SEAS ENTERTAINMENT PRESENTS

Masamune-kun's REVENGE 1

story by **HAZUKI TAKEOKA** art by **TIV**

TRANSLATION
Andrew Cunningham

ADAPTATION
Carol Fox

LETTERING AND LAYOUT
Jennifer Skarupa

LOGO DESIGN
Karis Page

COVER DESIGN
Nicky Lim

PROOFREADER
Holly Kolodziejczak

PRODUCTION MANAGER
Lissa Pattillo

EDITOR-IN-CHIEF
Adam Arnold

PUBLISHER
Jason DeAngelis

MASAMUNE-KUN'S REVENGE VOL. 1
©HAZUKI TAKEOKA · TIV 2013
First published in Japan in 2013 by ICHIJINSHA Inc., Tokyo.
English translation rights arranged with ICHIJINSHA Inc., Tokyo.

Seven Seas books may be purchased in bulk for educational, business, or
promotional use. For information on bulk purchases, please contact Macmillan
Corporate & Premium Sales Department at 1-800-221-7945 (ext 5442)
or write specialmarkets@macmillan.com.

Seven Seas and the Seven Seas logo are trademarks of
Seven Seas Entertainment, LLC. All rights reserved.

ISBN: 978-1-626922-25-9

Printed in Canada

First Printing: June 2016

10 9 8 7 6 5 4 3 2 1

FOLLOW US ONLINE: www.gomanga.com

READING DIRECTIONS

This book reads from *right to left*, Japanese style.
If this is your first time reading manga, you start
reading from the top right panel on each page and
take it from there. If you get lost, just follow the
numbered diagram here. It may seem backwards at
first, but you'll get the hang of it! Have fun!!

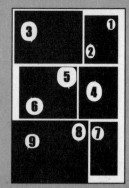